Old Testament Student Study Guide

Prepared by the
Church Educational System

Published by
The Church of Jesus Christ of Latter-day Saints
Salt Lake City, Utah

Table of Contents

A Testimony of Christ

Like all scripture, the Old Testament is a witness and testimony that God lives, that Jesus Christ is the Savior of all men, and that we must worship them and live their teachings to obtain peace in this life and eternal life after death.

President Spencer W. Kimball said, "Jesus Christ was the God of the Old Testament, and it was He who [spoke] with Abraham and Moses. It was He who inspired Isaiah and Jeremiah; it was He who foretold through those chosen men the happenings of the future" (in Conference Report, Apr. 1977, 113; or *Ensign*, May 1977, 76).

After his Resurrection, Jesus appeared to two men walking from Jerusalem to Emmaus. He quoted Old Testament prophecies about himself that filled the men with the Spirit and caused their hearts to burn with testimony (see Luke 24:13–32). As you study the Old Testament, look for truths that can teach you more about Jesus Christ and how to apply his gospel in your life. As part of your study, you will keep a notebook of insights and assignments. You may want to make a special place in your notebook for what you learn that specifically teaches about or testifies of Christ. You may also find your heart filled with testimony about Jesus Christ as you look for him in the Old Testament.

The Old Testament Story

The Old Testament begins with the creation of Adam and Eve, the first man and woman. It then briefly tells the history of Adam and Eve's posterity down to the time of Noah when a great flood destroyed all people and animals, except Noah and his family and the animals on the ark. After telling Noah's story, the Old Testament briefly records events leading up to the life of Abraham, who entered into covenants (sacred promises) with God and received special promises from God concerning his posterity. The promises God made to Abraham are called the "Abrahamic covenant" (see Bible Dictionary, s.v. "Abraham, covenant of"). The Abrahamic covenant continued with Abraham's son Isaac and grandson Jacob, whom the Lord renamed Israel. The Old Testament then records God's dealings with his covenant people, the descendants of Jacob, who are called the "house of Israel" or the "children of Israel."

Previewing the Old Testament—The Table of Contents

Look at "The Names and Order of All the Books of the Old and New Testament" in the front of your Bible. When the Old Testament was put together, the books were not always placed in chronological order. It would be a good idea to mark your table of contents so you can remember the different kinds of writings in the Old Testament. For example, put the following four names next to the books they refer to in your table of contents.

1. *The Law.* The books from Genesis to Deuteronomy are often referred to as "the law." Because Moses wrote them they are sometimes called "the five books of Moses." Genesis begins with the Creation of the world and Adam and Eve, and Deuteronomy finishes at the end of Moses' life. These five books tell about covenants God made with man and about the commandments men must live as their part of the covenant.

2. *The History.* The books from Joshua to Esther tell the continued history of the children of Israel for over six hundred years after Moses. These books are commonly called "the history." They are generally placed in chronological order; however, 1–2 Chronicles are essentially another writer's version of the same history found in 1–2 Kings.

3. *The Poetry.* The books from Job to Ecclesiastes are filled with teachings and revelations that are written in poetic form; thus, this section is known as "the poetry." The Song of Solomon is also contained in the poetry section although, according to the Prophet Joseph Smith, it is not an inspired writing (see Bible Dictionary, s.v. "Song of Solomon"). The book of Psalms contains words to sacred music of that time.

4. *The Prophets.* The books from Isaiah to Malachi contain the teachings of different prophets during the time the children of Israel had kings. They are not in historical order. We do not know the reason they are in their current order.

Benefiting from Your Study of the Old Testament

The Old Testament stories are some of the most famous in history. If we did not know them, much of the New Testament, Book of Mormon, and Doctrine and Covenants would not be as meaningful. But we must do more than just know the stories. We must learn true doctrine from them and apply that doctrine in our lives.

As you diligently study the Old Testament, you will find times when the Spirit will touch your heart and help you become more Christlike. For thousands of years the Old Testament has helped people with faith follow Heavenly Father's plan.

How to Use This Manual

As the title of this manual suggests, it is a guide in your study of the scriptures. This manual provides help in the following ways.

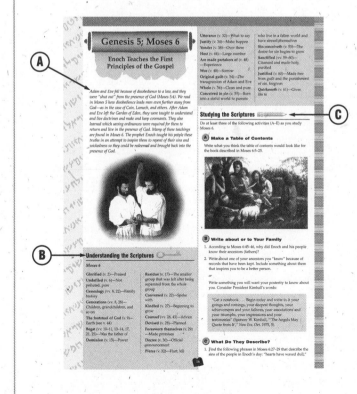

(A) Introduction

Printed below each scroll you will find introductions to the chapters in the scriptures you are assigned to read and explanations of the chapters you are not assigned to read. The "Introduction" section contains the following kinds of information:

- The historical setting
- An explanation of how the scripture block relates to the chapters before or after it
- Questions to think about before or during your reading to help you concentrate on the message of the scripture block

(B) Understanding the Scriptures

The "Understanding the Scriptures" section provides help for difficult words and phrases along with commentary that helps you understand ideas and concepts contained in the scriptures. Often this commentary includes statements by General Authorities.

(C) Studying the Scriptures

The "Studying the Scriptures" section contains questions and activities that help you discover, think about, and apply the principles of the gospel found in the scriptures. You will do these activities in a notebook or on your own paper since room to write is not provided in this manual.

The following steps will help you as you study the scriptures:

- Begin with prayer.
- Read the introduction to the chapter you will be studying and consider other "Before Reading" study skills (see p. 5).
- Read the assigned chapters. As you read, refer to the "Understanding the Scriptures" section of the manual for help. Use "During Reading" study skills (see p. 5). Use your notebook or paper to take notes and write questions. Write also about feelings or impressions that are important to you.
- Do the activities in the "Studying the Scriptures" section for the chapter you are studying. Sometimes you will get to choose which activities to complete. If you want to learn more about the Old Testament, complete all the activities.

Home-Study Seminary Program

If you are in a home-study seminary program, the reading chart that follows shows you what you should read each week of seminary. Remember that seminary is a daily religious education program, that prayerfully reading your scriptures should be a daily practice, and that you should work on your seminary assignments each school day even though you will not attend seminary each day. If you have more or less than thirty-six weeks in your seminary year, your teacher will tell you which chapters you should read in a week and which assignments to complete. Reading the scriptures and using this manual should take thirty to forty minutes each school day you do not attend seminary class.

Each week you should give your teacher the pages from your notebook that contain your thoughts about the scriptures and the questions you answered for that week. Your teacher will read and respond to them and return your notebook to you. You might choose to have two notebooks and use them every other week. You could also write in a loose-leaf binder and turn in the pages you did that week. When your teacher returns the pages, put them back into the notebook.

Daily Seminary Program

If you are in a daily seminary program, you will use this study guide as instructed by your teacher.

Studying the Scriptures

This manual is a guide to help you read, study, and understand the scriptures. Most of your study time will be spent reading and thinking about the scriptures, so this section has been included to help you get more out of that study.

Elder Howard W. Hunter, as a member of the Quorum of the Twelve Apostles, gave Church members valuable counsel on scripture study, which is summarized below. You may want to write these ideas on a card and put the card in a place where you can see it while you study.

- Read carefully to understand the scriptures.
- Study every day.
- Set a regular time every day when you will study.
- Study in a place where you can concentrate without distractions or interruptions.
- Study for a period of time rather than reading a certain amount of chapters or pages: sixty minutes is ideal, thirty minutes is a great accomplishment, yet fifteen minutes can be meaningful also.
- Have a study plan.
  (See Conference Report, Oct. 1979, 91–93; or *Ensign*, Nov. 1979, 64–65.)

Once you have followed this counsel, there are two other things you will find helpful as you study the scriptures: study helps found in the Latter-day Saint editions of the scriptures and using good study skills.

Old Testament Reading Chart

Days I Read Ten Minutes or More		Assigned Chapters I Read This Week
S M T W TH F S	Week 1	"Studying the Scriptures"
S M T W TH F S	Week 2	Abraham 3:22–28 Moses 1 2 3 4
S M T W TH F S	Week 3	Moses 5 6 7
S M T W TH F S	Week 4	Moses 8 Genesis 6:14–22 7 8 9:1–17 11:1–9
S M T W TH F S	Week 5	Abraham 1 2 Genesis 13 14:13–24 15 16 17
S M T W TH F S	Week 6	Genesis 18 21:1–21 22 23 (activity)
S M T W TH F S	Week 7	Genesis 24 25:19–34 27 28 29 30:1–24 32 33
S M T W TH F S	Week 8	Genesis 35 37 39 40 41
S M T W TH F S	Week 9	Genesis 42 43 44 45 46 49 50 JST, Genesis 50:24–38
S M T W TH F S	Week 10	Exodus 1 2 3 4 5 6 7 8 9 10
S M T W TH F S	Week 11	Exodus 12 13 14 15:22–27 16 17
S M T W TH F S	Week 12	Exodus 18 19 20–24
S M T W TH F S	Week 13	Activities for Exodus 25–27, 30 28 29 32 33 34
S M T W TH F S	Week 14	Leviticus 1 10 11 14 16 19 26
S M T W TH F S	Week 15	Numbers 6 9 11 12 13 14 16 21:4–9 22 23 24 27:12–23
S M T W TH F S	Week 16	Deuteronomy 4 6 7:1–6 8 10:10–22 26 28 30 32
S M T W TH F S	Week 17	Joshua 1 2 3 4 5:10–15 6 7 10 23 24
S M T W TH F S	Week 18	Judges 6 7 8 13 14 15 16 Ruth 1 2 3 4
S M T W TH F S	Week 19	1 Samuel 1 2 3 7 8 9 10
S M T W TH F S	Week 20	1 Samuel 13 15 16 17 24 26
S M T W TH F S	Week 21	2 Samuel 7 9 11 12 13 14
S M T W TH F S	Week 22	1 Kings 3 8 9:1–9 11 12 17 18 19
S M T W TH F S	Week 23	2 Kings 2 4 5 6 17 18 19 22 23
S M T W TH F S	Week 24	Selections from 1 and 2 Chronicles 2 Chronicles 15 20 Ezra 9 10 Nehemiah 1 6 8
S M T W TH F S	Week 25	Esther 1 2 3 4 5 6 7 8 9 10 Job 1 2 3 38 42
S M T W TH F S	Week 26	Psalm 22 23 24 Selected verses from Psalms and Proverbs Ecclesiastes 1 2 4 5 12
S M T W TH F S	Week 27	Isaiah 1 2 4 5 11 14
S M T W TH F S	Week 28	Isaiah 24 29 30:15–21 33:14–17 40 42:1–7 47:5–10
S M T W TH F S	Week 29	Isaiah 48 49 50 53 55 58 61:1–3 63:1–9 65:17–25
S M T W TH F S	Week 30	Jeremiah 1 7 9:23–24 16 17:5–8, 19–27 23 29:11–14
S M T W TH F S	Week 31	Jeremiah 30 31 33:15–18 52 Lamentations 1 5 Ezekiel 2 3
S M T W TH F S	Week 32	Ezekiel 11:16–20 18 20:33–44 33 34 37
S M T W TH F S	Week 33	Daniel 1 2 3 6
S M T W TH F S	Week 34	Hosea 1 2 3 13:9–14 Joel 2 Amos 3 4 5:4–6, 14–15 8:11–12 Obadiah 1:21
S M T W TH F S	Week 35	Jonah 1 2 3 4:1–11 Micah 3 5:2 6:7–8 Habakkuk 3:17–18 Zephaniah 3 Haggai 1
S M T W TH F S	Week 36	Zechariah 9:9 10 11:12–13 12:10 13:6 14 Malachi 3 4

Study Helps in the Latter-day Saint Editions of the Scriptures

Cross-References

A cross-reference is a scripture reference that will lead you to additional information and insight on the topic you are studying.

> 15 Neither do men light a ªcandle, and put it under a bushel, but on a candlestick; and it giveth light unto all that are in the house.
> 16 Let your ªlight so shine before men, that they may see your good ªworks, and ªglorify your Father which is in heaven.
> 17 ¶ Think not that I am come to ªdestroy the ªlaw, or the prophets: I am not come to destroy, but to fulfil.
> 18 For verily I say unto you, Till heaven and earth pass, one jot or one tittle shall in no wise pass from the ªlaw, till all be ªfulfilled.
> 19 Whosoever therefore shall ªbreak one of these least commandments, ªand shall ªteach men so, he shall be called the least in the kingdom of heaven: but whosoever shall do and ªteach them, the same shall be called great in the kingdom of heaven.
> 20 For I say unto you, That except your ªrighteousness shall exceed the

> 12c TG Persecution.
> 13a See Lev. 2: 13 and Num. 18: 19, where salt is a token of the covenant and was part of sacrifice ritual. TG Salt.
> 14a TG Mission of Early Saints.
> 15a Luke 11: 33 (33–34).
> 16a 3 Ne. 18: 24. TG Children of Light; Example; Light.
> b 1 Pet. 2: 12. TG Good Works.
> c John 15: 8.
> 17a D&C 10: 52 (52, 54).
> b TG Law of Moses.
> 18a TG Law of Moses.

> b D&C 1: 3
> 19a TG Sin.
> b JST Matt. (Appendi)
> c 2 Ne. 28:
> d TG Missio
> 20a TG Right
> b TG Scribe
> 21a TG Comm God.
> b TG Blood Murder.
> c GR subjec demnati
> 22a Prov. 29:
> 3 Ne. 12:
> TG Anger
> b JST Matt. 12: 22 o

For example, read Matthew 5:14–16 and notice footnote 16a. By looking up and reading the scripture referred to in the footnotes, what additional insights do you gain about what it means to "let your light so shine"? (Matthew 5:16).

Topical Guide and Bible Dictionary References

The Topical Guide (TG) contains an alphabetical list of hundreds of words and topics with scripture references in all four standard

> 25 And God made the beast of the earth after his kind, and cattle after their kind, and every thing that creepeth upon the earth after his kind: and God saw that it was good.
> 26 ¶ And God said, Let ªus ªmake ªman in our ªimage, after ªour ªlikeness: and let them have ªdominion over the fish of the sea, and over the fowl of the air, and over the cattle, and over all the earth, and over every creeping thing that creepeth upon the earth.
> 27 So God created man in his own ªimage, in the image of God created he him; male and ªfemale created he them.
> 28 And God blessed them, and God said unto them, Be ªfruitful, and ªmultiply, and ªreplenish the ªearth, and subdue it: and have ªdominion over the fish of the sea, and over the fowl of the air, and over every living thing that moveth upon the earth.
> 29 ¶ And God said, Behold, I have given you ªevery herb bearing seed, which is upon the face of all the earth, and ªevery tree, in the which is the fruit of a tree yielding seed; to you it shall be for ªmeat.
> 30 And to every beast of the earth, and to every fowl of the air, and to every thing that creepeth upon the earth, wherein there is life, I have

> 22a D&C 45: 58; 132: 63 (55–56, 63); Moses 2: 22; Abr. 4: 22.
> 24a TG Order.
> 26a Abr. 4: 27 (26–31); 5: 7. TG Godhead; Jesus Christ, Creator.
> b TG Creation.
> c TG Adam; Man, Physical Creation of.
> d Mosiah 7: 27; Ether 3: 15 (14–17); D&C 20: 18

> 46); Mos 28); Abr TG Man, Become Father.
> 27a TG God, poreal N
> b TG Wom
> 28a TG Child b TG Birth Marriage Marriage

works of the Church. The Bible Dictionary (BD) gives definitions and explanations for many biblical names and subjects. Although not referenced in the footnotes, you may want to check the index for the Book of Mormon, Doctrine and Covenants, and the Pearl of Great Price for additional references.

For example, read Genesis 1:26. As you do, you may wonder about the word us in "Let us make man in our image." Who helped God with the Creation? Notice the footnote that refers you to the Topical Guide. Find a scripture reference that clearly says Jesus Christ is the Creator. Look in the Bible Dictionary under "Christ" to find a list of other names he is known by.

Help with Words and Phrases

Words and phrases are labeled with the following notations:

- "HEB" defines a word in the Hebrew language (the original language of the Old Testament).
- "GR" defines Greek words (the original language of the New Testament).
- "IE" indicates that an expression is an idiom (a word or phrase used in a specific way when the scriptures were written but not commonly used today).

> 23b IE bribes. Ezek. 22: 12. TG Bribery.
> c HEB 'do not do justice to.' TG Judgment.
> 24a D&C 101: 58.
> 25a HEB return; i.e. repeatedly chastise.
> b Jer. 9: 7; Mal. 3: 3.
> 26a Jer. 33: 7 (7–8).
> b TG Counselors.
> c TG Jerusalem.
> 27a TG Zion.
> b HEB justice.
> c TG Conversion.
> 29a IE terebinth trees and gardens used in idol worship.
> 31a IE as a tuft of inflammable fibers.
> b Isa. 9: 16 (16–21).
> 2 1a Isaiah chapters 2–14

> are quoted from the brass plates by Nephi in 2 Ne. 12–24; there are some differences in wording which should be noted.
> b HEB khazah, meaning 'envisioned.' It means Isaiah received his message through a vision from the LORD.
> 2a TG Last Days.
> b Isa. 13: 2; Micah 4: 1 (1–3).
> c TG Jerusalem, New.
> d TG Dispensations; Restoration of the Gospel.
> e 1 Kgs. 8: 41 (41–42). TG Israel, Mission of; Nations.

What insight do you gain from knowing the Hebrew word for "saw" in Isaiah 2:1?

The Joseph Smith Translation of the Bible

The Lord commanded the Prophet Joseph Smith to study the Bible and seek revelation to obtain a more complete and true Biblical translation (see D&C 37:1; 73:3–4). Consequently, the Prophet Joseph Smith made many important changes to the Bible in places where it was not translated correctly (see Articles of Faith 1:8). We call these changes the "Joseph Smith Translation." The translation is abbreviated in the footnotes as "JST." Some Joseph Smith Translation changes are in the footnotes, while others are found in an appendix entitled "Joseph Smith Translation" on page 797 of the Latter-day Saint edition of the King James Version of the Bible.

> 11a TG False Prophets; Sorcery.
> b TG False Priesthoods.
> 13a JST Ex. 7: 13 And Pharaoh hardened his heart . . .
> 15a HEB to meet him.
> b Ex. 4: 17.
> 16a Ex. 5: 3.
> b TG Service.
> 17a OR Nile (so also in v. 18, 20, 21, 24, 25).
> b Rev. 11: 6 (5–6).
> c TG Plagues.

Read Exodus 7:10–13. What important help does the Joseph Smith Translation provide for these verses?

The Gazetteer and Maps

The gazetteer and maps, found in the appendix of the Latter-day Saint edition of the Bible, are helpful in finding places referred to in the scriptures.

Chapter Headings, Section Headings, and Verse Summaries

Chapter and section headings and verse summaries explain or give important background information to help you understand what you read. For example, what helpful information do you get by reading the section heading to Doctrine and Covenants 89?

Having the study helps found in Latter-day Saint editions of the scriptures is like having a small collection of reference books, available to you—all in one place!

Study Skills

Nephi said we ought to "feast" (2 Nephi 32:3) upon the scriptures, and Jesus commanded the Nephites to "search [them] diligently" (3 Nephi 23:1). This kind of study involves more than just quickly reading through the scriptures. The following ideas and skills will help you learn more when you study. They are divided into three different categories: before reading, during reading, and after reading.

Before Reading

Prayer

The scriptures were written by inspiration. Consequently, they are best understood when we have the companionship of the Spirit. In the Old Testament we learn about the priest Ezra, who "prepared his heart to seek the law of the Lord" (Ezra 7:10). We prepare our hearts to read the scriptures by praying each time we read.

Get Background Information

Understanding the historical background of the scriptures will help you gain greater insights as you read. The Bible Dictionary provides historical background and a brief overview of each book's content and main themes. The section headings in the Doctrine and Covenants provide a brief explanation of the historical background of the revelations. This manual also gives some background for many chapters in the scriptures. If you have time, you may also refer to other Church-approved books and manuals that have background on the scripture you are reading.

Ask Questions

Before you read it is helpful to ask yourself questions like "Who wrote these verses?" "To whom?" "Why is this teaching included in the scriptures?" "What do I want to know or learn as I read today?" and "What would the Lord want me to learn from these scriptures?" As you read the scriptures, look for answers to your questions. Remember that you can also use the study helps in the Latter-day Saint editions of the scriptures or look for answers in Church manuals or publications.

Read the Chapter Headings

Chapter headings are simple summaries of the main ideas in a chapter. Reading the chapter heading before you begin a chapter is not only a good study habit but will also help you prepare yourself to ask questions and look for answers as you read.

During Reading

Don't Be Afraid to Stop

Most nuggets of gold are not found on the surface of the ground—you must dig for them. Your scripture study will be much more valuable if you will slow down or stop and do some of the activities that follow.

Look up the Meanings of Words You Do Not Understand

Use a dictionary. Sometimes looking up a word you think you already know can give you additional insight. The "Understanding the Scriptures" sections of this manual will help you understand many difficult words and phrases.

Be aware that sometimes the Lord has inspired his prophets to include explanations in their writings that help us know the meaning of words and phrases. For example, read Mosiah 3:19 and ask yourself what it means to become like a child.

Use the Study Helps in the Latter-day Saint Editions of the Scriptures

See the section "Study Helps in the Latter-day Saint Editions of the Scriptures" on page 4.

Liken the Scripture

Using your own name in a verse helps make scriptural teachings more personal. For example, what difference does it make to use your own name in place of "man" in Moses 1:39?

Visualize

Picture in your mind what is taking place. For example, when you read Genesis 37, imagine how you might feel if you were one of the younger brothers in a family and all your older brothers hated or were jealous of you.

At times, the scriptures tell us to visualize. Read Alma 5:15–18 and stop to do as Alma suggests. Take some time to write about how you felt as you visualized those verses.

Look for Connecting Words

Connecting words include *and, but, because, therefore,* and *nevertheless.* As you read these words, notice what they help you understand about two or more ideas. Sometimes they show how two or more things are similar or different.

For example, if you think about what the word *because* indicates in Mosiah 26:2–3, you can learn an important truth about scripture study.

> 2 They did not believe what had been said concerning the resurrection of the dead, neither did they believe concerning the coming of Christ.
> 3 And now *because* of their "unbelief they could not *understand the word of God; and their hearts were hardened

Because indicates a cause and effect relationship between the people's disbelief and their ability to understand the scriptures and words of the prophets.

Now read Doctrine and Covenants 45:30–32 and note how the word *but* shows a contrast between the conditions of the wicked and the righteous in the latter days.

> 30 And in that generation shall the "times of the Gentiles be fulfilled.
> 31 And there shall be men standing in that "generation, that shall not pass until they shall see an overflowing *scourge; for a desolating *sickness shall cover the land.
> 32 But my disciples shall "stand in holy places, and shall not be moved; but among the wicked, men shall lift up their voices and *curse God and die.

Emphasizing the word *but* can give us assurance that the righteous will be spared some of the destructions before the Second Coming.

5

Look for Patterns

In 2 Nephi 31:2, Nephi said that he wanted to write a few words about the doctrine of Christ. Then in verse 21 he bore his testimony that he had just explained the doctrine of Christ. Knowing that Nephi taught the doctrine of Christ between verses 2 and 21, we should go back and study Nephi's words further to find out what the doctrine of Christ is.

Another example of finding patterns is to look for a prophet's explanation of cause and effect by watching for his use of the words *if* and *then*. In Leviticus 26, Moses prophesied of blessings or cursings that would come to the children of Israel. Look at verses 3–4, 18, 23–24, 27–28, and 40–42 and notice that Moses used the if-then pattern when he taught the children of Israel about what would happen if they obeyed or did not obey the Lord's commandments.

The repetition of a word or idea is another pattern to look for. For example, notice how many times in Genesis 39 the writer mentioned that the Lord was with Joseph.

Look for Lists in the Scriptures

Lists help you see more clearly what the Lord and his prophets teach. The Ten Commandments are a list (see Exodus 20). The Beatitudes in Matthew 5 are easily seen as a list. Finding other lists may require a little more effort. For example, make a list from Doctrine and Covenants 68:25–31 of what the Lord said parents are required to teach their children.

Ask Questions

Continue to ask questions like you were instructed to do in the "Before Reading" section above. As you read, you may rephrase questions you asked before reading or you may come up with completely different questions. Seeking answers to questions is one of the most important ways we gain greater understanding from our scripture study. One of the most important questions to ask is "Why might the Lord have inspired the writer to include this in the scriptures?" Look for the obvious clues writers sometimes leave when they say something like "and thus we see."

Answer Questions Given in the Scriptures

Many times the Lord asks and then answers a question. He asked the Nephite disciples, "What manner of men ought ye to be?" He then answered, "Even as I am" (3 Nephi 27:27).

On other occasions questions are asked but no answers are given—generally because the author thinks the answer may be obvious. Sometimes the writers don't answer, however, because the question asked may require some thinking and the answer may not be immediate. For example, read Mark 4:35–41 and give answers for the four questions in those verses as if you were there.

Look for Types and Symbolic Meanings

Prophets often use symbols and imagery to more powerfully communicate their messages. For example, parables are a way of telling a message simply and in a way that has a much deeper meaning. The story in a parable makes the lesson taught more memorable and meaningful.

The following suggestions may help you understand symbols in the scriptures:

1. Look for an interpretation in the scriptures. For example, Lehi had a vision in 1 Nephi 8. Nephi later had a vision in which he saw the things his father saw, along with the interpretations of the symbols in his father's vision (see 1 Nephi 11–14). Sometimes an interpretation can be found by using a cross-reference in your footnotes.

2. Think about the characteristics of the symbol and what the symbol might teach you. Alma used this skill in explaining the Liahona to his son (see Alma 37:38–47).

3. See if the symbol teaches you something about the Savior. The Lord told Adam that "all things bear record of [him]" (Moses 6:63). For example, how do the different elements in the story of Abraham's sacrifice of his son Isaac testify of the sacrifice of Jesus Christ?

Write

You should keep some paper or a notebook close by to write down ideas you want to remember, such as lists, special insights you get, or your feelings about something you read. To help you remember thoughts or insights the next time you read, you may want to write these ideas in the margins of your scriptures as well.

Many people like to mark important words and phrases in their scriptures. There is no right or wrong way to do this. Some people shade or underline important words and phrases that bring special meaning to a verse. Another way to mark scriptures is to write a cross-reference to another scripture in the margin. Doing this to several verses that treat the same topic gives you a chain of scriptures on a specific topic that you can find by finding any one of the scriptures in the chain. Marking scriptures can often help you find important verses more quickly.

After Reading

Ponder

To ponder is to think deeply about something, to weigh it out in your mind, asking questions and evaluating what you know and what you have learned. Sometimes the scriptures call this "meditating" (see Joshua 1:8). There are several good examples in the scriptures where important revelations came as a result of pondering, especially pondering the scriptures (see D&C 76:15–20; 138:1–11).

Liken the Scriptures to Yourself

To liken the scriptures to yourself is to compare them to your own life. In order to liken the scriptures to yourself, you need to ask questions like "What principles of the gospel are taught in the scriptures I just read?" and "How do those principles relate to my life?" An important part of likening the scriptures to yourself is listening to promptings of the Spirit, who the Lord promised "will guide you into all truth" (John 16:13).

For example, Nephi likened the scriptures to himself and his family by relating some of the principles Isaiah taught to their situation. He taught his brothers that they, like the children of Israel, had strayed from God—God had not strayed from them. He also taught them that if they would repent, the Lord would be merciful and forgive them (see 1 Nephi 19:24; 21:14–16). Nephi said that by likening the words of Isaiah to himself and his brothers, their belief in Jesus Christ as the Redeemer could increase (see 1 Nephi 19:23).

Reread

We obviously do not learn everything in a passage of scripture the first time we read it. In fact, it takes a lifetime of study to truly understand the scriptures. Often, we begin to see patterns, visualize better, and more deeply understand the scriptures after two or three readings. You may want to look for new teachings or ask different questions as you reread. Trying to rewrite a story or just a verse or two in your own words may help you discover whether or not you understood what you read and help you understand the scriptures better.

Write

Some people keep a journal in which they write the main idea of what they read, how they feel about what they read, or how they think what they read applies to their life. If you are using this manual for home-study seminary, you are required to keep a notebook to receive credit. This notebook will be like a scripture journal.

It is also good to talk to others about what you read. Writing down some notes so that you remember what you want to talk about and discussing what you learned will help you understand and remember more of what you read.

Apply

The real value of knowledge you gain from the scriptures comes when you live what you learn. Greater closeness to the Lord and feeling the peace he gives are just some of the blessings that come to those who live the gospel. In addition, the Lord said that those who live what they learn will be given more, while those who will not live what they learn will lose the knowledge they have (see Alma 12:9–11).

> "Feast upon the words of Christ; for behold, the words of Christ will tell you all things what ye should do" (2 Nephi 32:3).

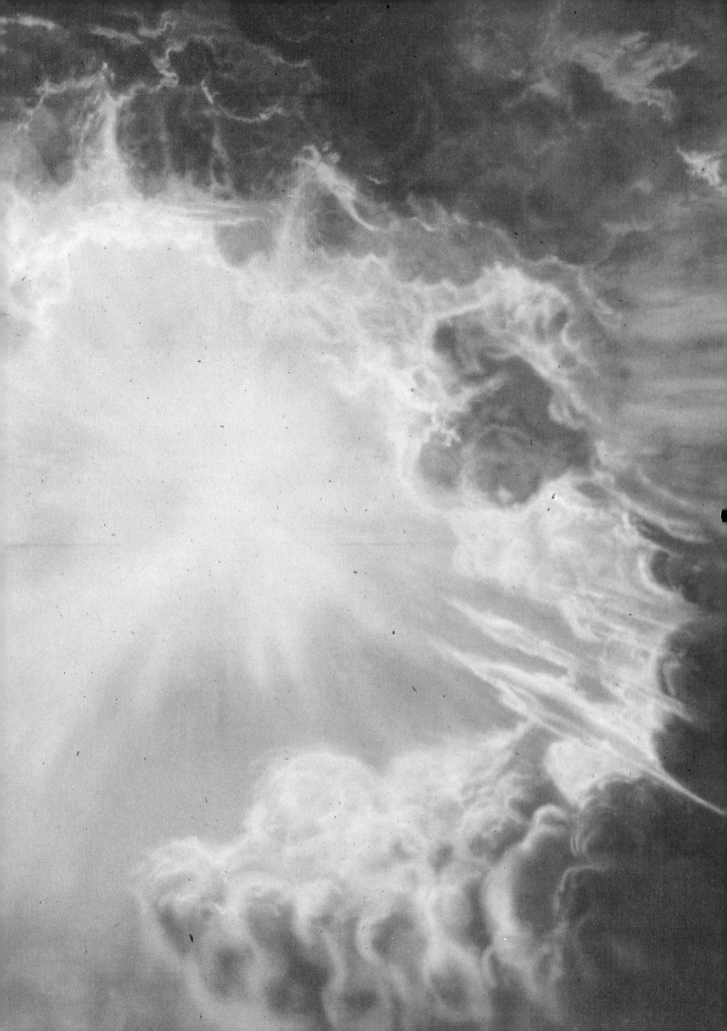

The Book of Genesis

The book of Genesis is the first of five books written by Moses. It covers roughly twenty-five hundred years of history—more than all the rest of the Bible, including the New Testament! Many of the most famous Bible stories come from Genesis, such as the Fall of Adam and Eve, Cain killing Abel, Noah and the Flood, the building of the Tower of Babel, Abraham nearly offering his son Isaac as a sacrifice, and Joseph being sold into Egypt. To learn more about the book, look up "Genesis" in the Bible Dictionary of the Latter-day Saint edition of the King James Version of the Bible.

The Book of Moses

Within a few months after the organization of the Church on 6 April 1830, the Lord commanded the Prophet Joseph Smith to make a "translation" of the Bible. From the Book of Mormon, the Prophet had learned that "many plain and precious things" were missing from the Bible (see 1 Nephi 13:23–28). His translation of the Bible involved restoring truths that were lost from the Bible because of the carelessness of those who copied the text or because wicked men took out truths they did not want people to know. A completed version of this translation of the Bible was never published in the Prophet Joseph Smith's lifetime. Today, however, we can read the changes he made, the most important of which are found in the footnotes and following the Bible Dictionary in the Latter-day Saint edition of the King James Version of the Bible.

So many changes were made in the Joseph Smith Translation (JST) of Genesis 1–6 that they were printed separately in the Pearl of Great Price and called the book of Moses. In Moses there are eight chapters. Moses 1 is like a preface to what we normally consider the beginning of the Bible and contains information not found in Genesis.

Because the book of Moses is a more complete and accurate version of the teachings in Genesis 1–6, this study guide will help you read, understand, and learn from the book of Moses.

The Book of Abraham

Because the revelations in Abraham relate to the earlier parts of the Bible, they are studied with the first part of Genesis and the book of Moses. In 1835 the Prophet Joseph received some ancient Egyptian writings that were found by archaeologists in Egypt. These writings included some of the writings and teachings of the prophet Abraham, which the Prophet Joseph Smith translated. They are also included in the Pearl of Great Price and are called the book of Abraham. The first two chapters are specifically concerned with Abraham's life and are discussed in this study guide with Genesis 11–12. The last three chapters of the book of Abraham contain revelations Abraham received concerning premortal life and the creation of the earth. You will begin your study of the Old Testament by reading the account of premortal life found in Abraham 3.

The following chart should help you see how inspired additions from the books of Moses and Abraham relate to the book of Genesis.

Inspired additions to the book of Genesis

THE BOOK OF MOSES	THE BOOK OF GENESIS	THE BOOK OF ABRAHAM
	No equivalent material in Genesis	3:1–28
1:1–42	No equivalent material in Genesis	
2:1–31	1:1–31	4:1–31
3:1–25	2:1–25	5:1–21
4:1–32	3:1–24	
5:1–59	4:1–26	
6:1–4	5:1–32	
6:5–68	6:1–13	
7:1–69		
8:1–13		
8:14–30	11:27–32	1:1–31
	12:1–13	2:1–5
		2:6–25

CONTENT COMPARISON

A M G

Abraham 3

The Premortal Life and Council in Heaven

After the Lord commanded Abraham to go to Egypt, he taught him truths about the planets, the sun, the moon, and the stars, all of which were important symbols in the Egyptian religion of the time. Abraham used these truths to teach the Egyptians the gospel by building upon what they already knew (notice the explanation of Facsimile No. 3 on page 41 of the Pearl of Great Price). Through a discussion of heavenly bodies and their motions, Abraham taught the Egyptians that the God he worshiped is greater than all other things in creation, because he is the Creator.

Understanding the Scriptures

Abraham 3:22–28

Intelligences that were organized (v. 22)—Spirit children of Heavenly Father

Prove (v. 25)—Test

First estate (vv. 26, 28)—Premortal life

Second estate (v. 26)—Earth life

Son of Man (v. 27)—Jesus Christ

Premortal world
Leaders are chosen in the first estate.

Mortal birth

Earth
Chosen leaders are tested in the second estate.

Abraham 3:22–23—Chosen before Birth

The Prophet Joseph Smith said, "Every man who has a calling to minister to the inhabitants of the world was ordained to that very purpose in the Grand Council of heaven before this world was" (*Teachings of the Prophet Joseph Smith*, sel. Joseph Fielding Smith [1976], 365). In other words, not only was Abraham chosen for certain assignments before birth, but so were you (see D&C 138:53–56).

Abraham 3:27–28—The Premortal Council in Heaven

For a more complete idea of what happened as part of the premortal council in heaven, read also Revelation 12:7–11; Doctrine and Covenants 76:25–28; Moses 4:1–4.

Studying the Scriptures

Do activity A and then do two of the other three activities (B–D) as you study Abraham 3:22–28.

A Scripture Mastery—Abraham 3:22–23

1. Write what Abraham learned about premortal life.

2. Read Doctrine and Covenants 138:53–56, which is part of a vision President Joseph F. Smith had of the spirit world. What information does the revelation in Doctrine and Covenants add to the revelation in Abraham 3:22–23? You may want to cross-reference these two scriptures to each other by highlighting the references in your footnotes or by writing the reference of one in the margin of the other.

3. In addition to what you read in Abraham 3 and Doctrine and Covenants 138, consider the statement from the Prophet Joseph Smith in the "Understanding the Scriptures" section, and describe how these doctrines of the premortal life affect you and how you feel knowing these things.

B Look for Important Words

1. Identify the words in Abraham 3:22–23 that tell who God would choose to be leaders on earth and when they were chosen. Write the words in your notebook; you may also want to circle them in your scriptures.

2. Find the phrase that most likely describes Jesus Christ in Abraham 3:24. Write it in your notebook and tell why that phrase describes him well.

C Write a Question

Write an important question people may ask that you think can be answered by Abraham 3:24–26.

D Apply the Doctrine

Choose one of the truths taught to Abraham in verses 22–28 and write about how it should, could, or will encourage you to live more righteously.

Moses 1

"This Is My Work and My Glory"

Although this is the first chapter of the Joseph Smith Translation, there is nothing like Moses 1 in Genesis. The teachings in Moses 1 belong at the beginning of Genesis because they tell how Moses learned the truths he wrote about in the book of Genesis. In addition, Moses 1 provides important information concerning Heavenly Father's plan for his children. Note that the revelation to Moses in Moses 1 occurred after the revelation at the burning bush (see Moses 1:18) but before Moses returned to Egypt (see Moses 1:26). Consequently, this revelation would come at some point in Exodus 3 or 4 if it were found in the Old Testament.

At some time in our lives we may ask, "Who am I?" "Where did I come from?" "Why am I here?" "How was life created on this planet? and why?" Moses asked questions like these, and God revealed answers. As you read, think about these questions and look for the answers the Lord gave Moses in this revelation, which includes chapter 1 as well as the rest of the book of Moses.

Understanding the Scriptures

Moses 1

Endure (v. 2)—Stay alive in

Cease (v. 4)—End, stop

Behold, beheld (vv. 5, 8, 25, 27)—See, seen

In the similitude of (vv. 6, 13, 16)—Like

Supposed (v. 10)—Thought

Withered (v. 11)—Lost all strength

Transfigured (vv. 11, 14)—Changed by the Holy Ghost (in a way that allows a mortal to see immortal beings)

Altogether withdrawn (v. 15)—Completely gone away

Hence (vv. 16, 18, 21–22)—Away to another place

Cease to call upon God (v. 18)—Stop praying

Inquire (v. 18)—Ask

Ranted (v. 19)—Spoke violently

Gnashing of teeth (v. 22)—Clenching of teeth in pain and anger

Thou wert (v. 25)—You were

Bondage (v. 26)—Slavery

Cast his eyes (v. 27)—Looked

Particle (v. 27)—Smallest part

Discerning, discerned (vv. 27–28)—To gain a more clear understanding and knowledge through more than the normal senses

Inhabitants thereof (vv. 28, 35–36)—People who live in a certain place

Content (v. 36)—Happy and at peace

Immortality (v. 39)—To live forever as a resurrected being

Eternal life (v. 39)—Exaltation; which is the kind of life God lives; to be with God and to be like him

Esteem (v. 41)—Value

Naught (v. 41)—Nothing

Moses 1:11—Moses Was Transfigured

"By the power of the Holy Ghost many prophets have been transfigured so as to stand in the presence of God and view the visions of eternity" (Bruce R. McConkie, *Mormon Doctrine*, 2d ed. [1966], 803). Other accounts of people being transfigured are found in 3 Nephi 28:13–17 and Doctrine and Covenants 76:11–12, 19–20.

Moses 1:23—Why These Things Are Not in the Bible

Moses 1:23 explains why the account of Moses overcoming Satan is not in our current Bible. It is interesting to note that the words *Satan* and *devil* do not appear in Genesis 1–6 in the Bible. *Satan* and *devil* appear over twenty times in the Joseph Smith Translation of these same chapters (Moses 1–8). One of the ways Satan tries to deceive people is to get them to believe he does not exist (see 2 Nephi 28:22).

Studying the Scriptures

Do at least two of the following activities (A–D) as you study Moses 1.

A Who Is God? Who Is Man?

1. Read Moses 1:1–11 and list what Moses learned about God.

2. List what Moses learned about himself in relation to God from those same verses. You may want to highlight these two lists in some way in your scriptures.

3. Explain how you think Moses felt about what he learned and why.

B Why Does It Matter?

1. How did Moses use what he learned about himself and God (see Moses 1:1–11) to overcome Satan? (see Moses 1:12–22).

2. How might you use Moses' example in Moses 1:12–22 to overcome temptation in your life?

C Scripture Mastery—Moses 1:39

Moses 1:39 tells us the whole reason behind God's works and creations. Note the definitions of *immortality* and *eternal life* found in "Understanding the Scriptures."

1. Rewrite this verse in your notebook, putting your own name in the place of "man."

2. Why is it important to know God's purposes?

3. What "work" has God done to bring to pass your immortality and eternal life?

4. What are you doing, or what could you do, with what God has done for you?

D Be a News Reporter

Pretend you are a reporter asked to interview Moses after his experiences in this chapter. Write down five questions you would ask him.

Genesis 1; Moses 2

The Creation

There are three accounts of the Creation in the scriptures: Genesis 1–2; Moses 2–3 (which is the Joseph Smith Translation of Genesis 1–2); and Abraham 4–5. This study guide provides help with studying the Joseph Smith Translation of Genesis but refers to Abraham for additional insight.

Some people believe that the earth was created by chance and that mankind came about by the accidental combining of the right elements over millions of years. In response, one writer said:

"When you can dump a load of bricks on a corner lot, and let me watch them arrange themselves into a house—when you can empty a handful of springs and wheels and screws on my desk, and let me see them gather themselves into a watch—it will [then] be easier for me to believe that all these thousands of worlds could have been created, balanced, and set in motion in their several orbits, all without any designing intelligence at all.

"Moreover, if there is no intelligence in the universe, then the universe created something greater than itself—for it created you and me" (Bruce Barton in E. Ernest Bramwell, comp. Old Testament Lessons [1934 seminary course], 4).

As you read, decide what you think Moses was trying to say in Moses 2 (Genesis 1) about the creation of man and all things on earth and in heaven.

Understanding the Scriptures

Moses 2

Mine Only Begotten (vv. 1, 26)—Jesus Christ

Without form (v. 2)—Not organized the way it is now

Void (v. 2)—Empty

Deep (v. 2)—Water

Firmament (vv. 6–8, 14–15, 17, 20)—Space

Herb (vv. 11, 29–30)—Plant

Yielding (vv. 11–12, 29)—Producing

Abundantly (vv. 20–21)—In a large amount

Fowl (vv. 21–22, 28, 30)—Birds

Be fruitful and multiply (vv. 22, 28)—Have children

Dominion (v. 26, 28)—Be in charge of, take care of

Replenish (v. 28)—Fill

Subdue (v. 28)—Have power over

Bearing (v. 29)—Producing

Meat (v. 30)—Food

Moses 2:1 (Genesis 1:1)—Jesus Christ Is the Creator

Moses 2:1; Abraham 3:22–25; 4:1 tell us that Jesus Christ, under the direction of the Father, created the earth. You can find many other scriptures that teach this truth in the Topical Guide under "Jesus Christ, Creator" (see p. 244).

Studying the Scriptures

A) Make a Chart

First Day	Fourth Day
Second Day	Fifth Day
Third Day	Sixth Day

Divide a page in your notebook into six parts and label each box like the one shown.

In each box, write about or draw pictures of the things God created on that day.

B) What It Is and What It Isn't

Notice that Moses 2 does not tell much about *how* the earth was created. What *does* it tell us? (see Moses 1:31–33, 39).

C) Scripture Mastery—Genesis 1:26–27 (Moses 2:26–27)

1. Compare Genesis 1:26–27 with Moses 2:26–27. How does Moses 2:26 help you understand the word *us* in Genesis 1:26?

2. In what ways is man different from all the other creations described in Genesis 1; Moses 2?

Genesis 2; Moses 3

The Creation of Eve

Genesis 2 (and Moses 3) completes the story of the Creation. In it we learn more about commandments God gave to Adam, about the relationship of Adam to all other creations, and about the creation of Eve, the first woman.

Understanding the Scriptures

Moses 3

Host (v. 1)—Great number of things

Sanctified (v. 3)—Made holy and sacred

Generations (v. 4)—Beginnings

Spiritually, spiritual (vv. 5, 7, 9)—Eternal, not subject to death

Naturally (vv. 5, 9)—Mortal, will eventually die

Till (v. 5)—Plow, to dig up

Flesh (vv. 5, 7)—Mortal life

Sphere (v. 9)—Condition

Compasseth (v. 11)—Goes around

Dress (v. 15)—Take care of

Freely eat (v. 16)—Eat without any consequences

Meet (vv. 18, 20)—Exactly right, perfectly matched, proper, fitting

Stead (v. 21)—Place

Cleave unto (v. 24)—Be closest to and stay with

Moses 3:4–9—Spiritual Creation

At the time described in Moses 3:5, all things were "spiritual," meaning they could not die. Elder Joseph Fielding Smith said: "Adam's body was created from the dust of the earth, but at that time it was a spiritual earth. . . .

". . . What is a spiritual body? It is one that is quickened by spirit and not by blood. . . .

". . . The forbidden fruit had the power to create blood and change his nature and mortality took the place of immortality" (*Doctrines of Salvation*, comp. Bruce R. McConkie, 3 vols. [1954–56], 1:76–77).

In other words, in the account we have of the Creation, we read that Adam and Eve had physical bodies, but they were "spiritual" physical bodies. When they fell, a change took place (as described in Moses 4), and all things became "natural," meaning Adam and Eve were subject to death. Adam and Eve then had "natural" physical bodies (see also 2 Nephi 2:22). You may want to highlight the words *spiritual* and *natural* in your scriptures and write their definitions in the margin of your scriptures.

The following diagram outlines the different stages in Adam's existence as described in Genesis 2; Moses 3.

Spirit Creation	Spiritual Creation	The Fall to Mortality
All things were first created as spirits (see Moses 3:5)	All things were next created physically, but in a spiritually unfallen condition (see Moses 2)	The Fall brought about a mortal, physical existence (see Moses 4:6–32)

Moses 3:15–17—The Fruit of the Tree of Knowledge of Good and Evil

The Lord gave Adam and Eve agency in the Garden of Eden. Agency, or the ability to make choices and be accountable for them, is necessary for everyone who desires to become like God. Consequently, Adam and Eve needed to exercise their agency and partake of the tree of knowledge of good and evil so they could progress to become like Heavenly Father. Partaking of the fruit of that tree not only helped Adam and Eve progress but made it possible for the rest of Heavenly Father's children to come to earth and to exercise their own agency (see 2 Nephi 2:22–27).

Some people have wondered why, since the Fall was necessary for eternal progression, God did not just place Adam and Eve in a fallen condition to begin with. But if Heavenly Father caused men to become mortal then he would ultimately be responsible for all the pain, sin, and sorrow that would come to man because of mortal life. Adam had to have the freedom to choose to eat the fruit and fall. Because of agency, man became responsible for his own destiny. Of course, Heavenly Father's plan also includes the means by which he can redeem all of his children from this fallen state, but they must again exercise their agency and choose to accept the plan. Because God gave Adam and Eve the gift of agency, and because Adam and Eve exercised their agency, we can make righteous decisions based on gospel principles and ultimately become like God.

Moses 3:20–24 (Genesis 2:20–24)—The Creation of Woman

In speaking to the women of the Church, President Gordon B. Hinckley said:

"You are an absolutely essential part of [Heavenly Father's] plan.

"Without you the plan could not function. Without you the entire program would be frustrated. . . . When the process of creation occurred, Jehovah, the Creator, under instruction from His Father, first divided the light from the darkness, and then separated the land from the waters. There followed the creation of plant life, followed by the creation of animal life. Then came the creation of man, and culminating that act of divinity came the crowning act, the creation of woman" (in Conference Report, Oct. 1996, 90; or *Ensign*, Nov. 1996, 67).

Studying the Scriptures

A Choose Important Words

Choose what you think are the four words in Moses 3:2–3 that help us best understand and appreciate the importance of the Sabbath day, and explain how they increase our understanding.

B Say It in Your Own Words

1. What commandment did Adam receive in Moses 3:15–17?
2. What did God say would be the consequences of breaking this commandment?

Genesis 3; Moses 4

The Fall

What happens if you plant vegetable seeds or seeds for beautiful flowers in a piece of ground and never care for them? Do vegetables ever take over and crowd out weeds? If care is not taken, why do weeds crowd out things that are more beautiful or useful?

Why do so many people find it easier to choose the wrong instead of the right? Why is there so much wickedness on the earth? Why do seemingly innocent people have so many trials?

The answers to these questions have to do with what we call the Fall. The Fall occurred when Adam and Eve partook of the fruit of the tree of knowledge of good and evil and were cast out of the Garden of Eden and the presence of God. As Adam and Eve's children, we inherit the consequences of their decision, which include living in a world outside of God's presence that is full of sin, trials, difficulties, and death. You will learn, however, that if Adam did not fall, we would never have been born and could never progress to receive the fulness of joy Heavenly Father offers his children. We are blessed to have a more complete story of the Fall of Adam and Eve in Moses 4 than we can find in the Bible. We are even more blessed to have the Book of Mormon, which explains the doctrine of the Fall more completely than any other book.

Understanding the Scriptures

Moses 4

Redeem (v. 1)—Saved from sin and death

Hearken (v. 4)—Listen and obey

Subtle (v. 5)—Sly

Beast (vv. 5, 20)—Animal

Beguile (vv. 6, 19)—Deceive

Thou beholdest (v. 9)—You see

Put enmity between thee and the woman (v. 21)—Cause you and the woman to strongly dislike and work against each other

Seed (v. 21)—Children

Bruise (v. 21)—Hurt

Conception (v. 22)—The process of beginning a pregnancy and giving birth to a child

Sake (v. 23)—Benefit

The sweat of thy face (v. 25)—Hard work

Lest he (v. 28)—So he cannot

Void (v. 30)—Without being fulfilled

Cherubim (v. 31)—A kind of heavenly being

Moses 4:4—Can Satan Deceive, Blind, and Make Captive?

Moses 4:4 describes the only way Satan can get power over you. You may want to write the following explanation in the margin of your scriptures: "The devil has no power over us only as we permit him. The moment we revolt at anything which comes from God, the devil takes power" (Joseph Smith, *Teachings of the Prophet Joseph Smith*, sel. Joseph Fielding Smith [1938], 181).

Moses 4:12—The Choice

It is important to know that Adam and Eve did not fully understand the impact of their choice until the events recorded in the first verses of Moses 5. In other words, the choice Adam made was based on his faith that it was the right thing to do. He had never been mortal or out of the presence of God and could not be certain what the consequence of his choice would be.

The tree of knowledge of good and evil

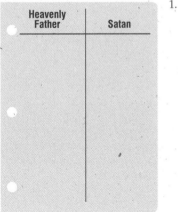

Adam's Choices

To Partake
Leave the garden and become subject to death, but with the opportunity to become as God is

Not to Partake
Remain in the garden in a changed condition without posterity and never die

Moses 4—The Fall

We cannot completely understand the importance of the Fall in Heavenly Father's plan unless we understand that because of the Fall, Adam and Eve would die both physically and spiritually (see Moses 3:17). Spiritual death means to be shut out of the presence of God (see Moses 5:4). Physical death is the separation of the spirit and the body. Although Adam and Eve did not immediately die physically when they ate the fruit, a change occurred in Adam and Eve that would cause them to eventually die. Eventually, they would die physically just as God said. Adam and Eve did not have the power to overcome physical or spiritual death. Knowing these truths helps us understand why they, and we as their children, need a Savior and the Atonement. Adam and Eve were taught about the Atonement after the Fall. We read some of those teachings in Moses 5.

Studying the Scriptures ▨

A Heavenly Father's Plan

Heavenly Father	Satan

1. Make a two-column chart in your notebook. Label the first column "Heavenly Father" and the second column "Satan."

Under each column, write specific words and phrases from Moses 4:1–4 that describe Heavenly Father or Satan. As you do this exercise it might be helpful to know that Heavenly Father presented his plan of salvation to his spirit children in the premortal world before the events that are described in these four verses occurred. Heavenly Father explained that we would be out of his presence and that a Savior would be provided for our redemption.

---

2. Write a paragraph that tells how Jesus and Satan differ. For example, what is different about their desires?

B Write a Journal Entry

Imagine you are Eve in the events of Moses 4. Write a journal entry as if you were Eve. Share the thoughts and feelings you would have had as you considered eating the fruit and what your motivations would have been when you finally ate it. Then write about how you would have felt after eating the fruit and about what the Lord said to you concerning the consequences of your choices.

or

Imagine you are Adam in the events of Moses 4. Write the thoughts and feelings you would have had when you found out Eve had eaten the fruit (see Moses 2:27–28; 3:23–24). Explain why you would have decided to eat the fruit—knowing the consequences (see Moses 3:16–17; 4:9), and how you would have felt about what the Lord said to you concerning the consequences of your choices. The following quotation may help you as you write: "Adam . . . was not deceived; on the contrary he deliberately decided to do as Eve desired, that he might carry out the purposes of his Maker" (James E. Talmage, *Articles of Faith* [1960], 69–70).

C Optional Activity

1. Briefly describe what happened to Adam and Eve as they were sent out of the Garden of Eden. Read Alma 12:21–37; 42:2–28 and find reasons the Lord said he kept Adam and Eve from eating the fruit of the tree of life shortly after eating of the tree of knowledge of good and evil.

2. What do the reasons the Lord gave tell us about what things are important to do in this life?

Genesis 4; Moses 5

Sacrifice and the Family of Adam

Being cast out of Eden and the Lord's presence must have been frightening for Adam and Eve. They had never experienced mortality. How could they return to the presence of God again?

Like Adam and Eve, we are cut off from the presence of God, so the same question applies to us.

Genesis tells the story of Adam and Eve being cast out of Eden and the presence of the Lord as if they had no hope of living in the Lord's presence again.

Fortunately, the book of Moses contains inspired additions to Genesis that tell how Adam was taught about the plan that was prepared before the creation of the world so he and his posterity could be redeemed, or freed, from the sin and death the Fall brought into the world.

In addition to truths about redemption and the Atonement, Moses 5 contains an account of how Satan and his followers from the premortal life attempted to influence the family of Adam to reject the message of redemption through Christ. As you read, notice what happened to those who refused to listen to the counsel of the Lord and instead followed the counsel of Satan.

Understanding the Scriptures

Moses 5

By the sweat of his brow (v. 1)—By his hard work

Divide two and two (v. 3)—Separate from their parents and marry (thus pairing up into twos)

Offer . . . an offering (v. 5; see also vv. 18–21)—To give a sacrifice to be burned

Firstlings (vv. 5, 20)—Firstborn lambs, cows, goats, and so on

Save (v. 6)—Except

Similitude (v. 7)—Likeness, a type or symbol

Redeemed (v. 9)—Saved from sin and death

Seed (v. 11)—Children

Redemption (v. 11)—To be freed from the results of sin and death

Carnal (v. 13)—Concerned with the needs, pleasures, and lusts of the body

Sensual (v. 13)—Concerned with the pleasures of the senses, or in other words, things you can touch, see, smell, and hear

Damned (v. 15)—Progress stopped

Firm decree (v. 15)—Statement that cannot be changed

Conceived and bare (vv. 16–17, 42)—Became pregnant and had a baby

Had respect unto (v. 20)—Approved of

Wroth (vv. 21–22, 26, 38)—Angry

His countenance fell, countenance fall (vv. 21–22)—He frowned, scowled

Abominations (vv. 25, 52)—Wicked actions

Yield unto thee her strength (v. 37)—Give you enough food

Fugitive, vagabond (vv. 37, 39)—Runaway, wanderer (meaning he was cut off from his family)

Vengeance (v. 40)—Punishment

Artificer in (v. 46)—Expert

Avenged (v. 48)—Satisfied, or to receive benefit from doing harm to, or injuring another

Administered (v. 49)—Given

Ministered not unto (v. 52)—Did not bless

Despised (v. 54)—Looked down on others, hated

Prevail (v. 55)—Have a great influence

Meridian of time (v. 57)—High point or most important time (This phrase refers to the time when Jesus Christ would come and perform his atoning mission.)

Confirmed (v. 59)—Given

Studying the Scriptures

Do at least three of the following activities (A–E) as you study Moses 5.

A Finish These Sentences (See Moses 5:4–11.)

1. Adam offered sacrifices because . . .

2. Adam learned from the angel . . .

3. Adam and Eve realized . . .

B Make a Comparison

In Moses 5:7–8, the angel explained to Adam what his sacrifices represented, and in Moses 5:9, the Holy Ghost explained the Savior's role as the ultimate redeeming sacrifice. Answer the following questions in your notebook: (1) Although we don't offer burnt sacrifices today, as Adam did, which ordinances do we participate in that serve the same purposes? (2) What do these ordinances have to do with redemption, doing all we do "in the name of the Son" (v. 8), and the sacrifice of the Only Begotten?

Adam's Day   =   ?   Our Day

C Gain Additional Understanding from the Book of Mormon

Moses 5:9–11 tells about some of the blessings Adam and Eve and their posterity received because of the Fall. Read 2 Nephi 2:19–27 and summarize what you learn from these two references about why the Fall of Adam and Eve was a necessary part of Heavenly Father's plan and how the Fall is a blessing to us.

D Answer Cain's Questions

Cain asked two important questions (see Moses 5:16, 34) that people today still ask. Write a letter explaining the correct answers to his questions.

E The Enticements of Satan

Read Moses 5:12–13 and consider Adam and Eve's actions and Satan's actions.

1. In what ways do you see Satan's influence in a similar way today?

2. What did Satan not "advertise" in his enticements? (see Moses 5:41, 52–54; see also Alma 30:60).

Genesis 5; Moses 6

Enoch Teaches the First Principles of the Gospel

Adam and Eve fell because of disobedience to a law, and they were "shut out" from the presence of God (Moses 5:4). We read in Moses 5 how disobedience leads men even further away from God—as in the case of Cain, Lamech, and others. After Adam and Eve left the Garden of Eden, they were taught to understand and live doctrines and make and keep covenants. They also learned which saving ordinances were required for them to return and live in the presence of God. Many of these teachings are found in Moses 6. The prophet Enoch taught his people these truths in an attempt to inspire them to repent of their sins and wickedness so they could be redeemed and brought back into the presence of God.

Understanding the Scriptures

Moses 6

Glorified (v. 2)—Praised

Undefiled (v. 6)—Not polluted, pure

Genealogy (vv. 8, 22)—Family history

Generations (vv. 8, 28)—Children, grandchildren, and so on

The footstool of God (v. 9)—Earth (see v. 44)

Begat (vv. 10–11, 13–14, 17, 21, 25)—Was the father of

Dominion (v. 15)—Power

Residue (v. 17)—The smaller group that was left after being separated from the whole group

Conversed (v. 22)—Spoke with

Kindled (v. 27)—Beginning to grow

Counsel (vv. 28, 43)—Advice

Devised (v. 28)—Planned

Foresworn themselves (v. 29)—Made promises

Decree (v. 30)—Official announcement

Pierce (v. 32)—Hurt, kill

Utterance (v. 32)—What to say

Justify (v. 34)—Make happen

Yonder (v. 38)—Over there

Host (v. 44)—Large number

Are made partakers of (v. 48)—Experience

Woe (v. 48)—Sorrow

Original guilt (v. 54)—The transgression of Adam and Eve

Whole (v. 54)—Clean and pure

Conceived in sin (v. 55)—Born into a sinful world to parents who live in a fallen world and have sinned themselves

Sin conceiveth (v. 55)—The desire for sin begins to grow

Sanctified (vv. 59–60)—Cleansed and made holy, purified

Justified (v. 60)—Made free from guilt and the punishment of sin, forgiven

Quickeneth (v. 61)—Gives life to

Studying the Scriptures

Do at least three of the following activities (A–E) as you study Moses 6.

A Make a Table of Contents

Write what you think the table of contents would look like for the book described in Moses 6:5–25.

B Write about or to Your Family

1. According to Moses 6:45–46, why did Enoch and his people know their ancestors (fathers)?

2. Write about one of your ancestors you "know" because of records that have been kept. Include something about them that inspires you to be a better person.

or

Write something you will want your posterity to know about you. Consider President Kimball's words:

> "Get a notebook. . . . Begin today and write in it your goings and comings, your deepest thoughts, your achievements and your failures, your associations and your triumphs, your impressions and your testimonies" (Spencer W. Kimball, "'The Angels May Quote from It,'" *New Era*, Oct. 1975, 5).

C What Do They Describe?

1. Find the following phrases in Moses 6:27–29 that describe the sins of the people in Enoch's day: "hearts have waxed dull," "ears are dull of hearing," "eyes cannot see afar off," "have denied me," "sought their own counsel in the dark," "devised murder," "have not kept the commandments [given to] Adam," and "foresworn themselves." You might want to underline or highlight these phrases in your scriptures.

2. Describe what you think is meant by "hearts waxed dull," "ears dull of hearing," "eyes that cannot see afar off," and what it means to "seek counsel in the dark."

3. Give the opposite of each description above so that they describe righteous people. In other words, through the gospel hearts can be ___, eyes can become ___, and so on.

D A Calling from the Lord

1. According to Moses 6:31, how did Enoch feel about his calling from the Lord?

2. Explain how you think Enoch felt after the things the Lord said and did in Moses 6:32–36.

3. Read Moses 7:13–19 and write about how the promises of the Lord to Enoch were fulfilled.

E How Do We Receive Our Inheritance from Heavenly Father?

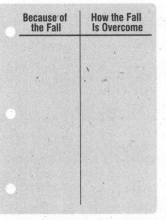

Because of the Fall	How the Fall Is Overcome

As children of God, we are entitled to inherit all that he has. When we sin, however, we become unclean, and no unclean thing can inherit the kingdom of God. The Lord taught Adam how to become clean and thus qualify to inherit eternal life. Enoch taught these same things to his people. Read Moses 6:48–68, and then make a chart like the one shown. List in the first column things that happened because of the Fall. List in the second column things that tell how to overcome the effects of the Fall.

Genesis 5; Moses 7

Zion Taken into Heaven

Have you ever wondered what God must be thinking and feeling as he watches the wickedness of his children on earth? Moses 7 helps us understand how God views his children, how he feels about their wickedness, and how wickedness will eventually be eliminated.

Understanding the Scriptures

Moses 7

Perished (v. 1)—Died

Torment (v. 1)—Suffering

Fiery indignation, fire of mine indignation (vv. 1, 34)—Intense punishment

Wrath (v. 1)—Anger

In battle array (v. 7)—Organized and prepared for fighting

Divide themselves (v. 7)—Spread out and settle

Land shall be barren, barrenness (vv. 7–8)—The land grows very little or nothing

Despised (v. 8)—Disliked and looked down upon

Flourish (v. 17)—Prosper

Residue (vv. 20, 22, 28, 43)—Remaining number

Abode (vv. 21, 64)—Place to live, house

Veiled (vv. 26, 56)—Covered

Particles (v. 30)—Smallest parts

Curtains are stretched out still (v. 30)—Creations are still continuing

Bosom (vv. 30–31, 63, 69)—Innermost parts, a symbol of being very close to something

Naught (v. 31)—Nothing

Is the habitation of thy throne (v. 31)—Is what lives in thy presence

Affection (v. 33)—Love

Mine eye can pierce them (v. 36)—My eyes can see right through to the very center of them

That which I have chosen, my Chosen (v. 39)—Jesus Christ

His bowels yearned (v. 41)—He felt very strong sorrowful emotions

Temporal (v. 42)—Physical

Meridian of time (v. 46)—High point or most important time (This phrase refers to the time when Jesus Christ would come and perform his atoning mission.)

Stay (v. 51)—Stop

Unalterable (v. 52)—Unchangeable

Remnant (v. 52)—Part

Gird up your loins (v. 62)—Prepare

Tribulations (v. 66)—Trials and afflictions

Moses 7:16–20—Building and Establishing Zion

President Spencer W. Kimball spoke of establishing Zion in our day:

"May I suggest three fundamental things we must do if we are to 'bring again Zion.' . . .

"First, we must eliminate the individual tendency to selfishness that snares the soul, shrinks the heart, and darkens the mind. . . .

"Second, we must cooperate completely and work in harmony one with the other. There must be unanimity in our decisions and unity in our actions. . . .

"'If the Spirit of the Lord is to magnify our labors, then this spirit of oneness and cooperation must be the prevailing spirit in all that we do' . . . (*Teachings of the Prophet Joseph Smith*, p. 1983.) . . .

"Third, we must lay on the altar and sacrifice whatever is required by the Lord. We begin by offering a 'broken heart and a contrite spirit.' We follow this by giving our best effort in our assigned fields of labor and callings. We learn our duty and execute it fully. Finally we consecrate our time, talents and means as called upon by our file leaders and as prompted by the whisperings of the Spirit" (in Conference Report, Apr. 1978, 122–24; or *Ensign*, May 1978, 81).

Sacrifice	Effort	Consecration
Cooperation		Unity
	Selflessness	

Studying the Scriptures

Do at least two of the following activities (A–D) as you study Moses 7.

A Scripture Mastery—Moses 7:18

Read Moses 7:4–27 and imagine what it would be like to have been part of Enoch's community. Write a letter to an imaginary friend who lives somewhere else and wants to know how to create a place as wonderful as Zion. Using the information in Moses 7, especially verse 18, tell your friend what it takes to establish and live in Zion. Encourage your friend and give advice on what a person your age could do to "eliminate selfishness" or accomplish one of the other things President Kimball suggested. Especially focus on what your friend could do first in his or her family and then in the Church and community.

B What Makes the Lord Weep?

1. In Moses 7:29–31 Enoch asked the Lord why he was weeping. Read verses 31–40 and write an answer to Enoch's question.

2. According to Moses 7:41, what did Enoch do when he understood the Lord's answer to his question?

3. What do you think the Lord and Enoch might weep about as they view the world today?

C Answer Enoch's Questions

Read Moses 7:42–67 and identify the questions Enoch asked the Lord. Write each question in your notebook followed by a summary of the Lord's answer.

D Explain the Imagery

In Moses 7:62, Enoch was told about the Restoration of the gospel in the latter days. He was told of two important things that would happen to help gather the "elect" from the whole earth to prepare for the Second Coming: "Righteousness will I send down out of heaven; and truth will I send forth out of the earth." Consider what you know about events that took place as part of the Restoration and explain what you think the Lord was referring to.

Genesis 6; Moses 8

Noah's Preaching

The scriptures speak of two separate times when the Lord would cleanse the earth of wickedness. The first was at the time of Noah (see Genesis 6) and the second will be at the Second Coming. Joseph Smith—Matthew 1:41–43, in the Pearl of Great Price, tells ways those two time periods will be like each other. The biggest difference in the two periods is that the earth was cleansed by water in the days of Noah, and at the Second Coming it will be cleansed by fire. These two events are a type of how we are cleansed by the baptism of water and the baptism of fire—the cleansing of the soul that occurs when we truly receive the gift of the Holy Ghost.

Genesis 6–9 tells the story of Noah and the Flood. As you read, look for reasons the Lord destroyed the wicked and why destroying them was the best possible thing he could do for the salvation of all his children. Also consider how the days of Noah might be compared to our day—the time before the earth is cleansed by fire.

Moses 8 is the Joseph Smith Translation of Genesis 5:23–32; 6:1–13, so you will want to read Moses 8 before reading Genesis 6:14–22. Notice that Moses 8 is the last chapter of Moses in the Pearl of Great Price. For the rest of the Old Testament, all references to the Joseph Smith Translation will be in your footnotes or at the back of your Bible (beginning on p. 777).

Understanding the Scriptures

Moses 8

The fruit of his loins (v. 2)—His descendant

Hearkened, hearken (vv. 13, 15, 20–21, 23–24)—Listen and obey

Sons of God (vv. 13, 21)—Those who made covenants with the Lord

Sons of men (v. 14)—Those who would not make or obey covenants with the Lord

Sold themselves (v. 15)—Married out of the covenant

Renown (v. 21)—Fame

Was lifted up (v. 22)—Was focused on and behaved

Imagination (v. 22)—Desire

Manifest (v. 24)—Known

Repented, repenteth (vv. 25–26)—Made feel very sorry

Grieved him (v. 25)—Made him feel very sorry

Found grace (v. 27)—Received blessings and power, was approved

Generation (v. 27)—Time

Flesh (v. 29)—People

Genesis 6

Pitch it (v. 14)—Cover it with a tar-like substance

Fashion (v. 15)—Way, pattern

Cubit (vv. 15–16)—The distance between an adult's

elbow and the tip of his longest finger (approximately forty-five centimeters or eighteen inches)

Stories (v. 16)—Levels

Moses 8; Genesis 6—Why the Lord Flooded the Earth

President John Taylor helped explain why the Lord decided to destroy all people on earth except the family of Noah. President Taylor suggested that the world was so wicked that children grew up with no choice but to be wicked. At that point where there is no chance to choose righteousness, sending innocent spirits from heaven to earth is no longer just. Consequently, the Lord destroyed all the wicked and began again with the family of Noah to raise up righteous men and women. "By taking away their earthly existence he prevented them from entailing [give as an inheritance] their sins upon their posterity and degenerating them [making them wicked], and also prevented them from committing further acts of wickedness" (in *Journal of Discourses*, 19:158–59). If God had not flooded the earth, his great plan could not be fulfilled. Read what Nephi said in 2 Nephi 26:24 about why the Lord acts as he does.

Studying the Scriptures

Do three of the following four activities (A–D) as you study Genesis 6; Moses 8.

A A Pattern for Fulfilling Our Calling from the Lord

1. In Doctrine and Covenants 4:2–4 the Lord said that one way we become sanctified and bring salvation to our souls is to work with all our might, mind, and strength to bring others to salvation. Noah is an excellent example of this process. Make a diagram in your notebook like the one below and fill it in with information you find in Moses 8:14–27. As you do this activity, notice how Noah magnified his calling from the Lord. Also pay special attention to how he was blessed with strength and power and came to know the Lord was pleased with him and his efforts.

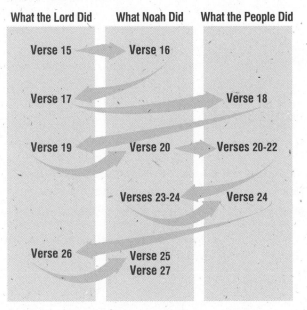

What the Lord Did	What Noah Did	What the People Did
Verse 15	Verse 16	
Verse 17		Verse 18
Verse 19	Verse 20	Verses 20-22
	Verses 23-24	Verse 24
Verse 26	Verse 25 Verse 27	

2. After you fill in the box for Moses 8:27, look up "grace" in your Bible Dictionary so you can more fully understand what it was that Noah received as a result of his diligent labors. Write a brief statement about grace below your diagram.

What Is the Difference?

1. Read Moses 8:13–14, 21 and the definitions for "sons of God" and "sons of men" in the "Understanding the

Scriptures" section above. Explain the difference between sons and daughters of God and sons and daughters of men. Include in your explanation who these four groups of people might be today.

2. According to Moses 8:15–22, explain what the Lord said about the sons of God marrying the daughters of men or the sons of men marrying the daughters of God and why you think it was so important.

C Explain to Someone Who Doesn't Understand

Use the information in the "Understanding the Scriptures" section above along with what you read in Moses 8 to answer the question "How could a loving God flood the world?"

D Figure It Out

Read Genesis 6:14–22 and figure out how big the ark was, and then compare the ark to something you are familiar with. Explain the ark's size in your notebook. (*Hint:* Look in your Bible Dictionary under "cubit" to help you make your calculations.)

Genesis 7

The Flood

Genesis 6 told about Noah before the Flood. Genesis 7 tells about Noah making final preparations before the Flood and what happened during the Flood.

Understanding the Scriptures

Genesis 7

Clean, not clean (vv. 2, 8)—Animals considered acceptable or unacceptable to eat and to be sacrificed to God

Keep seed alive (v. 3)—To allow them to reproduce

For yet (v. 4)—In

Fountains (v. 11)—Springs of water

Great deep (v. 11)—Ocean

Flesh (vv. 15–16, 21)—Animals (vv. 15–16), people (v. 21)

Prevailed (vv. 18–19, 24)—Flooded

Studying the Scriptures

A Find Out What Happened

1. Read 1 Peter 3:18–20; Doctrine and Covenants 138:6–11, 28–35 and describe what Jesus Christ did for the people destroyed in the Flood.

2. What does it teach you about the Savior to know he did the things described in 1 Peter and Doctrine and Covenants 138?

Genesis 8

The Rain Stops

Understanding the Scriptures

Genesis 8

Asswaged (v. 1)—Went down
Restrained (v. 2)—Stopped
Breed abundantly (v. 17)—Increase in number

Savour (v. 21)—Odor
Smite (v. 21)—Hurt

Studying the Scriptures

A Apply the Story

Using what you read in Genesis 6–8, list ways Noah and his family were saved from the Flood. Then write about comparisons between their actions and what we must do today to spiritually survive in preparation for the Second Coming.

| Noah's day | = | ? | Today |

Genesis 9

A New Start

Genesis 9 tells the story of Noah and his family leaving the ark and helping Heavenly Father fulfill his purposes for his children. Because they were the only family on earth, they were a family in a similar situation as Adam and Eve. Noah's family, however, had the benefit of knowing the temporal and spiritual history between Adam and the Flood. Considering what you know about why the Lord flooded the earth, what would you be very careful about doing in your life if you were in Noah's family? What would you be sure to teach your children?

The opportunity for Noah and his family to start over in a world cleansed of wickedness is symbolic of the opportunity we receive when we are baptized—we get a chance to start over again and be more diligent in following Heavenly Father's plan. Just like the rainbow became a reminder of God's love and mercy to Noah's family, the sacrament can be a frequent reminder of how the Lord has provided a way for us to gain eternal life through the Atonement.

Understanding the Scriptures

Genesis 9:1–17

Be fruitful, and multiply, and replenish the earth (v. 1)—Have children
Delivered (v. 2)—Given
Green herb (v. 3)—Plants

Sheddeth man's blood (v. 6)—Kills another person
Cut off (v. 11)—Destroyed
Token (vv. 12–13, 17)—Sign
For perpetual generations (v. 12)—From now on

Genesis 9—Help from the Joseph Smith Translation
As you read Genesis 9 you will get additional insight by reading each reference from the Joseph Smith Translation for this chapter.

Genesis 9:18–29—A Confusing Story about Noah
We likely do not have all the details of this story of Noah's drunkenness. We do know that the Lord never condemned Noah for this incident even though he condemned drunkenness elsewhere in scripture. In Old Testament times when juice of the grape (called wine) was stored, it would naturally ferment over time and could cause intoxication. But fermented grape juice is very different from what the Bible calls "strong drink." Strong drink was made from various fruits and grains and was intentionally intoxicating. Noah's drunkenness after drinking "wine" was likely unintentional.

We are also uncertain as to what happened in Genesis 9:22 when "Ham, the father of Canaan, saw the nakedness of his father" and why in verse 25 Noah cursed Canaan as a result. Some believe that the garment involved was taken because it had special religious significance and may have been a representation of Noah's priesthood. If Canaan or Ham took the garment, the cursing may be related to Abraham 1:26–27 where we read that the descendants of Ham were "cursed . . . as pertaining to the Priesthood" (v. 26).

The Prophet Joseph Smith added: "I referred to the curse of Ham for laughing at Noah, while in his wine, but doing no harm. Noah was a righteous man, and yet he drank wine and became intoxicated; the Lord did not forsake him in consequence thereof, for he retained all the power of his priesthood, and when he was accused by Canaan, he cursed him by the priesthood which he held, and the Lord had respect to his word, and the priesthood which he held, notwithstanding he was drunk, and the curse remains upon the posterity of Canaan until the present day" (*History of the Church*, 4:445–46).

When we seek to obtain or use the blessings of the priesthood dishonestly, we will be cursed, and we will lose opportunities, blessings, and power. For example, people who obtain the priesthood or priesthood ordinances by lying about their worthiness will not receive the blessings of those ordinances but will *lose* blessings. We cannot deceive the Lord.

Studying the Scriptures

A What Is Your "Rainbow"?

1. The Lord gave Noah a sign, or reminder, of the covenant he made. The sign helped Noah remember how merciful the Lord was to him. Write about something that reminds you how merciful the Lord is to you.

2. How can the sacrament be to us what the rainbow was to Noah?

Genesis 10

Noah's Descendants

Genesis 10 names the descendants of Noah's sons for several generations: Japheth (see vv. 2–6), Ham (see vv. 6–20), and Shem (see vv. 21–31). After this chapter, the Bible is mainly the story of some of Shem's descendants. The term Semite—usually referring to the Jews—means "a descendant of Shem."

Genesis 11

The Tower of Babel

Have you ever tried to communicate with someone who doesn't speak the same language as you? How much work would get done if all the students at a school spoke different languages and could not communicate? Genesis 11 tells us how and why we have different languages on the earth.

Understanding the Scriptures

Genesis 11:1–9

Throughly (v. 3)—Completely
Slime (v. 3)—Tar-like substance
Restrained (v. 6)—Kept

Confound (vv. 7, 9)—Confuse, mix up
Left off (v. 8)—Quit

Genesis 11:10–32—The Genealogy of Abraham

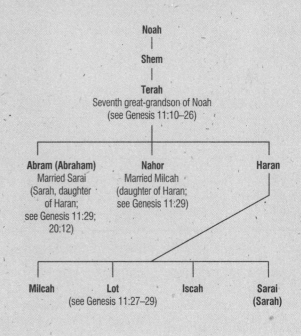

Noah
|
Shem
|
Terah
Seventh great-grandson of Noah
(see Genesis 11:10–26)

| Abram (Abraham) | Nahor | Haran |
| Married Sarai (Sarah, daughter of Haran; see Genesis 11:29; 20:12) | Married Milcah (daughter of Haran; see Genesis 11:29) | |

| Milcah | Lot | Iscah | Sarai (Sarah) |
| | (see Genesis 11:27–29) | | |

Studying the Scriptures

Do two of the following activities (A–C) as you study Genesis 11:1–9.

A Read and Compare

1. Read Genesis 11:1–4 and explain what the people of Shinar did in an attempt to reach heaven.

2. Read Acts 4:12; 2 Nephi 9:41–43; Mosiah 3:17; 5:10–15 and write about how we can get "a name" (Genesis 11:4) that will allow us into heaven.

B. Make a Connection to the Book of Mormon

Read Genesis 11:5–9 to find out how the Lord responded to the people's attempt to make a name for themselves and a tower reaching to heaven. Then read Ether 1:33–43 and summarize in your notebook what happened to one group of people at the time spoken of in Genesis.

C. What Do You Think?

Explain how you think the Lord's actions in Genesis 11:1–9 were a blessing to the people.

> As was mentioned in the introduction to Genesis (see "The Books of Genesis, Moses, and Abraham" on p. 9), Joseph Smith received more of the writings and teachings of the prophet Abraham by translating some papyrus he obtained while living in Kirtland, Ohio. The book of Abraham is not considered part of the Joseph Smith Translation of the Bible, but Abraham 1–2 does help us increase our understanding of events described in Genesis 12.

Abraham 1

Abraham Desires the Priesthood

Can people be righteous if they live in homes where righteousness is not encouraged or where they are persecuted by their own parents for being righteous? If so, what would those people have to do to overcome wicked influences? The great prophet Abraham, called the "Friend of God" (James 2:23), grew up in that very situation. During his lifetime he overcame the challenges he faced in his youth and was such a model of righteousness that God promised him that all who accept the true gospel would be called his children and that Jesus Christ would be born as one of his descendants. As you read about Abraham in the next few chapters of Abraham and Genesis, look for what he did to overcome his challenges and become one of the greatest prophets in history.

Understanding the Scriptures

Abraham 1

Residence (v. 1)—Place to live

Blessings of the fathers (v. 2) —Ordinances and covenants of the priesthood

Heir (v. 2)—A person entitled to receive blessings or an inheritance from another

because he or she is a child, close relative, or individual that the giver trusts

Conferred upon (v. 3)—Given

Appointment (v. 4)—Calling, ordination

Seed (v. 4)—Children, grandchildren, and so on

Heathen (vv. 5, 7)—Those who do not worship the true and living God

Offer, offering up (vv. 7–8, 11, 15)—Sacrificing

Endeavor, endeavored (vv. 7, 28, 31)—Try, tried

Virtue (v. 11)—Purity, obedience to laws and commandments of sexual purity

Laid violence upon me (v. 12) —Took me by force

Representation (v. 12)— Drawing

Commencement (v. 12)— Beginning

The fashion of them (v. 14)— What they look like

Figures (v. 14)—Writings and drawings

Signifies (vv. 14, 23)—Means

Kinsfolk (v. 16)—Relatives

From this descent sprang (v. 22)—From this individual came

Preserved (vv. 22, 24)— Continued

Patriarchal (vv. 25–26)—Father to son

Seeking earnestly (v. 26)— Trying very hard

Fain (v. 27)—Pretend to

Idolatry (v. 27)—Worship of false gods

Delineate (v. 28)—Show, describe

Chronology (v. 28)—History

Sorely tormented (v. 30)— Great distress or misery

Posterity (v. 31)—Children and grandchildren, descendants

Studying the Scriptures

Do two of the following activities (A–C) as you study Abraham 1.

A. What Blessings Do You Seek?

1. Elder Neal A. Maxwell said, "What we insistently desire, over time, is what we will eventually become and what we will receive in eternity" (in Conference Report, Oct. 1996, 26; or *Ensign,* Nov. 1996, 21). Read Abraham 1:2–4 and list the blessings Abraham "sought for" and "desired." You may also want to highlight them in your scriptures.

2. Choose something from this list that you also desire or seek, and explain why. You should notice that at the end of verse 2 we learn that Abraham did obtain what he sought. His life modeled how you can obtain the same blessings he sought.

B. Why Are the Righteous Persecuted?

1. Identify the reasons the three virgins and Abraham were persecuted, and compare those reasons to ways you think righteous people are sometimes persecuted.

2. Explain why you think it is worth it to live righteously even if you will be persecuted.

C. Write Verses in Your Own Words

Write Abraham 1:18–19 in your own words, identifying what the Lord promised Abraham as well as the responsibilities Abraham received.

Abraham 2

Abraham Receives Covenants from God

In Abraham 1 you read about Abraham's desire to obtain certain blessings from the Lord and about how he began to receive some of those blessings (see especially vv. 18–19). In Abraham 2 the Lord promised Abraham additional blessings. As you read, look for the things Abraham did to show his faithfulness and worthiness to receive such promises from God.

Understanding the Scriptures 🔑

Abraham 2

Wax sore (v. 1)—Become worse

Denominated (v. 4)—Named

Abated (v. 5)—Began to be over

Purposed (v. 6)—Planned

Bear my name (v. 6)—Be my representative (like a missionary), testify of me

Above measure (v. 9)—More than can be measured

Accounted (v. 10)—Considered

Earnestly (v. 12)—With great effort

Souls that we had won (v. 15)—People converted to the gospel

Situated (v. 18)—Located

Devoutly (v. 18)—Sincerely and diligently

Concluded (v. 21)—Decided

Sojourn (v. 21)—Live

Grievous (v. 21)—Hard on people

Fair (v. 22)—Beautiful

Abraham 2—Where Did the Story of Abraham Take Place?
See Bible map 2.

Abraham 2:8–11—The Abrahamic Covenant
You may read more about the Abrahamic covenant in the Bible Dictionary under "Abraham, covenant of." You will study more about the Abrahamic covenant in Genesis 17.

Abraham 2:22–25—She Is My Sister
Some people wonder why Abraham called Sarai his sister. The first and most important reason is that God told him to. It is also helpful to know that in the Hebrew language there are no separate words for granddaughter, grandson, cousin, niece, or nephew. The general terms *son, daughter, brother,* and *sister* were used for family relationships. Because Sarai was the daughter of Abraham's brother Haran, she would also be known as his sister.

It does seem strange that the Egyptians did not feel committing adultery with a man's wife was right, but they apparently had no problem with killing a man so they could "lawfully" marry his wife. It is important to note that if Abraham would have died at this time, the Lord's covenant with him could not have been fulfilled. Thus, the Lord told him what to say in this case in order to save his life and fulfill the covenant.

Studying the Scriptures ✏️

A Look for Evidence

1. Read Abraham 2:1–17 and find evidence that Abraham believed in and trusted God. List this evidence in your notebook.

2. Write about what you think someone else could find in your life that shows you follow God and believe and trust in him. Record examples from your life that are similar to ways

Abraham showed his faith in God, or note things in your life that you wish were similar to Abraham's example of faith.

B Use Every Word

Use *all* of the following words to write a sentence or two that summarize what the Lord promised to Abraham in Abraham 2:8–11: bless, seed, ministry, priesthood, gospel, father, families, salvation.

Genesis 12–13

Let There Be No Strife

Genesis 12 retells some of the same events you read about in Abraham 1–2. Genesis 12 adds the specific location where Abraham built an altar and worshiped the Lord (see Genesis 12:8) as well as details in the story of what happened when Abraham came into Egypt and told Pharaoh that Sarah was his sister (see Genesis 12:14–20).

You will notice that in the book of Genesis, Abraham is called "Abram" and Sarah is called "Sarai" until chapter 17. When you read Genesis 17 you will find out more about why their names were changed.

Abraham grew up in a family where his father persecuted him for being faithful to God. Lot's father (Haran) died even before Lot's grandfather (Terah). Both Abraham and Lot had trials. They spent much time together moving out of Ur, then to Egypt, and finally to the promised land of Canaan. Their lives turned out quite differently, however. We might wonder why Abraham's and Lot's lives were so different when they grew up in similar circumstances. As you read the next six to eight chapters of Genesis, look for choices that Abraham and Lot made and how those decisions affected them over time.

Understanding the Scriptures 🔑

Genesis 13

Bear (v. 6)—Hold (because there were not enough resources)

Strife (vv. 7–8)—Argument

Pray (v. 8)—Ask

Lifted up his eyes (v. 10)—Looked around

Breadth (v. 17)—Width

Removed (v. 18)—Moved

Studying the Scriptures ✏️

A Help a Friend

Write about how you could use the story of Abraham and Lot in Genesis 13:5–13 to help a friend solve a problem he or she has in getting along with a parent or other family member.

B Get Help from the New Testament

Read Hebrews 11:8, 10, 13–16 and tell what may have motivated Abraham to solve his problem the way he did in this chapter.

Genesis 14

Abraham Meets with Melchizedek

In Genesis 13:12 we read that Lot "pitched his tent toward Sodom." By Genesis 14:12 we learn that he "dwelt in Sodom." As a result, he became a prisoner in a battle between the various kings of the land at that time. Abraham was apparently not affected by the war until Lot was captured. Genesis 14:1–12 explains how the different kings formed military alliances in order to protect themselves and win battles. At this time, when one king did another king a favor, something was expected in return. As you read Genesis 14:13–24, notice what Abraham did to help Lot and how Abraham felt about receiving honor, power, money, or flattery from men with worldly power. Compare this reaction to how he received and honored a man with heavenly power and authority.

Understanding the Scriptures 🔑

Genesis 14:13–24

Confederate (v. 13)—Friendly and had an agreement to help one another

Pursued (vv. 14–15)—Chased

Divided himself against them (v. 15)—Split into groups to try to surround them

Smote (v. 15)—Attacked

Goods (vv. 16, 21)—Things that had been taken

Slaughter (v. 17)—Killing

Dale (v. 17)—Valley

Lift up mine hand (v. 22)—Made a promise or covenant

Shoelachet (v. 23)—Shoelaces

Save (v. 24)—Except

Studying the Scriptures ✏️

Do activity A and then do either activity B or C as you study Genesis 14:13–24.

A Who Was Melchizedek?

Notice that footnote 24a has a reference to JST, Genesis 14:25–40 (pp. 797–98). Read JST, Genesis 14:25–40; Alma 13:14–19; Doctrine and Covenants 84:14; 107:1–4; 138:41. Describe who Melchizedek was and why you think Abraham paid tithes to and received blessings from him.

B Make Your Own Conclusion

The city of Sodom was known for having wealth and many worldly pleasures and for its great wickedness. What did

Abraham's actions toward the king of Sodom teach us about his values and commitment to God? As you answer that question, consider what Abraham could have gained from the king of Sodom. Also consider the principle found in Moroni 10:30.

C Draw

Draw something that represents or symbolizes the story of Abraham in Genesis 14:17–24.

Genesis 15

A Covenant Confirmed

Earlier in Abraham's life, the Lord promised him many things concerning his posterity, including the promise that they would be as numerous as the "dust of the earth" (Genesis 13:16). By the time of the events in Genesis 15, Abraham and Sarah still did not have any children. In this chapter, the Lord helped Abraham know that his promises would still be fulfilled.

Understanding the Scriptures 🔑

Genesis 15

Steward (v. 2)—Servant in charge of other servants

One born in mine house (v. 3)—Someone born to one of my servants

Mine heir (v. 3)—The one who receives my possessions when I die

Bowels (v. 4)—Body

Abroad (v. 5)—Outside, an open space

Whereby (v. 8)—How

Heifer (v. 9)—Young cow

Divided them in the midst (v. 10)—Cut them in half

Carcases (v. 11)—Dead bodies

Horror (v. 12)—Feeling

Afflict (v. 13)—Trouble

Go to thy fathers (v. 15)—Die

Hither (v. 16)—Here

Iniquity (v. 16)—Sin

Genesis 15:6—Help from the Joseph Smith Translation

JST, Genesis 15:9–12 gives helpful additions to Genesis 15.

Genesis 15:9–17—What Was Abraham Doing in These Verses?

These verses in Genesis 15 describe an ancient Middle Eastern custom of making or "cutting" a covenant. After the individual making the covenant cut the animal (or animals) in two, he walked between the two pieces as if to say, "If I do not keep my covenant, may I become as this animal." In this case, the burning lamp represented the Lord's presence and gave Abraham assurance that the Lord would fulfill his covenant.

Studying the Scriptures

A Explain the Symbolism

Highlight the words in Genesis 15:1 that describe what the Lord said he was for Abram. Write about how the Lord is those same things for those who make and keep covenants with him.

B Finish These Sentences

1. Abraham was concerned that . . . (see vv. 3, 7–8)
2. The Lord reassured Abraham by . . . (see vv. 1, 17)

Genesis 16

Abraham Marries Hagar

In Genesis 15 we read about Abraham's doubts and concerns. In Genesis 16 we learn a little of how Sarah might have felt. The Lord commanded Sarah to give Hagar to Abraham for his wife and commanded Abraham to take Hagar as his wife (see D&C 132:34–35). Although it might have been difficult, when Sarah did this for Abraham, it showed how desirous she was to obey the Lord and fulfill his covenants. As you read this chapter think about how Hagar might have felt throughout this brief story.

Understanding the Scriptures

Genesis 16

Handmaid (v. 1)—Servant

Restrained me from bearing (v. 2)—Kept me from having children

Conceived (vv. 4–5)—Became pregnant

Mistress (v. 4, 8)—Woman who owns a servant

Into thy bosom (v. 5)—To you

Despised (v. 5)—Look down upon, hated

Fountain (v. 7)—Spring

Whither (v. 8)—Where

Submit thyself under her hands (v. 9)—Humble yourself and do whatever she says

Studying the Scriptures

A Recognizing God's Love

In the midst of a difficult trial, Hagar learned things that can help all of us endure trials. Write about what most impressed you in Genesis 16 that shows God's love for Hagar and how Hagar accepted his love. Footnotes 11*a* and 14*b* should be helpful as you respond.

Genesis 17

The Abrahamic Covenant

In Genesis 17 God blessed Abraham once again and gave him further promises concerning the blessings he and his posterity would receive. Like he does with us, the Lord gave Abraham promises and blessings step by step, a little more each time. All of the promises, blessings, and covenants given to Abraham, grouped together, are called the "Abrahamic covenant." In summarizing the promises of the Abrahamic covenant, Elder Russell M. Nelson said:

"The covenant . . . is of transcendent significance. It contained several promises:

"Abraham's posterity would be numerous, entitled to eternal increase and to bear the priesthood;

"He would become a father of many nations;

"Christ and kings would come through Abraham's lineage;

"Certain lands would be inherited;

"All nations of the earth would be blessed by his seed;

"That covenant would be everlasting—even through 'a thousand generations'" (in Conference Report, Apr. 1995, 42; or Ensign, May 1995, 33).

Elder Bruce R. McConkie explained how blessings were added upon Abraham:

"Abraham first received the gospel by baptism (which is the covenant of salvation); then he had conferred upon him the higher priesthood, and he entered into celestial marriage (which is the covenant of exaltation), gaining assurance thereby that he would have eternal increase; finally he received a promise that all of these blessings would be offered to all of his mortal posterity. (Abra. 2:6–11; D. & C. 132:29–50.) . . .

". . . Those portions of it which pertain to personal exaltation and eternal increase are renewed with each member of the house of Israel who enters the order of celestial marriage" (Mormon Doctrine, 13).

Because all Church members are the posterity of Abraham through the covenant, we should carefully consider the covenants the Lord made with Abraham and see how they apply to us.

Understanding the Scriptures

Genesis 17

Multiply thee exceedingly (v. 2)—Give you many descendants	**Make nations of thee, and kings shall come out of thee** (v. 6)—Nations and kings will be some of your descendants
Exceedingly fruitful (v. 6)—Many descendants	**Betwixt** (v. 11)—Between
	Bear (v. 17)—Have a child
	Left off (v. 22)—Quit

Genesis 17:9–14—Circumcision

The token or sign of the covenant God made with Abraham was circumcision. Circumcision symbolized cleanliness before God and was also a symbolic reminder of the promises the Lord made to Abraham regarding his posterity. You may read more about circumcision in your Bible Dictionary. Circumcision is not required today.

Studying the Scriptures

A Identify the Elements of the Covenant

A covenant is an agreement between two parties where both parties promise to do certain things. In a gospel covenant, God always sets the terms, or what must be done and received as part of the covenant, and man agrees to obey those terms.

1. What did the Lord ask Abraham to do in receiving this covenant? (see vv. 1, 10).

2. What did the Lord promise Abraham? (see vv. 2–8, 15–19). Make sure you read all of the Joseph Smith Translation references for these verses in your footnotes or in the appendix in your Bible, and include them as part of the list.

3. Read Genesis 12:1–3; 13:14–16; 15:1–7; Abraham 1:18–19; 2:9–11. Add the promises given to the list you began above.

B Organize the Elements

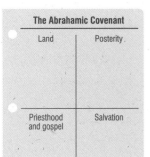

The Abrahamic Covenant	
Land	Posterity
Priesthood and gospel	Salvation

There are four basic categories of blessings in the Abrahamic covenant: land, posterity, priesthood and gospel, and salvation. Take the list you made in activity A above and organize them by category. If you feel a blessing applies to more than one category, list it under all applicable categories.

C What's in a Name?

Notice that Abraham's and Sarah's names were changed as part of the covenant (see Genesis 17:4–8; 15–16).

1. How would you feel receiving a name like the one Sarah received? Why? (see footnote 15a).

2. In what way was Sarah's name an additional testimony of the promises of God? Who is she a princess to and what does that teach us about who she can become?

3. Because members of the Church are the children of Abraham and Sarah, what can we learn about ourselves from the names God gave to this great couple?

4. In what ways does receiving a name have a part in the covenants we enter into today with the Lord to become his people? (see 2 Nephi 31:13, 17–20; Mosiah 18:8–10; Moroni 4:1–3).

5. What is the new name we receive when we are baptized and partake of the sacrament? What do you think is the significance of taking that name upon us?

Genesis 18

"Is Anything Too Hard for the Lord?"

In Genesis 17 the Lord promised Abraham that Sarah would bear a son. We read how Abraham reacted to that promise. In Genesis 18 we find out how Sarah reacted when she learned of this same promise.

Understanding the Scriptures

Genesis 18

Pass not away (v. 3)—Do not leave	**Do justice and judgment** (v. 19)—Live righteously and help others
Fetched, fetch, fetcht (vv. 4–5, 7)—Bring, brought	**Cry** (v. 20)—What is being said about the sin and wickedness
Morsel (v. 5)—Piece	**Grievous** (v. 20)—Terrible
Pass on (v. 5)—Leave	**See whether they have done altogether according to the cry of it** (v. 21)—Find out if they have done all the things people said they did
Hasten, hasted (vv. 6–7)—Hurried, hurry	
Meal (v. 6)—Flour	
Knead (v. 6)—Prepare it for baking	**Peradventure** (vv. 24, 28–32)—What if
Hearth (v. 6)—Place for cooking	**That be far from thee to do after this manner** (v. 25)—That is not the way you usually do things
Dress, dressed (vv. 7–8)—Prepare for eating	
According to the time of life (vv. 10, 14)—At the time when life can be conceived	**Dust and ashes** (v. 27)—Nothing compared to God
It ceased to be with Sarah after the manner of women (v. 11)—Sarah was too old to have a baby	**Left communing** (v. 33)—Finished speaking
Lord (v. 12)—Husband	

Genesis 18:1–22—Who Visited Abraham?

Genesis 18:1 indicates that the Lord appeared to Abraham. This does not mean that the Lord was one of the three men that visited him. The Joseph Smith Translation indicates that these three men were holy men who held the priesthood and were official representatives of the Lord.

Genesis 18:20—The Sins of Sodom and Gomorrah

When we read Genesis 19 we will learn that immorality was one of these cities' major sins. Ezekiel 16:48–50 helps us realize that the people of Sodom and Gomorrah were prideful, were unwilling to take care of the poor and needy among them, and were idle.

Genesis 18:23–33—The Wicked May Be Spared Because of the Righteous

Read Alma 10:20–23 to learn more about this principle of sparing the wicked.

Studying the Scriptures

A Answer the Lord's Question

1. Notice the question in Genesis 18:14 is not answered. Look in Luke 1:37 for an answer and then explain the answer.

2. Write about an experience that you or someone you know has had that shows "nothing is too hard for the Lord" (v. 14).

B Choose the Best Words

After reading Genesis 18:16–33, consider what you learn about the character of Abraham and the character of God. Choose from this passage two words you think best describe Abraham and two words you think best describe the nature of God.

Genesis 19

Sodom and Gomorrah

Genesis 14:12 states that Lot "dwelt in Sodom." In Genesis 18 messengers from God stayed with Abraham on their way to Sodom and Gomorrah, and Abraham learned about God's plan to destroy Sodom and Gomorrah. Genesis 19 tells the story of what happened when the messengers arrived to help Lot and his family leave Sodom and Gomorrah before its destruction.

Although Lot was able to escape before Sodom and Gomorrah were destroyed, some of his family members had become accustomed to the wicked ways of Sodom and Gomorrah. They were destroyed because they would not follow the counsel to leave.

Genesis 20–21

A Promise Fulfilled

In Genesis 20 God again told Abraham to save his life by saying Sarah was his sister. As a result, the Lord was able to help a man, Abimelech, and his family understand that Abraham was a prophet. The members of Abimelech's family were blessed because he believed that Abraham was a man of God and a prophet.

Sometimes our patience and faith are tested as we seek for the Lord's promises to be fulfilled. Genesis 21 contains the story of how God's promise to Abraham and Sarah that she would bear a son was fulfilled. The events in Genesis 21 occurred when Abraham was one hundred years old and Sarah was ninety. Could there be any question that the birth of their son was anything but a miracle and blessing from God?

Understanding the Scriptures

Genesis 21

Visited (v. 1)—Blessed

Given children suck (v. 7)—Breast fed a baby

Weaned (v. 8)—No longer fed with mother's milk

Bondwoman (vv. 10, 12–13)—Servant

Heir (v. 10)—Part of the family and receive goods from the father

Grievous (vv. 11–12)—Bad

Spent (v. 15)—Used up

Bowshot (v. 16)—The distance a person can shoot an arrow

Aileth (v. 17)—Is wrong with

Archer (v. 20)—Hunter with a bow and arrow

Studying the Scriptures

A Write a Letter

Imagine yourself in either Abraham's or Sarah's situation and write a letter to a friend, telling the story of Isaac's birth. Include details of the story back to the time when Sarah thought she could never bear children and describe how you would have felt during each part of the story. Include also the meaning of Isaac's name and how it relates to what happened (see Genesis 21, footnote 6a).

Genesis 22

The Sacrifice of Isaac

If the Lord asked you to give something up, what would be the one thing hardest for you to let go of? Would you do it? Why? Genesis 22 tells the story of one of the greatest tests God has ever given to anyone. Before reading chapter 22, read what the Lord said to Church members in Doctrine and Covenants 101:4–5. While you read Genesis 22, put yourself in either Abraham's or Isaac's place and consider what you would have been thinking at each point in the story.

Understanding the Scriptures

Genesis 22

Clave (v. 3)—Cut

Yonder (v. 5)—To another place

Fearest (v. 12)—Reverence, love, and respect

Thicket (v. 13)—Bush, bushes

Stead (v. 13)—Place

Possess the gate of (v. 17)—Have power over

Genesis 22—Why Did the Lord Ask Abraham to Sacrifice Isaac?

"Why did the Lord ask such things of Abraham? Because, knowing what his future would be and that he would be the father of an innumerable posterity, he was determined to test him. God did not do this for His own sake; for He knew by His foreknowledge what Abraham would do; but the purpose was to impress upon Abraham a lesson, and to enable him to attain unto knowledge that he could not obtain in any other way. That is why God tries all of us. It is not for His own knowledge; for He knows all things beforehand. He knows all your lives and everything you will do. But He tries us for our own good, that we may know ourselves. . . . He required Abraham to submit to this trial because He intended to give him glory, exaltation and honor; He intended to make him a king and a priest, to share with Himself the glory, power and dominion which He exercised" (George Q. Cannon, in Conference Report, Apr. 1899, 66).

Elder Neal A. Maxwell applied these truths to us when he said our lives "cannot be both faith-filled and stress-free. . . .

"Therefore, how can you and I really expect to glide naively through life, as if to say, Lord, give me experience, but not grief, not sorrow, not pain, not opposition, not betrayal, and certainly not to be forsaken. Keep from me, Lord, all those experiences which made Thee what Thou art! Then let me come and dwell with Thee and fully share Thy joy!" (in Conference Report, Apr. 1991, 117; or *Ensign*, May 1991, 88).

The Prophet Joseph Smith suggested that sacrifice is one of the ways we obtain greater faith. For example, how do you think your faith in God would have grown if you had experienced what Abraham had? He would not have grown in faith if he had refused to offer the sacrifice God commanded. Joseph Smith said, "A religion that does not require the sacrifice of all things never has power sufficient to produce the faith necessary unto life and salvation" (*Lectures on Faith* [1985], 69).

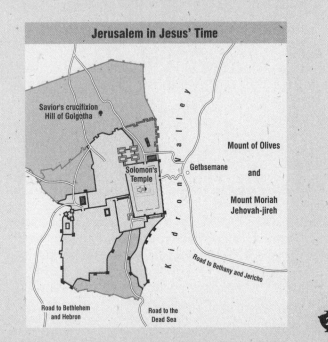

Jerusalem in Jesus' Time

Savior's crucifixion Hill of Golgotha

Solomon's Temple

Kidron Valley

Gethsemane

Mount of Olives

and

Mount Moriah Jehovah-jireh

Road to Bethany and Jericho

Road to Bethlehem and Hebron

Road to the Dead Sea

Genesis 22:14—Where Was Jehovah-jireh and What Does Its Name Mean?

Abraham called the place where he built the sacrificial altar "Jehovah-jireh," which was a prophecy that the Lord would later be seen on this same mountain. Commonly called Mount Moriah (see Genesis 22:2), this same group of hills was the site of Solomon's Temple and the Savior's Crucifixion.

Studying the Scriptures

Do three of the following five activities (A–E) as you study Genesis 22.

A A Type of Christ

1. Read Jacob 4:3–5 and explain what we learn about the story of Abraham and Isaac.

Abraham and Isaac	The Sacrifice of the Son of God

2. List as many details as you can about the story of Abraham and Isaac that teach us something about the Atonement of Jesus Christ. You may want to organize the information in a chart like the one shown.

B Find and Note Examples

1. Make a list of all the evidence you can find in Genesis 22:1–14 that demonstrates Abraham's obedience, faithfulness, and dedication to God.

2. Choose one item from your list that especially impresses you and write about how you could apply it in your life.

C Ponder and Write about Sacrifice

1. Why do you think Abraham was willing to offer his son as a sacrifice?

2. What does the Lord ask you to offer as a sacrifice? (see 3 Nephi 9:19–20).

3. Why would a person be willing to offer sacrifices to God?

As you consider your answers to these questions, consider the following teaching of the Prophet Joseph Smith: "For a man to lay down his all, his character and reputation, his honor, and applause, his good name among men, his houses, his lands, his brothers and sisters, his wife and children, and even his own life also . . . requires more than mere belief . . . that he is doing the will of God; but actual knowledge, realizing that, when these sufferings are ended, he will enter into eternal rest, and be a partaker of the glory of God" (*Lectures on Faith*, 68; see also Paul's teaching in Hebrews 11:17–19).

Ⓓ Compare the Promises

Read the promises of God to Abraham in Genesis 12:2–3; 13:14–16; 15:5; 17:2, 4, 7. Compare them to what God promised Abraham in Genesis 22:15–18. In what ways are they the same or different?

Ⓔ Ponder and Write about How Testing and Trying Experiences Strengthen Our Faith

How do trials like this one of Abraham and Isaac strengthen our faith in Christ? Some of the insights in the "Understanding the Scriptures" section above may help you answer.

Genesis 23

Sarah Dies

In Genesis 23 we read that Sarah died. Sarah was the first of Abraham's family to be buried in the land God promised him.

Studying the Scriptures

Ⓐ Introduce Abraham

Imagine that you are conducting a meeting and Abraham is the featured speaker. Write how you would introduce him, and include what you think are the most important and impressive details about his life.

Genesis 24

A Wife for Isaac

What do you think are the most important qualities to consider in choosing someone to marry? Whom would you trust to choose a marriage partner for you?

President Spencer W. Kimball said: "The greatest single factor affecting what you are going to be tomorrow, your activity, your attitudes, your eventual destiny . . . is the one decision you make . . . when you ask that individual to be your companion for life. That's the most important decision of your entire life! It isn't where you are going to school, or what lessons you are going to study, or what your major is, or how you are going to make your living. These, though important, are incidental and nothing

compared with the important decision that you make when you ask someone to be your companion for eternity" (The Teachings of Spencer W. Kimball, *Edward L. Kimball, ed. [1982], 301).*

Choosing a marriage partner is important for everyone, but especially for those who desire the blessings of the Abrahamic covenant, which includes the promise of an eternal family. If a husband and wife both accept and keep the Abrahamic covenant, which is fully received in the temple, they can have the blessing of an eternal family. As you read, notice the efforts made to enable Isaac to marry in the covenant and how the Lord helped in the process. Consider what effort you are willing to make to marry in the covenant and how the Lord might help you.

Understanding the Scriptures 🔑

Genesis 24

Kindred (vv. 4, 7, 38, 40)— Family, relatives

Peradventure (vv. 5, 39)— What if

Thither (vv. 6, 8)—There, in that place

Thence (v. 7)—There

Oath (vv. 8, 41)— Commandment and promise

Hand (v. 10)—Care

Good speed (v. 12)—Success

Trough (v. 20)—Place where animals drink

Held his peace (v. 21)— Waited and stayed quiet

Wit (v. 21)—Know

Lodge (vv. 23, 25)—Stay

Provender (vv. 25, 32)—Food for animals

Who hath not left destitute (v. 27)—Who has given

Ungirded (v. 32)—Unloaded

Errand (v. 33)—Assignment

Proceedeth (v. 50)—Comes

Raiment (v. 53)—Clothing

Hinder (v. 56)—Get in the way, stop

Enquire at her mouth (v. 57) —Ask her and let her answer for herself

Meditate (v. 63)—Prayerfully think about things

Eventide (v. 63)—Evening

Vail (v. 65)—Cloth covering for the face, traditionally worn in this society by an unmarried woman

Studying the Scriptures ✏️

Ⓐ What Kind of Person Do You Want to Marry?

1. Make a list of what you learned about Rebekah from Genesis 24 that you think made her a good wife for Isaac.

2. Write about the one item on your list you would most like your spouse to have or be and explain why.

Genesis 25

What Is the Value of the Covenant?

Genesis 25 tells us that after Sarah died, Abraham took another wife and had more children. This chapter also tells about his death and burial. A brief list of Ishmael's descendants is given, and then the chapter focuses on the story of the birth of Esau and Jacob, the twin sons of Isaac and Rebekah. The story of Esau and Jacob raises important questions that each of us should ask ourselves: How do I feel about being born with the Abrahamic covenant as my inheritance? How much do I value that covenant?

Understanding the Scriptures 🔑

Genesis 25:19–34

Intreated (v. 21)—Prayed to

Barren (v. 21)—Could not have children

Why am I thus (v. 22)—Why is this happening

Separated from thy bowels (v. 23)—Born

Garment (v. 25)—Clothing

Cunning (v. 27)—Skillful

Venison (v. 28)—Meat from animals hunted by Esau

Sod (v. 29)—Cooked by boiling

Pottage (vv. 29–30, 34)—Stew

Faint (vv. 29–30)—Tired and hungry

Genesis 25:30–34—Esau Sold His Birthright

In the culture of this time period, the firstborn son received a "birthright," which included the right to preside in the family and a double portion of his father's goods and land when his father died. The birthright son then could take care of the rest of the family, including his father's widow. The revelation Rebekah received concerning her two sons probably prepared her to understand that this tradition would not necessarily apply in their family. Receiving the birthright of the covenant did not come because of birth order but because of righteousness. The story in Genesis 25:29–34 can help us see why Rebekah was told to expect the younger to receive the birthright. Some people criticize Jacob for "taking advantage" of his brother; however, we do not know the whole story. The story does show what little value Esau placed on the birthright and blessings of being the firstborn son in the covenant line of Abraham and to show that Jacob desired those blessings.

Studying the Scriptures ✏️

A) How Does It Happen Today?

Esau traded away something that would be of great value to him in the future (his birthright), for something of little value that could be obtained right away and satisfied an immediate appetite (hunger). Write about ways you see people today trading eternal opportunities and blessings for something worldly or something that satisfies an appetite.

Genesis 26–27

Jacob Received Covenant Blessings

In Genesis 26 we read about how the Lord prospered Isaac and renewed the Abrahamic covenant with him (see vv. 3–5, 23–25). Chapter 26 also tells of other experiences Isaac had that were

like what happened to his father Abraham (see vv. 6–11, 19–22, 26–31). The concluding verses of the chapter tell how Esau decided to marry out of the covenant and how that decision saddened Isaac and Rebekah.

Some people think they can receive blessings without obeying the commandments relating to those blessings. They are mistaken (see D&C 130:20–21). In Genesis 25:29–34 we read how Esau cared more about satisfying his immediate personal appetites than about the responsibilities and blessings of being the firstborn son in the covenant. In Genesis 26:34–35 Esau again showed how little he valued the covenant when he chose a wife outside of the covenant. Knowing these two things about Esau is helpful in understanding what happened in Genesis 27. We must realize that Esau had not qualified for the blessings Isaac desired to give him.

You should also note that the blessings promised to Jacob in Genesis 27 were conditional—meaning they were only promised to Jacob if he lived faithful to the covenant. The blessings were not automatic. As you continue to read Genesis 28–35, look for what Jacob did to see that the promised blessings were fulfilled.

Understanding the Scriptures 🔑

Genesis 27

Quiver (v. 3)—Arrow holder

Savoury (vv. 4, 7, 9, 17, 31)—Good tasting

Fetch (vv. 9, 13–14, 45)—Get

Goodly raiment (v. 15)—Nice clothing

Badest (v. 19)—Asked

Discerned him not (v. 23)—Could not tell it was him

Fatness (vv. 28, 39)—Prosperity

Scarce (v. 30)—Barely

Subtilty (v. 35)—Deceit

Supplanted me (v. 36)—Taken my place or things

Sustained (v. 37)—Blessed

Dominion (v. 40)—The opportunity to establish yourself in the land

Break his yoke from off thy neck (v. 40)—Not be his servant

Touching (v. 42)—Concerning

Purposing (v. 42)—Planning

Fury (v. 44)—Anger

Genesis 27—A Stolen Blessing?

Even though Isaac thought he was blessing Esau, when he realized he had blessed Jacob he did not change the blessing or curse Jacob (see Genesis 27:33). Apparently, Isaac recognized that the Lord inspired him to bless the right person. The story of Jacob and Isaac helps us realize that the Lord inspires his servants to accomplish his will in spite of their weaknesses or incomplete knowledge of a situation.

Jacob was promised blessings at the time of the events in Genesis 27, but those blessings were not fulfilled until he was obedient to the commandments that allowed those blessings to come into his life.

Studying the Scriptures ✏️

A) Give Counsel to Esau

Imagine that you are Esau's friend and have the opportunity to speak with him after the events of Genesis 27. Considering what you've learned from Genesis 25–27, help Esau understand why Jacob received the covenant blessings and suggest what Esau should do.

Genesis 28

Jacob's Sacred Experience

In Genesis 27 Isaac blessed Jacob that he would have prosperity and would rule over his older brother Esau. The greatest blessings Jacob could obtain, however, were the blessings of the covenant given to his grandfather Abraham and his father Isaac. In Genesis 28 the Lord taught Jacob more about the covenant and its blessings.

Understanding the Scriptures

Genesis 28

Charged (vv. 1, 6)—Commanded

Lighted upon (v. 11)—Came to

Ascending (v. 12)—Going up

Descending (v. 12)—Going down

Keep (v. 15)—Watch over and bless

Dreadful (v. 17)—Holy

Pillar (vv. 18, 22)—Altar

Genesis 28:10–28—Jacob at Bethel

We are not exactly sure what the ladder looked like in Jacob's dream. In any case, the ladder symbolizes "stepping up" into heaven through means provided by God and administered by his servants (angels).

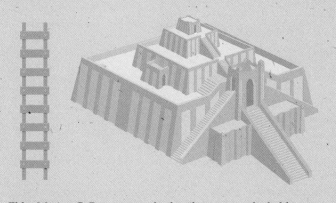

Elder Marion G. Romney taught that the steps on the ladder represent covenants we make with God that bring us closer to him. He also said, "Temples are to us all what Bethel was to Jacob" ("Temples—The Gates to Heaven," *Ensign,* Mar. 1971, 16). Temples are "mountains of the Lord" where we go to lift ourselves above the things of this world, draw nearer to God and heaven, and learn how to enter his presence eternally. The ordinances we receive in the temple are essential to our exaltation; thus, the temple is the "gate" to God and eternal life.

Studying the Scriptures

Do one of the following activities (A–B) as you study Genesis 28.

A Identify the Promises

Isaac promised Jacob (see vv. 3–4)	The Lord promised Jacob (see vv. 13–15)	Jacob promised the Lord (see vv. 20–22)

In Genesis 28 Isaac promised Jacob certain blessings, the Lord promised Jacob certain blessings, and Jacob promised the Lord he would do certain things. Identify the promises in this chapter and put them in a chart similar to the one shown.

B Draw Your Ladder to Heaven

1. Draw a ladder (of either style shown above) in your notebook. Label the rungs or steps with ordinances you must receive and covenants you must make with God in order to obtain eternal life.

2. Show your drawing to your parents or Church leaders to see if you've left anything out.

3. Write about what you are doing in your life right now to obtain these covenants, or what you are doing to be worthy of the blessings of the covenants you have already entered into.

Genesis 29

The Children of Jacob, Part 1

In Genesis 32 you will read how the Lord changed Jacob's name to Israel. We often speak in the Church of the "twelve tribes of Israel," which refers to the twelve sons of Jacob (Israel) and their descendants. Genesis 29–30 tells the story of Jacob's marriages and the birth of eleven of his twelve sons.

Understanding the Scriptures

Genesis 29

High day (v. 7)—The sun is high in the sky, midday

Kept (v. 9)—Watched over

Tidings (v. 13)—News

Abode (v. 14)—Lived

Nought (v. 15)—Nothing

Tender eyed (v. 17)—Eyes that are delicate and lovely

Beautiful and well favoured (v. 17)—Attractive in every way

Go in unto her (v. 21)—Be her husband (literally, to go into her tent and live with her)

Wherefore (v. 25)—Why

Beguiled (v. 25)—Deceived

Fulfil her week (vv. 27–28)—Stay married to her and wait until the week-long marriage celebration ends before doing anything else

Opened her womb (v. 31)—Blessed her to have children

Barren (v. 31)—Could have no children

Left bearing (v. 35)—Stopped having children

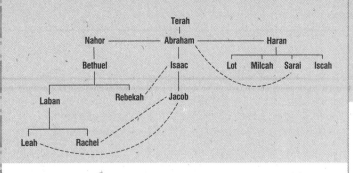

Genesis 30:25–43—Jacob Is Prospered

In Genesis 30 we read that Jacob sought to return to the land of his father. He asked Laban if he could take with him the things he had obtained by his work. In a miraculous way, the Lord prospered Jacob so he was able to have much more than Laban was willing to give him.

Studying the Scriptures

A The Children of Jacob

Make a chart of the sons of Jacob that looks like the one below. You will also need to look at Genesis 29:31–35 to complete the chart. Jacob's last son, Benjamin, was not born until later in Jacob's life; the story of Benjamin's birth is in Genesis 35. You may want to leave room on your chart and write him in later. Put the sons in the order they were born according to the scriptures. Your footnotes will be very helpful in completing the chart. You may also want to highlight or underline each son when his name first appears in the verses, and also underline the meaning of his name in the footnotes. If you mark your scriptures this way, you can see each name quickly the next time you read.

Name of Child	Mother	Meaning of Name	Reason Why Name Was Given
Reuben	Leah	Look, a son	Leah was pleased that she could have a son for Jacob, even though she felt unloved.
Simeon			
Levi			

Studying the Scriptures

Do either activity A or B as you study Genesis 29.

A Put Yourself in Their Place

Imagine you are Jacob, Leah, or Rachel. Write to a close friend or family member living in another place and describe the story from Genesis 29 as if you were that person.

B What Is the Price of a Good Marriage?

1. Anciently, a man paid a woman's father for the right to marry his daughter. Because Jacob had little or nothing, what did he do to pay for the right to marry Leah and Rachel?

2. Explain why you would or would not be willing to do what Jacob did in order to have a certain spouse.

3. Write about what you think the "price" of a good, eternal marriage is today.

Genesis 30

The Children of Jacob, Part 2

Genesis 31

Jacob Leaves Padan-aram

In Genesis 31 the Lord commanded Jacob to return to the land of his birth, which was promised to him by covenant. When Jacob left for home, Laban and his sons and servants were upset. They felt Jacob took possessions with him that belonged to Laban, and they were jealous of the way God had prospered Jacob. Laban was also angry because Jacob took away his daughters. We also read, however, that Laban treated Jacob and his own daughters unfairly during the twenty years Jacob lived among them. In fact, he even denied his daughters their rightful inheritance of property. In an attempt to claim her inheritance, Rachel left the land of her father with his small images, which contained a legal description of her property. Laban chased after Jacob and his family, and they discussed how Laban treated Jacob and why he decided to return home. Finally, Laban and Jacob made a promise that they would not hurt each other and that Jacob would treat kindly Laban's daughters and grandchildren.

Understanding the Scriptures

Genesis 30

Envied (v. 1)—Was jealous of

Stead (v. 2)—Place

Fruit of the womb (v. 2)—Children

Bear upon my knees (v. 3)—Have children for me as my servant

Prevailed (v. 8)—Overcome

Mandrakes (vv. 14–16)—See Bible Dictionary, s.v. "mandrakes"

Hearkened unto (v. 17)—Heard

Hire (v. 18)—Reward

Endued (v. 20)—Blessed

Dowry (v. 20)—Present, or reward

Opened her womb (v. 22)—Blessed her to have children

Reproach (v. 23)—Shame and sadness

Genesis 32

Jacob Travels toward Home

What was the relationship between Jacob and Esau when Jacob left to find a wife? (see Genesis 27:41–45). If you were Jacob, how would you feel about going home? What would you do about your situation?

Genesis 32–33 tells the story of Jacob's return and what he did to prepare to meet Esau. As you read, consider what you can learn from this story about how to repair a relationship that has gone bad.

Understanding the Scriptures 🔑

Genesis 32

Host (v. 2)—Army, camp

Sojourned (v. 4)—Lived

Distressed (v. 7)—Worried

Company (vv. 8, 21)—Group

Staff (v. 10)—Walking stick that was also a shepherd rod to help control animals

Lodged (vv. 13, 21)—Slept, stayed

That which came to his hand (v. 13)—His possessions

Drove (vv. 16, 19)—Groups of animals

Betwixt (v. 16)—Between

Foremost (v. 17)—First in line

Appease (v. 20)—Try to calm

Peradventure (v. 20)—If

Ford (v. 22)—River

Prevailed not (v. 25)—Could not win

Hollow of his thigh (vv. 25, 32)—Socket of his hip

Prevailed (v. 28)—Overcome, won

Preserved (v. 30)—Saved

Halted (v. 31)—Limped

Sinew (v. 32)—A tendon connecting muscle to the bone

Studying the Scriptures ✏️

(A) Apply the Words of Modern Prophets

Consider the following statement from President Spencer W. Kimball, and then write about how it might apply to some of the things that Jacob did in Genesis 32:1–23.

"If we will sue for peace, taking the initiative in settling differences—if we can forgive and forget with all our hearts—if we can cleanse our own souls of sin, accusations, bitterness, and guilt before we cast a stone at others—if we forgive all real or fancied offenses before we ask forgiveness for our own sins—if we pay our own debts, large or small, before we press our debtors—if we manage to clear our own eyes of the blinding beams before we magnify the motes in the eyes of others—what a glorious world this would be!" (in Conference Report, Oct. 1949, 133).

(B) What Does It Mean?

1. Read Enos 1:1–5 in the Book of Mormon and tell what you think it means to "wrestle" before the Lord.

2. Why do you think Jacob was wrestling before the Lord? (You can find help in verses 9–12.)

3. What does Jacob's name tell you about his wrestle before God? (Make sure you read footnote 36*a* of Genesis 27 for the meaning of his name.)

Genesis 33

Jacob Meets Esau

Understanding the Scriptures 🔑

Genesis 33

Foremost (v. 2)—In front

Hindermost (v. 2)—Behind

Graciously (vv. 5, 11)—Kindly

Blessing (v. 11)—Gift

Urged (v. 11)—Encouraged

Before (v. 12)—In front of

Tender (v. 13)—Young

Overdrive (v. 13)—Walk them too fast and far

Pass over before (v. 14)—Go a different way

Lead on softly (v. 14)—Move slowly

Parcel (v. 19)—Plot of land

Erected (v. 20)—Made

Studying the Scriptures ✏️

(A) Esau's Point of View

Write the story found in Genesis 32–33 as if you were Esau. Include your feelings about Jacob twenty years ago and your feelings about him at the time of the story. Use information in Genesis 33 to keep the story as accurate as possible.

Genesis 34

Vengeful Acts of Jacob's Sons

The last part of Genesis 33 says that Jacob settled for a time in an area called Shechem. Genesis 34 tells the story of how a man named Shechem forced Dinah, Jacob's daughter, to have sexual relations with him. This angered Dinah's brothers. Two of them, Simeon and Levi, carried out a plan that resulted in the death of Shechem and other men of his city. Jacob was very upset about their vengeful actions.

Genesis 35

Jacob Returns to Bethel

In Genesis 28 Jacob had a very important spiritual experience at a place he named Bethel. At that time, the Lord promised to be with Jacob so that he could return and worship the Lord again in his homeland. Twelve children and over twenty years later, he returned to that sacred spot where he had another important spiritual experience. As you read, think about all you've learned about Jacob, all that had happened since his last visit to Bethel, and how Jacob's experiences might affect the way he felt about what God promised him this time at Bethel.

Understanding the Scriptures

Genesis 35

Strange gods (vv. 2, 4)—Idols, statues

Distress (v. 3)—Troubles

Terror (v. 5)—Fear, respect

A company of (v. 11)—Many

Come out of thy loins (v. 11) —Be your descendants

Pillar (vv. 14, 20)—Altar

Travailed (v. 16)— Experienced the pains of having a baby

Labour (vv. 16–17)—The pain and work of giving birth

Lay (v. 22)—Had sexual relations

Studying the Scriptures

A) Prepare to Go to the House of the Lord

In Hebrew, *Beth-el* means "House of God" (see Genesis 28, footnote 19a). Bethel was to Jacob what temples are to us today. Knowing that, what can Genesis 35:1–5 teach us about going to the temple?

B) Compare What the Lord Said to Jacob to What He Has Said to Others

Read what the Lord said to Abraham in Genesis 12:1–3; 15:17–21; 17:1–8; 22:15–18. How do those words compare to what the Lord said to Jacob in Genesis 35:9–12?

Genesis 36–37

Joseph and the Coat of Many Colors

Genesis 36 lists the names of many of Esau's descendants (Esau is also called "Edom" in verses 1, 43). Esau's posterity were neighbors to Jacob (Israel) throughout the history of the Bible and were called "Edomites."

The birthright son became the leader of the family upon his father's death. He also assumed responsibility for caring for other family members. In order to fulfill his responsibilities, he was given a double amount of land and goods in his inheritance. Because of the covenant God made with Abraham, the birthright son also had spiritual responsibilities. (For more information, see the Bible Dictionary, s.v. "birthright.")

Usually the firstborn son received the birthright. Reuben, however, made himself unworthy of this honor (see Genesis 35:22; 1 Chronicles 5:1). As firstborn son of Rachel, Jacob's second wife, Joseph was given the birthright. The "coat of many colors" Jacob gave to Joseph (see Genesis 37:3) is thought to represent the fact that Joseph received the birthright (see William Wilson, Old Testament Word Studies [1978], s.v. "colour," 82).

Remember that although Joseph was the firstborn son of Rachel, he was the eleventh son born. Even though he was worthy, we can imagine how the ten older brothers must have felt about him receiving the birthright blessings. As you read each part of Genesis 37, think about how you would have felt if you were Joseph at that time.

Understanding the Scriptures

Genesis 37

Lad (v. 2)—Boy (meaning the boy Joseph)

Their evil report (v. 2)—A report that they (the brothers) had done evil

Peaceably (v. 4)—Kindly

Binding sheaves (v. 7)—Tying stalks of wheat into bundles

Sheaf (v. 7)—Bundle of wheat

Made obeisance (vv. 7, 9)— Bowed down

Reign (v. 8)—Rule

Dominion (v. 8)—Power

Rebuked (v. 10)—Tried to correct or scold

Envied (v. 11)—Were jealous of

Observed (v. 11)— Remembered

Vale (v. 14)—Valley

Conspired (v. 18)—Planned

Devoured (vv. 20, 33)—Eaten

Delivered (v. 21)—Saved

Rid (v. 22)—Save

Company (v.25)—Group

Spicery and balm and myrrh (v. 25)—Precious things to sell

Conceal (v. 26)—Hide

Content (v. 27)—Agreed

Merchantmen (v. 28)—Businessmen

Rent (vv. 29, 33–34)—Tore

Put sackcloth upon his loins (v. 34)—Dressed in rough clothing (a tradition that showed his sadness)

Studying the Scriptures

Do two of the activities below (A–C) as you study Genesis 37.

A Choose a Title for a Biography

If you were writing a biography of Joseph's life up to the end of Genesis 37, what would you title it? Explain why.

B Joseph's Trials

1. List the challenges in Genesis 37 that Joseph faced.

2. How do you think Joseph felt about his challenges?

3. How are Joseph's challenges like the ones young people face today?

C Gain Insight from the Book of Mormon

1. Explain why you think Jacob "refused to be comforted" (v. 35).

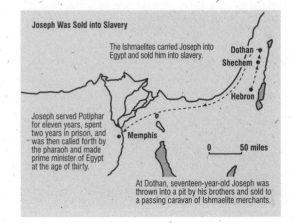

Joseph Was Sold into Slavery

The Ishmaelites carried Joseph into Egypt and sold him into slavery.

Dothan
Shechem
Hebron

Joseph served Potiphar for eleven years, spent two years in prison, and was then called forth by the pharaoh and made prime minister of Egypt at the age of thirty.

Memphis

0   50 miles

At Dothan, seventeen-year-old Joseph was thrown into a pit by his brothers and sold to a passing caravan of Ishmaelite merchants.

2. Jacob kept a piece of Joseph's coat that his sons brought to him. Later, when he learned that Joseph was still alive, he prophesied about Joseph's descendants. Read this prophecy in Alma 46:24–25 and explain it in your own words. This prophecy not only refers to the people of the Book of Mormon but also to you if you are from the tribes of Ephraim or Manasseh (Joseph's sons).

Genesis 38–39

Joseph's Righteousness

Genesis 38 tells the story of Judah, the fourth son of Jacob (Israel), and his example of wickedness. We read that he married out of the covenant and did not care for his family as he should have. We also read that he broke the law of chastity with his daughter-in-law, although he didn't know that it was her at the time.

In contrast, Genesis 39 tells us how Joseph sought to do good. Even though Joseph was a faithful young man, he experienced great trials. It was possible that he would never see his family again. How would you feel in a similar situation? Far away from anyone of your faith, what would you do about your religious beliefs and practices?

On one occasion, the Prophet Joseph Smith told Elder George A. Smith: "Never be discouraged. . . [I]f I were sunk in the lowest pit of Nova Scotia, with the Rocky Mountains piled on me, I would hang on, exercise faith, and keep up good courage, and I would come out on top" (in John Henry Evans, Joseph Smith: An American Prophet *[1933], 9). As you read Genesis 39, look for how Joseph was an example of the Prophet Joseph's statement.*

Understanding the Scriptures

Genesis 39

Pharaoh (v. 1)—King of Egypt

Of the hands of (v. 1)—From

Prosperous, prosper (vv. 2–3, 23)—Successful and blessed

Hand (vv. 3–4, 6, 8, 22)—Control

Found grace (v. 4)—Was favored and treated kindly

Overseer (vv. 4–5)—Leader, someone put in charge

Save (v. 6)—Except

Goodly (v. 6)—Strong

Well favoured (v. 6)—Handsome

Lie (vv. 7, 10, 12, 14)—Have sexual relations

Committed (vv. 8, 22)—Given

Garment (vv. 12–13, 15–16)—Outer clothing

Mock (vv. 14, 17)—Insult

His lord (v. 16)—Potiphar

His wrath was kindled (v. 19)—He became angry

Looked not to (v. 23)—Did not worry about

Genesis 39:7–20—Joseph and Potiphar's Wife

President Ezra Taft Benson explained Joseph's actions this way: "When Joseph was in Egypt, what came first in his life—God, his job, or Potiphar's wife? When she tried to seduce him, he responded by saying, 'How then can I do this great wickedness, and sin against God?' (Genesis 39:9).

"Joseph was put in prison because he put God first. If we were faced with a similar choice, where would we place our first loyalty? Can we put God ahead of security, peace, passions, wealth, and the honors of men?

"When Joseph was forced to choose, he was more anxious to please God than to please his employer's wife. When we are required to choose, are we more anxious to please God than our boss, our teacher, our neighbor, or our date?" (in Conference Report, Apr. 1988, 4; or Ensign, May 1988, 4–5).

Studying the Scriptures

A Find a Repeated Idea

1. Read verses 2–3, 21, 23 and find a phrase that is similar in all four verses. (You may want to underline the phrase in your scriptures.) Why do you think it was important for Joseph to know this to be true?

2. What did Joseph do in Genesis 39 that allowed the phrase in verses 2–3 to still be true in verses 21, 23?

B Scripture Mastery—Genesis 39:9

1. What reasons did Joseph give for resisting Potiphar's wife's invitation to be immoral?

2. What impresses you most about Joseph's statement and actions? How could you use the same ideas to resist temptation in your own life?

Genesis 40

Joseph in Prison

As you read Genesis 40–41, look for more ways that "the Lord was with Joseph" (Genesis 39:21). Consider that none of Joseph's successes would have happened if Joseph had given in to the temptation of Potiphar's wife. Notice as you read how the Lord turned what seemed to be a bad situation into a good one.

Understanding the Scriptures

Genesis 40

Butler (vv. 1–2)—Servant

Wroth against (v. 2)—Angry at

Ward (vv. 3–4, 7)—Prison

Charged Joseph with them (v. 4)—Made Joseph responsible for them

Continued a season (v. 4)—Stayed

Each man according to the interpretation of his dream (v. 5)—Each man's dream had a different meaning

Interpreter, interpretation, interpreted (vv. 8, 12, 16, 18, 22)—Someone who tells the meaning of something, to tell the meaning of something

Budded (v. 10)—Grew flowers or leaves

Lift up thine head (v. 13)—Bring you out of prison and into favor

Think on (v. 14)—Remember

Uppermost (v. 17)—Top

Bakemeats (v. 17)—Baked foods

Studying the Scriptures

A Dreams and Interpretations

Make a chart like the one below and write in it the dreams of the butler and baker and the interpretations Joseph gave.

	Contents of the Dream	Interpretation
Butler		
Baker		

B Give Your Opinion

Based on what you know about Joseph's life so far, explain why you think he was able to interpret the dreams in this chapter.

Genesis 41

Joseph and the Pharaoh

How would you feel if you were called to appear before the leader of your country and give him advice? What would you be thinking and what would you say? What would you do if you became a leader of your country, second only to the president, king, queen, or prime minister? As you read Genesis 41, see what Joseph did in these situations and compare his actions to what you would do.

Understanding the Scriptures

Genesis 41

Well favoured (vv. 2, 4, 18)—Strong, healthy

Kine (vv. 2–4, 18–20, 26–27)—Cows

Fatfleshed (v. 2)—Fat, healthy

Ill favoured (vv. 3–4, 19–21, 26–27)—Weak, sickly

Lean fleshed (vv. 3–4, 19)—Skinny, not healthy

Brink (v. 3)—Edge, bank

Rank (vv. 5, 7)—Ripe

Blasted (vv. 6, 23, 27)—Dried

Devoured (vv. 7, 24)—Ate

Raiment (v. 14)—Clothing

Hastily (v. 14)—Quickly

Withered (v. 23)—Weakened, dried up and hardened

Declare (v. 24)—Explain

Consume the land (v. 30)—Use up all the food the land can produce, land cannot produce enough

Grievous (v. 31)—Terrible

Established (v. 32)—Done

Discreet (vv. 33, 39)—With good judgment

Plenteous years (v. 34)—Years with much food

Store (v. 36)—Storage, to save

Against (v. 36)—To prepare for

Forasmuch as (v. 39)—Because

In the throne (v. 40)—As the king

Arrayed (v. 42)—Dressed

Vestures (v. 42)—Clothing

Laid up (v. 48)—Stored

Left (v. 49)—Quit

Toil (v. 51)—Labor

Fruitful (v. 52)—Prosperous

Dearth (v. 54)—Famine

Famished (v. 55)—Starving

Waxed sore (v. 56)—Became terrible

Studying the Scriptures

Do two of the following activities (A–C) as you study Genesis 41.

A Describe or Draw

Describe or draw a picture of Pharaoh's two dreams and tell what they meant, according to Joseph.

B Finish These Sentences in Your Own Words

1. After Pharaoh told Joseph his dream, Joseph . . .

2. Joseph suggested . . .

3. Pharaoh made Joseph . . .

4. Joseph had two sons . . .

C What Do You Suppose He Was Thinking?

1. Describe what you believe Joseph might have been thinking and feeling about his life at the end of chapter 41 considering the ways the Lord blessed him since the time he was with his family in Canaan.

2. What advice do you think Joseph would give to others about their trials?

3. How would things be different if Joseph had given in to Potiphar's wife?

Genesis 42

Joseph's Brothers Go to Egypt

Suppose someone betrayed you and caused you great financial problems where you lost nearly all your possessions. You later recovered and became quite wealthy. After becoming wealthy, you learned that the person who had earlier harmed you was now very poor and nearly starving. How would you feel? What would you do? Why?

Joseph's story in Genesis 42–45 is much like the situation just described. His story should cause us to think about how we deal with those who have wronged us. As we read, we might also look at the story from the point of view of those who did wrong. How were they given the opportunity to change, and how does the Lord give us similar opportunities? Look for these ideas as you read chapters 42–45.

Understanding the Scriptures

Genesis 42

Lest peradventure mischief befall him (v. 4)—Because something bad might happen to him

Made himself strange unto them (v. 7)—Did not tell them who he was

Nakedness of the land (vv. 9, 12)—How little food is able to grow (implying that Joseph's brothers came to see if the Egyptians were weak because of the lack of food)

One is not (vv. 13, 32)—One is dead

Hereby (vv. 15, 33)—In this way

Hence (v. 15)—Back home

Hither (v. 15)—Here

Into ward (v. 17)—Under arrest

Bound (v. 19)—Kept

Verified (v. 20)—Proved true

Verily (v. 21)—Truly

Anguish (v. 21)—Pain

Besought (v. 21)—Begged for mercy

Distress (v. 21)—Punishment

His blood is required (v. 22)—We will be held responsible for what we did to him

Communed (v. 24)—Talked

Provision, provender (vv. 25–26)—Food

Laded (v. 26)—Loaded

Espied (v. 27)—Saw

Befell, befall (vv. 29, 38)—Happened

Traffick (v. 34)—Buy and sell

Bereaved (v. 36)—Taken away

Mischief (v. 38)—Something bad

Studying the Scriptures

A What Was Happening to Joseph's Brothers?

"Remorse and deep sorrow then are preliminary to repentance. . . .

". . . Suffering is a very important part of repentance. One has not begun to repent until he has suffered intensely for his sins" (Spencer W. Kimball, *The Teachings of Spencer W. Kimball*, 87–88).

Considering the statements above, find and write about things in Genesis 42 that show how Joseph's brothers were beginning the process of repentance for what they did to him. Continue to look for these as you read Genesis 43–44.

Genesis 43

Joseph's Brothers Return to Egypt

At the end of Genesis 42, Jacob (Israel) was determined not to send Benjamin to Egypt even though Simeon was still being held there. As you read Genesis 43, look for what changed Jacob's mind. What do you think happened when Joseph saw his younger brother?

Understanding the Scriptures 🔑

Genesis 43

Solemnly protest unto (v. 3)—Warn

Wherefore dealt ye so ill (v. 6)—Why were you so cruel

State (v. 7)—Condition

The tenor of these words (v. 7) —These kinds of words

Surety (v. 9)—Responsible. Judah promised Israel that he would stay in Canaan and give his life for Benjamin if Benjamin didn't return from Egypt.

Lingered (v. 10)—Waited

Balm, honey, spices, myrrh, nuts, almonds (v. 11)—Precious things

Oversight (v. 12)—Mistake

Bereaved (v. 14)—Deprived, left without

Slay (v. 16)—Kill an animal for food

Seek occasion (v. 18)—Find a reason to punish

Bondmen (v. 18)—Slaves

Steward (v. 19)—Servant in charge

Made obeisance (v. 28)—Kneeled before him and bowed their heads in humility

Bowels did yearn (v. 30)—Felt strong emotions of love

Made haste (v. 30)—Hurried

Refrained (v. 31)—Controlled his emotions

Messes (v. 34)—Food

Studying the Scriptures ✏️

A Find the Fulfillment of Prophecy

Read again the dreams of Joseph found in Genesis 37:5–10. Write about specific ways these dreams were fulfilled in Genesis 42–43, including specific verses you believe fulfilled these dreams.

Genesis 44

Joseph Tests His Brothers

Early in the story of Joseph and his brothers, it did not seem that the older brothers cared much about what happened to their younger brothers, nor did it seem like they worried much about the feelings of their father. As you read, notice how those feelings changed.

Understanding the Scriptures 🔑

Genesis 44

Divineth (v. 5)—Makes predictions about the future

Bondmen (v. 9)—Servants

Rent (v. 13)—Tore

Wot (v. 15)—Know

Divine (v. 15)—Know what you are doing without anyone telling me

Clear (v. 16)—Make innocent

Iniquity (v. 16)—Sin

Mischief befall him (v. 29)—Bad things happen to him

Bound up in (v. 30)—Very closely tied to

Surety (v. 32)—Responsible

Studying the Scriptures ✏️

A How Is This Story a Symbol?

President Brigham Young taught that "Joseph was foreordained to be the temporal saviour of his father's house, and the seed of Joseph are ordained to be the spiritual and temporal saviours of all the house of Israel in the latter days" (in *Journal of Discourses,* 7:290). The Prophet Joseph Smith was a direct descendant of Joseph, son of Jacob; most members of the Church are of the lineage of either Ephraim or Manasseh, Joseph's two sons. How are Joseph's modern descendants (the Church) spiritually doing for the house of Israel what he temporally did for his family anciently?

B How Is Judah a Type of Christ?

Describe how Judah's actions in Genesis 44:18–34 were like the future actions of his descendant Jesus Christ.

Genesis 45

Joseph Reveals Himself to His Brothers

In Genesis 45, Joseph finally made himself known to his brothers. Before you read, predict how his brothers, the Egyptians, and Joseph's father Jacob (Israel) will react. Read and see what actually happened.

Understanding the Scriptures 🔑

Genesis 45

Refrain himself (v. 1)—Control his emotions

Grieved (v. 5)—Troubled

Earing nor harvest (v. 6)—Growing or gathering food

Deliverance (v. 7)—Way of escape

Nourish (v. 11)—Feed

Fame thereof (v. 16)—Story

Regard not (v. 20)—Do not worry about

Provision (v. 21)—Food

Raiment (v. 22)—Clothing

Revived (v. 27)—Became strong

Studying the Scriptures ✏️

Do either activity A or B as you study Genesis 45.

A Write a Journal Entry

Write an imaginary journal entry for Joseph at the end of the day he revealed himself to his brothers. Include what you think he realized about his life twenty years after being sold into Egypt, including the difficult trials he experienced.

B What Do You Think They Said?

In Genesis 45:25–27 Joseph's brothers told Jacob the story of what happened when they were in Egypt. They certainly needed to fill in some parts of the story, however, like what *really* happened to Joseph when Jacob thought he had died. Imagine you are Judah and write what you would have said to Jacob on this occasion. Include the following information in what you write: how your feelings have changed over the years (for example, compare Genesis 37:23–34 with Genesis 43:3–10; 44:14–34), which events changed your feelings, how you feel about things in the past, and how you feel about what happened on your trips to Egypt, especially the final time when Joseph revealed himself.

Genesis 46

Father and Son Reunited!

Jacob thought his son was dead. After twenty years he learned that Joseph was alive and that he would get the opportunity to see this beloved son again. We can only imagine what the reunion was like (read about it in Genesis 46:28–30). This chapter also includes a list of the names of all of Jacob's (Israel's) descendants who went and lived in Egypt (see vv. 8–27).

Understanding the Scriptures 🔑

Genesis 46

Visions (v. 2)—Dreams

Direct his face (v. 28)—Show the way

Trade (vv. 32, 34)—Work

Occupation (v. 33)—Work

Abomination (v. 34)—Considered bad

Studying the Scriptures ✏️

A Joseph: A Type of Christ

One special way some ancient prophets bore witness of Christ was by the way they lived or by the things that happened to them. By carefully looking at the lives of the prophets we see patterns, or types, of what would happen to the Savior or what the Savior would do or say. Joseph's life in Egypt had many of these types.

Review the story of Joseph (see Genesis 37–46). List as many details as you can about Joseph's life that either are like what happened to Jesus Christ or that teach us something about the Savior. You may want to discuss this activity with others to create a large list. Some students have found as many as fifteen to twenty different things in the scriptures about Joseph that are a type of Christ.

Genesis 47–48

Jacob Adopts Joseph's Sons

Genesis 47 tells about what occurred during the last five years of the famine. The famine got so bad that people traded their personal property and land for food. Because of this trading, Pharaoh gradually became the owner of nearly everything in the country.

By the end of Genesis 47, Jacob was ready to die. He had just one request: to be buried in the land God promised him, his fathers, and his posterity.

Before he died, Jacob needed to assign birthright responsibilities. Generally, the firstborn son received the birthright blessing and responsibilities. Isaac, however, was not actually the first child of Abraham. Jacob was not the firstborn of Isaac. Joseph was nearly the last son born to Jacob. Yet all three of these men received the birthright blessings. In Genesis 48, Ephraim received the birthright instead of his older brother Manasseh. There is no account of why Ephraim was selected. We know that God chooses according to his laws and purposes (see D&C 130:20–21). Although Ephraim received the birthright, the blessings of Manasseh are also great because of what was promised to all the posterity of Joseph (see Genesis 49:22–26; Deuteronomy 33:13–17). In addition, both of these sons were "adopted" by Jacob (see Genesis 48:5). Because of the birthright, Joseph was entitled to a double portion of the inheritance from his father Jacob. Ephraim was assigned to preside, or lead, the family of Israel. Ephraim and Manasseh were each given one part of the double portion of inheritance and became two of the "tribes of Israel."

Genesis 49

Patriarchal Blessings for Israel's Sons

Genesis 49 contains the blessings given by the prophet and patriarch Jacob (Israel) to his twelve sons before he died. Especially notice the blessings given to Judah, whose descendants include Jesus Christ, and the blessings given to Joseph, whose descendants are the people of the Book of Mormon and most Church members since the Restoration.

To better understand this chapter, it is helpful to know that it was written in poetry in the original Hebrew. The poetic form most often used in the scriptures, especially in the Old Testament, is called "parallelism." In this form, the writer, or speaker, says something and then repeats it using different words. Note the two phrases at the end of verse 11:

• "He washed his garments in wine."

• "[He washed] his clothes in the blood of grapes."

Understanding the Scriptures

Genesis 49

Befall (v. 1)—Happen to

The excellency of (v. 3)—The highest in

Dignity (v. 3)—Honor

Unstable (v. 4)—Reckless

Excel (v. 4)—Be great

Defiledst (v. 4)—Made unclean (see Genesis 35:22)

Couch (v. 4)—Bed

Instruments of cruelty (v. 5)—Weapons of violence

Habitations (v. 5)—Place where one lives

Selfwill (v. 6)—Selfishness, lack of control of one's emotions

Whelp (v. 9)—Offspring

Prey (vv. 9, 27)—Victim, conquered and taken by force to be eaten

Couched (vv. 9, 14)—Laid down

Rouse him up (v. 9)—Awake him

Sceptre (v. 10)—Right or authority to rule

Binding (v. 11)—Tying

Foal (v. 11)—Young donkey

Haven (v. 13)—Harbor, safe place

Bear (v. 15)—Carry

Tribute (v. 15)—Forced labor

Adder (v. 17)—Snake

Royal dainties (v. 20)—Rare things given to kings

Hind (v. 21)—Female deer

Bough (v. 22)—Large branch

Sorely grieved (v. 23)—Greatly humbled

Abode in strength (v. 24)—Stayed strong

Have prevailed (v. 26)—Are greater

Progenitors (v. 26)—Ancestors

Utmost (v. 26)—Farthest

Ravin (v. 27)—Eat greedily, take food by violence and force

Devour (v. 27)—Eat up

Spoil (v. 27)—Things taken by force

Charged (v. 29)—Commanded

Yielded up the ghost (v. 33)—Died

Jacob's blessings to Judah and Joseph

Judah   **Joseph**

Studying the Scriptures

Do two of the following activities (A–C) as you study Genesis 49.

A Identify the Blessings

Underline the names of the twelve sons of Israel in your scriptures so that you can quickly see where to find each son's blessing. Write about the special things promised to Judah and Joseph; two blessings seem to stand out above the others.

B Patriarchal Blessings

The blessings given in Genesis 49 are like patriarchal blessings. Explain what your patriarchal blessing means to you.

or

Explain why we receive a patriarchal blessing and what the requirements are to receive one.

C How Was This Prophecy Fulfilled?

Explain what verse 22 in Genesis 49 means. To help you, read 1 Nephi 5:14–16; Jacob 2:25, which tell which tribe the Book of Mormon people are from. Also keep in mind that Elder LeGrand Richards said that the "everlasting hills" in Genesis 49:26 refer to the Americas (see Conference Report, Apr. 1967, 20).

Genesis 50

Jacob and Joseph Die

The Bible is a record of the house of Israel. Genesis means "beginnings." Genesis is the book of beginnings where we read of the beginning of the world and the beginning of the house of Israel. Genesis 50 is the final chapter of Genesis and tells of Israel's (Jacob's) death; in this way, Genesis 50 is the "end of the beginning."

A large part of Genesis 50 is not in the Bible, but the part not included was revealed to the Prophet Joseph Smith and is found in JST, Genesis 50:24–38. This account prepares us to better understand Exodus because it mentions Moses and his work.

Understanding the Scriptures 🔑

Genesis 50

Embalm, embalmed (vv. 2–3, 26)—Prepare for burial

Threshingfloor (v. 10)—Place to separate wheat grain from the stalks

Lamentation (v. 10)—Very sad words and weeping

Requite (v. 15)—Repay

JST, Genesis 50:24–38

Fruit of my (thy) loins (vv. 24, 26–27, 30–31)—My descendants

Branch (vv. 24–25)—Group

Manifest (v. 25)—Known

Seer (vv. 26–27, 29–30, 33)—Prophet

Esteemed (v. 27)—Respected

Confounding, confounded (vv. 31, 33)—Overthrow or destroy

Laying down of contentions (v. 31)—Ending arguments

Preserve (v. 34)—Protect from destruction

Confirmed (v. 37)—Made certain

Studying the Scriptures ✏️

Do two of the following activities (A–D) as you study Genesis 50, including the Joseph Smith Translation.

A Why Were They Worried?

1. Why do you think Joseph's brothers did what they did in Genesis 50:14–21?

2. What Christlike example did Joseph set?

B Identify the Elements of Joseph's Prophecy

List things from JST, Genesis 50:24–38 that Joseph prophesied would happen to the family of Israel.

C Find the Phrases

1. JST, Genesis 50:31 speaks of the Bible and the Book of Mormon. What term refers to the Bible and what term refers to the Book of Mormon?

2. What did Joseph say the Book of Mormon would (and will) do?

D Who Is This Seer?

Identify the seer referred to in Genesis 50:30–33, and explain what Joseph prophesied this seer would do.

The Book of Exodus

The book of Exodus is the second of the five books of Moses. In Exodus we read about Moses' birth, his calling as a prophet, and how he led the children of Israel out of Egypt. *Exodus* means "exit" or "departure."

of how the prophet Moses led the Israelites in a miraculous escape from slavery.

We also learn about notable events in religious history like the Passover, the parting of the Red Sea, and the giving of the Ten Commandments. From the teachings in Exodus, we can gain faith that the Lord will lead his people to him by raising up prophets to teach and lead them, by giving them his law, by inviting them to enter covenants to keep that law, and by giving them temples where they can receive covenants and more fully worship him. The Lord promises that those who are true and faithful can enter his presence.

Why Read Exodus?

There are many reasons the book of Exodus is significant to Latter-day Saints today. The first half of Exodus tells the inspiring story

Getting Ready to Study Exodus

There is a period between the end of Genesis and the beginning of Exodus that is not written about in the Bible. During that time, the children of Israel increased in number and prospered in the land assigned to them by the pharaoh who ruled at the time of Joseph. After some years, a new line of pharaohs who did not have respect for Joseph's family came to power and enslaved the Israelites.

The first part of Exodus tells the story of Moses and the role he played in delivering the children of Israel from bondage (see chapters 1–18). The rest of Exodus tells about how worship and religious laws and covenants were reestablished among the children of Israel. These laws and covenants were given to prepare the Israelites to enter the land God promised them as descendants of Abraham (see chapters 19–40).

Unfortunately, the Israelites often complained about God's dealings with them, which led them to rebellion and disobedience. Their complaining and rebellion kept them from receiving all the blessings the Lord desired to give them. As you read, you may be amazed at how merciful the Lord was to the Israelites—even when they complained against him. (For more information on the book of Exodus, see the Bible Dictionary, s.v. "Exodus, book of.")

Exodus 1

Courageous Midwives

What do you do when you know something is wrong but you are told by powerful and important people to do it anyway? Exodus 1 gives an example of a group of women faced with that kind of a situation.

Understanding the Scriptures

Exodus 1

Deal wisely with them (v. 10)—Govern them in a way that will benefit us

Taskmasters (v. 11)—Person who assigns hard jobs

Serve with rigour (vv. 13–14)—Treat cruelly by requiring very hard work

Bitter (v. 14)—Difficult

Midwives (vv. 15–21)—Women who help deliver babies

Stools (v. 16)—Places where women gave birth

Feared God (vv. 17, 21)—Honored and cared more about God than other things

Lively (v. 19)—Strong and healthy

Ere (v. 19)—Before

Studying the Scriptures

Do either activities A and B or activity C only as you study Exodus 1.

A Finish These Sentences

1. Pharaoh made life more difficult for the children of Israel because . . .

2. Pharaoh commanded the midwives to . . .

3. The midwives disobeyed Pharaoh's commands because . . .

B Identify the Principle

Read Doctrine and Covenants 3:7–8. How does it apply to what the midwives did? You may want to write "Exodus 1:15–22" in the margin next to verses 7–8.

C Apply the Principle

1. Write about whether you think it is easier to fear what friends think or to fear God, and explain why.

2. Name a way you think people your age fear man more than God. Write a letter in your notebook to a person with this challenge to help him or her understand what should be done. Use what you learned in Doctrine and Covenants 3:7–8 and the story in Exodus 1 in what you write.

Exodus 2

Moses' Early Life

In the Church we know that "a man must be called of God" before he can represent God to the people (Articles of Faith 1:5). Acts 7 records that Moses apparently knew he would be the one to help deliver the Hebrews from Egypt. As you read Exodus 2, look for ways the Lord prepared Moses to do a great work for his people and what Moses might have learned from his experiences. Thinking about Moses' experiences may also help you think about some ways you may serve the Lord in your life. How are you preparing yourself for these responsibilities now? What are you doing to make the most of these preparatory experiences?

Understanding the Scriptures

Exodus 2

Goodly (v. 2)—Beautiful, pleasant-natured, and intelligent

Took for him an ark of bulrushes (v. 3)—Made for him a waterproof basket out of reeds or palm leaves

Maidens (v. 5)—Servants

Smiting (vv. 11, 13)—Hit with the intent to injure

Strove (v. 13)—Fought

Content (v. 21)—Pleased

Sighed (v. 23)—Groaned

By reason (v. 23)—Because

Had respect (v. 25)—Knew of their circumstances

Studying the Scriptures ▰▱▱

Ⓐ Get Help from the New Testament

Read Acts 7:22–29; Hebrews 11:24–27. Then complete the following activities.

1. Explain how the situation in which Moses was raised specially prepared him to deliver the children of Israel.

2. Explain what Moses was trying to do when he killed an Egyptian (see Exodus 2:11–12).

Ⓑ Moses' Preparation

In order to more fully understand what happened to Moses while in Midian, read Exodus 2:15–22. Read the other name for Reuel in Exodus 3:1 (see Exodus 2:18). Then read Doctrine and Covenants 84:6 to see what Reuel had to offer Moses. List in your notebook the three experiences Moses had in Midian that you think were important ones in preparing him for his work with the children of Israel.

Exodus 3

The Burning Bush

Have you ever been given an assignment you felt you could not successfully complete because you felt inadequate? If you have had this experience, why did you try? If you haven't, what would it take for you to try? Exodus 3–4 tells about when the Lord called Moses to deliver the children of Israel from Egypt. We read that Moses felt he wasn't good enough to deliver his people, and then we read what the Lord did to reassure and help him. What does Ether 12:27 teach you about the Lord's promise to you as well as to Moses?

Understanding the Scriptures ⚷

Exodus 3

Kept (v. 1)—Watched over

Consumed (v. 2)—Burned up

Draw not nigh hither (v. 5) —Do not come closer

By reason (v. 7)—Because

Token (v. 12)—Sign

Visited (v. 16)—Watched over

Beseech (v. 18)—Ask, plead

I will stretch out my hand (v. 20)—I will use my power

Sojourneth (v. 22)—Stays

Exodus 3:11–16—"I Am That I Am"

"I Am That I Am" is a form of "Jehovah," one of the names of Jesus Christ. Moses and the Israelites understood the name to mean that God is eternal and not created by man, as were other gods of the day. This name was a way for the Lord to identify himself as the all-powerful true and living God. The Israelites came to greatly reverence this name and declared that speaking it was blasphemy.

Whenever this name occurs in the Old Testament's Hebrew text, Jehovah is most often translated as "LORD." In the New

Testament a group of Jews sought to kill Jesus because he testified that he was the "I Am" who spoke to Moses and other prophets (see John 8:58). This New Testament reference confirms that Jesus Christ is Jehovah, the God of the Old Testament.

Studying the Scriptures ▰▱▱

Ⓐ Learn More about God

Exodus 3 tells us about God revealing himself to Moses and calling him to be a prophet. By studying chapter 3 we not only learn about what Moses was called to do, but we also learn something about God himself.

1. Describe what you learn about God from what he said and did in Exodus 3.

2. How might the truths you learned about God from this chapter help someone who is in the bondage of sin (as Israel was in bondage to Egypt) or who is required to accomplish a difficult task (as Moses was).

Exodus 4

Moses Returns to Egypt

Refer to the introduction to Exodus 3.

Understanding the Scriptures ⚷

Exodus 4

Into thy bosom (vv. 6–7)— Next to your chest

Leprous (v. 6)—Having leprosy, a skin disease

Eloquent (v. 10)—Good at speaking

Heretofore (v. 10)—In the past

Dumb (v. 11)—Someone who can't speak

Wherewith (v. 17)—With it

Note: Remember to use the footnotes in the Latter-day Saint edition of the King James Version of the Bible to aid you in understanding what you read.

Studying the Scriptures ▰▱▱

Ⓐ What If They Won't Believe Me?

Moses' Fears, Doubts, and Concerns	How the Lord Resolved the Concern

Make a chart like the one shown. Fill in the chart with what you learn in Exodus 4 about Moses' concerns about his assignment and what the Lord did to help resolve his concerns.

Exodus 5

Hard-Hearted Pharaoh

When we do what is right we are not always immediately rewarded or may not be immediately successful in the ways we desire. To do what we know is right when the rewards are not immediate or when things seem to get worse instead of better is an important test of faith (see Ether 12:6).

At the end of Exodus 4 we read that Moses returned to Egypt and showed signs and wonders to his people. They believed in him and appeared anxious to follow him in his role as deliverer. As you read Exodus 5 notice how and why the attitudes of the people changed. Also think about what you would do in a similar circumstance.

Understanding the Scriptures 🔑

Exodus 5

Hold a feast unto me (v. 1)—Worship me

Pestilence (v. 3)—Epidemic, plague

Burdens (vv. 4–5)—Forced work or labor

Ye make them rest from their burdens (v. 5)—You are causing them to stop working

Heretofore (vv. 7–8, 14)—In the past

Lay upon (v. 8)—Assign

Diminish/minish ought thereof (vv. 8, 11, 19)—Make any smaller

Idle (vv. 8, 17)—Lazy

Regard (v. 9)—Pay attention to

Vain words (v. 9)—Things that are not true or that will not happen

Stubble (v. 12)—The short, small stalks left after cutting a field of wheat, barley, and so on

Fulfil your works/task (vv. 13–14)—Do what was required

Wherefore dealest thou thus (v. 15)—Why are you doing this

Made our savour to be abhorred (v. 21)—Made Pharaoh hate us

Studying the Scriptures ✏️

Do activity A, then do either activity B or C.

A Summarize the Chapter

Summarize Exodus 5 following the example below. Finish each sentence in your own words.

Moses and Aaron asked Pharaoh . . .
    and so
Pharaoh responded by . . .
    and so
The Israelites said to Pharaoh . . .
    and so
Pharaoh said . . .
    and so
The Israelites said to Moses and Aaron . . .

B Write an Imaginary Journal Entry

Record what you would have written at the end of Exodus 5 if you had experienced what Moses and Aaron did.

C Explain an Important Idea

Write to the Israelites, telling why the Lord sometimes allows circumstances to get harder for us rather than making them easier when we do what is right. You may use any scripture, ancient or modern, in your answer, or you may use General Authority statements you might have access to.

Exodus 6

I Am the Lord

At the close of Exodus 5 both Moses and the children of Israel were discouraged; it seemed like obeying God only caused them more trials. Exodus 6 contains the Lord's promises that he would deliver and sustain them.

Understanding the Scriptures 🔑

Exodus 6

Pilgrimage (v. 4)—Land where they stayed or wandered

Redeem (v. 6)—Deliver from slavery

Stretched out arm (v. 6)—This phrase is a symbol of power

Heritage (v. 8)—A lasting possession or inheritance

Anguish of spirit (v. 9)—Discouragement

Charge (v. 13)—Stewardship

Studying the Scriptures ✏️

A Find Messages of Encouragement

Choose what you think are the two encouraging things the Lord said to the Israelites in Exodus 6. Explain why you think both messages were encouraging to the children of Israel and could be encouraging to someone with trials and challenges today. Make sure you read the Joseph Smith Translation for Exodus 6:3.

Exodus 7–10

The Plagues

In Exodus 5 the Lord gave Pharaoh the opportunity to simply let the children of Israel go, but Pharaoh refused. Exodus 7

begins a series of confrontations Moses and Aaron had with Pharaoh. Moses and Aaron asked Pharaoh to let the Israelites go, declaring that if he did not, God would display his power by plaguing or causing problems for Egypt. As a result, the signs God sent are known as "the plagues of Egypt." Exodus 7–10 records nine different plagues. A tenth plague will be discussed in Exodus 11–13.

The fact that the Lord plagued Egypt so many times shows how merciful he is. Instead of immediately destroying Pharaoh and the Egyptians, he gave them many chances to acknowledge him and his power. The Lord's purpose is to have all of his children turn to him. Only after nine impressive displays of the Lord's power and Pharaoh completely hardening his heart did the Lord prepare the destructive tenth plague.

To help you see this story as a whole, "Understanding the Scriptures" will help you with words and phrases by chapter, and "Studying the Scriptures" will combine all four chapters into one section.

Understanding the Scriptures

Exodus 7

Armies (v. 4)—Divisions or groups of people

Stretch forth mine hand (v. 5)—Show my power

Fourscore (v. 7)—Eighty (a "score" is twenty)

Sorcerers (v. 11)—People who attempt to work magic with the help of evil spirits

Enchantments (vv. 11, 22)—The practice of sorcery

Hitherto (v. 16)—Up until now

Lothe (v. 18)—Hesitate

Vessels (v. 19)—Containers

Exodus 7—How Could the Pharaoh's Magicians Perform "Miracles"?

President Joseph Fielding Smith, then President of the Quorum of the Twelve Apostles, said, "All down through the ages and in almost all countries, men have exercised great occult and mystical powers, even to the healing of the sick and the performing of miracles. Soothsayers, magicians, and astrologers were found in the courts of ancient kings. They had certain powers by which they divined and solved the monarch's problems, dreams, etc. . . .

". . . The Savior declared that Satan had the power to bind bodies of men and women and sorely afflict them [see Matthew 7:22–23; Luke 13:16]. . . . It should be remembered that Satan has great knowledge and thereby can exercise authority and to some extent control the elements, when some greater power does not intervene" (*Answers to Gospel Questions*, 5 vols. [1957], 1:176, 178).

Exodus 8

All thy borders (v. 2)—The whole country

Abundantly (v. 3)—In great number

Kneading-troughs (v. 3)—Place to make bread

Intreat (vv. 8–9, 28–30)—Ask, beg

Respite (v. 15)—Relief

Grievous (v. 24)—Large, heavy

Deceitfully (v. 29)—Dishonestly

Exodus 9

Pestilence (v. 15)—Epidemic, plague

Exaltest (v. 17)—Lift up, be proud and stubborn

Foundation (v. 18)—Beginning

Regarded not (v. 21)—Paid no attention to, did not respect

Abroad (vv. 29, 33)—Out

Exodus 10

Wrought (v. 2)—Done

Coast (vv. 4, 14, 19)—Land, area

Residue (v. 5)—What is left

Snare (v. 7)—Problem, something to cause trouble for

Herb (vv. 12, 15)—Plant

Rested (v. 14)—Remained, stayed

Dwellings (v. 23)—Homes

Be stayed (v. 24)—Not go

Until we come thither (v. 26)—Until we get there

Studying the Scriptures

A Why Did God Send Plagues?

Read Exodus 7:1–7; 9:16 and tell what the Lord said about why he would show signs and miracles.

B Find the Plagues

Make a chart like the following and fill it in with information you find about each of the nine plagues.

Reference	Plague	What Moses and Aaron Did Before the Plague	The Effect of the Plague on the Egyptians	The Effect of the Plague on the Isrealites	How Pharaoh or His Servants Responded to the Plague
Exodus 7:14-25					
Exodus 8:1-15					
Exodus 8:16-19					
Exodus 8:20-32					
Exodus 9:1-7					
Exodus 9:8-12					
Exodus 9:13-35					
Exodus 10:1-20					
Exodus 10:21-29					

Exodus 11–12

The Passover

Exodus 11 is a continuation of the face-to-face meeting between Moses and Pharaoh that occurred at the end of Exodus 10. While still in the presence of Pharaoh, Moses received a revelation about the tenth and final plague. He declared to Pharaoh that the final plague would be the death of the firstborn in all the land. Pharaoh responded to Moses as he had before—he hardened his heart and ignored Moses' warning. Moses then left, seeing Pharaoh's "face again no more" (Exodus 10:29; see also v. 28).

The tenth and final plague described in Exodus 11–12 was a great tragedy for the Egyptians. The final plague was also one of the most significant events in Israelite history when God showed his power as he delivered his people. To all who believe in Jesus Christ, this event— known as the Passover—is one of the most powerful symbols of Christ found in the Old Testament and can strengthen our testimony of his Atonement. As you read, look for how God's miraculous deliverance of the Israelites from Egyptian bondage can be compared to Christ's Atonement and think of how Jesus Christ delivers us from the spiritual bondage of sin.

12:35–36). As you read further in Genesis, you will find out what the Lord will have them do with these riches.

Exodus 12:1–20—Animal Sacrifice a Similitude of Christ

President Joseph Fielding Smith said: "When the Israelites left Egypt, the Lord gave them the passover. They were to take a lamb without blemish; they were not to break any of its bones. They were to kill it, cook it, and eat it with bitter herbs and unleavened bread. This feast they were to remember annually thereafter until Christ should come. This was also in the similitude of the sacrifice of Jesus Christ. If you stop to consider it, it was at the time of the passover that our Lord was taken and crucified in fulfillment of the promises that had been made that he would come to be our Redeemer.

"All these things point to his coming and to his ministry. In fact sacrifice goes right back to the days of Adam. Animal sacrifices were to be without blemish, for it was in the similitude of the sacrifice of Jesus Christ, and pointed to his coming. We do not learn much in the Book of Genesis what sacrifice was for, because the plain things pertaining to sacrifice have been removed" (*Doctrines of Salvation*, comp. Bruce R. McConkie, 3 vols. [1954–56], 1:22).

Understanding the Scriptures

Exodus 12

Blemish (v. 5)—Defect or fault

Keep it up (v. 6)—Take care of it

Strike (vv. 7, 22)—Put, hit, mark

Flesh (v. 8)—Meat

Unleavened bread (vv. 8, 15, 17–18, 20)—Bread made without yeast

Bitter herbs (v. 8)—Plants that taste bitter

Sodden . . . with water (v. 9) —Boiled

Loins girded (v. 11)—Putting a belt around one's cloak

Execute judgment (v. 12) —Judge

By an ordinance (vv. 14, 17)— As a sacred ritual or permanent law

Leaven (vv. 15, 19)—Yeast

Save (v. 16)—Except

Even (v. 18)—Sunset

Draw out (v. 21)—Select

Hyssop (v. 22)—An herb

Bason (v. 22)—Bowl-like container

Lintel (vv. 22–23)—Top crosspiece of a door frame

Suffer (v. 23)—Allow

Observe (v. 24)—Do, preserve or protect

Service (vv. 25–26)— Ceremony, ordinance

Were urgent (v. 33)—Eager for them to leave

Tarry (v. 39)—Stay

Victual (v. 39)—Food and other supplies

Sojourning, sojourn, sojourneth (vv. 40, 48–49)— Temporary dwelling, to live somewhere for a time

Hosts (v. 41)—People

Observed (v. 42)— Remembered and treasured

Stranger (v. 43)—Non-Israelite

Ought (v. 46)—Anything

Exodus 11:2—Why Would the Lord Ask the Israelites to Borrow Things When They Were Leaving?

The word *borrow* is not used here the way we would normally use it. The Hebrew word for borrow means to ask or request. In other words, the Israelites asked payment for service they gave to the Egyptians over the years. Because of recent plagues, the Egyptians were soft enough in their hearts to give liberally (see Exodus

Studying the Scriptures

(A) Learn about Christ from the Passover

The Passover is a type, or symbol, of the Atonement of Jesus Christ. Make a chart like the one shown here. Using Exodus 12:1–20, 43–49, list the elements of the Passover and then write what you think those elements represent as they apply to Christ, his Atonement, and our deliverance through repentance from the bondage of sin and worldliness. The following scripture references may help you as you look for meanings to symbols: Jeremiah 51:6; John 19:30–36; 1 Peter 1:18–20; Mosiah 27:24–26; Alma 5:21, 27, 57; 34:8–10; Doctrine and Covenants 19:16–19, 31.

Try to find at least the following elements: new calendar, lamb (without blemish), blood on the doorposts, unleavened bread, eaten with bitter herbs. There is a small section in the front of this study guide entitled "Look for Types and Symbolic Meanings" (on p. 6) that will help you interpret or find the spiritual significance of scriptural symbols. The first two elements are provided for you as examples.

Verse	Elements of the Passover	Spiritual Significance or Interpretation
2	Calendar changed; the Passover marked the first month of the year	Through our repentance and the Atonement of Jesus Christ, we can make a "new beginning."
3	A lamb	The blood of the Lamb of God, or Jesus Christ, cleanses us if we repent.

B What about Today?

Following his Resurrection, Jesus Christ gave instructions regarding sacrifices and offerings under the law of Moses.

1. Read Matthew 26:17–30 and tell which ordinance the Lord asked us to participate in today that helps us remember the same spiritual things that the Passover did in ancient times.

2. Read 1 Corinthians 5:7–8 and tell why we no longer observe the Passover.

Exodus 13

The Firstborn

Suppose you were condemned to die in another land. Before your execution, someone made arrangements, at great cost, to purchase your freedom. How would you feel about that individual? What would your relationship to that person be for the rest of your life? This scenario is like the situation of the firstborn males in Israel. They would die as part of the tenth plague unless they had the blood of a lamb on their doorposts. The blood literally redeemed, or saved, them from death. Exodus 13 records what the Lord said to these firstborn who from that time forward, in a sense, lived on "borrowed time" because they were unable to save themselves. Only through the blood were they spared from death.

Understanding the Scriptures

Exodus 13

Sanctify (v. 2)—Set apart to the Lord and made holy

Openeth the womb (v. 2)— Firstborn

In his season (v. 10)—At the time the Lord said

Openeth the matrix (vv. 12, 15)—Firstborn

Firstling (vv, 12–13)— Firstborn

Redeem (vv. 13, 15)—Pay for. In other words, a lamb is sacrificed in the place of something else to recognize that which was saved belongs to the Lord.

Frontlets (v. 16)—A decorative band or ribbon worn across the forehead

Studying the Scriptures

A The Firstborn

1. Imagine you are a father in Israel in the days of Moses. Write what you would say to your firstborn son about who he is and why special things are done for him and expected of him. Pay special attention to Exodus 13:1–3, 8–16 as you consider what you will say.

2. Read 1 Corinthians 6:20; 1 Peter 1:18–19; 2 Nephi 2:8; 9:7–9; Doctrine and Covenants 18:10–12 and write about how you are like the firstborn in Israel. Also write about what you can do to always remember what the Lord has done and show him your gratitude for the redemption provided through his Atonement.

Exodus 14

Crossing the Red Sea

One of the blessings of having trials in life is that trials often prompt us to turn to the Lord for help (see Ether 12:27). When we receive the Lord's power and help, our faith and confidence to trust him in future trials increase. We must remember that in most instances, divine help comes only after we exercise faith by first doing all we can (see Ether 12:6). When help does come, it generally comes in a manner that helps us see the hand of the Lord.

In Exodus 13:17–18 the Lord told Moses which direction to lead the children of Israel on their way to the promised land. He said he would not lead the Israelites in the straightest and most direct course because they did not yet have enough faith to face the Philistines, who would seek to prevent them from entering the land. We can find comfort knowing that the Lord will not give us challenges greater than we can handle (see 1 Nephi 3:7). He will, however, allow us to experience challenges he knows we can overcome in order to build our faith and confidence. Exodus 14 tells about one such challenge. After their faith was tested, the Israelites experienced a miracle that once again demonstrated the power of God as he helped them overcome what seemed to be an impossible circumstance.

Understanding the Scriptures 🔑

Exodus 14

Entangled (v. 3)—Confused, lost

I will be honoured upon Pharaoh (vv. 4, 17–18)—The Lord is saying that people will be more likely to honor him as God because of what he will do to Pharaoh and the Egyptian army.

Host (v. 4)—Army

With an high hand (v. 8)—Defiant

Thus (v. 11)—In this way

Hold your peace (v. 14)—To be silent

To them (v. 20)—The Egyptians

To these (v. 20)—The Israelites

The morning watch (v. 24)—From 2:00 A.M. until sunrise

Drave them heavily (v. 25)—Drove with difficulty

Studying the Scriptures ✏️

Do activity A or B as you study Exodus 14.

Ⓐ Give Some Advice

Use specific ideas and phrases from chapter 14 to write a letter of advice to someone who recently converted to the Church or has become active who is having a difficult time with former friends and ways and seems to be drifting back to them.

Ⓑ Make a Match

The Time of Moses	Today
Leaving Egypt	Baptism
Traveling through the wilderness	Forsaking the ways of the world
Passing through the Red Sea	Receiving the gift of the Holy Ghost
A pillar of cloud and fire to watch over, guide, and protect the Israelites	Living in a world where things that promote spirituality are hard to find

Match items in the first column to items in the second column and explain how they are related. If you need some help, read 1 Corinthians 10:1–4. You may want to write 1 Corinthians 10:1–4 in the margin next to the beginning of Exodus 14.

Exodus 15

Murmuring, Part 1

How do you express happiness and gratitude? What do you do to show the Lord how you feel? Exodus 15 tells how the Israelites wrote and sang a song to the Lord after their miraculous escape at the Red Sea. Not long after their deliverance, the children of Israel experienced another

challenge. Read Exodus 15:22–27 to find out how they faced this next challenge.

Understanding the Scriptures 🔑

Exodus 15:22–27

Murmured (v. 24)—Complained

Ordinance (v. 25)—Law

Statute (vv. 25–26)—Commandment

Proved (v. 25)—Tested

Studying the Scriptures ✏️

Ⓐ What Is Your Favorite Hymn?

When the Israelites were happy and grateful they sang to the Lord. Which hymn makes you feel closer to God? Explain why. Use the lyrics of the hymn in your explanation.

Ⓑ What Are You Going to Do about It?

1. Read Exodus 15:22–27 and compare what the people did and what Moses did when they realized there was no water.

2. What can you learn from the different ways Moses and the people responded to this challenge?

Ⓒ Optional Activity

Read Exodus 15:22–27; Alma 36:17–21 and explain what spiritual meaning the physical experience at Marah could have.

Exodus 16

Murmuring, Part 2

Exodus 15 records that the children of Israel "murmured," or complained, about Moses and the Lord when they had a problem. It is hard for us to understand how they could have complained so quickly after the great miracle of the Red Sea. We must remember, however, that although slavery limited the Israelites' freedom, slavery also provided the Israelites' necessities of life in a way similar to that of a person in prison. Because the children of Israel had limited freedom to make choices, they were spiritually immature. Because the Lord is interested in our growth, he wants—even requires—that we make choices. As we need his help, he provides help for us in a way that requires us to do difficult things that build and strengthen us. To murmur against the Lord is to show that we lack faith that he knows what is best for us.

Exodus 16–17 contains much murmuring by the children of Israel. As you read these chapters, look for what the Lord taught the children of Israel to strengthen them and give them greater reason to trust him.

Understanding the Scriptures

Exodus 16

Would to God (v. 3)—We wish

Flesh pots (v. 3)—Pots of meat

Rate (v. 4)—Amount

Even (vv. 6, 12)—Sunset

Flesh (vv. 8, 12)—Meat

Host (v. 13)—Large group

Wist (v. 15)—Knew

Omer (vv. 16, 18, 22, 32, 36)—About five pints (two liters)

Mete (v. 18)—Measured

Leave of it (v. 19)—Keep or save any of it

Bred worms (v. 20)—Became wormy or filled with maggots

Wroth (v. 20)—Angry

Lay up, laid up (vv. 23–24)—Stored

Bade (v. 24)—Commanded

Studying the Scriptures

A What Was the Purpose of Manna?

1. According to Exodus 16:4, what was one of the purposes of manna?

2. Based on what you read in chapter 16, how do you think manna could accomplish the purpose verse 4 gives?

B Manna Was a Type of Christ

Read John 6:31–35, 48–51 and write about how manna is like Jesus Christ and how we are like the children of Israel. You may be interested to know that in Hebrew *Bethlehem* (the city where Jesus was born) means "house of bread."

C Who Are You Really Complaining Against?

When you murmur against your leaders, who are you really murmuring against? (see Exodus 16:8; D&C 84:36).

Exodus 17

Murmuring, Part 3

As you read Exodus 17, consider this: Being thirsty and wanting a drink of water are not sins. So why was the Lord displeased with the children of Israel?

Understanding the Scriptures

Exodus 17

Prevailed (v. 11)—Was winning

Rehearse (v. 14)—Tell

Note: Remember to look in your footnotes for help with difficult words and phrases.

Studying the Scriptures

Do activity A or B as you study Exodus 17.

A What Would You Say?

If you were given five minutes to speak to the Israelites after the events recorded in Exodus 17, what would you say to them, and why?

B How Does It Happen Today?

Compare what people wanted to do to the prophet Moses in Exodus 17:4 with what Aaron and Hur did for Moses in verses 10–13.

Exodus 18

Keeping Moses from Wearing Away

How do you react when people criticize you? What if they are right? Do you accept their opinions and change or do you argue just to save your pride? Moses was a great prophet set over all the people. Notice, however, what happened in Exodus 18 when someone criticized how Moses acted and suggested how he could change. In this case, the person who criticized Moses had nothing to gain personally; he was only interested in helping someone he loved.

Understanding the Scriptures

Exodus 18

Did obeisance (v. 7)—Bowed down in respect

Travail (v. 8)—Trouble

Statutes (v. 16)—Commandments

Causes (v. 19)—Problems

Provide (v. 21)—Choose

Covetousness (v. 21)—Desire for the things of others

Studying the Scriptures

Moses tried to do it all.

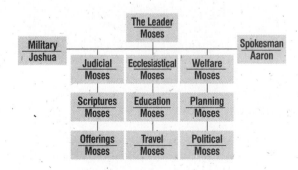

The Lord taught Moses the organization of leadership over the children of Israel.

	The Leader Moses	
Ruler of 1,000	Ruler of 1,000	Ruler of 1,000

Ruler of 100 | Ruler of 100 | Ruler of 100 | Ruler of 100 | Ruler of 100 | Ruler of 100 | Ruler of 100 | Ruler of 100 | Ruler of 100 | Ruler of 100

Ruler of 50 | Ruler of 50

Ruler of 10 | Ruler of 10 | Ruler of 10 | Ruler of 10 | Ruler of 10 | Ruler of 10 | Ruler of 10 | Ruler of 10 | Ruler of 10 | Ruler of 10

Ⓐ Keeping Moses from "Wearing Away"

Make a chart like the one shown and fill in information from what you read in Exodus 18:13–26.

The situation	
Why there is a problem	
The proposed solution	
The benefits of implementing the solution	
What Moses did	

Ⓑ What Do We Learn from Moses' Example?

What do we learn about Moses from the way he responded to Jethro's criticism?

Exodus 19

At Mount Sinai

Moses was on Mount Sinai when the Lord called him to deliver the Israelites from Egyptian bondage (see Exodus 3). The Lord promised Moses that after he led the children of Israel out of Egypt, they would "serve God upon this mountain," meaning Mount Sinai" (Exodus 3:12). After the miracle at the Red Sea, Moses wrote a song in which he said that the Lord led the Israelites out of Egypt so they could be in his "Sanctuary," which is "in the mountain of thine inheritance" (Exodus 15:17).

From the time Moses was called as a prophet, it was part of God's plan to lead the children of Israel to Mount Sinai—a place made holy by the Lord. According to the Doctrine and Covenants, Moses sought to bring his people into the presence of the Lord through the ordinances of the priesthood (see D&C 84:19–24). Today we might say he wanted to take them to the temple to receive power from on high. For Moses and the children of Israel, Mount Sinai was a temple—a place where the Lord could make himself known to his people. Keep this in mind as you read Exodus 19.

Understanding the Scriptures

Exodus 19

Peculiar (v. 5)—"'valued treasure,' 'made' or 'selected by God'" (Russell M. Nelson in Conference Report, Apr. 1995, 44; or *Ensign,* May 1995, 34).

Sanctify, sanctified (vv. 10, 14, 22–23)—Make holy, pure, and clean

Against (vv. 11, 15)—In preparation for

Bounds (vv. 12, 23)—Limits

Take heed to yourselves (v. 12)—Be careful

Border (v. 12)—Boundary

Descended (v. 18)—Came down

Ascended (v. 18)—Went up

Charge, chargedst (vv. 21, 23)—Command

Lest (vv. 21–22, 24)—Unless

Gaze (v. 21)—See

Break forth upon them (vv. 22, 24)—Appear to them

Exodus 19—The Exodus As a Symbol of Our Journey Back to the Presence of God

The following diagram shows an outline of the journey of the children of Israel as a group and how their journey is a type of the one we make as we seek to return to the presence of God.

The world	Baptism	The Holy Ghost	Journey through the world toward God	The temple	Celestial kingdom
The land of Egypt	The Red Sea	The cloud and pillar of fire	The wilderness	Mount Sinai	The land of promise

Bounds set to keep the people from the presence of God until they are worthy

Studying the Scriptures

Ⓐ Moses Goes up and down Mount Sinai

Exodus 19 contains the account of three times Moses went up and came down Mount Sinai. Moses ascended Sinai to speak with the Lord, and then traveled down the mountain to deliver the words of the Lord to the people. At the same time, Moses tried to prepare the people to be worthy enough to also ascend the mountain and commune with the Lord. The following diagram may help you organize the chapter by outlining Moses' trips up and down Sinai.

Summarize what happened on each of the occasions noted above. Read in Exodus 20–23; 24:1–8 what happened on the next occasion Moses went up Mount Sinai.

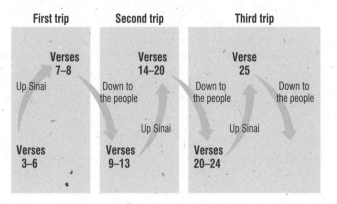

First trip	Second trip	Third trip
Verses 7–8 Up Sinai	**Verses 14–20** Down to the people	**Verse 25** Down to the people	Down to the people
Verses 3–6	Up Sinai **Verses 9–13**	Up Sinai **Verses 20–24**

B Prepare for the Temple

Elder J. Ballard Washburn, of the Seventy, said, "We cannot go to His holy house unworthily without bringing upon ourselves the judgments of God. For God will not be mocked" (in Conference Report, Apr. 1995, 12–13; or *Ensign*, May 1995, 11–12).

1. List the truths Moses or the Lord said in Exodus 19 that emphasize the importance of what Elder Washburn taught.

2. Why is it important to be worthy before entering the temple? (see D&C 97:15–17 for important help).

Exodus 20

The Ten Commandments

On one of the three trips Moses made up Mount Sinai (see Exodus 19), God taught him the commandments we read about in Exodus 20. These teachings are widely known as the Ten Commandments. The Lord said later that the Ten Commandments are the "words of the covenant," or the requirements to receive the covenant (see Exodus 34:28). Consequently, the Ten Commandments were given to the Israelites for their acceptance before they were allowed to go up Mount Sinai. The Ten Commandments at that time were much like the standards required today to obtain a temple recommend.

Later, the Ten Commandments were written on stone tables, placed in the ark of the covenant (which you will read about later), and called "the testimony." Having a testimony of the principles of the Ten Commandments is basic to understand the gospel principles which the Savior and the Prophet Joseph Smith later taught (see Deuteronomy 10:1–5).

Elder Bernard P. Brockbank, Assistant to the Quorum of the Twelve Apostles, said, "The God-given Ten Commandments are still a basic part of God's way of life and a basic part of the gospel of the kingdom. The way we live and respect the Lord and his commandments in the home has a relationship to the degree of

Glory that we will merit in the hereafter. If all mankind would live the Ten Commandments, we would have self-respect, peace, love, and happiness on this earth" (in Conference Report, Oct. 1971, 41; or Ensign, Dec. 1971, 63).

Understanding the Scriptures

Exodus 20

Graven (v. 4)—Carved, chiseled, created

Image (v. 4)—Object of worship

Likeness (v. 4)—Picture, statue, or other representation

Iniquity (v. 5)— sin

Vain (v. 7)—For no worthy purpose

Bear (v. 16)—Speak or give

Hewn (v. 25)—Cut and fitted

Studying the Scriptures

A Scripture Mastery—Exodus 20:3–17

The fourth and fifth commandments (see Exodus 20:8–12) tell us what we *should* do. The other commandments tell us what *not* to do. Rewrite these "thou shalt not" commandments as "thou shalt" statements so you can see ways to keep each commandment.

B What Do You Think?

Which of the Ten Commandments do you think the world needs to pay more attention to today? Why?

C How Did They Respond?

1. What did the children of Israel do after hearing and seeing the things in Exodus 19–20? (see also Exodus 20:18–21).

2. Why do you think some people choose to not get any closer to God or to draw away from him?

Exodus 21–23

An Eye for an Eye, and a Tooth for a Tooth

Exodus 21–23 contains specific, case-by-case applications of God's laws. For example, "thou shalt not kill" is one of the Ten Commandments, but what if you hurt someone badly? Or what if you kill an animal versus a human? Exodus 21–23 discusses many of these kinds of questions and also describes the punishment that may come from breaking a commandment. The punishments given are the maximum penalty for a violation and are not necessarily automatic. This Old Testament principle was replaced by the gospel of Jesus Christ (see Matthew 5:38–48).

Exodus 24

Seventy Elders See God

Moses explained God's laws to the children of Israel in Exodus 20–23. For them to progress any further, they first needed to commit themselves to live those laws. Exodus 24 tells of the commitment the Israelites made that prepared them to receive the higher laws associated with the temple. Consequently, the Lord again called Moses up to Sinai for a fourth time to receive further information about ordinances that would allow the people to enter his presence.

Understanding the Scriptures

Exodus 24

One voice (v. 3)—With unity of feeling

Behold (v. 8)—This is

Nobles (v. 11)—Leaders

He laid not his hand (v. 11)—God's power did not

hurt the Israelites. Normally, seeing God would be more than they could endure.

Minister (v. 13)—Helper

Studying the Scriptures

A How Important Are Covenants?

1. After Moses gave the people God's laws, what did they covenant to do? (see Exodus 24:3–8).

2. According to Exodus 24:9–11 what happened to seventy elders in Israel because they made this covenant?

3. What has the Lord promised will occur as you make and keep covenants with him? (see Mosiah 18:8–10; D&C 20:77, 79). How do these promises relate to what happened to Moses and the seventy elders?

Exodus 25–27, 30

The Tabernacle

Exodus 25–27, 30 contain the Lord's instructions to Moses about building the tabernacle. The tabernacle was a sacred place

to the children of Israel just as the temple is a sacred place to us today. This tabernacle was designed to be portable because the children of Israel moved often while in the wilderness. The instructions for building the tabernacle are very detailed, helping us understand that everything about a temple is important to the Lord as he teaches and inspires his people. A temple's structure and furnishings teach us important principles that make us want to feel closer to him and keep his commandments. The following tabernacle diagrams label each item or element in the tabernacle. Also included are some suggestions of what these elements help teach us about God and his plan for his children.

Information from Exodus 25–27, 30 about the tabernacle replaces the usual sections entitled "Understanding the Scriptures" and "Studying the Scriptures." Each item below includes a studying-the-scriptures type activity for you to complete in your notebook that should help you better understand how the tabernacle and its furnishings taught principles of the gospel.

The Tabernacle

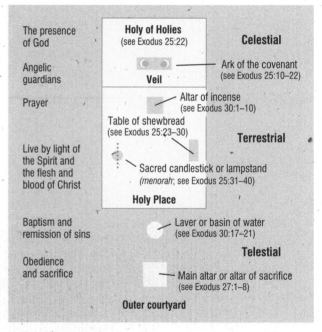

The presence of God	**Holy of Holies** (see Exodus 25:22)	**Celestial**
Angelic guardians	**Veil**	Ark of the covenant (see Exodus 25:10–22)
Prayer	Altar of incense (see Exodus 30:1–10)	
	Table of shewbread (see Exodus 25:23–30)	**Terrestrial**
Live by light of the Spirit and the flesh and blood of Christ	Sacred candlestick or lampstand (*menorah*; see Exodus 25:31–40)	
	Holy Place	
Baptism and remission of sins	Laver or basin of water (see Exodus 30:17–21)	
		Telestial
Obedience and sacrifice	Main altar or altar of sacrifice (see Exodus 27:1–8)	
	Outer courtyard	

Ark of the covenant

Only authorized people were allowed to touch the ark of the covenant (see Exodus 25:10–22), so there were poles attached to it so it could be carried. Inside the ark were the stone tables containing the law written by the Lord. Later, a pot of manna and Aaron's budding rod were also placed inside it. The lid represents the presence of God and is called the mercy seat. Once a year the priest performed an ordinance at the mercy seat to make atonement for the people (see the information for Leviticus 16 on p. 60). What did the Lord say to Moses in Exodus 25:22 about the mercy seat?

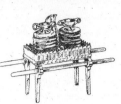

Table of shewbread

The table of shewbread (see Exodus 25:23–30) held twelve large loaves of bread. The bread was changed each Sabbath and eaten by the priests. Although Exodus does not say so, Jewish tradition holds that wine was also placed on the table. What could the bread and wine represent?

Sacred candlestick or lampstand

The candlestick or lampstand (see Exodus 25:31–40) is a famous symbol of the Jewish faith and is frequently called by its Hebrew name *menorah*. The seven candle cups at the top were filled with pure olive oil, into which a wick was placed and lit. The number seven represents wholeness or perfection among the Hebrews. The parable of the ten virgins that Jesus told gives a clue about what oil in a lamp represents (see Matthew 25:1–13; D&C 45:56–59). Write what you think the oil symbolized.

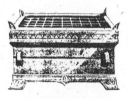

Main altar or altar of sacrifice

All burnt offerings were performed on the altar of sacrifice (see Exodus 27:1–8). Sacrifice was the first thing an individual did when entering the tabernacle if he desired to progress any further. What does the Lord ask of his people today by way of sacrifice? (see 3 Nephi 9:19–20). Which of the first principles and ordinances of the gospel did this altar represent? (see Articles of Faith 1:4). Elder Neal A. Maxwell said, "The real act of personal sacrifice is not now nor ever has been placing an animal on the altar. Instead, it is a willingness to put the animal that is in us upon the altar—then willingly watching it be consumed! Such is the 'sacrifice unto [the Lord of] a broken heart and a contrite spirit.' (3 Nephi 9:20.)" (*Meek and Lowly* [1987], 94).

Altar of incense

Hot coals were placed on the altar of incense (see Exodus 30:1–10) each morning and evening when the high priest burned incense. Read Psalm 141:2; Revelation 5:8; 8:3–4 and explain what you think this altar represented.

Laver or water basin

The priests used the laver for washing (see Exodus 30:18–21) in preparation for entering the holy places of the tabernacle. In Moses' time the laver was simply a large basin; however, when Solomon built a permanent temple he placed the laver on the backs of twelve oxen. What do you think the Lord was trying to teach his people by putting the laver in front of the entrance to the holier places of the tabernacle?

Exodus 28–29

The Priests in the Temple

Exodus 28–29 contains the Lord's revelations to Moses concerning the priests who worked in the tabernacle performing ordinances for the people. These revelations include instructions on how to set apart and consecrate the priests, what they were to wear, and what some of their duties were. As with the tabernacle, considering the symbolism of what was done can teach us more about the gospel and what the Lord expects of us.

Understanding the Scriptures

Exodus 28

Minister unto (v. 1)—Serve

Bear (vv. 29–30)—Carry

For a memorial (v. 29)—To remember

Exodus 29

Perpetual statute (v. 9)—Everlasting ordinance

Savour (vv. 18, 41)—Smell

Mingled (v. 40)—Mixed

Hin (v. 40)—About six liters

Sanctified, sanctify (vv. 43–44)—Make holy

Ephod
(see Exodus 28:6–12)

Breastplate
(see Exodus 28:15–30)

Robe
(see Exodus 28:31–35)

Mitre
(see Exodus 28:36–38)

Studying the Scriptures ✏️➤

Do two of the following activities (A–C) as you study Exodus 28–29.

Ⓐ How Were They Called?

Read Exodus 28:1; Hebrews 5:1, 4; Articles of Faith 1:5. Explain how Aaron and his sons were called to be priests and how the way they were called is a pattern for all who receive a priesthood office in the Church.

Ⓑ Outline a Sacred Ceremony

Exodus 29:1–21 describes how a priest was consecrated, or set apart, to work in the tabernacle. Outline the ceremony by describing what happened according to the following verses:

- First event (see v. 4)
- Second event (see vv. 5–6)
- Third event (see v. 7)
- Fourth event (see vv. 10–14)
- Fifth event (see vv. 15–18)
- Sixth event (see vv. 19–21)

Ⓒ What Is the Symbolism?

Aaron and his sons had their ears, hands, and feet consecrated with blood. We know that blood symbolized the Atonement of Christ, which has the power to make us holy. What do ears, hands, and feet symbolize, and what does that symbolism teach us about preparing to attend to temple duties?

Exodus 31

Men Called to Work on the Tabernacle

Exodus 31 tells how the Lord called skilled men to help build the tabernacle and its furnishings. Moving the kingdom of God forward requires many different kinds of talents. Therefore, skill in building, the arts, business, and so on can all help build the Lord's kingdom when we dedicate those talents to him. Exodus 31 also contains the Lord's reminder to Israel to refrain from work on the Sabbath—even work on his tabernacle.

Exodus 32

The Golden Calf

Exodus 24 tells how Moses went up Mount Sinai and communed with the Lord for forty days. Moses consequently received the revelations found in Exodus 25–31. Before Moses went up the mountain, the children of Israel covenanted with God to keep the commandments revealed up to that time through Moses, including the Ten Commandments. As was mentioned earlier, the Israelites' committing to live the Ten Commandments was important so they could receive the greater blessing Moses asked the Lord for on Mount Sinai. If the Israelites broke the Ten Commandments, they would lose additional blessings the Lord desired to give them. Unfortunately, that is exactly what happened.

Understanding the Scriptures 🗝️

Exodus 32

Fashioned (v. 4)—Formed
Graving (v. 4)—Engraving
Molten (vv. 4, 8)—Made of melted metal
Stiffnecked (v. 9)—Proud
Wrath (vv. 10, 12)—Anger
Consume (vv. 10, 12)—Destroy

Besought (v. 11)—Plead with, to ask with great feeling
Mischief (vv. 12, 22)—An evil or bad purpose
Mastery (v. 18)—Victory
Strawed (v. 20)—Spread
Blot (vv. 32–33)—Remove

Note: Remember to look for changes in the Joseph Smith Translation of this and other chapters.

Exodus 32:26—"Who Is on the Lord's Side?"

Elder George Albert Smith, then a member of the Quorum of the Twelve Apostles, stressed the importance of staying on the Lord's side: "There is a division line well defined that separates the Lord's territory from Lucifer's. If we live on the Lord's side of the line Lucifer cannot come there to influence us, but if we cross the line into his territory we are in his power. By keeping the commandments of the Lord we are safe on His side of the line, but if we disobey His teachings we voluntarily cross into the zone of temptation and invite the destruction that is ever present there. Knowing this, how anxious we should always be to live on the Lord's side of the line" ("Our M. I. A.," *Improvement Era*, May 1935, 278).

Studying the Scriptures ✏️➤

Ⓐ Did They Have a Short Memory?

Read Exodus 20:3–6; 24:3; 32:1–6, 8 and answer the following questions:

1. Which of the Ten Commandments did the children of Israel break in Exodus 32?
2. Why do you think they did what they did?

Ⓑ Apply the Principle

1. In what ways are people today tempted to become impatient with God's way of doing things and break his commandments?
2. How could this lack of patience be considered worshiping a false god?

C Learn about Sin and Repentance

In Exodus 32:19–29 Moses swiftly called the people to repentance. From how Moses acted and what happened, what lessons can we learn about the effects of sin and the requirements of repentance?

Exodus 33

Moses Sees the Lord Again

Because the children of Israel broke their covenant with the Lord by worshiping the golden calf, they made themselves unworthy to have the Lord's presence with them. The Lord did not abandon his people, however. Even though the children of Israel could not be in his presence, in Exodus 32:34 the Lord promised that his angel would go with them to the promised land. Exodus 33 contains stories that show the difference between the Israelites' relationship with the Lord and Moses' relationship with the Lord. This difference should lead us to ask ourselves if we desire and will seek the Lord's full blessings or if we will just let the prophets and other Church leaders have significant spiritual experiences. If we desire the Lord's full blessings, what must we do?

Understanding the Scriptures 🔑

Exodus 33

Depart, and go up hence (v. 1)—Leave the place you are in

Tidings (v. 4)—News

Ornaments (vv. 4, 6)—Decorative clothing and jewelry

Tabernacle (vv. 7, 10)—A tent. (This is not the tabernacle described in Exodus 33:25–27, 30.)

Without (v. 7)—Outside

Carry (v. 15)—Lead

Gracious (v. 19)—Kind and compassionate

Clift (v. 22)—Split

Studying the Scriptures ✏️

A What Did They Lose?

1. Find the word the Lord used in both verses 3 and 5 of Exodus 33 to describe the children of Israel. You will probably want to highlight it in your scriptures. What does the word symbolize?

2. According to verses 7–11, what blessings did the children of Israel lose because of the attitude described above?

3. Write a brief example of how someone today could lose great blessings because of this same attitude.

B Be a Missionary Using a Scripture Mastery Verse

Your investigators say they do not believe the Joseph Smith story of the First Vision because they say the Bible says man cannot see God. They may read to you Exodus 33:20. Explain how you would answer them using Exodus 33:11; JST, Exodus 33:20; and two other Bible scriptures showing that man can in fact see God. You may need to use the study helps in your scriptures. Write the references you find in your scriptures next to Exodus 33:11.

Exodus 34

The Lesser Law

At Mount Sinai Moses received laws, commandments, ordinances, and covenants from the Lord that were written on stone tablets. When Moses came down from Sinai and saw the children of Israel worshiping the golden calf, he threw the tablets on the ground and broke them (see Exodus 32:15–19). The Israelites had not proved worthy to receive all that was written on them.

We may also lose great blessings if we are disobedient. The Lord was patient with the children of Israel, however, and gave them opportunities to repent and return to him. Because the Lord desires to help us, he frequently gives additional or new, more strict commandments that allow us the opportunity to repent and eventually receive the full blessings he desires to give us. Exodus 34 records additional commandments the Lord gave to the disobedient children of Israel.

Understanding the Scriptures 🔑

Exodus 34

Hew, hewed (vv. 1, 4)—Cut

By no means (v. 7)—In no way

Clear (v. 7)—Declare innocent

Pardon (v. 9)—Forgive

Terrible (v. 10)—Awe-inspiring

Take heed to thyself (v. 12)—Be careful

Snare (v. 12)—Trap

Groves (v. 13)—Places where false gods are worshiped

Jealous (v. 14)—Having deep

feelings and expecting faithfulness

Whoring (vv. 15–16)—Unfaithful to God

Molten (v. 17)—Made of melted metal

Openeth the matrix (v. 19)—Is firstborn

Empty (v. 20)—Without paying a redemption price

Thrice (vv. 23–24)—Three times

Tenor (v. 27)—Pattern

Studying the Scriptures ✏️

A Get Help from the Joseph Smith Translation

Read the Joseph Smith Translation for Exodus 34:1–2 and write about how the second set of tablets was different from the first.

Why Were They Different?

Read Mosiah 13:29–30; Doctrine and Covenants 84:19–27 and write about why the second set of tablets was different from the first.

Exodus 35–40

The Tabernacle Is Built and Dedicated

Exodus 35–40 tells how the children of Israel carried out the Lord's commands given in Exodus 25–30 concerning the tabernacle. Much of what is written in Exodus 35–40 is worded like Exodus 25–30 to show that the Israelites tried to keep the Lord's commands exactly.

Studying the Scriptures

A — What Happened at the Dedication of the Tabernacle?

Read Exodus 40:24–38 and write about what happened when the tabernacle was finished.

The Book of Leviticus

Leviticus is the third of the five books of Moses (see "The Books of Genesis, Moses, and Abraham" on p. 9). We assume the instructions in Leviticus were revealed to Moses either while he was on Mount Sinai or sometime shortly after the events described in Exodus because part of the instructions deal with sacrifices to be offered in the tabernacle. *Leviticus* means "having to do with the Levites." The Lord chose the tribe of Levi to take care of the tabernacle, work in it, and help the rest of the house of Israel perform ordinances in that sacred place. Much of Leviticus gives instructions concerning the ordinances to be performed in the tabernacle, the qualifications of the priesthood holders who would perform those ordinances, and the duties of the people with regard to the ordinances.

A "Handbook" for the Levites

Because Leviticus is a "handbook" for the Levites serving in the tabernacle, it contains many detailed instructions concerning different kinds of sacrifices and religious practices that may seem strange or unfamiliar to the modern reader. If you look past these unfamiliar practices, you can learn important truths about sin, repentance, forgiveness, holiness, and the Atonement of Jesus Christ.

Getting Ready to Study Leviticus

OVERVIEW OF LEVITICUS		
	Chapters	**Description**
Part 1	Leviticus 1–16	Becoming justified, which means to be forgiven of sin and worthy before God
	Leviticus 1–7	Sacrifices that atone for sin or express a willingness to be committed to God
	Leviticus 8–10	Laws for priesthood holders who assist in the offerings
	Leviticus 11–15	Laws of cleanliness for the people
	Leviticus 16	Explanation of the Day of Atonement when the whole house of Israel could be cleansed

Part 2	Leviticus 17-27	Becoming sanctified, which is to become more holy and godly
	Leviticus 17	Personal holiness
	Leviticus 18	Holiness in family relations
	Leviticus 19–20	Holiness in social relations and as a congregation
	Leviticus 21–22	Holiness of the priesthood
	Leviticus 23–25	Celebrations and sacred events that encourage holiness
Part 3	Leviticus 26	Blessings that come from obeying the laws of God
Part 4	Leviticus 27	Consecrating possessions to the Lord

Leviticus 1

The Burnt Offering

The Apostle Paul taught that the law of Moses was a "schoolmaster to bring us unto Christ" (Galatians 3:24). In other words, the purpose of the law of Moses was to help the Israelites focus their attention on principles that would point them to Jesus Christ (see Jacob 4:4–5; Jarom 1:11; Alma 34:13–14). The law of Moses was very strict and required many specific performances designed to help the children of Israel continually remember God and their duty toward him. For example, killing an animal as a sacrifice for sin reminded an individual that the consequences of sin are "deadly." On the other hand, the innocent animal who died in the place of the person who sinned also served as a symbol of what would occur when the sinless Savior would come to earth and have his blood shed for us, saving us from sin.

Leviticus 1 gives instructions for a burnt offering. The priests made this offering twice a day. Individuals could also make a burnt offering to show their devotion and commitment to God. Many of the instructions concerning the burnt offering are the same as for other offerings explained in Leviticus. The biggest difference between the burnt offering and other offerings is that to make a burnt offering the entire animal was burned on the altar, symbolizing total commitment or surrender to God.

As you read, think about different ways the burnt offering can teach us about the Atonement of Jesus Christ and how it reminded the Israelites of their duty to God.

Understanding the Scriptures 🔑

Leviticus 1

Blemish (vv. 3, 10)—Mark or imperfection of any kind

Flay (v. 6)—Skin

Wrung (v. 15)—Drained

Crop (v. 16)—Stomach

Cleave it (v. 17)—Cut it open

Divide it asunder (v. 17)—Cut it completely in half

Studying the Scriptures ✏️

Ⓐ Find the Symbols of Repentance

Highlight the specific requirements of the burnt offering found in Leviticus 1:1–9 that are listed in the following chart. Make the chart in your notebook and explain what each element of the burnt offering teaches us about repentance through the Atonement of Jesus Christ.

Requirement	What You Learn about Repentance or Jesus Christ's Atonement
You must make "your offering" (Leviticus 1:2), meaning you can't offer something that belongs to someone else.	
You must offer an animal that is a "male without blemish" (v. 3).	
You must make the offering of your "own voluntary will" (v. 3).	
You must first bring your offering to "the door of the tabernacle," which tabernacle represents the place where God dwells (v. 3).	
You must put your hand on the head of the sacrificial animal and then kill it yourself (see vv. 4–5).	

You must "flay," or skin, the offering (v. 6).	
The priests lay the "head," "fat," "inward" organs, and the "legs" on the altar (vv. 8–9).	
The sacrifice is completely burned by the fire (see v. 9).	

Leviticus 1:8–9 speaks of offering various parts of the animal's body. The head represents our thoughts. The legs represent our walk, or the direction we are going. The "inwards" represent our feelings, desires, and motivations. The fat represents our strength and health. What is symbolized by the events in verses 8–9? (see also D&C 59:5).

Leviticus 2–7

Other Offerings

Leviticus 2–7 describes in detail the different sacrifices the Israelites were to offer. Leviticus 2 describes the meat, or meal offering. Leviticus 3 describes the peace offering. Leviticus 4–5 describes the different kinds of sin and trespass offerings. Leviticus 6–7 contains additional instructions concerning all of the various offerings. The Bible Dictionary explains these sacrifices and their relationship to each other (s.v. "sacrifices").

Studying the Scriptures ✏️

Ⓐ The Law of Sacrifice

The sacrifices described in Leviticus are no longer required of Church members today. The principles taught by the sacrifices, however, are still true and must be a part of our lives if we want to be right with God.

1. Read 3 Nephi 9:19–20 and write what the Lord said we sacrifice instead of animals.

2. Give examples of how you think you can do what Jesus commanded in 3 Nephi 9:19–20.

Leviticus 8–9

The Consecration of Aaron and His Sons

Leviticus 8–9 records the actual setting apart of Aaron and his sons to serve in the priest's office in the tabernacle (see Exodus 28–29). The setting apart was followed by a dramatic display of the Lord's glory, showing that he approved of what was done.

Leviticus 10

Priesthood Holders Must Be Holy

Leviticus 10 is one of the few chapters in the book of Leviticus that tells a story instead of simply giving instructions. It contains a powerful message about faithfulness in the priesthood. As you read, consider this question: How does the Lord feel about the way we perform sacred ordinances?

Understanding the Scriptures

Leviticus 10

Took either of them his (v. 1)—Each took his own

Censer (v. 1)—Container for burning incense

Strange (v. 1)—Forbidden

Held his peace (v. 3)—Did not speak

Rend (v. 6)—Tear

Bewail (v. 6)—Feel sad about

Due (vv. 13–14)—Payment or wages

Wave breast (vv. 14–15)—An animal's breast held up

and waved as part of the peace offering ceremony

Heave shoulder (vv. 14–15)—An animal's shoulder held up and presented before the Lord as part of the peace offering ceremony

Bear (v. 17)—Carry

Iniquity (v. 17)—Sin

Befallen (v. 19)—Happened to

Content (v. 20)—Satisfied

Leviticus 10:12–20—Why Didn't Aaron Eat the Meat from the Offering?

Moses noticed that Aaron and his sons Eleazar and Ithamar did not eat the sin offering the way they were instructed. In response,

Aaron told Moses that he didn't feel right about eating the meat after what happened to his other sons because of their disobedience. This answer satisfied Moses. We should not participate in certain ordinances, like the sacrament, when we have not repented or when our priesthood leader has counseled us not to. If one desires to repent and improve, has not committed serious sins that have not yet been resolved with his bishop, and is not under priesthood restriction, the person is worthy to partake of the sacrament.

Studying the Scriptures

A Give Counsel on Properly Respecting the Priesthood

The Lord obviously does not strike dead all unrighteous, disrespectful priesthood holders today. In Leviticus 10, however, it was important that the Lord give this forceful lesson since Aaron's sons treated the priesthood lightly so soon after the dramatic display of God's glory at their setting apart (see Leviticus 9). To emphasize the importance of properly respecting the priesthood, use Leviticus 10:1–7; Doctrine and Covenants 121:36–38 to give counsel to a young man who might be considering playing a "practical joke" as part of his involvement with the sacrament.

B Why Not?

1. What did the Lord command Aaron and his living sons not to do? (see Leviticus 10:8–11).

2. What reason did the Lord give for this commandment?

Leviticus 11

A "Word of Wisdom" for the Israelites

On any given day, people may forget to pray or neglect to work or worship, but they seldom forget to eat. Since one purpose of the law of Moses was to provide continual daily reminders to the Israelites of their duty to God, the law included instructions concerning what the children of Israel could and could not eat. Leviticus 11 contains these instructions. The rules and instructions are commonly known as "kosher laws." Kosher comes from a Hebrew word that means "religiously clean." Like the Word of Wisdom revealed in our day, the kosher laws promoted good health, but their major purpose was to teach obedience. This law of health, like the Word of Wisdom today, helped set God's people apart from the world in habits and practices, which was another purpose of the law of Moses, and helped them become clean and holy.

Understanding the Scriptures

Leviticus 11

Parteth/divideth the hoof (vv. 3–7, 26)—Has a split hoof

Clovenfooted (vv. 3, 7, 26)—Foot divided into two parts

Coney (v. 5)—A hare-like animal like the rock badger

Hare (v. 6)—Rabbit

Swine (v. 7)—Pig

Carcase (vv. 8, 11, 24–28)—Dead body

Ossifrage, and the osprey (v. 13)—The Hebrew words

for these animals seem to mean they are some kind of birds of prey

Kite (v. 14)—Perhaps some kind of bird of prey

Cuckow (v. 16)—Cuckoo bird

Cormorant (v. 17)—Perhaps some kind of bird of prey

Beareth (vv. 25, 28, 40)—Carries

Ought (v. 25)—Any

Studying the Scriptures

Do two of the following activities (A–C) as you study Leviticus 11.

A) Is It Kosher?

Kosher means proper or sanctified by Jewish law. List the following animals in your notebook: snail, sheep, mouse, locust, stork, pig, cow, camel, eagle, shark. For each animal, write whether they were "kosher" or "not kosher" for Israelites to eat, and then explain why. For each reason, give a verse from Leviticus 11 that supports your answer.

B) Review the Word of Wisdom

Read Doctrine and Covenants 89:5–17 and list what the Lord commanded Church members in our day to eat or not eat.

Compare these instructions to Leviticus 11 where the Lord taught the children of Israel what they could and could not eat.

C) Why Does It Matter?

Why do you think the Lord has commanded his people not to eat certain things? (If you need help, see Leviticus 11:43–47; 1 Corinthians 6:19–20; D&C 89:1–4, 18–21).

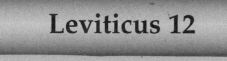

Leviticus 12

Clean and Unclean

In Leviticus chapters 12–15 the Lord gave instruction on what was "clean" and "unclean" under the law of Moses regarding bodily functions and diseases. Leviticus 12 explains the laws that applied to women after they gave birth. For a period of time they were considered "unclean," but the Lord also outlined specific ordinances that could make them ceremonially "clean" again after a certain period of time. Mary, the mother of Jesus, followed these ordinances after Jesus was born (see Luke 2:21–24, 39).

Some people are puzzled by the idea that natural bodily functions make someone unclean. We must understand, however, that under the law of Moses, "unclean" did not mean dirty or disgusting but simply not acceptable to participate in sacred ordinances. Remember also that the law of Moses was designed to provide outward physical reminders found in daily life to remind the Israelites of deeper spiritual truths.

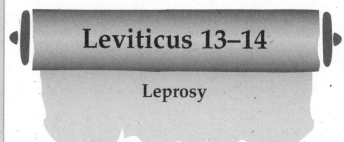

Leviticus 13–14

Leprosy

Leviticus 13–14 addresses the disease of leprosy. From the descriptions in these chapters, it appears that leprosy included several different infectious skin diseases. For more information about leprosy, see "leper" and "leprosy" in the Bible Dictionary.

Understanding the Scriptures

Leviticus 14

Tarry abroad out (v. 8)—Stay outside

Log (vv. 10, 12, 15, 21)—About one-half of a liter

Studying the Scriptures

A) Compare the Cleansing of Leprosy to the Cleansing of Our Sins

Because leprosy was so visible and involved the decay or corruption of the body, it served as an excellent symbol of sinfulness. Sin corrupts someone spiritually the way leprosy corrupts someone physically. Leviticus 14 describes what a man must do to be ceremonially, or religiously, clean after being healed of leprosy. We can see parallels between the process of being cleansed of leprosy and how we overcome the effects of sin.

Before you study Leviticus 14, you should know that when an individual acquired leprosy, he was required to live outside the camp. The same is true of sin. When we sin, we cut ourselves off from full communion with the Lord and his Church. For example, we may not be permitted to take the sacrament or receive a temple recommend.

The steps in becoming ceremonially clean of leprosy are found in the following groups of verses. Read each group of verses from Leviticus 14, summarize each step, and explain how the steps teach the process of sin and repentance. With each group of verses you will find a question to help you focus your thinking.

1. Verses 2–3. If leprosy symbolizes sin, who might the priest represent?

2. Verses 4–8. You should know that (a) cedar wood is known as something that helps preserve other things from decay and corruption; (b) the color scarlet is red, reminding us of blood, which is the symbol of life and the Atonement; (c) hyssop was used in the Old Testament as a purifying plant; and (d) blood and water are symbols of birth (see

Moses 6:59). Considering this information, what do you think is symbolized in these verses?

3. Verse 9. Newborns usually have little or no hair, except for on their heads. What might the message of this verse be? (see 3 Nephi 11:37).

4. Verses 10–14. Recall similar symbolism in Exodus 28–29. How might the symbolism apply here?

5. Verses 15–18. The olive tree is an emblem of peace and purity, and the olive oil became a symbol of the Holy Ghost and doing righteous deeds and acts of service (see D&C 45:56–57). How is this part of the process of becoming clean from sin? (see 2 Nephi 31:17).

6. Verses 19–20. Ultimately, what makes repentance possible?

Leviticus 15–16

The Day of Atonement

The first fifteen chapters of Leviticus all have something to do with how individuals became "right" with God through sacrifice or how they become ceremonially "clean" before him by obedience to his laws of cleanliness. Leviticus 15 contains further instructions about how human functions relate to being clean or unclean under the law of Moses. We must realize, however, that there is no real forgiveness of sins without sincere repentance and the Atonement of Christ. Leviticus 16 describes a sacred ceremony that the Lord commanded the Israelites to perform once a year at a specific time that symbolized how Jesus Christ would atone for the sins of all people. While the rites described in Leviticus 1–15 were individual in application, the Day of Atonement described in Leviticus 16 symbolized atonement for the sins of the whole Israelite nation and was a day when the entire house of Israel fasted and rested.

Understanding the Scriptures 🗝

Leviticus 16

Linen (v. 4)—White cloth

Breeches (v. 4)—Underclothing

Girdle (v. 4)—Sash

Cast lots (vv. 8–10)—To throw marked stones or a die for the purpose of randomly choosing something. When holy men cast lots, it was an expression of faith that God would oversee an event and make his will known. In Leviticus 16, one stone was marked for the Lord and another for the

scapegoat. When Aaron threw the stones, depending on how they landed, one goat was chosen to be sacrificed and the other was chosen to be the scapegoat.

The testimony (v. 13)—The ark of the covenant

Hallow (v. 19)—Make sacred

Reconciling (v. 20)—Atoning for

Stead (v. 32)—Place

Leviticus 16:10—The Scapegoat

Scapegoat was the name given to the goat that "escaped" into the wilderness, never to return, with the blood, or sins, of the people

on him. The scapegoat symbolized that through the Atonement all of Israel's sins could be forgiven, never to return.

Studying the Scriptures ✏

(A) A Sacred and Important Ceremony

Leviticus 16:3–28 contains instructions for the priest on the Day of Atonement. The following outline gives six general steps involved in the ceremony. Write answers to the questions about each step.

1. What is symbolized by what the Lord asked Aaron to do in verse 4? (see vv. 3–5). (*Hint:* Make sure you know what "linen" is.)

2. Why did Aaron need two goats? (see vv. 6–10).

3. Why do you think Aaron needed to make atonement for himself before making atonement for the people? (see vv. 11–14). How is this step different from when Christ performed his Atonement? (see Hebrews 9:6–14; Alma 34:8–12).

5. Why would Aaron need to cleanse the holy place of the temple? What does this requirement tell you about the importance of cleanliness in the sight of God and about the power of the Atonement? (see vv. 15–19).

6. How do *both* goats (the one used for the offering and the one used as scapegoat) represent Christ and his Atonement? (see vv. 20–22).

7. What do Aaron's responsibilities and the responsibilities of the man who led the scapegoat into the wilderness symbolize? (see vv. 20–22; see also D&C 36:5–6).

Leviticus 17–18

Avoid Idolatrous Practices

Leviticus 17–18 records the Lord's instructions to the Israelites about practices that would clearly separate them from the false religions of their time. Leviticus 17 contains instructions on what to do when the Israelites killed an animal. Even when an animal was not going to be offered as a sacrifice, the Israelites had to present it before the Lord at the tabernacle. This practice helped prevent any sacrifice to false gods and helped the Israelites to remember that all they had came from the Lord. The Lord also commanded the Israelites in Leviticus 17 not to eat blood. Blood is a common symbol for life, and some false religions of the day included the drinking of blood as part of their religious rituals. By this practice the believers sought to extend their own lives. The Lord gave Israel various sacrifices symbolizing the great sacrifice of Jesus Christ, in which his blood would be shed to give eternal life to all who would believe in him and obey his commandments (see Leviticus 17:11).

Leviticus 18 contains the Lord's warning to the Israelites that immoral sexual behavior could cause the destruction of nations and that the Israelites would be destroyed if they participated in these practices.

Leviticus 19–20

"Be Holy for I Am Holy"

Leviticus 19–20 records the Lord's emphasis on being holy. The word for holy in Hebrew is "qadash," which means to be sanctified, consecrated, and dedicated or to be separated from the world and worldliness. Not only did the Lord command the Israelites to be holy, but in these two chapters he gave specific examples of things they could do in their daily lives to obey this commandment. Each of these specific practices helped remind the Israelites to separate themselves from the world and its ungodly practices. Jesus later explained the basic principle behind holiness when he taught his Apostles that he would not take them out of the world but would keep them from evil (see John 17:14–16).

As you read, determine the principle behind each commandment the Lord gave. In what ways has he asked us to live these principles today as we strive to be "not of the world"?

Understanding the Scriptures

Leviticus 19

Fear (v. 3)—Love and respect

Ought (v. 6)—Anything

Bear (v. 8)—Have responsibility for

Profaned (vv. 8, 12)—To desecrate the sacred

Gleanings (v. 9)—What is left after the field is harvested the first time

Defraud (v. 13)—Cheat

Avenge (v. 18)—Seek revenge

Gender (v. 19)—Mate

Diverse (v. 19)—Different

Sow (v. 19)—Plant

Mingled (v. 19)—Mixed (two different kinds)

Betrothed (v. 20)—Engaged

Redeemed (v. 20)—Paid for and made free

Scourged (v. 20)—Whipped

Uncircumcised (v. 23)—Unholy

Enchantment, observe times (v. 26)—Different kinds of fortune telling

Round the corners of your heads (v. 27)—Refers to a kind of haircut used by those involved in false religions

Them that have familiar spirits (v. 31)—Those who claim to communicate with the spirits of the dead

Wizards (v. 31)—Men who call up the spirits of the dead

Hoary (v. 32)—White

Sojourn (v. 33)—Stay

Vex (v. 33)—Mistreat and make angry

Meteyard (v. 35)—Measurement of length

Ephah, hin (v. 36)—Units of measure (see Bible Dictionary, s.v. "weights and measures")

Studying the Scriptures

A Find the Principle

If you consider the principle behind each commandment in Leviticus 19, nearly every commandment in the chapter applies

to Latter-day Saints today. Some are obvious (like the ones in vv. 11–12), but others seem strange to us. Choose two of the commandments in Leviticus 19 that seem to be specifically for the people of that day. Identify the principles behind the commandments and rewrite them to apply to our time. For example, in verse 19 the Lord said not to have a field with two different kinds of plants or a piece of clothing with two different kinds of fabric in it. Through these commandments, the Lord reminded Israel that they could not mix themselves with the world and remain holy. Today we might apply this principle to the idea of dating or marriage. We should date members of the Church and marry within the covenant.

B Scripture Mastery—Leviticus 19:18

Read Jesus' commandment in Matthew 22:35–39. What did the Lord say in Leviticus about the importance of this commandment?

Leviticus 21–22

Holiness of the Priesthood

Leviticus 21–22 contains commandments regarding the holiness of the priests, their families, and the sacrifices they offered. Today we also have special standards for those who serve on missions and in positions of authority, as well as standards for the way our ordinances are performed.

Leviticus 23–25

Holy Days and Events

Leviticus 23 tells how the Lord established five holy times when all Israel was to make a special effort to be holy and draw closer to him. These times were on the Sabbath (see vv. 1–3); at the Feast of the Unleavened Bread, or Passover (see vv. 4–14); at the Feast of Weeks, or Pentecost (see vv. 15–23); on the Day of Atonement (see vv. 26–32); and at the Feast of the Tabernacles (see vv. 33–44). For more information about these times, see "feasts" in the Bible Dictionary.

Leviticus 25 is related to chapter 23 in theme. In Leviticus 25 we read that the Lord commanded the Israelites to not only have a Sabbath every seventh day but to declare every seventh year a Sabbath year. In this Sabbath year they were not to grow crops but were to let the land rest. Furthermore, after seven times seven years (forty-nine years), the fiftieth year was to be a special Sabbath year, called the jubilee year. Not only were the Israelites not to plant or harvest during the jubilee, but they were to forgive all debts and free all slaves. Jubilee helped remind Israel that since God was merciful to them, they were to be merciful to others and the land.

Leviticus 24 contains some instructions for using the candlestick and the table of shewbread in the tabernacle. Chapter 24 then relates the story of an individual who blasphemed the name of God and was put to death since blasphemy was specifically prohibited in the commandments God gave the children of Israel. Part of the explanation for his punishment includes the famous phrase "eye for eye, tooth for tooth" (v. 20).

Leviticus 26–27

Blessings or Cursings

Having explained what he expected of the Israelites regarding religious cleanliness and holiness, the Lord concluded the book of Leviticus with an explanation of the consequences of obeying or disobeying these commandments (see Leviticus 26). The Lord also gave some concluding counsel about fully consecrating oneself to the Lord's service.

Understanding the Scriptures

Leviticus 26

Yield (vv. 4, 20)—Give

Threshing (v. 5)—Harvesting of grain

Reach (v. 5)—Last

Vintage (v. 5)—Grape harvest

Ye shall eat old store, and bring forth the old because of the new (v. 10)—You will still be eating from last year's storage when the new comes in, and you will have to move the old to make room for the new

Abhor (vv. 11, 15, 30, 43–44)—Dislike and neglect

Upright (v. 13)—Free

Consumption, and the burning ague (v. 16)—Diseases

Pursueth (vv. 17, 36–37)—Chases

Contrary (vv. 21, 23–24, 27, 41)—In opposition

Desolate (vv. 22, 33, 35, 43)—Empty

Pestilence (v. 25)—Plagues, diseases

Staff (v. 26)—Supply

Chastise (v. 28)—Discipline, correct

Waste (vv. 31, 33)—Devastate

Desolation (vv. 31–32)—Destruction

Heathen (vv. 33, 38, 45)—Those who don't know the true and living God

Faintness (v. 36)—Lack of courage

Studying the Scriptures

(A) Identify Choices and Consequences

Make a chart on your paper with two columns like the one below. Label one column "If" and one column "Then."

If	Then
Choices the Israelites Could Make	Consequences for Those Choices

1. As you read Leviticus 26, find the word *if*. You may want to mark or circle it in your scriptures. Write in the "If" column the things the Lord said Israel could do.

2. Find the word *then* somewhere close after the *if*s you found in the first step. Mark or circle it in your scriptures. List in the "Then" column what the Lord said would happen if Israel made certain choices. Continue through the chapter and find more "if-then" connections.

The Book of Numbers

Wanderings in the Wilderness

The book of Numbers was named when it was translated into Greek because it contains the account of two occasions when Moses "numbered," or counted, the people of Israel (see Numbers 1–4; 26). Some Hebrews call it *Vayedabber* (the first word in the book in Hebrew), which means "And He spoke." This name seems appropriate since Numbers contains over 150 accounts of God speaking to Moses. The book is more commonly called *Bemidbar* in Hebrew, which means "In the wilderness," describing the setting of nearly the entire book. Although the title "Numbers" sounds rather plain, the book actually contains some very significant and inspiring stories of Israel's forty-year wandering in the desert of Sinai.

Getting Ready to Read Numbers

Numbers contains several stories of the murmuring, complaining, and rebellion of even Moses' closest associates and family members. The Lord gave the children of Israel the opportunity to enter their land of promise about a year after they left Egypt, but they feared, murmured, and rebelled, so they lost the opportunity. As you read you should consider that we, like the children of Israel, have a prophet today. How do we receive his counsel? What are the consequences of following or not following the prophet's counsel?

The book of Numbers can be divided into three sections: (1) leaving Sinai (see chapters 1–10), (2) journeying in the wilderness (see chapters 11–21), and (3) preparing to enter the promised land (see chapters 22–36).

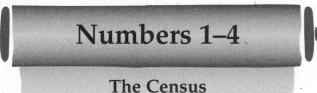

Numbers 1–4

The Census

Numbers 1–4 relates how Israel was numbered by tribe or family. Joseph's tribe received a double inheritance because of the birthright. This double inheritance was divided between Joseph's two sons Ephraim and Manasseh. As a result, these two sons were given status as separate tribes in Israel (see Genesis 48:5), making thirteen tribes in Israel. The tribe of Levi had a special calling to hold the priesthood and perform ordinances under the law of Moses. Because of this calling, they lived among all the other tribes and were not counted in the same way. Israel was generally considered to have twelve tribes—plus the Levites. Numbers 1–2 tells that the twelve tribes were counted and organized into groups for marching and camping. Numbers 3–4 records how the Levites were counted and given their assignments.

Numbers 3–4 also explains that all the firstborn among the children of Israel belong to the Lord because they were saved only through the Lord's mercy when they put blood on their doorpost at the time of the tenth plague in Egypt (see Exodus 12–13). The Lord explained, however, that instead of having the firstborn of every family serve him full-time, he would have Levites serve in their place. To show they recognized that the Levites served in their place, each firstborn son in the other twelve tribes was required to pay a certain amount of money each year to support the Levites' work in the tabernacle. This was called "redemption money" (see Numbers 3:44–51).

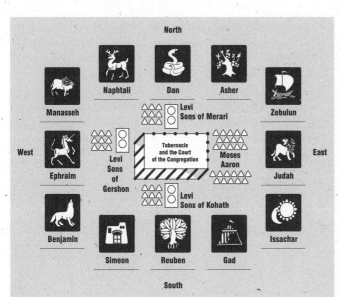

A It Could Be You

Read Numbers 3:12–13; 4:40–41 and the explanation of Numbers 1–4 above to learn what the Lord said about the firstborn in all Israel. Then read 2 Nephi 9:6–9, and explain how we could be compared to the firstborn in Israel. In other words, without the Atonement of Christ, what would happen to us? (see also 1 Corinthians 6:19–20; 1 Peter 1:18–19).

B What Should You Do?

Considering what you learned in activity A, how should knowing who we belong to affect our priorities? What does the Lord ask us to do that could be compared to "redemption money"?

Numbers 5–8

Additions to the Law of Moses

Numbers 5–6 contains additional instructions the Lord gave concerning disease (see 5:1–4), repentance (see 5:5–10), what a husband is to do when he thinks his wife has been unfaithful to him (see 5:11–31), those who make a special vow to serve the Lord (Nazarites; see 6:1–21), and a blessing priests should pronounce upon the people (see 6:22–27). In Numbers 7–8 we read about offerings that were made at the dedication of the tabernacle and the setting apart of the Levites to perform their special priesthood callings.

This study guide pays special attention to Numbers 6, which describes the laws of the Nazarite. In Hebrew nazir *means "one consecrated or devoted." Thus, when people committed themselves in a special way to the Lord, or if their parents committed them to the Lord, they were called "Nazarites."*

Understanding the Scriptures

Numbers 6

Separate, separation, separateth (vv. 2–8)—To dedicate to God, to be separate from the world

Vow (vv. 2, 5)—Promise

Come at (v. 6)—Touch

On this wise (v. 23)—In this way

Lift up his countenance (v. 26)—Turn his face

Numbers 6:22–27—A Blessing for Israel from Its Leaders

The Lord's anointed still frequently offer blessings to entire congregations or the Church as a whole. For example, consider the following blessings given by three different Presidents of the Church at general conferences:

"Now, in the authority of the sacred priesthood in me vested, I invoke my blessing upon the Latter-day Saints and upon good people everywhere.

"I bless you with increased discernment to judge between Christ and anti-Christ. I bless you with increased power to do good and to resist evil. I bless you with increased *understanding* of the Book of Mormon" (Ezra Taft Benson, in Conference Report, Apr. 1986, 100; or *Ensign*, May 1986, 78).

"And now, my beloved brothers and sisters, through the power and authority of the priesthood vested in me and by virtue of the calling which I now hold, I invoke my blessings upon you. I bless you in your efforts to live a more Christlike life. I bless you with an increased desire to be worthy of a temple recommend and to attend the temple as frequently as circumstances allow. I bless you to receive the peace of our Heavenly Father in your homes and to be guided in teaching your families to follow the Master" (Howard W. Hunter, in Conference Report, Oct. 1994, 119; or *Ensign*, Nov. 1994, 88).

"We leave a blessing upon you, even an apostolic blessing. We bless you that the Lord may smile with favor upon you, that there may be happiness and peace in your homes and in your lives, that an atmosphere of love and respect and appreciation may be felt among husbands and wives, children and parents. May you 'look to God and live' (Alma 37:47) with happiness, with security, with peace, with faith" (Gordon B. Hinckley, in Conference Report, Apr. 1995, 118; or *Ensign*, May 1995, 88).

Studying the Scriptures

Do two of the following activities (A–D) as you study Numbers 6.

A Write an Advertisement

Write an imaginary advertisement to recruit men to become Nazarites. Your ad should include at least three things the Lord expected of a Nazarite (pay special attention to Numbers 6:3–7).

B Who Were Some Famous Nazarites?

Read the following scriptures and name three people who were Nazarites: Judges 13:5, 24; 1 Samuel 1:11, 19–20, 28; Luke 1:13–15.

C Apply It to Today

What are we asked to do today to dedicate ourselves to God that makes us different from many other people in the world?

D Think of a Blessing from Your Leaders

Choose one of the blessings from the "Understanding the Scriptures" section above that you would like to receive, and explain why. What must you do to receive that blessing?

Numbers 9

The First Passover in the Wilderness

Numbers 9 marks the beginning of the second year of the Israelites' journey from Egypt to the promised land. Chapter 9

tells what the children of Israel should do to stay committed to the Lord and how they could know he was with them. How do we show the Lord today that we are committed to him, and how does he let us know he is with us?

Understanding the Scriptures

Numbers 9

His appointed season (vv. 2–3, 7, 13)—The Lord's chosen time

Even (vv. 3, 11, 15)—Sundown

Forbeareth (v. 13)—Decides against

Bear (v. 13)—Be responsible for

Sojourn (v. 14)—Live

One ordinance (v. 14)—The same rules and practices

Reared up (v. 15)—Set up

Abode (vv. 17–18, 21)—Stood still

Tarried (vv. 19, 22)—Stayed

Charge (vv. 19, 23)—Commandments

Numbers 9:6–14—Who Should Participate in the Passover?

It is interesting to note that in Numbers 9 some men who had come in contact with a dead body, perhaps by simply being the ones who may have buried a dead relative, were not allowed to participate in the Passover. According to the law of Moses, they were "unclean." The Lord revealed to Moses, however, that the Passover was so important that even those who were unclean because they touched a dead body should participate. Furthermore, the Lord said that it was a very serious sin to be fully clean and qualified and to refuse to participate in the Passover meal.

Since the Savior instituted the sacrament to replace the Passover, we might consider some personal applications. For example, we should take every available opportunity to worthily participate in the ordinance of the sacrament. To have the opportunity and then refuse to attend our sacrament meetings is a sin. Partaking of the sacrament is so important that the Lord wants us to participate even though we may have some personal blemishes in our life. Our priesthood leaders can counsel us about when we should or should not partake of the sacrament, which is the principle behind what happened in chapter 9.

Studying the Scriptures

A Always Remember

The first half of Numbers 9 tells about the first anniversary of the Passover in Egypt. Consider the following key words and phrases and describe how they relate to the Passover (you may want to look back to your study of Exodus 12):

1. Fourteenth day of the first month

2. Unleavened bread and bitter herbs

3. No broken bones

B How Did the Lord Lead Them?

1. Describe how Numbers 9:15–23 says the Lord led the children of Israel.

2. What do you think the children of Israel learned by being led through the wilderness in this way?

3. How does the Lord lead his people today?

Numbers 10

Leaving Sinai

Numbers 10 tells of the camp of Israel's first movement away from Mount Sinai after a lengthy stay there. When the Israelites left, they met Moses' brother-in-law and invited him to join them—just as we should invite others to join us in our journey back to God.

Numbers 10 also explains that the tabernacle—representing the place where the Lord dwells—was the focus of their attention as they journeyed.

Numbers 11

The Israelites Driven by Their Appetites

Consider how the following questions apply to the Israelites as you read Numbers 11: How do you feel when you do something good for another person and they complain in response? What would happen if the Lord gave you everything you asked for without any consideration of whether or not what you asked for was good for you?

Understanding the Scriptures

Numbers 11

Kindled (vv. 1, 10, 33)—Stirred up

Uttermost (v. 1)—Outer

Quenched (v. 2)—Put out

Mixt multitude (v. 4)—Non-Israelites

Fell a lusting (v. 4)—Felt strong desires to satisfy their appetites (in this case, desire for food other than manna)

Flesh (vv. 4, 13, 18, 21, 33)—Meat

Our soul is dried away (v. 6)—We have lost our appetite (for manna)

Coriander (v. 7)—A plant related to parsley

Bdellium (v. 7)—Resin, a waxy substance

Mortar (v. 8)—Bowl-like container

As the taste of fresh oil (v. 8)—Like the taste of something cooked in oil

Afflicted (v. 11)—Troubled

Conceived, begotten (v. 12)—Given birth to

Swarest (v. 12)—Promised

Bear (vv. 14, 17)—Carry

Thus (v. 15)—In this way

Wretchedness (v. 15)—Extreme unhappiness

Against (v. 18)—In preparation for

Loathsome (v. 20)—Sickening

Despised (v. 20)—Turned away from, shown no appreciation for

Footmen (v. 21)—Men over twenty years old who can be soldiers

Suffice (v. 22)—Fill, satisfy

Enviest thou (v. 29)—Are you jealous

Two cubits (v. 31)—Approximately three feet (one meter)

Ten homers (v. 32)—Approximately three liters

Ere (v. 33)—Before

Lusted (v. 34)—To seek after things having to do with bodily appetites

Numbers 11:29—Moses Wished That All the People Were Prophets

The Prophet Joseph Smith said, "God hath not revealed anything to Joseph, but what He will make known unto the Twelve, and even the least Saint may know all things as fast as he is able to bear them" (*Teachings of the Prophet Joseph Smith*, sel. Joseph Fielding Smith [1976], 149).

Studying the Scriptures

Do three of the following activities (A–E) as you study Numbers 11.

A Some Complaints and Criticisms Today

Imagine you felt the way the Israelites did in Numbers 11:1–9. Write a note of complaint to Moses that reflects what you think the people were saying at the time.

B Write a Response

Use what Moses said in Numbers 11:10–15 and what you have learned about this journey so far and write how you might respond to the Israelites' complaint if you were their leader.

C What Happens When We Complain?

Look at Numbers 11:1–4; Jude 1:14–16 and tell what eventually happens to people who complain or murmur against the Lord and his servants. Notice in Numbers 11:20 what the Lord said the children of Israel were really doing when they complained against Moses.

D Find Important Words

Find what you think are three important words or phrases that describe what the seventy men did and why they were called in response to Moses' discouragement.

E What Is the Lesson?

Read Galatians 5:16–17 and tell how these verses express what could be considered the main idea of Numbers 11. Think about the meaning of the word *lust* and what the Lord did to the seventy elders in response to the situation.

Numbers 12

Sustaining or Rejecting the Prophet

One of the wonderful things about the Lord's Church is that it makes available the gifts of the Spirit to all who worthily seek them. This truth was demonstrated in Numbers 11 when the Lord's Spirit came upon seventy Israelite men and they prophesied. While anyone may experience these gifts, there still must be order in God's kingdom. He calls men to preside and he gives them special inspiration needed to govern the Church. To experience spiritual gifts does not mean that we are no longer subject to the priesthood leaders God has chosen to preside over us.

Having received spiritual gifts or knowledge, some members begin to see themselves as better than those who preside over them. This pride often leads to criticism of a leader and an unwillingness to follow counsel. Unless critical people humble themselves and repent of their feelings, they soon find themselves cut off from the Spirit and on the road to apostasy. Numbers 12 not only teaches the principle of supporting our leaders but it also shows that even those who should know better may fall to this temptation.

What is the most difficult thing you ever had to do to keep the Lord's commandments or receive a promised blessing from him? Why did you do it? What would have happened if you hadn't?

When the Lord delivered the Israelites from Egypt, he said he would lead them into the land of Canaan, which was the land promised to Abraham, Isaac, and Jacob and their posterity forever. After many miracles and over a year of difficult travels in the wilderness, the Israelites finally arrived at the borders of this promised land. Numbers 13–14 tells the story of twelve men, one from each tribe, who were sent to find out what the land looked like and who lived there. We also read about their report to the people and what the people decided to do about what they heard.

As you read Numbers 13–14, ask yourself the following question: When faced with what seems to be a very difficult task from the Lord, do I react with fear or with faith? If most people around you chose fear over faith, how might you be affected? (see D&C 30:1–2). The way you respond tells how much you trust the Lord—how much you believe that if he gives a commandment or a promise he has also prepared a way for you to accomplish it (see 1 Nephi 3:7).

Understanding the Scriptures 🔑

Numbers 12

Apparently (v. 8)—Clearly

Dark speeches (v. 8)—Things difficult to understand

Similitude (v. 8)—Bodily form

Behold (v. 8)—See

Leprous (v. 10)—Having leprosy (a skin disease; see Bible Dictionary, s.v. "leprosy")

Alas (v. 11)—Please

Beseech (vv. 11, 13)—To plead with

Studying the Scriptures ✏️

(A) What Happens When We Criticize the Prophet or Other Church Leaders?

1. What lessons do you think are symbolized by what happened to Miriam?

2. How is Miriam's punishment related to what we read in Doctrine and Covenants 1:14?

Numbers 13–14

Scoping Out the Promised Land

Understanding the Scriptures 🔑

Numbers 13

Oshea, Jehoshua (vv. 8, 16)—Joshua

Bare (v. 23)—Carried

Two (v. 23)—Two men

Staff (v. 23)—Straight stick

Stilled (v. 30)—Quieted

Stature (v. 32)—Size

Numbers 14

Prey (vv. 3, 31)—Something captured

Rent their clothes (v. 6)—Tore their clothes as a sign of great sorrow

Bade (v. 10)—Requested

Provoke, provoked (vv. 11, 23)—Make angry

Ere (v. 11)—Before

Pestilence (v. 12)—Plague, disease

Clearing the guilty (v. 18)—Letting the guilty go without punishment

Pardon, pardoned (vv. 19–20)—Forgive

Carcases (vv. 29, 32–33)—Dead bodies

Fall (v. 29)—Die

Save (v. 30)—Except

Despised (v. 31)—Rejected

Wasted (v. 33)—Dead and decayed

Slander (v. 36)—Bad report

Presumed (v. 44)—Knowingly moved on without permission (an act of defiance)

Discomfited (v. 45)—Clearly defeated

Studying the Scriptures

Do two of the following activities (A–D) as you study Numbers 13–14.

(A) Create an Advertisement

Create an advertisement from the point of view of Joshua or Caleb to encourage the Israelites to enter the promised land.

(B) Convince the Israelites

1. Give the reasons why most of the Israelites did not want to enter the promised land.

2. Use the events and teachings you already read about in Genesis, Exodus, Leviticus, or the first part of Numbers to convince the Israelites to go forward and enter their land of promise.

(C) Compare Events in the Story

1. Summarize the response of the children of Israel to the report of the spies (found in Numbers 14:1–4).

2. Read Numbers 14:28–33 and compare what the children of Israel said to what the Lord said about their lack of faith.

(D) "We Can Do This on Our Own"

What did the Israelites decide to do and why didn't they succeed?

Numbers 15

Obtaining Forgiveness

After the main body of Israelites showed their lack of faith (see Numbers 13–14) and sinned against the Lord, it is not surprising that Numbers 15 speaks about sacrificial offerings necessary for forgiveness of sins. Numbers 15 specifically speaks of sinning "presumptuously," which means to sin knowing that what you are doing is wrong (compare Numbers 14:44 with Numbers 15:30–31). Numbers 15 closes with a commandment that could help Israel always remember the importance of obeying the commandments.

Numbers 16

Rebellion against the Prophet

Sometimes people think that they don't really have to follow the teachings of the prophets because they think prophets are human just like the rest of us and are just giving their opinion on

things. Elder Harold B. Lee, then a member of the Quorum of the Twelve Apostles, said, "I want to bear you my testimony that the experience I have had has taught me that those who criticize the leaders of this Church are showing signs of a spiritual sickness which, unless curbed, will bring about eventual spiritual death" (in Conference Report, Oct. 1947, 67). Some years later, as President of the Quorum of the Twelve Apostles and a member of the First Presidency, President Lee said, "Your safety and ours depends upon whether or not we follow the ones whom the Lord has placed to preside over his church" (in Conference Report, Oct. 1970, 153).

Those whom the Lord chooses to preside over us are given sacred keys to receive revelation in directing the Church and directing us in righteousness. How we respond to our leaders reflects our feelings for and faith in our Heavenly Father. Read what the Lord said to latter-day Israel in Doctrine and Covenants 1:14; 121:16–17; 124:45–46. Look for how Numbers 16 dramatically illustrates the truth of these statements.

Understanding the Scriptures

Numbers 16

Renown (v. 2)—Well-known people

Censers (vv. 6, 17–18, 37–39)—Containers to burn incense

Separated (v. 9)—Chosen

Company (vv. 11, 16)—Group, family

Wroth, wrath (vv. 15, 22, 46)—Angry, anger

About (v. 24)—Near

Appertain, appertained (vv. 30, 32–33)—Belong

Provoked (v. 30)—Made angry

Clave asunder (v. 31)—Split apart

Yonder (v. 37)—Away from the camp

Hallowed (vv. 37–38)—Holy or sacred

Broad plates (vv. 38–39)—Metal sheets (from the metal of the censers)

Brasen (v. 39)—Bronze, copper

Studying the Scriptures

(A) Tell the Story in Your Own Words

1. Write the story of Numbers 16 in your own words.

2. Explain how this story is an example of President Harold B. Lee's statements in the introduction to this chapter.

Numbers 17–19

A Follow-up to a Tragic Incident

You will be able to understand Numbers 17–19 more completely when you read thinking about what happened in Numbers 16. The real issue in chapter 16 was that a group of men felt they should be able to perform certain priesthood ordinances that were assigned to only the priests, which at this time were Aaron and his sons. This rebellion resulted in the rebels' death. Many who followed the rebels also died.

Note that the punishment of death inflicted as a result of serious sin was the Lord's way of teaching ancient Israel, and us, that serious or continuous sin may result in spiritual death since fully repenting is much more difficult.

Numbers 17 tells how the Lord provided a miracle for those who survived so they could know that God chose Aaron and authorized him to perform the priesthood ordinances of their day.

Numbers 18 describes additional duties that belonged only to Aaron and his sons who were ordained to the priest's office. Numbers 18 also describes duties that belong to other Levites, showing the difference between the priest's office and all other duties of the Levitical priesthood.

Finally, Numbers 19 explains rules and commandments concerning what to do with dead bodies, which surely was an issue after the events in Numbers 16.

Numbers 20

Thirty-Eight Years of Frustration

Numbers 20 recounts events that occurred approximately thirty-eight years after the rebellion incident in Numbers 16. We do not know what occurred during those years or why we don't have a record of that period. Perhaps nothing was recorded because nothing really changed over those years. For example, Numbers 20 begins with a story of Israel murmuring against Moses and Aaron, which is exactly where the story left off thirty-eight years before. This time the story is a little different, however, in that Moses and Aaron became so frustrated that they used poor judgment in how they responded to the people. Because they used poor judgment the Lord chastised them and told them they would not be privileged to lead the children of Israel into the promised land.

By reading Deuteronomy 1:37; 3:25–28 we learn that Moses was chastised because of his disobedience. By punishing Moses the Lord powerfully taught the children of Israel that obedience was required to enter the promised land—even (perhaps especially) if one happened to be the prophet. If Moses had varied from the Lord's commands and gone unpunished, this hard-hearted people might possibly have excused their own sins on a greater matter by saying they saw Moses vary from the Lord's commands and go unpunished. As evidence that the Lord did not seriously condemn Moses, we read in other scripture that he was translated into heaven without tasting death and that he appeared on earth at very important occasions to confer priesthood keys to future generations (see Luke 9:28–36; Alma 45:19; D&C 110:11).

Numbers 20 also contains an account of Israel attempting to pass peacefully through the land of Edom and being met with resistance. The land of Edom was the land of Esau's (Jacob's brother) descendants. You may want to look at map 3 in the back of the Latter-day Saint edition of the King James Version of the Bible to trace the path of the Israelites.

The beginning of Numbers 20 tells of the death of Moses' sister, Miriam; the end of the chapter tells about the death of Moses' brother, Aaron, and of Aaron's son Eleazar becoming the high priest.

Numbers 21

The Brass Serpent

Like Miriam and Aaron in Numbers 20, it is likely that many of the Israelites died during the thirty-eight years of dwelling in the wilderness. The Lord said, however, that all who were over twenty years old at the beginning of the exodus (except for Joshua and Caleb, who gave positive reports of the promised land) would die before the camp of Israel entered the promised land. Numbers 21 records an incident where many more died. This story is especially significant because it involves a type of Christ—the brass serpent. Because an entire generation of Israelites would not look upon the serpent, they died physically and spiritually and were denied entrance into the promised land. This event appears to have separated those whose faith was weakest from those whose faith was strong, because the rest of Numbers 21 tells how the Israelites conquered those who opposed them and successfully moved toward the promised land. When the Israelites were stronger in faith, they had much more success.

Understanding the Scriptures

Numbers 21

Loatheth (v. 5)—Dislikes, hates

Light bread (v. 5)—Manna

Studying the Scriptures ✏️

A · Tell the Story in Your Own Words

Imagine you are a Primary teacher. Tell the story of Numbers 21:4–9 in words that children could understand. Draw a picture or two you could show the children while you tell the story.

B · Find Important Interpretations from Other Scriptures

Make a chart like the one below and fill it in with insights that relate to the event in Numbers 21.

Scripture Reference	Who Spoke	What He Said
John 3:14–16		
1 Nephi 17:40–41		
Alma 33:18–22		
Helaman 8:13–15		

Numbers 22–24

The Story of Balaam

How much money would someone have to pay you to do something you knew wasn't right? Numbers 22–24 tells the story of a man who had to make that decision. His name was Balaam. He was a soothsayer (one who professes to foretell the future) who believed in, or at least knew about, the God of Israel to the degree that he could be influenced by the Spirit. The king of Moab tried to hire Balaam to curse Israel so the Moabites could defeat them in battle. As you read, think about what you would have done if you had been Balaam and what you might have learned from the experience.

Understanding the Scriptures 🔑

Numbers 22

Distressed (v. 3)—Worried

Lick up (v. 4)—Eat, consume

Abide over against (v. 5)—Settled next to

Prevail (v. 6)—Win

Rewards of divination (v. 7)—Money for prophesying

Lodge (v. 8)—Stay

Hinder (v. 16)—Stop

Smote, smitten (vv. 23, 25, 27–28, 32)—Hit

Perverse (v. 32)—Wrong, wicked

Numbers 23

Defy (vv. 7–8)—Go against

Reckoned (v. 9)—Counted, considered, noticed

But the utmost part (v. 13)—Only part

Enchantment, divination (v. 23)—Fortune telling

Wrought (v. 23)—Done

Numbers 24

Nigh (v. 17)—Near

Sceptre (v. 17)—A staff a ruler holds to signify his power. In this case the capital *S* refers to the Messiah, who is the ruler of Israel.

Valiantly (v. 18)—Strong and courageously

Have dominion (v. 19)—Rule

Wasted (v. 22)—Destroyed

Numbers 22:20–35—Why Was God Angry at Balaam for Doing What He Was Told?

The Lord told Balaam that if the Moabite princes asked him to accompany them again he should go *only to say the words the Lord would tell him to say* (see Numbers 22:20). Verse 21 records that Balaam simply got up the next morning and started on his way. Some have noted that it appears that Balaam had his heart set on the money offered for his services (see 2 Peter 2:15); he left without any intention of following the Lord. Consequently, he had an experience with his ass and an angel with a drawn sword that demonstrated he should listen to the Lord. At the end of his experience, the Lord reminded Balaam once more that he could go with the princes but only if he would say the words the Lord would give to him (see Numbers 22:35).

Studying the Scriptures ✏️

Do two of the following activities (A–C) as you study Numbers 22–24.

A · Is Your Integrity for Sale?

Just like Balak wanted Balaam to go against what he knew was right for money (see Numbers 22), how do you see people today going against what they know is right for money or the opportunity to be "promoted . . . unto very great honour"? (v. 17).

or

Write about someone you know who gave up money and honor to do what he or she knew was right.

B · Give a Character Reference

Imagine you are Balak, and another king in the area wrote you because he was thinking about hiring Balaam to curse his enemies. Write what your response would be and include what happened the three times he asked Balaam to curse Israel (first time: Numbers 23:1–13; second time: Numbers 23:14–30; third time: Numbers 24:1–13).

C · Interpret the Prophecy

In Numbers 24:17 who do you think is the "Star of Jacob" and the "Sceptre of Israel"? (see also vv. 14–16, 18–29). Why do you think so?

Numbers 25–26

Cursing Israel

Although Balaam did not curse Israel in Numbers 22–24, his desire for the riches the Moabites offered was too much for him to resist. Numbers 31:7–8, 15–16; Revelation 2:14 lead us to believe that Balaam taught the Moabites that they could not defeat Israel as long as Israel was righteous, so Balaam told the Moabites to tempt Israel with immorality and idolatry and cause them to lose the help of the Lord. Consequently, Numbers 25 tells about the final plague that killed many Israelites before the camp of Israel entered the promised land. This plague came upon them because of immoral acts with Moabite women.

By the end of the plague, nearly all who left Egypt as adults were dead. Numbers 26 is another numbering, or census, of the next generation of Israelites thirty-nine years after their fathers rejected the opportunity to enter the promised land and were cursed to wander and die in the wilderness.

Numbers 27

Choosing a New Leader for Israel

Obviously, Moses could not be with the children of Israel forever. Consider the following questions as you read Numbers 27:12–23: What kind of leader would the Israelites need when Moses was gone? How are leaders chosen in the Church today? Why is the way they are selected important?

Understanding the Scriptures 🗝

Numbers 27

Gathered unto thy people (v. 13)—Die

Strife (v. 14)—Rebellion

Sanctify (v. 14)—Honor

A charge (vv. 19, 23)— Instructions, responsibilities, and blessings

Studying the Scriptures ✏️➡

A ▸ **We Believe . . .**

What principles of the fifth Article of Faith were used in choosing Joshua as a leader in Israel?

Numbers 28–30

Old Commandments Still Apply

Numbers 28–30 tells how Moses reminded a new generation of Israelites that they were under the same obligation to keep the sacrifices, feast days, laws, and commandments that the Lord gave at the beginning of the journey nearly forty years earlier.

Numbers 31

Balaam Dies

Numbers 31 records how the Lord sent the army of Israel against the Midianites because the Midianites sought to destroy the Israelites through immorality and idolatry. Among the slain was the soothsayer Balaam who turned against the Lord and his people. To show gratitude for their victory, the armies of Israel dedicated to the Lord much of what they captured.

Numbers 32

Land for Reuben and Gad

While the children of Israel were on the east side of the Jordan River waiting to cross over into Canaan, the tribes of Reuben and Gad asked Moses if they could have their inheritance on the east side because they thought the land looked good for cattle. Moses told them the other tribes would be upset if they did not help conquer the land on the west of the Jordan (Canaan); the main

body of Israelites felt that conquering Canaan's inhabitants would be hard enough with all twelve tribes. Reuben and Gad agreed to send their men to help with the conquest until every tribe had an inheritance. They would, however, leave their women, children, and cattle behind on the eastern shore. Moses agreed to this arrangement and also gave half the tribe of Manasseh an inheritance on the east of the Jordan as well (see Bible map 5).

Numbers 33–36

Instructions for the Promised Land

Numbers 33–36 contains additional instructions the Lord gave to the Israelites as they camped near the borders of their promised land.

Numbers 33 records that the Lord had Moses record forty separate journeys the Israelites had taken to get to Canaan, perhaps to remind the Israelites of how fortunate they had been in their travels. We are not able to geographically identify most of the places on the list. The Lord then commanded the Israelites to completely drive out or destroy the inhabitants of Canaan so they would not be a spiritual plague to them.

Numbers 34 tells how the Lord outlined the borders of the land the Israelites were to conquer and how he named the men who would be in charge of dividing the land among the twelve tribes and the families of those tribes.

Numbers 35 contains the Lord's commandment that special cities be created throughout Canaan for the Levites. This would allow the Levites to be among all the tribes and perform ordinances for them. The Lord also named some of these cities as cities of refuge for those who had slain another person. Having these places of refuge would help prevent anyone taking revenge on these people before proper justice could be accomplished.

Numbers 36 contains counsel from the Lord concerning marrying within one's own tribe so that land inheritances might stay within the same tribe.

The Book of Deuteronomy

A Repetition of the Law

Deuteronomy is the final book of Moses. The events in Deuteronomy occurred approximately forty years after the Lord brought the Israelites out of Egypt. Because they refused to exercise faith in the Lord thirty-nine years earlier, all Israelites—except Moses, Joshua, and Caleb—who were adults at the time they left Egypt died in the wilderness (see Numbers 13–14).

At the time Moses wrote Deuteronomy, the children of those who had died were prepared to enter their promised land. The prophet

Moses knew he would not enter with them, but he was given the opportunity to instruct and counsel this generation of Israelites before he left. Moses gave the "speeches" recorded in Deuteronomy on the plains of Moab, just east of the Jordan River and the promised land. After teaching the people one last time, Moses was translated, or taken into heaven without tasting death (see Alma 45:19).

Getting Ready to Study Deuteronomy

The first four chapters of Deuteronomy are a "remembering" of Israelite history. On over twenty additional occasions in Deuteronomy, Moses told the people to "remember" or "forget not" certain important teachings to help them remain faithful. Note the following about Deuteronomy:

- The Ten Commandments are repeated in Deuteronomy 5.

- Deuteronomy is quoted over a hundred times in the New Testament. Two notable instances include when Jesus used three verses from Deuteronomy to dismiss the temptations of Satan (see Deuteronomy 6:13, 16; 8:3; Matthew 4:1–11) and when Jesus quoted a verse from Deuteronomy in response to the question "Which is the great commandment in the law?" (Matthew 22:36; see also vv. 35, 37–38; Deuteronomy 6:5).

To find out more about the book of Deuteronomy, see "Deuteronomy" in the Bible Dictionary.

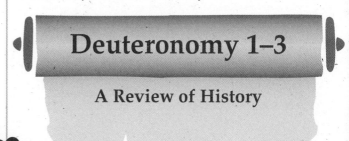

Deuteronomy 1–3

A Review of History

Deuteronomy 1–3 records how Moses introduced his message to the children of Israel by reviewing their previous forty-year history. In many ways this review is a good summary of the book of Numbers. Moses used examples from this history of Israel throughout the rest of Deuteronomy to emphasize certain ideas.

Deuteronomy 4

"Take Heed to Thyself"

Deuteronomy 4 tells how Moses used the Israelites' history to teach them about their duty to God and their religion. Moses also said that his teachings applied to all future generations of Israelites, and he told parents to teach their children the truths he taught them.

Understanding the Scriptures

Deuteronomy 4

Statutes (vv. 1, 5–6, 8, 14, 40, 45)—Laws, commandments, and ordinances

Diminish ought (v. 2)—Take away anything

Cleave (v. 4)—Stay close to

Nigh (v. 7)—Near

Take heed (un)to thyself/yourselves (vv. 9, 15, 23)—Be careful about what you do

Keep (v. 9)—To be careful

Horeb (v. 10)—Another name for Mount Sinai

Driven (v. 19)—Directed

Thence (v. 29)—That place

Tribulation (v. 30)—Trouble

Forsake (v. 31)—Abandon

On this side Jordan toward the sunrising (vv. 41, 47)—On the east of the Jordan River

Deuteronomy 4:9, 15, 23—How Do We Apply the Counsel "Take Heed to Thyself"?

Elder M. Russell Ballard, a member of the Quorum of the Twelve Apostles, suggested a way to apply this idea. In a talk to the youth of the Church, he said: "I encourage you to take time each week to be by yourself, away from television and the crowd. Have your scriptures with you, and as you read, ponder, and pray, take an honest look at your life. Evaluate where you stand with the promises you have made with Heavenly Father. If you have a problem, talk it over with the Lord in earnest and humble prayer. Counsel with your parents; they will help you. Your bishop and your Young Men and Young Women adult leaders will help. They love you and want you to be at peace with yourself so you can partake of the sacrament worthily each week. When all is said and done, however, only you know if you are living true to your covenants made with God" (in Conference Report, Apr. 1993, 7; or *Ensign*, May 1993, 8).

Studying the Scriptures

A Be a Missionary

Your friend who is not a member of the Church says that Christians should use *only* the Bible for scripture. To prove her point she quotes to you Revelation 22:18–19. Look up these verses and compare them to Deuteronomy 4:2. Write a note to your friend that explains how these two scriptures are alike and what would happen if you used Deuteronomy the same way she used Revelation 22. Also explain what these scriptures really mean.

B Notice a Pattern in the Scriptures

Find and mark the similar phrase in Deuteronomy 4:9, 15, 23. How do these three verses help us understand who is responsible for our keeping the commandments? (Notice also the statement from Elder Ballard in the "Understanding the Scriptures" section for how to apply this counsel.)

C Use the Scriptures to Help Someone Who Has Sinned

Use the ideas in Deuteronomy 4:25–31 to give advice and hope to someone who has strayed from what he or she knows to be right. Write your advice in your notebook.

Deuteronomy 5

The Ten Commandments

Deuteronomy 5 contains Moses' review of the Ten Commandments originally recorded in Exodus 20. Moses emphasized that these Ten Commandments are important to each generation of Israelites because they are the foundation of righteousness among God's covenant people.

Deuteronomy 6

The Great Commandment

Do you have a scripture that has been a special strength and guide to you? Why has it had this influence? How often do you remember it? How often do you share it with others?

Deuteronomy 6 contains a passage that is one of the Jews' most frequently quoted scriptures. This passage is also what Jesus called "the first and great commandment" (Matthew 22:38; see also vv. 36–37). As you find and read this passage, ask yourself why this is the great commandment. Why is this the "first and great commandment" when it was given hundreds of years after the Ten Commandments? Deuteronomy 6 also includes Moses' explanations concerning how the Israelites should observe this commandment and why.

Understanding the Scriptures 🔑

Deuteronomy 6

Frontlets (v. 8)—A band or ribbon worn across the forehead

Preserve (v. 24)—Save

Deuteronomy 6:4–5—The First and Great Commandment

In Hebrew the word *hear* is *shema*. Consequently, the Jews call Deuteronomy 6:4–5 the *Shema*. When asked which was the greatest commandment in all the law, Jesus quoted the *Shema* (see Matthew 22:36–38). President Ezra Taft Benson, President of the Church, explained why it must be first: "When we put God first, all other things fall into their proper place or drop out of our lives. Our love of the Lord will govern the claims for our affection, the demands on our time, the interests we pursue, and the order of our priorities" (in Conference Report, Apr. 1988, 3; or *Ensign*, May 1988, 4).

Deuteronomy 6:8–9—How Did the Israelites Apply This Instruction?

By the time of Jesus, many Jews interpreted Deuteronomy 6:8–9 in a very literal way. They wrote verses 4–5 on small scrolls, put the scrolls in small boxes called "phylacteries," and tied one box on their arms and another around their heads so that the box was over the forehead. They also put one of these scrolls in a small container called a "mezuzot" and nailed the mezuzot to the right doorpost of their homes.

Phylactery   Mezuzot

Studying the Scriptures ✏️

Ⓐ Cross-Reference

Write the reference Matthew 22:35–38 next to Deuteronomy 6:4–5 (the *Shema*). Read the verses in Matthew and summarize what Jesus said about the *Shema*.

Ⓑ How Can You Remember?

1. List the things Moses told the people to do in Deuteronomy 6:7–9 so they could better remember and keep the commandment in verses 4–5.

2. Write about ways *you* could better remember this same commandment. Choose and put into practice at least one of the ideas you thought of.

Ⓒ Write a Question

Write what you think is an important, meaningful question that can be answered by Deuteronomy 6:24.

Deuteronomy 7

Marry in the Covenant

The people in the land of Canaan were extremely wicked. Because of their wickedness, the Lord commanded the Israelites to completely destroy them. Deuteronomy 7 records that Moses explained a very important reason why the Israelites should follow this commandment and how the Lord would bless them in such a challenging task.

Studying the Scriptures ✏️

Ⓐ What Would You Say?

A friend asks your advice on marrying someone who is not a member of the Church. Write how you could use Deuteronomy 7:1–6 to counsel your friend.

Deuteronomy 8

Remember!

Elder Spencer W. Kimball, when he was a member of the Quorum of the Twelve Apostles, said: "When you look in the dictionary for the most important word, do you know what it is? It could be 'remember.' Because all of you have made covenants . . . our greatest need is to remember" (Circles of Exaltation [address to religious educators, 28 June 1968], 8). Deuteronomy 8 recounts what Moses told the covenant people of Israel about things they needed to remember and why. He also told them what would happen if they forgot those things.

Understanding the Scriptures 🔑

Deuteronomy 8

Multiply (vv. 1, 13)—Increase in number

Chasteneth (v. 5)—Corrects and disciplines

Scarceness (v. 9)—Going without, famine

Rock of flint (v. 15)—Very hard rock

Deuteronomy 8:2—Some Purposes of Wandering for Forty Years in the Wilderness

Compare Deuteronomy 8:2 to Abraham 3:24–25 where the Lord explained a purpose of earth life. Israel's journey in the wilderness was a type or symbol of our mortal life.

Studying the Scriptures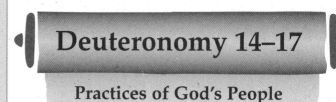

A What Is the Message?

Determine the main ideas of Moses' message in Deuteronomy 8 by looking at the following group of verses and choosing one key word from each group that you feel identifies the most important idea in that group. Briefly explain why you chose the word you did. Make the following chart in your notebook to help you organize the information.

Verses	Key Word	Explanation
1		
2		
3		
4–6		
7–10		
11–17		
18–19		
20		

Deuteronomy 9–10

The Lord Will Help

One of the primary reasons the previous generation of Israelites refused to enter the promised land was that they were afraid of the people who already lived there. Deuteronomy 9–10 tells that Moses assured the Israelites that the Lord would help them destroy the Canaanites and enter the promised land. Moses warned the Israelites, however, to not be prideful about the help they would receive.

Understanding the Scriptures 🔑

Deuteronomy 10:12–22

Regardeth not persons (v. 17)—Treats everybody by the same principles

Taketh reward (v. 17)—Accept bribes

Cleave (v. 20)—Be closely attached

Threescore (v. 22)—Sixty (a "score" is twenty)

Deuteronomy 9:3–6—Why Were the Israelites Able to Drive the Canaanites Out of the Land?
See 1 Nephi 17:32–38.

Studying the Scriptures 🔑

A What Does the Lord Require?

1. What did the Lord say he required of Israel, and why? (see Deuteronomy 10:12–22).

2. List what you learn about God in these verses that would help you want to do what he requires.

Deuteronomy 11

Blessings or Cursings— You Choose

The Fall and the Atonement preserved the agency of all mankind (see 2 Nephi 2:25–27). Agency is a great blessing, but there are risks involved because it requires that we must accept and be responsible for the consequences of our decisions. Deuteronomy 11 says that Moses put before Israel "a blessing and a curse" (v. 26). In other words, Moses told the children of Israel that they could receive blessings or cursings depending on how they chose to live in the promised land. The outcome was up to them.

Deuteronomy 12–13

Avoid Evil Practices

Deuteronomy 12–13 contains Moses' warning to the Israelites about worshiping false gods. The covenant people were to be different from all other nations and avoid not only false practices but apparent involvement with false practices. In chapter 12 Moses told the Israelites to avoid the places where false gods were worshiped and warned them about imitating the practices of false religions. In chapter 13 Moses warned the Israelites about people who participate in or might lead them to the worship of false gods.

Deuteronomy 14–17

Practices of God's People

Deuteronomy 14–17 contains reminders of the Lord's previous commandments. Chapter 14 contains laws concerning food (see also Leviticus 11). Chapter 15 contains commandments regarding the release of debts and slaves every seventh year (see Leviticus 25). Chapter 16 records the Lord's reminder to the Israelites about the importance of participating in the major feasts: Passover, Pentecost (the Feast of Weeks), and Tabernacles. Commandments concerning these feasts were given previously in Exodus 12, 23; Leviticus 23; Numbers 28. Chapter 17 contains instructions for certain sacrificial practices, for dealing with those who worship false gods, and for judging others. Chapter 17 also gives instructions to future Israelites should they ever decide to have a king. In each of these chapters, all the instructions the Lord gave were to help separate Israelites from worldly practices.

Deuteronomy 18

True and False Prophets

The Canaanite people held many superstitions. Such superstitions often attract people because these practices seldom require any standard of conduct and often promise results such as worldly success or healing by "magic" without any effort on the part of the individual. Deuteronomy 18 tells how Moses warned the Israelites not to follow any of these practices. Moses also counseled them that the true source of guidance is the true and living God who speaks through his prophets—not through an idol or performer of the magical or mystical arts. He told the people how they could discern a true prophet.

Deuteronomy 19–25

Specific Laws for a Chosen People

Deuteronomy 19–25 contains specific laws and commandments concerning many different areas of daily life, including farming, family relationships, warfare, religious cleanliness, and doing business. Some of these laws may sound odd, but each is based on some principle the Lord wanted Israel to remember. By giving these rules and commandments, the Lord provided continual, sometimes daily, reminders of principles he wanted the Israelites to learn. For example, in Deuteronomy 22:9 the Lord told the Israelites not to sow a field with two different kinds of seeds. Sowing seeds was an important part of life, and whenever they sowed they were reminded that as Israelites, they were not to mix their seed with another, or, in other words, they were not to marry out of the covenant. Some of the principles

behind the laws in Deuteronomy 19–25 may be harder to see than others, but if we read these chapters and seek for the principle that could be drawn from each specific practice, we may find that these laws are not so strange at all—especially for a people "slow to remember the Lord their God" (Mosiah 13:29).

Deuteronomy 26

Our Debt to God

Does the Lord get some benefit when we pay our tithing? Why does he ask us to pay it? What does paying tithing do for us? What do you think is the difference between people who willingly pay their tithing and people who pay their tithing grudgingly? Think about these questions as you read what Moses taught the children of Israel in Deuteronomy 26.

Understanding the Scriptures

Deuteronomy 26

Profess (v. 3)—Declare

Note: Remember to look in your footnotes for help with words and phrases.

Studying the Scriptures

A Make a List

From Deuteronomy 26 list what Moses said the Lord had done for Israel.

B Write a Thank You Note

Consider all the Lord has done for you. If you need help thinking of some of his blessings, read Mosiah 2:21–25. Write how we can show our gratitude to the Lord for his blessings to us.

Deuteronomy 27–28

Blessings and Cursings

In Leviticus 26 the Lord set before Israel the blessings they could receive if they kept his commandments and the punishments they would receive if they disobeyed. Deuteronomy 27–28 tells how Moses spoke to the Israelites about these same blessings and commandments since they were children at the time of the events in Leviticus 26. This time, however, Moses gave more detailed instructions and used an "object lesson." The object lesson began with a command to go to two mountains in the land of Canaan, Mount Ebal and Mount Gerizim, which were

very close together. Six tribes were assigned to one mount where they were told to declare the promised blessings while the other six tribes stood on the other mount and responded by proclaiming the cursings. This event was to help remind the children of Israel that they were privileged to choose their future by their obedience.

Think about the following statement of President Joseph F. Smith, then President of the Quorum of the Twelve Apostles, as you read Deuteronomy 28: "These are the promises that the Lord made to the people of Israel anciently, if they would hearken unto His words and obey His laws.

"Now, I want to say to you without any hesitancy . . . that the words [in Deuteronomy 28:1–13] are as applicable to you as they were to the children of Israel. You are modern Israel and they were ancient Israel. The same God spake through His servant Moses that speaks today through His servant [the prophet]. Obedience to the laws of God will produce the same results today that it did anciently" (in Conference Report, Oct. 1899, 45).

Understanding the Scriptures 🔑

Deuteronomy 28

Fruit of thy body (vv. 4, 11, 18, 53)—Children

Fruit of thy ground (vv. 4, 11, 18)—Harvest of crops

Fruit of thy cattle (vv. 4, 11)—Offspring of your cows

Plenteous (v. 11)—To have many

Vexation (v. 20)—Confusion and frustration

Rebuke (v. 20)—Reprimand, scold

Pestilence (v. 21)—Plagues, diseases

Cleave (vv. 21, 60)—Stay close to

Consumption (v. 22)—Sickness

Inflammation (v. 22)—Swelling

Blasting (v. 22)—Plant disease

Fray (v. 26)—Frighten

Grope (v. 29)—To walk cautiously using your hands to feel in front of you because you cannot see

Betroth (v. 30)—Make an agreement to be married

A proverb and a byword (v. 37)—A thing people look down on and make fun of

Dress (v. 39)—Take care

Fierce countenance (v. 50)—Fearful looks

Besiege (v. 52)—Attack

Continuance (v. 59)—Lasting

Studying the Scriptures ✏️

Do at least two of the following activities (A–D) as you study Deuteronomy 28.

Ⓐ How Does It Apply Today?

Deuteronomy 28:1–13 tells of blessings Israel will receive if they are faithful. Tell what you think each blessing means for the people of today, and record them in your notebook in a chart like the one below.

Verse	The Blessing	How the Principle Applies Today
1	Set above all nations	
3	Blessed in the city and field	
4	Blessed in fruit of the body, ground, animals	
5	Blessed in basket and store	
6	Blessed in coming in and out	
7	Protected from enemies	
8	Blessed in all undertakings	
9	Be established as a holy people	
10	Called by the name of the Lord	
12	The Lord will open his good treasure	
13	Made the head not the tail	

Ⓑ Which One Would You Like?

From the list of blessings above, write which one you would like to receive and explain why.

Ⓒ Consider the Curses

Deuteronomy 28:15–68 contains a very long section of curses. As you read them, choose two that you have seen happen to people who do not obey God's commandments, and write about them. Your examples may come from people you know or know about or from the scriptures. You need not identify the people you know.

Ⓓ Optional Activity

If God loves us, why must we suffer if we don't repent? (see D&C 19:17). The following scriptures may help you answer this question: Alma 39:7; 42:16–24; Helaman 12:2–3; Doctrine and Covenants 90:36; 95:1–2.

◀ # Deuteronomy 29–30 ▶

Returning to the Lord

Deuteronomy 29–30 contains the conclusion of Moses' address to the Israelites. He continued to explain the blessings that come from obedience and the cursings that come from disobedience. Deuteronomy 30 tells what the Lord would do for the Israelites if they fell away from him and then repented, and what they would have to do if they desired to be acceptable to him again. From this chapter we learn that the Lord is very merciful and longsuffering with his children.

Understanding the Scriptures

Deuteronomy 30

Call them to mind (v. 1)—Remember them

Captivity (v. 3)—Bondage, slavery

Studying the Scriptures

A. Make a Chart

Deuteronomy 30:1–10 contains the Lord's counsel to the Israelites about what to do if and when the curses spoken of in Deuteronomy 28 came upon them. Notice that there are several things the Lord said the people must do and several promises of what the Lord would do.

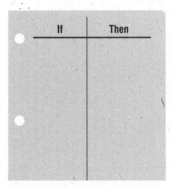

Make two columns on a page in your notebook. Label one column "If," and the other column "Then." Under "If," list the things the Lord said the Israelites must do in their cursed condition (see vv. 1–2, 6, 8, 10). In the "Then" column list what the Lord promised to do for the Israelites (see vv. 3–7, 9).

B. Apply These Teachings

Which verses would you use from Deuteronomy 30 to help someone who had sinned and strayed from the Church? Explain how you would use the verses.

Deuteronomy 31–32

The Song of Moses

After Moses taught this new generation of Israelites the laws of God and the consequences of obedience and disobedience to those laws, he was ready to leave them. Before he left, however, he encouraged them and their new leader, Joshua, to love and obey God above all other things. At this time, the Lord revealed to Moses a song that he was to teach the Israelites (see

Deuteronomy 32:1–43). The song would help them remember the Lord and the commandments Moses taught them.

Understanding the Scriptures

Deuteronomy 32

Distil (v. 2)—Come down

Ascribe (v. 3)—The act of acknowledging

Requite (v. 6)—Repay

Bounds (v. 8)—Limits

Jeshurun (v. 15)—A name meaning "the upright one," referring to Israel as a people

Abhorred (v. 19)—Strongly disliked

Vanities (v. 21)—Self-serving, selfish acts

Mischiefs (v. 23)—Troubles, evils

Void (v. 28)—Empty

Gall (v. 32)—Bitter

Vengeance (vv. 35, 41, 43)—Judgment

Recompence (v. 35)—Repayment

Vain thing (v. 47)—Something of little value

Studying the Scriptures

A. Find a Song Title

Deuteronomy 32 is called the "song of Moses." As you read through the chapter, look for phrases that you think could be a good hymn title. List at least four titles.

B. How Does Music Help You Stay Righteous?

1. Of all that the Lord could have given the Israelites, why do you think he gave them a song to help them remember him and to be a testimony to them?

2. Write in your notebook the words of a Church hymn or song that helps you want to keep the commandments and remember the Lord. If you don't have the words memorized, try to learn them this week so you can sing the song to yourself in time of need.

C. Optional Activity

1. Notice how many times the word *rock* is used in the song of Moses. According to 1 Corinthians 10:1–4, what is the Rock?

2. List what this song says about the Rock.

Deuteronomy 33

Blessings for Each Tribe

Like Jacob (Israel) did in Genesis 48–49, Moses blessed each of the tribes of Israel before he left them. The blessing for the seed of Joseph (Ephraim and Manasseh) is especially interesting (see Deuteronomy 33:13–17). The blessing of the tribes of

Joseph tells of their future prosperity and of their role in pushing together the rest of God's children "to the ends of the earth" (v. 17). As part of the scattering of Israel, the children of Joseph were scattered to all parts of the earth. In our day they are being gathered back to the Church of Jesus Christ, thus fulfilling this prophetic blessing of Moses.

Deuteronomy 34

Farewell to Moses

You have now covered over three hundred pages in the Bible that the prophet Moses wrote, which is more than any other

Old Testament prophet wrote. Deuteronomy 34 says that Moses died; however, as was noted earlier (see p. 71), Alma 45:19 teaches us that Moses did not die but was translated. See "Moses" in the Bible Dictionary for more information concerning Moses' translation.

Studying the Scriptures

A Write a Life Sketch

When famous people die, the newspapers usually do a brief life history, or "sketch," that outlines things that occurred in their lives, emphasizing notable achievements. If you were a newspaper writer of Moses' day, what would you include in Moses' life sketch? Include what impressed you significantly as you studied the life and teachings of Moses.

The Book of Joshua

A Covenant Fulfilled

The book of Joshua is named for its main character, Joshua. The book tells the story of how God fulfilled his covenant to give the children of Israel their promised land of Canaan.

In Hebrew, "Joshua" means "the Lord saves" or "the Lord gives the victory." The Greek form of this name translated into English is "Jesus." This name has interesting symbolism since the book of Joshua is the record of Joshua leading the children of Israel into their promised land, and Jesus Christ leads us into the "promised land" of eternal life.

A Book of Wars

The book of Joshua gives many accounts of how the children of Israel fulfilled the covenants of the Lord by conquering their enemies in war. We may wonder how God can say to a people, "Thou shalt not kill," and then tell those same people to destroy the entire population of certain cities. While we do not completely know the mind of God in these matters, we do know the following:

1. The events in the book of Joshua occurred at a time when nations fought in the name of their god. When the Israelites triumphed over the Canaanites by the power of the Lord, their victory was a witness that he is the true and living God. You will notice that nearly every account in the books of Joshua and Judges shows how the Israelites won their battles in some miraculous way, helping both the Israelites and their enemies know that the Lord God had won the battle, not any man or strategy. In addition, the Lord did not allow Israel to become rich through capturing the goods of the people they conquered (as you will read in Joshua 7).

   The Lord often reminded the Israelites that the land belonged to him, but was given to them for their use as his people. The destruction of the wicked and idolatrous nations of Canaan is a lesson to all people that this is one way God may punish the wicked, and it reminds us of the great destruction of the wicked that will occur at the time of judgment.

2. The prophet Nephi taught that the Lord "doeth not anything save it be for the benefit of the world" (2 Nephi 26:24). The prophet Ezekiel recorded that the Lord does not delight in the death of the wicked (see Ezekiel 18:32; 33:11). Therefore, when the Lord commanded the Israelites to drive out or destroy the Canaanites, he was doing what was most beneficial to all involved, based on their circumstances.

3. The iniquity of the Canaanites had reached a fulness (see Leviticus 18:3, 24–25; Deuteronomy 18:10–12; 1 Nephi 17:32–35). This fulness means they were willing to kill the prophets and the Saints (see 2 Nephi 26:3). While Saints in all days are expected to live in ways different from the world around them, in this case it would be very difficult for the Israelites to live the righteous life the Lord asked of them if they were side-by-side with the extraordinary wickedness of the Canaanites. When the wickedness of a society is so great that the rising generations have no opportunity to choose to live righteously, then God mercifully destroys the society from the earth for the sake of future generations. We learned this from the story of Noah and the Flood.

4. God's ways are not our ways (see Isaiah 55:8–9). When we consider that it is his work "to bring to pass the immortality and eternal life of man" (Moses 1:39) and that he is the Creator and has power over his creations, including the ability to save them, then we can have faith that God's actions help fulfill his work. Because we are limited in our understanding, we are not able to see things from God's point of view.

Getting Ready to Study Joshua

One of the early themes of the book of Joshua is that of strictly following the Lord's instructions. When the armies of Israel were obedient, they were successful. When they were not, they failed. The consequences of obedience helped the Israelites realize that it was the Lord's help that gave them the victory.

The book of Joshua can be divided into three general sections:

- The conquering of Canaan
- How Joshua divided the land
- Joshua's final instructions and testimony

Joshua 1

"Be Strong and of a Good Courage"

Consider how inadequate and humble Joshua may have felt when he was called to lead the children of Israel after Moses— one of the greatest prophets in history. As you read Joshua 1, look for what the Lord told Joshua to encourage him in his new calling. Think about how you might apply this counsel to callings the Lord gives you and in your life's experiences.

Understanding the Scriptures

Joshua 1

Minister (v. 1)—Servant, assistant

Tread (v. 3)—Walk

Stand before (v. 5)—Overcome, defeat, or replace

Forsake (v. 5)—Turn away from

Shalt not depart out of thy mouth (v. 8)—Always in your mind

Meditate therein (v. 8)—Think about it

Dismayed (v. 9)—Discouraged

On this side (vv. 14–15)—East of

Pass before your brethren armed, all the mighty men of valour (v. 14)—Have the great soldiers march in front of the people with their weapons.

According (v. 17)—Just

Studying the Scriptures

Do two of the following activities (A–C) as you study Joshua 1.

(A) Be Strong and Courageous

1. Find the verses where the Lord told Joshua to be strong and have courage. You may want to highlight them in your scriptures.
2. Write about how you can be strong and of good courage.

(B) Scripture Mastery: The Importance of Relying on the Scriptures

In your notebook, draw a poster that you think would best represent the message of Joshua 1:8. Make sure your poster includes what we should do with the scriptures (the book of the law) and what blessings are promised if we do.

(C) How Would You Feel?

1. How important is it to a prophet for his people to sustain him?

2. If you could speak briefly to the prophet of the Church today, what would you say about how you are trying to sustain him?

Joshua 2

Spies in Jericho

Alma taught that faith is putting your trust in God (see Alma 36:3). As you read Joshua 2, look for ways people in this chapter demonstrate their faith.

Understanding the Scriptures

Joshua 2

Harlot's (v. 1)—Prostitute's

Wist not whence they were (v. 4)—Did not know where they came from

Gate (v. 5)—An opening in the city wall

Whither (v. 5)—Where

Wot (v. 5)—Know

Pursue, pursued, pursuers (vv. 5, 7, 16, 22)—Chase, chased, chasers

Stalks (v. 6)—Long bundles

The way to Jordan unto the fords (v. 7)—To the places where one may cross the Jordan River

Your terror is fallen upon us (v. 9)—We are afraid of you

House (v. 12)—Family

Token (v. 12)—Sign that you will keep your word

Our life for yours (v. 14)—You have saved our lives and we will save yours in return.

Cord (v. 15)—Rope

Scarlet (v. 18)—Red

His blood shall be upon his head (v. 19)—He will be held responsible for his own death.

His blood shall be on our head (v. 19)—We will be held responsible for his death.

Quit of (v. 20)—Free from

Befell (v. 23)—Happened to

Joshua 2:1—Why Did the Spies Stay at the Home of a Harlot?

When we read something in the Bible that doesn't seem to make sense, we must remember what we know about the Lord and his teachings. For example, he has asked us to be chaste and to avoid situations and people that would encourage us to be unchaste. Knowing that fact, we can be sure that either "harlot" means something other than what we normally think or that this harlot had repented. What happened in this story leads us to believe that she was a good woman who had faith in God. We also should consider the spies' situation. People would be less likely to notice foreigners staying in a harlot's home than if the strangers stayed somewhere else.

Studying the Scriptures

Do activity A or B as you study Joshua 1.

A Rahab the Good

After reading Joshua 2; Hebrews 11:30–31; James 2:24–25, imagine you were one of the spies and write an explanation giving evidence of how Rahab demonstrated faith and explaining why you think the Israelites should save her when they conquer Jericho.

B A Scarlet Thread

What do you think the scarlet thread could represent? What did the Israelites do when they were in Egypt that was like this scarlet thread? (see Exodus 12:7, 13).

Joshua 3–4

Crossing the Jordan River

What helps you to have faith and confidence in our living prophets and apostles? Why is it important to have faith and confidence in them? Joshua 3–4 records what the Lord did that witnessed to those who desired to know that he was with Joshua as he had been with Moses.

Understanding the Scriptures

Joshua 3

Host (v. 2)—Camp

Bearing (v. 3)—Carrying

Pass over (v. 6)—Cross the Jordan River

Magnify (v. 7)—Make great

Brink (v. 8)—Edge

Hereby (v. 10)—By this

The waters of Jordan shall be cut off from the waters that come down from above (v. 13)—The Jordan River will stop flowing downstream.

They shall stand upon an heap (v. 13; see also v. 16)—The water upstream will be stopped and become higher, a place will open up for the armies of Israel to cross the Jordan River.

Brim (v. 15)—Edge

Failed (v. 16)—Stopped

Right against (v. 16)—Very close to

Clean (v. 17)—Completely

Joshua 4

Midst (vv. 3, 5, 8–10, 18)—Middle

Lodging, lodged (vv. 3, 8)—Resting, camping

Cut off (v. 7)—Stopped

Hasted (v. 10)—Hurried

Pitch (v. 20)—Set up

Studying the Scriptures

Do two of the following activities (A–C) as you study Joshua 3–4.

A Make a Journal Entry

Imagine you are watching the Levites carrying the ark. Write your journal entry for the day described in Joshua 3–4. Include how you feel about Joshua as a prophet of God.

B How Does It Happen Today?

In what ways does the Lord help confirm to us today that the President of the Church is a prophet of God?

C A Memorial

In Joshua 4 the Lord commanded Joshua to make a memorial of stones. Write in your notebook what you think a plaque placed on the memorial might say.

Joshua 5

A Special Visitor

Joshua 5 records some events that took place when the camp of Israel was in the promised land on the west side of the Jordan River. The Israelites showed their commitment to the Lord, and he showed them he was still with them as they faced their next challenge—the conquering of the land of Canaan.

Understanding the Scriptures

Joshua 5:10–15

Parched (v. 11)—Dried

Ceased (v. 12)—Stopped

Over against (v. 13)—In front of

Adversaries (v. 13)—Enemies

Host (v. 14)—Army

Studying the Scriptures

A Captain of the Lord's Host

1. It is not clear who the "captain of the Lord's host" is in Joshua 5:13–15, but verse 14 tells us that Joshua "fell on his face . . . and did worship." Other people in the scriptures have reacted like Joshua did: Cornelius, meeting Peter (see Acts 10:25–26); John, visited by an angel (see Revelation 19:10;

22:9); and Nephi's brethren toward Nephi (see 1 Nephi 17:55). Read also Exodus 3:1–6 where Moses saw the Lord. How do these incidents compare to what happened with Joshua and "the captain"? What might these incidents teach us about who visited Joshua?

2. Why do you think it was important for Joshua to have this experience at this time?

B Optional Activity

Write about a time when the Lord gave you added strength as you faced a challenge.

Joshua 6

The Walls Came Tumbling Down

In Joshua 2 we read about how two Israelites spied on Jericho, were protected by Rahab, and then brought back their report to Joshua. Joshua 6 tells how the Israelite army conquered the city and how Rahab was saved as the spies had promised.

Understanding the Scriptures

Joshua 6

Straitly (v. 1)—Tightly

Mighty men of valour (v. 2)—Trained soldiers or warriors

Bear before (v. 4)—Carry in front of

Bid you (v. 10)—Tell you to

Accursed (vv. 17–18)—Utterly destroyed by God

Kindred (v. 23)—Family

Without (v. 23)—Outside

In his firstborn (v. 26)—By losing his firstborn child to death

In his youngest son (v. 26)—By losing his youngest son to death

Noised (v. 27)—Talked about

Joshua 6—Seven

Notice how many times the number seven is used in this story. In Hebrew, seven (*sheva*) means "whole, complete, or perfect." By using the number seven the Lord emphasized that if Israel wholly kept his commandments and their covenants with him, they would be successful.

Studying the Scriptures ✏️

A Describe the Battle of Jericho

Briefly describe the battle of Jericho, making sure to include the following words: surround, trumpet, seven, ark, and Rahab.

B How Did They Feel? What Did They Think?

Write something you think each of the following people thought or felt as a part of the conquest of Jericho: an Israelite priest with a trumpet, a soldier in the army, a cousin to Rahab, and a citizen of Jericho. Jericho was the first city the armies of Israel battled after entering the land of Canaan. What do you think the children of Israel should have learned from how they won this battle that could have helped them as they continued their conquest of the promised land?

Joshua 7

Conquering the City of Ai

What happens when we sin and try to hide it? (see D&C 121:37). Even though other people may not know we are hiding our sins, who does know? What happens to our spiritual progress when we try to hide our sins? Joshua 7 records how the children of Israel learned a very important and impressive lesson about the importance of obedience and how it effects others, and that we cannot hide our disobedience from the Lord.

Understanding the Scriptures 🗝️

Joshua 7

Trespass (v. 1)—Sin

Accursed thing (vv. 1, 11–13, 15)—Things God commanded to be destroyed

Smote (v. 5)—Killed

Rent (v. 6)—Tore

Eventide (v. 6)—Evening

Content (v. 7)—Satisfied

Sanctify (v. 13)—Make clean and holy

Taketh, take (vv. 14–18)—Chooses, choose

Thus and thus (v. 20)—These are the things.

Spoils (v. 21)—Material possessions left after the people were destroyed

Shekels (v. 21)—Pieces (see Bible Dictionary, s.v. "weights and measures")

Coveted them (v. 21)—Wanted them

Joshua 7:22–26—Was Achan's Family Killed with Him?

The language of Joshua 7 makes it unclear as to whether Achan's family was killed with him or whether they were required to watch while he was killed and the accursed spoils burned. It is possible, however, that they were killed, especially if they helped Achan hide the things he took. The whole camp was commanded not to take anything from the city.

A Consequences of Sin

1. Elder Dean L. Larsen said, "There is no such thing as private sin" (in Conference Report, Apr. 1983, 49; or *Ensign*, May 1983, 35). In what ways does the story of Achan demonstrate this truth? For example, how did Achan's sin affect thirty-six Israelites and their families? Include in your answer how his sin affected all the camp of Israel, including Joshua, and how it affected Achan's family.

2. Think of and write about a modern example of how what seems to be a person's "private sin" can actually affect many others.

Joshua 8

Conquering Ai

Joshua 8 records how the Lord commanded Joshua to return and destroy the city of Ai after he resolved the situation caused by Achan's sin. Joshua 8 also tells how Joshua fulfilled the commandment given in Deuteronomy 27 to have Israel recite the blessings and cursings that might come to them.

Joshua 9

Tricked by the Gibeonites

By the time of the events in Joshua 9, the Israelites' fame was spreading through the land. One group of people, the Gibeonites, decided to trick the Israelites into making a peace treaty with them. Without asking the Lord for his approval, the Israelites made the treaty. They were angry when they found out the Gibeonites had tricked them, but they still honored the agreement. The people felt that honoring a promise was very important. The treaty incident taught the Israelites to counsel more with the Lord in their doings (see also Alma 37:37).

Joshua 10

The Sun and Moon Stand Still

The news of what the Israelites did in the land continued to spread. Joshua 10 tells about what several different groups of people tried to do to stop the Lord's people. We also read about what the Lord did to help his people overcome their enemies. As you read, think about who your "enemies" are as you try to obtain eternal life. In what ways can you follow Joshua's example? In what ways can you compare what the Lord did for Joshua to what the Lord can do for you?

Understanding the Scriptures 🗝️

Joshua 10

Slack not thy hand from thy servants (v. 6)—Do not turn away from helping us.

Men of valour (v. 7)—Trained soldiers or warriors

Stones (v. 11)—Hail

Hasted not (v. 13)—Was not quick

Keep (v. 18)—Guard

Smite the hindmost of them (v. 19)—Attack them from behind

Suffer (v. 19)—Allow

Fenced cities (v. 20)—Cities with strong walls

Moved his tongue (v. 21)—Spoke

Dismayed (v. 25)—Discouraged

Remain, remaining (vv. 28, 30, 33, 37, 39–40)—Stay alive

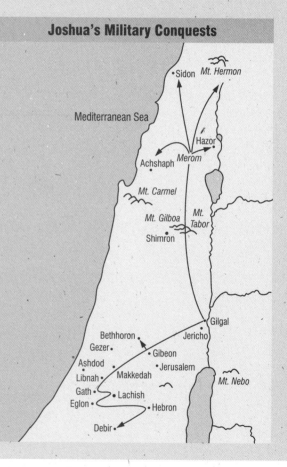

Joshua's Military Conquests

Studying the Scriptures ✏️

A Extra Help from the Lord

1. What two extraordinary acts did the Lord cause to help the Israelites battle their enemies?

82

2. What help do we have today to withstand temptations and wickedness? (You may want to read 1 Nephi 14:12–14 for some ideas.)

B Liken the Scriptures to Yourself

1. Read Joshua 10:24–25 and compare what you read to what the Lord said in 1 Corinthians 15:21–26; Doctrine and Covenants 76:58–62, 101–6; 103:5–8. Describe what Joshua told the captains to do and how it is a symbol of what Jesus will do for his people.

2. How can we prepare ourselves to be worthy of the Lord's help and protection?

Joshua 11–21

The Conquest of Canaan Continues

Joshua 11 describes more battles Joshua and the Israelites won. Chapter 11 also mentions that the Israelites "made war a long time" with some of the kings. We do not know why conquering these particular cities took the Israelites longer than conquering some of the first cities they battled against. Joshua 12 contains a list of the cities and kings the Israelites destroyed, and Joshua 13:1–14 contains a list of some of the cities and kings they did not destroy or drive out. We do not know exactly why these groups were not destroyed or driven out.

Beginning in Joshua 13 and continuing through Joshua 21 we read about how the land was divided between the tribes of Israel. Look in the map section of your scriptures to see the approximate boundaries of the land each tribe received (see Bible map 5).

Joshua 22

Settling the East Side of the Jordan

Before he was translated, Moses gave land on the east side of the Jordan River to the tribe of Reuben, the tribe of Gad, and half of the tribe of Manasseh if they would help the other tribes obtain the land on the west side of the Jordan River. This was accomplished by the time of the events in Joshua 22.

Joshua 22 tells about these two and one half tribes going back to receive their land inheritance on the east side of the Jordan. The other tribes misunderstood something they did on their way as breaking the law of Moses and they nearly had a war. But the leaders of the tribes came together and solved the problem peacefully. Like these ancient people, we should also find out the whole story before we judge others.

Joshua 23–24

"Choose You This Day"

As a young man, Joshua came out of Egypt and was a servant to Moses. He witnessed the plagues in Egypt, the miracles in the wilderness, and the murmuring and rebellions of the Israelites. Finally, he led the armies of Israel in their miraculous victories over the cities and kings of Canaan. Joshua 23–24 records the last sermon of this great (and now quite old) leader in Israel. Having studied a little about his life and his experiences, what do you think the major theme of his talk was?

Understanding the Scriptures

Joshua 23

Expel (v. 5)—Thrust them out

Cleave unto (vv. 8, 12)—Hold closely to

Take good heed (v. 11)—Pay close attention

Remnant of these nations (v. 12)—The survivors of the nations of Canaan

Scourges in your sides (v. 13) —Wounds, like the effect of a whip

Going the way of all the earth (v. 14)—To die

Joshua 24

The Flood (vv. 2–3, 14–15)— The Jordan River

Multiplied his seed (v. 3)— Increased the size of his family

I sent the hornet before you (v. 12)—I allowed your reputation to frighten others.

Consume (v. 20)—Destroy

Incline (v. 23)—Stretch out

Set them a statute and an ordinance (v. 25)—Gave them laws to be received by covenants

Studying the Scriptures

A Diagram Joshua's Advice

Make two diagrams in your notebook like the ones below to represent what Joshua told the Israelites in Joshua 23. In the first diagram, list under "Actions" what Joshua told Israel to do; then list under "Consequences" the blessings promised. In the second diagram, list under "Actions" what Joshua told Israel *not* to do, and then list under "Consequences" what would happen because of their disobedience.

Actions		Consequences
Joshua 24:6–8, 11	→	Joshua 24:9–10

Actions		Consequences
Joshua 24:12, 16	→	Joshua 24:15–16

1. List the ways the Lord had blessed the Israelites mentioned in Joshua 24:1–13.

2. Because of all that the Lord did for the family of Israel, what did Joshua ask them to do in verses 14–15?

3. How could Joshua's counsel in verse 15 bless your life today?

The Book of Judges

The book of Judges tells the history of Israel between the death of Joshua and the selection of Samuel as a prophet. While the book of Judges contains stories from Israelite history, these stories do not necessarily appear in historical order and are certainly not complete in relating Israelite history. Judges contains stories of idolatry and lawlessness that have parallels to our society today. Some of the stories are strange, tragic, or contain disgusting elements, and we wonder how the Israelites could be so wicked. But we also see the hand of the Lord as he helped Israel—even though they were mostly a spiritually weak people during these times. The book of Judges is a testimony that the Lord can help us in our weakness if we will turn to him.

Who Were the "Judges"?

"Judges" refers to leaders in the tribes of Israel who were chosen by God or the people to deliver the Israelites from their enemies. The judges were more like military leaders than actual judges who deal with issues of law. The people made them heroes, although the righteous judges tried to teach that the Lord is the real leader of Israel (see Judges 8:23; 11:27).

Who?	What Did They Do?
Ehud	Killed the enemy's king
Deborah	A prophetess who inspired the armies of Israel
Gideon	Relied on the Lord to lead Israel to victory with a very small army
Jephthah	Chosen by the people to lead Israel to victory, but made a foolish promise
Samson	Foreordained for a great work, but wasted his gifts

A Main Theme

After the Lord led the Israelites into their promised land with miraculous power, they did not continue to progress in their faith and commitment. They did not drive out all of the Canaanites and even began to adopt some of the Canaanites' evil practices. Consequently, the children of Israel lost their unity and broke up into tribes and families. A cycle of apostasy and deliverance occurred over and over in the book of Judges (see the illustration below). This cycle began when people blessed by God forgot him and became involved in practices he forbids, such as the religions of the Canaanites. The resulting sin and wickedness had consequences. One important consequence was that the Israelites lost the Lord's protection against their enemies and were taken into bondage. Finally, after their sincere humility and repentance, the Lord delivered his people and prospered them again.

What Can We Learn from the Book of Judges

Why would the Israelites let themselves go through this cycle over and over again—twelve times in the book of Judges alone? Individuals and groups of people in our day get caught in this cycle as well. President Spencer W. Kimball said: "Few men have ever knowingly and deliberately chosen to reject God and his blessings. Rather, we learn from the scriptures that because the exercise of faith has always appeared to be more difficult than relying on things more immediately at hand, carnal man has tended to transfer his trust in God to material things. Therefore, in all ages when men have fallen under the power of Satan and lost the faith, they have put in its place a hope in the 'arm of flesh' and in 'gods of silver, and gold, of brass, iron, wood, and stone, which see not, nor hear, nor know' (Dan. 5:23)—that is, in idols" ("The False Gods We Worship," *Ensign,* June 1976, 4). Look for this cycle as you read the book of Judges.

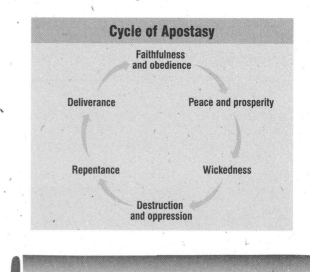

Cycle of Apostasy

Faithfulness and obedience

Peace and prosperity

Wickedness

Destruction and oppression

Repentance

Deliverance

Judges 1

Who Shall Fight for Us?

The first verse of Judges 1 contains the basic question of the book: "Who shall go up for us against the Canaanites first, to fight against them?" From what we read in the book of Joshua, the answer ought to be clear: the Lord. As President Kimball said in the quotation found above: "The exercise of faith has always appeared to be more difficult than relying on things more immediately at hand." This certainly seems true for the people in the book of Judges. The Israelites strayed from the faith and looked to mortal men and armies—instead of the Lord—to deliver them.

Judges 1 introduces another main idea in the book of Judges by telling us about the groups of people not driven out by the tribes of Israel. Instead of driving out and destroying these peoples, Judges 1 says the Israelites made treaties with them. The chart below shows how this was the first step in leaving God and embracing idolatry.

Disobedience Leads to Idolatry

Allowing the Canaanites to remain in the land

↓

Treaties, tribute, and tolerance

↓

Intermarriage

↓

Idolatry

Judges 2–3

Ehud Delivers Israel

Following the pattern of the chart above, Judges 1 describes how the Israelites did drive out the Canaanites and then how they made treaties with them. Judges 2–3 describes how the children of Israel then fell into idolatry because of intermarriage with the Canaanites. The cycle continued and they were eventually relieved with the help of a judge named Ehud.

Several times in Judges 2–3 we read that the Israelites "angered" the Lord. In fact, we learn that the Lord's anger was "hot" (see Judges 2:14, 20; 3:8). While this may sound harsh, knowing a little about the gods Baal and Ashtaroth might help us understand why the Lord was so angry. Baal was the male god of fertility, and Ashtaroth was his female companion and goddess of fertility. "Worship" included base violations of the law of chastity. All violations of the law of chastity are serious sins and spiritually destructive, but to do them in the name of worship is especially abominable to Heavenly Father.

Judges 4–5

Deborah the Prophetess

Judges 4–5 tells about how Israel was delivered from the bondage of their enemies under the direction of a woman named Deborah, who was both a judge and a prophetess. She prophesied that a woman would destroy the enemy's leaders. The prophecy was fulfilled when a non-Israelite woman named Jael killed the leader of the enemy army. The people learned that if they trusted the Lord, he could deliver them.

Judges 5 contains the words of a song the Israelites sang about this important event. Music can be a powerful way of praising God (see also D&C 25:12).

Judges 6–8

Gideon

Judges 6–8 tells the story of a great judge named Gideon who was raised up by the Lord to deliver the Israelites after they once again fell into apostasy.

Understanding the Scriptures

Judges 6

Hand (vv. 1–2, 9, 14)—Power

Prevailed (v. 2)—Stayed in power

Sown (v. 3)—Planted crops

Sustenance (v. 4)—Food

Greatly impoverished (v. 6)—Very poor

Oppressed (v. 9)—Persecuted

Threshed wheat (v. 11)—Separated wheat kernels from the outer casing of chaff

Befallen (v. 13)—Happened to

Kid (v. 19)—Young goat

Ephah (v. 19)—A little over a bushel (see Bible Dictionary, s.v. "weights and measures")

Flesh (vv. 19–21)—Meat

Consumed (v. 21)—Completely burned

Perceived (v. 22)—Realized

Fleece (vv. 37–40)—Piece or clump of the hide of a sheep or goat with the wool attached

Judges 6:17—"Shew Me a Sign"

The Lord commands us not to seek signs; rather we are to exercise faith and obedience before receiving a witness (see Ether 12:6; D&C 63:7–12). In this case, Gideon is not so much seeking a sign as he is trying to determine if the messenger who visited him was a true messenger, since he lived in a day and time of false religions and worship and did not want to be deceived by a messenger from a false source.

Judges 7

Pitched (v. 1)—Camped

Vaunt (v. 2)—Boast

Victuals (v. 8)—Food and provisions

Retained (v. 8)—Kept

Lay along (v. 13)—Collapsed

Save (v. 14)—Except

Companies (vv. 16, 20)—Groups

Pitchers (vv. 16, 19)—Jars

Beginning of the middle watch (v. 19)—After 10:00 P.M. (see Bible Dictionary, s.v. "watches")

Judges 8

Chide with (v. 1)—Contend

Gleaning (v. 2)—What is left after the harvesting is done

Vintage (v. 2)—Best grapes

Their anger was abated (v. 3)—They quit being angry.

Faint (vv. 4–5)—Tired and hungry

Secure (v. 11)—Not suspecting an attack

Discomfited (v. 12)—Defeated

Prey (v. 24)—Things that were captured

Ephod (v. 27)—A piece of clothing that fits over the neck, shoulders, and chest (see Bible Dictionary, s.v. "ephod")

Whoring after (vv. 27, 33)—Worshiping something instead of God

Subdued (v. 28)—Overcome

Of his body begotten (v. 30)—That he fathered

Concubine (v. 31)—A woman who was a servant and was also married to her master

Studying the Scriptures

Do three of the following activities (A–E) as you study Judges 6–8.

A First Things First

1. According to Judges 6:25–32, what was the first thing Gideon did as he attempted to deliver the Israelites from the Midianites?

2. Why do you think the Lord commanded Gideon to do this first?

B What Do You Think?

Why do you think the Lord reduced the size of the Israelite army before they went to battle?

C Finish These Sentences

Finish these sentences in your own words by using what you learned in Judges 7.

1. Gideon chose the 300 men who . . .

2. A man told Gideon about his dream in which . . .

3. The men in the army used their pitchers and trumpets to . . .

D A King?

1. Imagine you were selected to nominate Gideon as king of Israel. What would you say about him to convince others he would make a good king?

2. Write what you think Gideon would say after you nominated him (see Judges 8:22–23).

E What Was the Lesson?

How is the story of Gideon in Judges 6–8 an example of Doctrine and Covenants 1:19?

Judges 9–10

The Cycle Continues

Judges 9 tells about Abimelech, son of Gideon, who took advantage of his father's popularity and became king of Shechem. The story helps us see the problems in ignoring the Lord and solely putting our trust in man to lead and rule us.

Judges 10 records that Israel continued worshiping idols. Consequently, they lost the protection of the Lord and were conquered by their enemies. They then began to cry to the Lord for help. In this case, the Lord sternly rebuked the people when they cried for help. He told them to go "cry unto" the idols they worshiped and see if those gods would provide deliverance (see Judges 10:13–14).

Judges 11–12

The Story of Jephthah

Following the pattern of leaders in the book of Judges, Jephthah was an unlikely leader. He was the son of a harlot and once he was grown was thrust out of his family and home by his half brother. The Lord used this person from a lowly position, however, to deliver Israel from her enemies. He had faith in God and forsook idols, which gave him the strength of the Lord in his efforts.

Judges 13

The Birth of Samson

Have you ever asked your parents about the events surrounding your birth? What were their thoughts as they prepared to receive you in their life? What were their hopes for you as you grew? Judges 13 tells about the events of Samson's birth. As you read, look for what Samson's parents thought and hoped during the time surrounding his birth.

Understanding the Scriptures 🔑

Judges 13

Conceive (vv. 3, 5, 7)—Become pregnant

Unclean thing (v. 4)—Against the law of Moses (see Bible Dictionary, s.v. "clean and unclean")

No razor shall come upon his head (v. 5)—He will not cut his hair.

Countenance (v. 6)—Appearance

Very terrible (v. 6)—Creating a sense of humility and respect for the visitor

Nazarite (v. 7)—A special calling under the law of Moses (see Numbers 6:1–21)

Intreated (v. 8)—Prayed to

How shall we order the child? (v. 12)—By what rules or commandments should we raise the child?

Beware (v. 13)—Pay special attention or obey

Observe (v. 14)—Do

Detain thee (vv. 15–16)—Make you wait

Kid (vv. 15, 19)—Young goat

Do thee honour (v. 17)—Give you credit

Studying the Scriptures ✏️

A. A Special Calling

Describe how the following terms had something to do with Samson's special birth and calling: barren, drink, razor, angel, burnt offering.

B. Write a Letter

Imagine you are Samson's aunt or uncle and that Samson is now in his teen years. Based on what you read in Judges 13, write Samson a letter to help him understand what wonderful parents he has.

Judges 14–15

One Mistake After Another

Although Samson was born with great promises and blessings, Judges 14–15 tells us how he misused those God-given gifts. The blessings Samson was promised were just like the blessings promised us in our patriarchal blessings: the promises and blessings are only fulfilled when we live worthy of them (see D&C 130:20–21). As you read, think about what Samson's actions teach us about his focus in life.

Understanding the Scriptures 🔑

Judges 14

Occasion (v. 4)—An opportunity to confront

Had dominion (v. 4)—Ruled

Rent (v. 6)—Tore

Carcase (vv. 8–9)—Dead body

Expound, expounded (vv. 14, 19)—Explain, explained

Entice (v. 15)—Persuade, urge

Spoil (v. 19)—Goods

Judges 15

Chamber (v. 1)—Room

Firebrands, brands (vv. 4–5)—Torches

Be avenged (v. 7)—Get revenge

Fast (v. 13)—Tight

Judges 14:6, 19; 15:14—"The Spirit of the Lord Came Mightily upon Him"

In these instances, when we read that "the Spirit of the Lord" was upon Samson, it means that at one time he was living worthy to have the Spirit, which he lost as he became prideful and disobedient.

Studying the Scriptures ✏️

A. What's the Problem?

1. Make a chart like the following in your notebook, and fill it in with information you learn from the scripture reference listed:

Reference	What Samson Did	Why
Judges 14:5–6		
Judges 14:19		
Judges 15:1–5		
Judges 15:6–8		

2. Write about what you think Samson's biggest weakness was (see Judges 14–15).

Judges 16

Samson and Delilah

After reading Judges 13–15, what lessons do you think Samson could have learned from his experiences? As you read Judges 16, see if he really did learn those lessons.

Understanding the Scriptures 🔑

Judges 16

Compassed him (v. 2)—Surrounded him

Thread of a tow (v. 9)—Piece of string or flax

Occupied (v. 11)—Used

Vexed (v. 16)—No longer patient

Wist (v. 20)—Knew

Fetters (v. 21)—Chains

Grind (v. 21)—Make flour from grain

Sport (vv. 25, 27)—To make people laugh

Borne (v. 29)—Held

Studying the Scriptures

A Apply the Words of Modern Prophets and Apostles

How could Samson have benefitted from the following advice? Write your answer in your notebook. President N. Eldon Tanner of the First Presidency said: "I would like to say to you again, remember these three words: keep the covenants. And I think I am safe in saying to you that if you and your families will keep these covenants, you will be happy, you will be successful, you will be respected, you will have good families that you can take back into the presence of our Heavenly Father. All you will have to do is remember three words: keep the covenants, the obligations that you have taken upon yourselves, the pledges that you have made. Keep the covenants" (in Conference Report, Oct. 1966, 99).

B Not Very Obedient

Read Numbers 6:1–9 and list the requirements of a Nazarite. Next to each requirement, write a scripture reference from

Judges 14–16 that demonstrates a time when Samson disobeyed that requirement, and then briefly explain what he did.

Judges 17–21

Israel Suffers for Disobedience

Judges 17–21 can be tied together with a statement made in Judges 17:6 and then repeated as the last verse of Judges in 21:25: "In those days there was no king in Israel: every man did that which was right in his own eyes." The writer seemingly showed us the truth of these verses by what he wrote in Judges 17–21. These chapters describe some of the worst times in Israel's history and perhaps prepare us to understand why Israel thought they needed a king (which occurs early in the next book, 1 Samuel). Unfortunately, Israel didn't realize they could have made the Lord their king and that he would have given them peace and provided a way to solve the problems facing them. In this case, we must learn from Israel's mistakes rather than their successes.

The Book of Ruth

This short, significant story took place during the time of the book of Judges. Unlike most of the stories in the book of Judges, however, it is hopeful, full of faith, and has a happy ending.

The Faith of a Convert

It is especially interesting to note that Ruth was not an Israelite by birth but was a Moabite (see Bible Dictionary, s.v. "Moab"). Ruth married an Israelite of the tribe of Judah who lived in Moab during a famine. From the book of Ruth we can learn about the faith of a convert to the true gospel. We also learn that the love and mercy of the Lord are extended to those who desire it, even if they grew up outside of the covenant.

A Noble Posterity

You might be interested to know that Ruth's descendants include David, who was a king in Israel, and the Lord Jesus Christ. As you read, look for what Ruth did that showed her to be a worthy ancestor of the Savior.

Ruth 1

"Where You Will Go, I Will Go"

What is the most important thing that you ever gave up because of your commitment to the true gospel? As you read Ruth 1, think about what Ruth gave up.

Understanding the Scriptures

Ruth 1

Sojourn (v. 1)—Live

Left (v. 3)—Alone, widowed

Left of her two sons (v. 5)—Lost two sons to death

Visited (v. 6)—Blessed

Turn again (v. 11)—Go back

Tarry (v. 13)—Wait

Clave unto (v. 14)—Stayed with

Intreat (v. 16)—Ask

Whither (v. 16)—Wherever

Lodge, lodgest (v. 16)—Live

Stedfastly minded (v. 18)—Very determined

Moved about them (v. 19)—Talked among themselves

Afflicted (v. 21)—Caused to suffer

Studying the Scriptures

A Meeting Challenges

1. List at least three trials faced by people in Ruth 1.

2. Choose one trial that is like one you have faced, and briefly describe it.

3. What can you learn about facing your challenges from the examples in this chapter?

Ruth 2

Ruth Meets Boaz

President Spencer W. Kimball said, "God does notice us, and he watches over us. But it is usually through another person that he meets our needs" ("The Abundant Life," Ensign, July 1978, 4). Look for this idea as you continue reading the story of Ruth.

Ruth 3–4

Ruth and Boaz Marry

Ruth 3–4 records several customs that are not practiced today. The following explanations may help you as you read:

- Under the law of Moses, the nearest relative was responsible to take care of widows, including marrying those who could still have children (see Deuteronomy 25:5–10).

- Ruth followed certain customs in Ruth 3 to let Boaz know she was available for marriage. Nothing immoral took place. When Ruth asked Boaz to take her under his "skirt," she was saying in effect "Please take care of me."

- There was a man more closely related to Ruth than Boaz, but he was unwilling to accept the responsibilities of caring for Naomi and Ruth—especially the responsibility to marry Ruth. So Boaz was able to accept the responsibility.

Understanding the Scriptures

Ruth 2

Kinsman (vv. 1, 20)—Relative

Glean, gleaned (vv. 2–3, 7–8, 15–19, 23)—Pick up grain left over after the harvest

Reapers (vv. 3–7, 9, 14)—People who harvest crops

Light on (v. 3)—Go to

Kindred (v. 3)—Family

Sheaves (vv. 7, 15)—Stalks and ears of grain

Hence (v. 8)—Here

Abide (v. 8)—Stay

Vessels (v. 9)—Containers

Drawn (v. 9)—Pulled up from a well

Nativity (v. 11)—Birth

Recompense (v. 12)—Reward

Wings (v. 12)—Protection

Hither (v. 14)—Here, to this place

Reached (v. 14)—Gave

Sufficed (vv. 14, 18)—Full

Reproach (v. 15)—Shame

Of purpose (v. 16)—On purpose

Rebuke (v. 16)—Stop or reprimand

Even (v. 17)—Sundown

Beat out (v. 17)—To separate the grain from the chaff

Ephah (v. 17)—A little over a bushel (see Bible Dictionary, s.v. "weights and measures")

Reserved (v. 18)—Kept apart from, saved

Wrought, wroughtest (v. 19)—Produced

Near of kin (v. 20)—Closely related

Ruth 2—"Gleaning" the Fields of Boaz

According to the law of Moses, farmers were not to harvest all their crops, but they were to leave some in the field so that the poor could go through and harvest some food (see Leviticus 19:9–10).

Understanding the Scriptures

Ruth 3

Winnoweth (v. 2)—Separates the grain from the chaff

Threshing floor (v. 2)—Place where winnowing is done

Anoint (v. 3)—Perfume

Raiment (v. 3)—Clothing

Mark (v. 4)—Find out

Bade (v. 6)—Asked or commanded

Virtuous (v. 11)—Pure in thought and action

Requirest (v. 11)—Are requesting

Howbeit (v. 12)—However

Fall (v. 18)—Turn out

Ruth 4

Turn aside (v. 1)—Leave what you are doing and come speak with me.

Parcel (v. 3)—Piece

Advertise (v. 4)—Make something known

Redeem (vv. 4, 6)—Purchase or fulfill one's part of an agreement

Raise up the name of the dead (vv. 5, 10)—Provide children for a relative who has died

Mar (v. 6)—Ruin

Former (v. 7)—Earlier

Plucked (v. 7)—Took off

Testimony (v. 7)—The sign or witness of a formal agreement

Conception (v. 13)—Becoming pregnant

Restorer (v. 15)—One who replaces or gives back a thing or returns something to its original condition

Nourisher (v. 15)—One who feeds another and takes care of their needs

Studying the Scriptures

A What Do You Think?

Explain why you think Boaz was so kind to Ruth.

Studying the Scriptures

A Choosing a Husband or Wife

Give examples from Ruth 1–4 that show what qualities Boaz had as a husband (if you are a woman), or what qualities Ruth had as a wife (if you are a man).

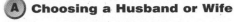

1. How might the things Boaz did for Ruth be similar to what Christ did (and does) for us?

2. How are Ruth's actions an example of what we can do to "come unto Christ"?

The First Book of Samuel

Prophets or Kings?

The book of 1 Samuel begins with the story of Samuel's birth and contains an account of his ministry. The book describes the ministry of a prophet to the kings of Israel, so 1 Samuel is essentially the story of the nation of Israel as well. The Israelites rejected the Lord's counsel to trust in him and be ruled by judges and prophets and instead asked for a king. Notice that the title of this book in your Bible says it is "Otherwise Called the First Book of the Kings."

Getting Ready to Study 1 Samuel

Samuel obviously did not write 1–2 Samuel, since we read of his death before the end of 1 Samuel. The book of 1 Samuel was written by someone in the time of King Solomon. For more information about 1 Samuel, see the Bible Dictionary, s.v. "Samuel, books of."

Important People in 1 Samuel

Eli and Samuel

Saul

Jonathan

David and Goliath

1 Samuel 1

"For This Child I Prayed"

President Spencer W. Kimball said, "Someday, when the whole story of this and previous dispensations is told, it will be filled with courageous stories of our women, of their wisdom and their devotion, their courage, for one senses that perhaps, just as women were the first at the sepulchre of the Lord Jesus Christ after his resurrection, our righteous women have so often been instinctively sensitive to things of eternal consequence" (in Conference Report, Apr. 1978, 6; or Ensign, May 1978, 5).

Samuel's mother, Hannah, could certainly be considered one of the women President Kimball referred to. As you read 1 Samuel 1, look for instances that show her greatness. Consider what it means for children to have parents like Hannah and Elkenah. Learning about them gives us examples to follow when we become parents.

Understanding the Scriptures

1 Samuel 1

Gave . . . portions (v. 4)—The law of Moses allowed the priest to keep some of the meat of a sacrifice offering for food. Some of the rest was returned to the family after the meat was cooked on the altar. Each family member received "portions," or parts, of what was returned to the family.

Worthy portion (v. 5)—Greater part

Adversary (v. 6)—Enemy, meaning the other wife, who was her rival

Provoked her sore (v. 6)—Continually tried to upset her

Fret (v. 6)—Unhappy and worried

Grieved (v. 8)—Sad

Bitterness (v. 10)—Sadness

Sore (v. 10)—Much

Vow (vv. 11, 21)—Promise

Affliction (v. 11)—Trouble or misery

No razor come upon his head (v. 11)—Not cut his hair (see Bible Dictionary, s.v. "Nazarite")

Abundance of my complaint and grief (v. 16)—Great pain and sadness

Petition (vv. 17, 27)—Request

Countenance (v. 18)—Face, expression

Knew his wife (v. 19)—Conceived a child with his wife

Weaned (vv. 22–24)—No longer fed by a mother's milk. Among the Israelites at this time, mothers usually breast-fed their children for three years.

Establish (v. 23)—Fulfill

Abode (v. 23)—Stayed home

Suck (v. 23)—Milk from the breast

Lent (v. 28)—Given

Studying the Scriptures

Do two of the following activities (A–C) as you study 1 Samuel 1.

A How to Meet Challenges

From the events you read about in 1 Samuel 1, what can you learn from Hannah to apply to your own life's experiences?

B What Do You Think It Would Be Like?

Describe what you think it would be like to be Hannah's child. Include in your answer some qualities you read about in 1 Samuel that show what kind of mother Hannah was.

C How Do You Dedicate Yourself to God?

Because Hannah dedicated Samuel to the Lord's service, Samuel would grow up with the priests and work with the tabernacle all his life. Obviously we do not dedicate our children to the Lord in the same way today; however, what do you think you could do as a parent to give your children the feeling Samuel had growing up, the feeling that he belonged to the Lord and was specially dedicated to the Lord's service all his life?

1 Samuel 2

Eli's Sons

Why should parents correct their children when the children do wrong? What happens if they are not corrected? How does the Lord feel about children being neglected? An additional example of parents' influence on the lives of their children can be found in 1 Samuel 2.

Understanding the Scriptures

1 Samuel 2

Exalted (v. 1)—Lifted high, increased

Arrogancy (v. 3)—Pride

Weighed (v. 3)—Judged

Girded (v. 4)—Clothed, covered

Ceased (v. 5)—Stopped

Barren (v. 5)—Unable to bear children

Waxed feeble (v. 5)—Become weak

Pillars (v. 8)—Posts (*Note:* This is poetic language. The people did not think and the Bible does not teach that the earth literally sits on posts.)

Keep the feet (v. 9)—Protect and care for

Prevail (v. 9)—Overcome

Adversaries (v. 10)—Enemies

Anointed (vv. 10, 35)—Chosen

Sons of Belial (v. 12)—Worthless, wicked men

Fleshhook (vv. 13–14)—Tool with which priests could reach the sacrifice and remove pieces of the meat

Abhorred (v. 17)—Hated

Girded (v. 18)—Clothed

Ephod (vv. 18, 28)—Part of the attire of a high priest (see Bible Dictionary, s.v. "ephod")

Seed (v. 20)—Children

Lay (v. 22)—Have sexual relations

Intreat (v. 25)—Plead for mercy

Habitation (vv. 29, 32)—House

Despise (v. 30)—Look down upon

Esteemed (v. 30)—Valued

Cut off thine arm (v. 31)—Punish by taking away your strength. Arm is symbolic of strength.

Consume thine eyes (v. 33)—Be constantly on one's mind

In the flower of their age (v. 33)—A young age

I will build him a sure house (v. 35)—I will give him continued posterity.

Crouch to him (v. 36)—Bow down

1 Samuel 2:12–17, 22—The Sins of Eli's Sons

According to the law of Moses, the priests were to receive certain portions of the sacrifice to eat, but they were only to receive it after the fat was burned on the altar, and they were to receive no additional pieces. When Eli's sons took what did not belong to them and took it before they should have, they were robbing God of his offering and cheating the people. Notice that because of Eli's sons' actions, the people disliked offering sacrifices (see 1 Samuel 2:17). To make things worse, verse 22 says they committed fornication with women who came to the temple.

Studying the Scriptures

Do two of the following activities (A–D) as you study 1 Samuel 2.

A A Song for the Lord

1. Choose what you think would be a good title for Hannah's song in 1 Samuel 2:1–10.

2. Choose something Hannah said about the Lord in this song that impresses you, and explain why.

B Applying the Story Today

After reading 1 Samuel 2:12–17, explain what you think modern Aaronic Priesthood holders could learn from this story. Especially consider what verse 17 says.

C Be a Prosecuting Attorney

You have been assigned to bring Eli and his sons to justice. Read 1 Samuel 3:13 and list the crimes you would charge them with and the evidence you have that they are guilty.

D The Duties of Parents

Read Mosiah 4:14–15; Doctrine and Covenants 68:25–31; 93:40–43 and list what the Lord commands parents to teach their children.

1 Samuel 3

Samuel Hears the Lord

In 1 Samuel 2 we read that the Lord was displeased with Eli. The Lord told Eli that he would raise up another prophet. Chapter 3 tells about Samuel's calling to replace Eli as priest and also to be a prophet to Israel.

As you read about what happened to Samuel, ask yourself the following questions: When and how might the Lord make his will known to me? How do I respond to the guidance and inspiration he gives?

Understanding the Scriptures

Samuel 3

Precious (v. 1)—Rare, not happening often

Ere (v. 3)—Before

Perceived (v. 8)—Realized, understood

Vile (v. 13)—Wicked

Restrained them not (v. 13)—Did not stop them

Purged (v. 14)—Removed, taken away

Whit (v. 18)—Bit

Fall to the ground (v. 19)—Not come true

Studying the Scriptures

A The Calling of a New Prophet

1. According to 1 Samuel 3:1, why did the Lord need to call a new prophet?

2. What can we learn from Samuel's example about how to respond when the Lord, through his servants, calls us to serve?

1 Samuel 4–6

The Ark of the Covenant

When we keep the commandments, we grow in confidence and faith in God. When we do not keep the commandments, we begin to lose confidence and faith and often turn to outward things to make up for our lack of inner strength. The Israelites were in that situation in 1 Samuel. Chapter 4 tells us that the Israelites believed they could defeat their enemies if they took the ark of the covenant with them to battle. They did not understand that the ark, like a temple, was an outward symbol of deep spiritual meaning and that it only blessed the Israelites when they were faithful to the Lord and his covenants, which the ark represented. In other words, God could deliver the Israelites from their enemies if they were true to him, but instead they looked to a symbol of him, believing that the physical object itself had supernatural power. To their great disappointment, the Israelites not only lost their battle but allowed the Philistines to take possession of the ark of the covenant.

Although the Israelites were wrong to use the ark of the covenant in a superstitious way, the ark remained an important symbol of the Israelite religion, and the Lord desired it to be placed in his tabernacle. Thus, 1 Samuel 5–6 tells about what happened to the Philistines after they captured the ark that made them decide to later return it to the Israelites.

1 Samuel 7

Repentance Brings the Victory

After losing their battle with the Philistines by trying to use the ark as a symbol of good luck, the Israelites had two choices.

They could try getting another god to save them (which is what many superstitious people did), or they could repent and exercise more faith and trust in the living God, instead of the symbol of the living God. As you read 1 Samuel 7, notice what Samuel counseled the people to do and what happened when the people followed his counsel.

Understanding the Scriptures 🔑

1 Samuel 7

Fetched up (v. 1)—Took

Sanctified (v. 1)—Made clean according to the law of Moses

Lamented after the Lord (v. 2) —Sought the Lord with sorrow for what had happened to them

Strange (v. 3)—Gods not known to the children of Israel

Drew water, and poured it out before the Lord (v. 6)—An act of filling a container with water and pouring it out in a specific manner.

Judged (vv. 6, 15–17)—Led or governed

Subdued (v. 13)—Defeated

Coasts (v. 14)—Borders

Studying the Scriptures ✏️

A What Saves?

1. Read 1 Samuel 4:3 and explain what the people thought would save them.

2. What do people today believe will save them?

3. What did Samuel do in 1 Samuel 7, and what did he ask the people to do so they could be saved from their enemies?

4. In what ways could we use these same things to overcome our challenges and temptations today? Give an example.

1 Samuel 8

"Give Us a King"

The Israelites' success against the Philistines is told in 1 Samuel 7. After their victory, it seems that the Israelites would be more willing to do what Samuel asked of them, But they were still weak in faith. The Israelites did not want to follow Samuel. They demanded a king! They had rejected the Lord as their king. Chapter 8 of 1 Samuel records that the Lord comforted Samuel, telling him the people had not rejected Samuel, but had rejected the Lord. Later, they changed from believing the ark of the covenant was the source of their protection to believing that having a strong leader was their key to success.

Other surrounding nations had kings. Through the prophet Moses, however, the Lord told Israel they were a "peculiar" people to him, meaning they were specially chosen and set apart from the world to be his people and to do the work of saving the rest of his children. Much of the law of Moses helped remind

Israelites that they were different from other nations and promised them great blessings if they remained different and did not seek the acceptance and riches of the world. Of course the Israelites' desire to be like those around them was not just a problem in ancient times. Today there are some Church members who want to live like the people around them who do not share the same beliefs and standards. Often the ways of the world are quite attractive.

Without a strong testimony that God lives and that he gives us commandments for our good, we may choose to act a certain way because "everyone else is doing it" and lose the blessings of being God's covenant people. In 1 Samuel 8 we are taught that the attractiveness of worldly practices tempted the Israelites and threatened their standing as a "peculiar people."

Understanding the Scriptures 🔑

1 Samuel 8

Lucre (v. 3)—Money

Bribes (v. 3)—To accept money or favors as payment to do something illegal or dishonest for someone else

Howbeit yet (v. 9)—But

Manner (vv. 9, 11)—Judgment or justice

Goodliest (v. 16)—Strongest, best

Studying the Scriptures ✏️

Do two of the following activities (A–D) as you study 1 Samuel 8.

A What Will Happen?

The Lord had Samuel explain to the people what would happen if they had a king. Using 1 Samuel 8:10–18, write what would happen in each of the following cases if Israel had a king. For each, give a scripture reference that supports your answer.

1. The king decides that he needs more servants on his staff.

2. The king is offended by another king and decides to go to war to defend his honor.

3. The king sets the budget for his expenses and decides he needs more money.

4. The people are unhappy with the king and he learns of their complaints.

B Motivations

1. Read 1 Samuel 8:1–9, 19–22 and explain why the people wanted a king.

2. What was wrong with their reason for desiring a king?

C Prepare an Outline for a Talk

Suppose you are asked to give a talk on what Latter-day Saints can learn from 1 Samuel 8. List three main ideas you would include in your talk.

D "Know This, That Every Soul Is Free"

What does 1 Samuel 8 teach you about the Lord, knowing that he still allowed the Israelites to have a king? (Alma 29:4–5 may help with your answer.)

1 Samuel 9–10

Saul Anointed King

In 1 Samuel 8 the people of Israel said they wanted a king, even though the prophet Samuel counseled them against it. Chapter 9 in 1 Samuel teaches us how much the Lord loves his people when we realize that even though the people of Israel did not follow the Lord's counsel, he still helped them by inspiring his prophet to choose and train a king for them. As you read, look for what you can learn about callings from the Lord.

Understanding the Scriptures

1 Samuel 9

Goodly, goodlier (v. 2)—Pleasant, agreeable

Leave (v. 5)—Quit

Take thought for (v. 5)—Worry about

Spent (v. 7)—Gone

Bidden, bid (vv. 13, 22, 27)—Invited, invite

Communed (v. 25)—Spoke

Pass on (v. 27)—Continue traveling

1 Samuel 10

Vial (v. 1)—Container

Sepulchre (v. 2)—Grave

Left the care (v. 2)—Quit worrying about

Salute (v. 4)—Greet

Garrison (v. 5)—Fort, army station

Adversities and tribulations (v. 19)—Trials and troubles

Taken (vv. 20–21)—Chosen

1 Samuel 9–10—The Prophet Chooses a King for Israel

Following the same pattern we use in the Church today, Saul was called by one having authority from the Lord (see Articles of Faith 1:5), he was set apart by one having authority, he was trained, and he was presented to the people for their sustaining vote (see 1 Samuel 10:24).

Studying the Scriptures

Do two of the following activities (A–C) as you study 1 Samuel 9–10.

A Write a News Report

Imagine that you were a faithful Israelite news reporter who followed Saul through all the experiences of 1 Samuel 9–10. Write a brief article describing why Saul is a good choice for Israel's king. Use scripture references to support your ideas.

B Write a Journal Entry

Based on what you learned from 1 Samuel 9–10, write how you think Saul might have felt after his experience of being called as king in Israel. Pay special attention to 1 Samuel 9:21; 10:6, 9, 20–27.

C Apply the Words of Modern Prophets and Apostles

How does the following statement quoted by President Harold B. Lee relate to what happened in 1 Samuel 10:26–27: "That person is not truly converted until he sees the power of God resting upon the leaders of this church, and until it goes down into his heart like fire" (in Conference Report, Apr. 1972, 118; or *Ensign*, July 1972, 103).

1 Samuel 11

Saul Leads Israel to Battle

The story of Samuel calling Saul and presenting him to the people as their leader is told in 1 Samuel 9–10. Chapter 11 of 1 Samuel contains an account of Saul successfully leading Israel against their enemies. Because Israel was successful, the people gained confidence in Saul's abilities to lead them.

1 Samuel 12

The Lord Is Still King

After the Israelites defeated their enemies in 1 Samuel 11, the people might have been tempted to say to Samuel, "We told you that a king would be good for us." However, 1 Samuel 12 records what Samuel said to the Israelites to make sure they resisted this temptation. He reminded Israel that the Lord had delivered them from their enemies—no matter who their mortal leader was. Even though the Lord let them have a man for their king, he was still the real king of Israel (see 1 Samuel 12:12). Samuel promised the people that if they rebelled against the Lord, they would lose his helping hand—no matter how great their earthly king.

1 Samuel 13

Saul Acts Foolishly

Suppose you were one of twenty Church members on an island and the only priesthood holders were deacons in the Aaronic Priesthood. Would it be acceptable for those deacons to administer the sacrament rather than let all the members go without that important ordinance? Why not? In 1 Samuel 13 we read about a situation like this.

Understanding the Scriptures 🔑

1 Samuel 13

Garrison (vv. 3–4, 23)—Fort

Strait (v. 6)—Difficult situation

Distressed (v. 6)—Worried

Salute (v. 10)—Greet

Supplication (v. 12)—Fervent prayer and sacrifice

Spoilers (v. 17)—Men assigned to destroy crops, homes, cattle, and so on

Smith (v. 19)—Craftsman

Goads (v. 21)—Spears

Passage (v. 23)—Way to get through the mountains

1 Samuel 13:8—"According to the Set Time That Samuel Had Appointed"

In 1 Samuel 10:8, Samuel asked Saul to meet him in Gilgal, where Samuel would offer sacrifices for him.

Studying the Scriptures ✏️

(A) If He Could Do It Over Again

Sometimes we wish we could relive a certain situation and choose differently. Rewrite the story in 1 Samuel 13:1–16 so

that it tells the story in a way that what Saul did pleased the Lord and Samuel.

1 Samuel 14

A Foolish Oath

When we are disobedient and do not repent, we lose the companionship of the Holy Ghost. Without the Holy Ghost we are more likely to make poor decisions. Saul's actions in 1 Samuel 14 are an example of this principle.

The account in 1 Samuel 14 describes how Saul, hoping to inspire his men and receive help from God, commanded the army of Israel to fast in preparation for their battle against the Philistines. To enforce the command, Saul said that any man who ate would be put to death. He did not know, however, that his own son, Jonathan, was not present when he gave the command. Jonathan ate some honey, and Saul prepared to take the life of his son. Fortunately, the people pled with Saul and he did not carry out this foolish oath.

1 Samuel 15

The Importance of Obedience

Elder Bruce R. McConkie said, "Obedience is the first law of heaven, the cornerstone upon which all righteousness and progression rest" (Mormon Doctrine, 2d. ed. [1966], 539). As you read 1 Samuel 15, consider what it teaches about the principle of obedience.

Understanding the Scriptures 🔑

1 Samuel 15

Laid wait (vv. 2, 5)—Hid in preparation for attack

Spare (v. 3)—Save

Fatlings (v. 9)—The secondborn of animals

Vile and refuse (v. 9)—Worthless and unclean according to the law of Moses

Fly upon the spoil (v. 19)—Rushed to take all the good things

Delicately (v. 32)—Humbly

1 Samuel 15:2–3—Why Completely Destroy the Amalekites?

There are very few times in scripture that God commanded a people be destroyed. The Amalekites were extremely cruel to the dren of Israel when they came out of Egypt (see Deuteronomy 25:17–19). They picked out the weak, sick, and elderly that struggled along at the back of the march and killed these stragglers.

Studying the Scriptures

Do two of the following activities (A–C) as you study 1 Samuel 15.

(A) Make a Comparison

Compare what Samuel told Saul to do (see 1 Samuel 15:1–3) with what Saul actually did (see 1 Samuel 15:4–9).

(B) Excuses

1. What excuses did Saul give for what he did instead of being obedient to what he was commanded to do?

2. Write a letter to Saul explaining why his excuses for disobedience are not acceptable. Make sure you respond to each of his excuses.

(C) The Real Reason

1. Finally in 1 Samuel 15:24, Saul confessed why he did what he did. Identify some reasons people give today for their acts of disobedience. How are they similar to Saul's response?

2. What do you think can help strengthen us from falling into the temptation to justify our actions?

1 Samuel 16

The Lord Chooses a New King

Because of Saul's disobedience, he was told that another king would be chosen for Israel (see 1 Samuel 13:13–14; 15:26–28). If you were choosing the new king, what would you be looking for? As you read 1 Samuel 16, notice what the Lord said to Samuel about choosing a new king.

Understanding the Scriptures

1 Samuel 16

Heifer (v. 2)—A young cow
Countenance (vv. 7, 12)—Appearance
Cunning (vv. 16, 18)—Skilled

Prudent (v. 18)—Understanding
Comely (v. 18)—Handsome
Kid (v. 20)—Young goat

1 Samuel 16:14–15—"An Evil Spirit from the Lord"

The Joseph Smith Translation changed 1 Samuel 16:14–15 to indicate that the evil spirit was *not* of the Lord.

Studying the Scriptures

(A) Scripture Mastery—1 Samuel 16:7

What does 1 Samuel 16:7 teach us about the way the Lord looks at us and the way we should look at others?

(B) The Power of Music

1. Music has great power to influence our feelings. What did David's music do for Saul?

2. We should realize that what David's music did for Saul was only temporary. What would have given those feelings to Saul more permanently?

3. How do people today use music in the same way Saul did?

4. Name a hymn or song that helps you feel the influence of the Holy Ghost.

1 Samuel 17

David and Goliath

The story of David and Goliath is one of the most well-known of any in the Bible. As you read the story in 1 Samuel this time, look for what David considered his source of strength and courage. Also ask yourself questions like these: What effect could the events in chapter 16 have on the events in chapter 17? Why was it significant that David defeated Goliath after he had been "anointed" by the Lord's prophet?

Chapter 17 of 1 Samuel may help you think of answers to these questions as well: What "Goliaths" are there in your life? What covenants have you entered into with the Lord that can give you strength to overcome your "Goliaths"? How can what David did to show his faith in the Lord's promises apply to situations in your life?

Understanding the Scriptures 🗝

1 Samuel 17

Set the battle in array (vv. 2, 8, 21)—Put the soldiers in their places for battle

Champion (vv. 4, 51)—A man who represents the whole army and fights a representative from the other army to decide the winner of a battle

Six cubits and a span (v. 4)—Measurements of length (see Bible Dictionary, s.v. "weights and measures")

Coat of mail (vv. 5, 38)—Armor made of small metal pieces husked together

Shekels (vv. 5, 7)—A measurement of weight (see Bible Dictionary, s.v. "weights and measures")

Bearing (v. 7)—Carrying

Defy (vv. 10, 25–26)—Challenge, make fun of

The man went among men for an old man (v. 12)—He was considered old.

Ephah (v. 17)—A little over a bushel (see Bible Dictionary, s.v. "weights and measures")

Look how far thy brethren fare (v. 18)—See how your brethren are doing.

Take their pledge (v. 18)—Bring back a report of how they are doing.

Trench (v. 20)—Battle lines

Reproach (v. 26)—Shame

After the former manner (v. 30)—Like before

Assayed to go (v. 39)—Tried to see if it would work

Proved (v. 39)—Used

Scrip (v. 40)—Bag

Disdained (v. 42)—Insulted him as being unworthy to stand up against him

Staves (v. 43)—Sticks

Hasted (v. 48)—Hurried

Studying the Scriptures ✏

Do two of the following activities (A–C) as you study 1 Samuel 17.

Ⓐ What Did They Say?

1. Write down one thing each of the following people said in 1 Samuel 17: Goliath, Jesse, Eliab, David, and the men of Israel.

2. Write what you think are the two significant things David said or did in 1 Samuel 17, and explain why.

Ⓑ Draw a Picture

Use information in 1 Samuel 17 to draw some part of the David and Goliath story.

Ⓒ Make a List

1. List what you think are the three biggest temptations facing people your age in the Church in your area.

2. Make a list of five ideas or quotations from 1 Samuel 17 that you would use in a talk entitled "Overcoming Our Personal Challenges."

1 Samuel 18–23

Saul Seeks David's Life

After defeating Goliath, David became a national hero. He was invited to live with Saul, where he worked closely with Saul and where he became close friends with Saul's son Jonathan. Saul grew jealous of David's popularity, however, and attempted to kill David several times and to get David's enemies to kill him.

In 1 Samuel 18–23 Saul was trying to take David's life and David continued to flee and hide from Saul. Throughout these incidents, David kept his friendship with Jonathan. On several occasions, Jonathan helped protect David from danger.

From these chapters, we see a growing difference between David, who sought to be right with God, and Saul, whose disobedience and unwillingness to repent left him cut off from God's influence. Saul grew increasingly wicked and murderous while David received the help of the Lord unto deliverance.

By the end of these chapters, David had gained many followers who looked forward to the day when he would be king in Israel.

1 Samuel 24

Respect for the Lord's Anointed

Several instances where Saul tried to take David's life are recorded in 1 Samuel 18–23. In 1 Samuel 24 we are told about a time when David had the opportunity to take Saul's life but did not. The reasons he did not can teach us an important lesson concerning our respect and loyalty to those called by the Lord.

Understanding the Scriptures 🗝

1 Samuel 24

Smote him (v. 5)—Made him feel guilty

Stayed his servants (v. 7)—Kept his men from attacking

Wherefore hearest thou (v. 9)—Why do you listen to

Bade (v. 10)—Encouraged

Cut off my seed (v. 21)—Kill my children and their children

Hold (v. 22)—Place of safety and hiding

Apply David's reason for not killing Saul to a situation today where friends are criticizing a Church leader in your presence. Write how you would answer this.

1 Samuel 25–26

Love Your Enemies

David demonstrated that he would be kind to Saul, who had tried to kill him. In 1 Samuel 25 David was taught about giving others the same consideration as he did Saul. David and his men asked for some supplies from a man named Nabal; Nabal treated them rudely. In response, David and his men prepared to attack. Nabal's wife, Abigail, heard about what was happening and acted wisely to keep David from attacking and killing her husband. In the process David realized his revengeful actions were not right. A short time later, Nabal died, and the problem was solved anyway. After Nabal's death David married Abigail as one of his wives.

When Jesus gave the Sermon on the Mount, he told the people to "love your enemies" and "bless them that curse you" (Matthew 5:44). Over a thousand years earlier, David practiced these principles in the way he dealt with Saul. As you read, think about the following statement by President Howard W. Hunter and how it might apply not only to this chapter but, more importantly, to our lives today:

"Think of what this admonition alone [to love your enemies] would do in your neighborhood and mine, in the communities in which you and your children live, in the nations which make up our great global family. I realize this doctrine poses a significant challenge, but surely it is a more agreeable challenge than the terrible tasks posed for us by the war and poverty and pain the world continues to face.

"How are we supposed to act when we are offended, misunderstood, unfairly or unkindly treated, or sinned against? What are we supposed to do if we are hurt by those we love, or are passed over for promotion, or are falsely accused, or have our motives unfairly assailed?

"Do we fight back? Do we send an ever-larger battalion? Do we revert to an eye for an eye and a tooth for a tooth, or . . . do we come to the realization that this finally leaves us blind and toothless?" (in Conference Report, Oct. 1992, 23; or Ensign, Nov. 1992, 18).

1 Samuel 26

Trench (vv. 5, 7)—Protected area in the middle of the camp

Cruse (vv. 11–12, 16)—Container

Ⓐ Make a Comparison

Read first what Saul tried to do to David in 1 Samuel 18:10–11; 19:9–12; 24:1–2, and then review what David did to Saul in 1 Samuel 24; 26. What does David's statement in 1 Samuel 26:23 tell us about why he did what he did in 1 Samuel 26? Think of a way you could apply David's example in your life and begin doing it today.

1 Samuel 27

David among the Philistines

After the events of 1 Samuel 26 David still did not trust Saul. In 1 Samuel 27 David fled and lived among the Philistines for a period of time. Chapter 27 also tells how during that time he tried to fulfill the Lord's original commands to the Israelites to eliminate all the idolatrous and wicked people from the land.

1 Samuel 28

Saul's Spiritual Darkness

Perhaps the lowest point in Saul's life is recorded in 1 Samuel 28. Because Saul could not get any revelation from God concerning how he should lead Israel, he went to a witch to see if he could get some help from spiritualists, or those who seek to contact the spirits of the dead for advice and counsel. In chapter 28 the witch claimed to have brought forward the prophet Samuel from the dead. President Joseph Fielding Smith said that it should be obvious that dead prophets do not respond to the call of witches and that the entire event was under the influence of the devil, who certainly must have been pleased with what had occurred in Saul's life (see Answers to Gospel Questions, 5 vols. [1957–66], 109).

1 Samuel 29–31

David's Success and Saul's Death

In 1 Samuel 29–31 is recorded how the Philistines decided to once again attack the Israelites. Worried about whether David might turn against them, they asked him to leave their land.

David and his men left. Upon leaving, David and his men continued to destroy the idolatrous enemies of Israel. When David obtained goods and cattle, he sent portions of them to each of the cities in Judah. In this way David began to build support for the time when Saul would die and he would lead Israel.

The book of 1 Samuel ends with the death of the first king in Israel. Saul saw that they were going to lose the battle against the Philistines. Rather than die at the hands of the Philistines, Saul asked his armourbearer to take his life, but the armourbearer would not. So Saul leaned on his own sword and took his own life.

The Second Book of Samuel

The Story of the Second King

As noted in the title of this book in your Bible, the book of 2 Samuel is "Otherwise Called the Second Book of the Kings." The story of Saul is found in 1 Samuel along with the story of the first king in Israel, and 2 Samuel is the story of the second king, David. Samuel could not have written the book of 2 Samuel since he died before the end of 1 Samuel. For more information on 1–2 Samuel, see the Bible Dictionary, s.v. "Samuel, books of."

Important People in 2 Samuel

Ishbosheth—Son of Saul who claimed the kingdom after his father's death

Abner—Leader of Saul's army who first supported Ishbosheth but then joined with David

Joab—Leader of David's army who killed Abner

Mephibosheth—Son of Jonathan who was disabled and honored and protected by David

Bathsheba—Woman with whom David committed adultery

Uriah—Bathsheba's husband whom David had killed so he could marry his wife

Nathan—Prophet in the days of David

Ammon—Son of David who was killed by his brother Absalom

Absalom—Son of David who killed his brother and tried to take the kingdom from his father

2 Samuel 1–3

After Saul's Death

In the last chapter of 1 Samuel, we read that Saul tried to get his armourbearer to kill him. When the man wouldn't, Saul fell upon his own sword and died. In 2 Samuel 1 the story is told of a man who thought he could gain David's favor by claiming to

be the one who killed Saul. This man also brought before David the crown and bracelet that signified that Saul was king. When David found out that Saul and Jonathan were dead, he mourned. He also had the man killed who took credit for Saul's death. The last verses of 2 Samuel 1 are the words of a psalm, or song, that David wrote for the occasion.

David was then directed by the Lord to go to the land of Judah. There, the people made him king of Judah. During that same time period, the captain of Saul's army helped make Saul's son Ishbosheth the king over the rest of Israel. Some fighting between David's men and the men of Ishbosheth is explained in 2 Samuel 2–3. These chapters help us understand that David had no desire to act in a revengeful way against his enemies.

2 Samuel 4–5

David Becomes King

In 2 Samuel 4 it is recorded that eventually men seeking favor from David killed Ishbosheth and brought his head to David. David had these men killed for their actions. Even with all Saul tried to do to him, David loved and honored Saul and his family. With Ishbosheth dead, the rest of the leaders in Israel came to David and asked him to be their king.

Chapter 5 of 2 Samuel then tells about how David captured the city of Jerusalem—a city that seemed nearly impossible to conquer in those days because it was located on a natural hill surrounded by three deep valleys. Jerusalem was very easy to

...end because of these valleys. Jerusalem was an important city to obtain because it included Mount Moriah where Abraham went to sacrifice Isaac. David made Jerusalem the capitol city of Israel.

2 Samuel 6

The Ark of the Covenant Comes to Jerusalem

After the Israelites got the ark of the covenant back from the Philistines, they put the ark in a safe place and guarded it from being captured again. In 2 Samuel 6 it tells how David established Jerusalem as the capitol city of Israel and decided to house the ark of the covenant there to symbolize that the Lord was with them in their capitol.

2 Samuel 7

David Wants to Build a Temple

How would you feel if you thought up and planned to do something for the Lord and his Church that you thought was very special and then found out he wanted you to do something else? Chapter 7 of 2 Samuel records that this is essentially what happened to David. As you read, notice how David responded to what the Lord said to him.

Understanding the Scriptures 🔑

2 Samuel 7

Rest (vv. 1, 11)—Peace

Curtains (v. 2)—Portable tent, tabernacle

Afflict (v. 10)—Trouble

Which shall proceed out of thy bowels (v. 12)—Your direct offspring or descendants

Chasten (v. 14)—Discipline for the purpose of loving correction

Rod (v. 14)—A stick, branch, or twig

Stripes (v. 14)—To be struck with a stick or whip

Is this the manner of man (v. 19)—Is this the way you deal with man

Confirmed (v. 24)—Established, made sure

2 Samuel 7:11—What Kind of House Was the Lord Promising to Build David?

The "house" David wanted to build for the Lord was a temple. The "house" the Lord promised to build David was a posterity—especially a posterity of rulers. Although David was not permitted to build the temple (see activity A below), the Lord did build the house he promised to David. The kings of Judah were descendants of David, as was the King of Kings—Jesus Christ—who interestingly enough promised to help all who follow him obtain "mansions" in the world to come (see John 14:1–3).

Studying the Scriptures ✏️➡️

A) Insight from Other Scripture

Read 1 Chronicles 22:7–8 and explain why the Lord did not want David to build a permanent temple.

B) How Did David Feel?

1. Reread the introduction to 2 Samuel 7 and think about how you would feel if you were in a situation similar to David's. Then read 2 Samuel 7:18–29 and tell how David felt about what the Lord told him.

2. Write in your notebook and mark in your scriptures the parts of verses you think best express David's feelings.

3. Explain why you think David felt the way he did.

2 Samuel 8–10

David's Political and Personal Success

In 2 Samuel 8, 10 is a description of how David continued to conquer the land promised by God to the Israelites. The Lord commanded the Israelites to conquer people in the land promised them from the time of Joshua, but David was the one who finally fulfilled the command most fully. At the same time, the record says he ruled his own people with fairness. Chapter 9 of 2 Samuel contains a great example of David's justice in the account of how he fulfilled his promise to Saul's son Jonathan to take care of Saul's family.

Understanding the Scriptures 🔑

2 Samuel 9

Lame (vv. 3, 13)—Walk with difficulty

Did reverence (v. 6)—Paid respect by bowing down

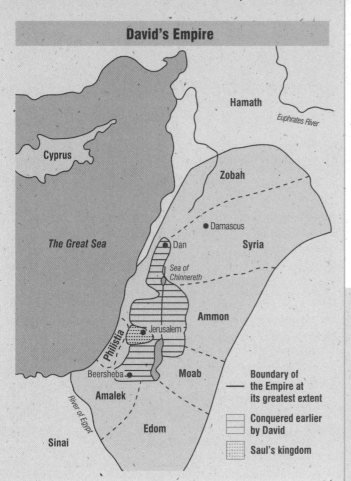

David's Empire

Hamath

Euphrates River

Cyprus

Zobah

• Damascus

The Great Sea

Dan

Syria

Sea of
Chinnereth

Ammon

Jerusalem

Philistia

Beersheba

Moab

Amalek

River of Egypt

Edom

Sinai

— Boundary of
the Empire at
its greatest extent

▤ Conquered earlier
by David

▦ Saul's kingdom

Studying the Scriptures ✏️

A What Do You Think?

Why might some people have been surprised that David would do what he did in 2 Samuel 9 for one of Saul's descendants?

B Find a Scripture

Use your scripture helps to find a scripture verse that teaches us to act as David did in 2 Samuel 9. Write the scripture in your notebook and explain why you chose it. A good way to find a scripture is to look in the Topical Guide under a word that describes David's actions. You may find one of those words in the footnotes. Write the reference in the margin of 2 Samuel 9 in your Bible.

2 Samuel 11–12

David's Tragic Mistakes

Sometimes we don't recognize the importance of some of the "little" decisions we make in our lives. Elder Gordon B. Hinckley gave an example of the importance of little decisions when he told about an experience he had working for a railroad company. He said he received a call from New Jersey that a passenger train arrived without the baggage car.

"We discovered that the train had been properly made up in Oakland, California, and properly delivered to St Louis. . . . But in the St. Louis yards, a thoughtless switchman had moved a piece of steel just three inches.

"That piece of steel was a switch point, and the car that should have been in Newark, New Jersey, was in New Orleans, Louisiana, thirteen hundred miles away" (in Conference Report, Oct. 1972, 106; or Ensign, Jan. 1973, 91).

When you first read about David, he appeared to be the model for a king in Israel. Chapters 1–10 of 2 Samuel record the great success he had as the leader of the country. As you read 2 Samuel 11–12, look for "switch points" in David's life that put him on a different "track" than the one he started on in his younger years.

Understanding the Scriptures 🔑

2 Samuel 11

Expired (v. 1)—Ended

Besieged (v. 1)—Attacked

Purified from her uncleanness (v. 4)—Ceremonially clean according to the part of the law of Moses having to do with menstrual cycles and pregnancy

Conceived (v. 5)—Became pregnant

Retire (v. 15)—Retreat, don't support

Charged (v. 19)—Commanded

2 Samuel 12

Lay in his bosom (v. 3)—Lay down to sleep right next to him

Dress, dressed (vv. 4–5)—Prepare, prepared

Wayfaring (v. 4)—Traveling

Despised (vv. 9–10)—Taken lightly

Blaspheme (v. 14)—Express great disrespect of the Lord and his religion

Vex (v. 18)—Be upset

Under (v. 31)—To work with

2 Samuel 12:1—"The Lord Sent Nathan unto David"

When repentance is true and sincere, the sinner confesses to God, to those he or she has offended, and to his or her priesthood leader when the sin is as serious as David's was (see D&C 58:42–43). David's discussion with Nathan, however, happened after the birth of the baby David fathered with Bathsheba. Therefore, the discussion must have been at least nine months after David's first transgression. Furthermore, the Lord had to send Nathan to David instead of David going to Nathan to confess. What do you learn about David's remorse and repentance if, after such a long time, Nathan had to come to David to confront him about his sin?

Studying the Scriptures ✏️

Complete two of the following activities (A–E) as you study.

A Switch Points

Make the following chart in your notebook, and then fill in the blanks with information you learn from 2 Samuel 11 as well as with your own thoughts. There may be more than one item in the middle column.

Decisions That Changed David's Life		
Verses	What David did	What David should have done
1		
2		
3		
4		
6–8, 14–17		
26–27		

B Switch Points Today

You probably noticed that each "switch point" brought David closer and closer to sin. Write a short letter as if you were writing to someone your age and warn him or her about "switch points" you believe will be faced that could lead to immoral actions. A *For the Strength of Youth* booklet (34285) may provide some suggestions. Also use David's story to help this person see the consequences of such choices.

C Interpret the Parable

Explain Nathan's parable in 2 Samuel 12:1–4 as it applied to David. Tell what each specific part of the parable represents.

D Feelings of Remorse

Sometime after his discussion with Nathan, David wrote Psalm 51. Read Psalm 51 and write what you think David would say to someone who believes that sin is nothing to worry about because you can always repent (see also D&C 132:38–39).

E A Big Change

Compare the kind of man David was when he fought Goliath to the kind of man he was in 2 Samuel 11–12 when he committed serious sins. Why do you think there is such a difference? How can people change so drastically?

2 Samuel 13–14

The Sins of David's Children

Sin always affects those around us—especially our families. Often the parents' example has an impact on the way their children behave. Even more, when parents set a bad example, correcting the same bad behavior in their children is very difficult. As you read 2 Samuel 13–14, think about how the actions of David's sons are similar to his own. Consider also what you might have done if you were in these situations.

Understanding the Scriptures

2 Samuel 13

Fair (v. 1)—Beautiful

Vexed (v. 2)—Frustrated, obsessed

Subtil (v. 3)—Devious

Lean (v. 4)—Tired and upset

Folly (v. 12)—Mistake

He will not withhold me from thee (v. 13)—He would let you marry me

Divers (vv. 18–19)—Many different

Apparelled (v. 18)—Clothed

Regard not this thing (v. 20)—Don't make a public display

Desolate (v. 20)—Extremely sad

Chargeable (v. 25)—A burden

Pressed (v. 27)—Urged; kept asking

Longed (v. 39)—Wanted

2 Samuel 14

The king's heart was toward Absalom (v. 1)—David loved and thought about Absalom.

Feign (v. 2)—Pretend

Aileth (v. 5)—Troubles

Strove (v. 6)—Fought

Slew (vv. 6–7)—Killed

Heir (v. 7)—One who lived

Quench my coal (v. 7)—Put out my fire (A phrase that means "leave me without hope")

Remainder (v. 7)—Children

Charged (v. 8)—An order, a decree

Faulty (v. 13)—Guilty of the same thing

Fetch (v. 13)—Bring

Devise (v. 14)—Think and plan

Banished (vv. 13–14)—Sent away

Expelled (v. 14)—Cast out

Therefore (v. 15)—This is the reason

Discern (v. 17)—See the difference between

Polled (v. 26)—Shaved

2 Samuel 13—Amnon Hated His Sister Instead of Loving Her

President Ezra Taft Benson said, "There is no lasting happiness in immorality. . . . Just the opposite is true. There may be momentary pleasure. . . . But quickly the relationship will sour. Guilt and shame set in. . . . Love begins to die. Bitterness, jealousy, anger, and even hate begin to grow. All of these are the natural results of sin and transgression.

"On the other hand, when we obey the law of chastity and keep ourselves morally clean, we will experience the blessings of increased love and peace, greater trust and respect for our marital partners, deeper commitment to each other, and, therefore, a deep and significant sense of joy and happiness" ("The Law of Chastity," in *Brigham Young University 1987–88 Devotional and Fireside Speeches* [1988], 51).

Studying the Scriptures

A Read and Answer

Read 2 Samuel 14:14 and answer this question: What "means" (plans) has God "devised" (created) to help those who are "banished" (out of his presence) so they are not permanently "expelled" (driven out) from him?

2 Samuel 15–18

Absalom Seeks to Be King

The last verses of 2 Samuel 14 tell how Absalom was lovingly received by his father David in Jerusalem. Chapter 15 of 2 Samuel tells how Absalom went about getting the people's support to overthrow David as king. When David heard that Absalom gained favor among the people, he saw the events as a punishment from God for things he had done. He left Jerusalem in the attitude of humility, hoping the Lord would be merciful to him.

The story of Absalom's attempt to set himself up as the new king is told in 2 Samuel 16–17. He received some of David's counselors and servants who hoped to gain political favor. One of them encouraged Absalom to sleep with his father's concubines as a symbol that he was now the king. This fulfilled one of Nathan's prophecies (see 2 Samuel 12:11–12).

Finally, Absalom was encouraged to go out and fight David and David's men. The story of how Joab found and killed Absalom is in 2 Samuel 18. David wept when he heard the news. Perhaps one of the reasons David wept was that he saw his own sins reflected in the lives of his children.

2 Samuel 19–20

Continued Troubles for David

Chapter 19 of 2 Samuel begins by telling of David's continued sorrow for the death of Absalom. Joab told King David that many people were confused that he wept over the death of someone who attempted to overthrow him as king and go to battle against him. Joab said that David appeared to love his enemies and hate his friends. The rest of 2 Samuel 19 tells how David took Joab's counsel and attempted to deal kindly with both friends and former enemies. For example, the tribe of Judah generally supported Absalom.

David invited Judah to support him once again and said he would put one of them in charge of his army. This, however, angered both Joab and the other tribes of Israel. A rebellion by the other tribes in Israel as they attempted to put another man in as king is recorded in 2 Samuel 20. David's men, led by Joab, stopped the rebellion—after Joab killed the man David put in charge of the army.

Chapters 19–20 of 2 Samuel leave us with the impression that while David's desires are usually good, the wise judgment he had as a young man had left him.

2 Samuel 21–23

More about David

The story in 2 Samuel 21 is either not translated correctly or shows that David truly fell deep into apostasy. Never would God approve of putting one's grandsons to death for something their grandfather did. The idea that God demanded human sacrifice to end a famine is simply false doctrine, like the doctrine of idol worship.

Chapters 22–23 of 2 Samuel are not really the continuation of David's history but appear to be placed at the end of 2 Samuel by the writer to summarize some things about David and his kingdom. Chapter 22 of 2 Samuel is a psalm of David. Chapter 23 tells about David's "mighty men," or the men of his army.

2 Samuel 24

More of David's Mistakes

Chapter 24 is the final chapter of 2 Samuel; it records that David was determined to number, or count, the people in Israel. The record states that the Lord was displeased with him for doing this. Apparently, David was numbering the people to see how successful he really was as king. The Lord, however, was the one who gave David strength to conquer Israel's enemies. David's sin was in taking credit for Israel's success.

In the last part of 2 Samuel 24, David bought a threshing floor from a man. On that threshing floor David offered sacrifice to the Lord for his sins. This threshing floor is the traditional place where Abraham offered Isaac, and was the place where David's son Solomon built the temple. Today a Moslem mosque sits on this place and is called the "Dome of the Rock."

Overview of the Book

First Kings is the third book in the group of four books that tells the history of Israel during the time they were ruled by kings. The book begins with Solomon being chosen as king after David. It covers approximately one hundred twenty years of history, ending with the story of Ahab, one of the more wicked kings in Israel's history. Our Father in Heaven confronts Ahab by sending someone more than equal to the task, Elijah the prophet. Often revered as Israel's greatest prophet, Elijah displays the power of God over the false god Baal in dramatic fashion on Mount Carmel. Although 1 Kings tells some political history, the book is more a history of how political leaders kept the covenants God made with Israel, especially regarding idolatry. The major focus is on those kings who were most notable in either keeping or not keeping the covenant and on the prophets who preached to them. We can learn lessons from both the good and bad examples in 1 Kings.

Baal Worship

Worship of the idol Baal is mentioned many times in 1–2 Kings. Baal was the false god of many of Israel's neighbors. Those who worshiped him believed he helped their crops grow and their herds increase. This false religion, inspired of Satan, included immoral activities in its worship and was referred to by prophets as "the shame" (see Bible Dictionary, s.v. "Baal"). At various times, many Israelites forsook God and defiled themselves by this religion rather than worshiping the true and living God.

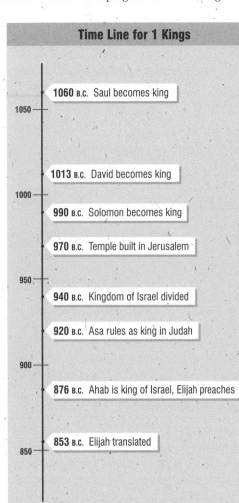

Time Line for 1 Kings

1060 B.C. Saul becomes king

1050

1013 B.C. David becomes king

1000

990 B.C. Solomon becomes king

970 B.C. Temple built in Jerusalem

950

940 B.C. Kingdom of Israel divided

920 B.C. Asa rules as king in Judah

900

876 B.C. Ahab is king of Israel, Elijah preaches

853 B.C. Elijah translated

850

Note: All dates are approximate.

---

1 Kings 1–2

The Death of David

As David grew older, many wondered who would take his place when he died. Chapter 1 of 1 Kings tells about one of David's sons, Adonijah (younger brother of Absalom), who wanted very much to be the next king. He had the support of Joab, David's military leader, and Abiathar, the priest. But David had promised Solomon (Bathsheba's son) that he would be the next king. The prophet Nathan, along with Bathsheba, reminded David of this and encouraged him to publicly declare Solomon as the next king of Israel. It is of special note that David had Solomon ride on his mule as a sign to the people that he was David's successor.

When Adonijah found out about the public anointing of Solomon, he was afraid Solomon might kill him. Solomon promised Adonijah, however, that he would not hurt him. In 1 Kings 2 Adonijah tried again to become king by seeking to marry one of David's wives after he died. For this act of treason he was put to death.

The account of David's death is also in 1 Kings 2. Before David died, he gave Solomon instructions, including directions to punish Joab for the innocent lives he took and Abiathar for supporting Adonijah as king.

Studying the Scriptures

A Prepare a Talk

Suppose that you were assigned to talk on "Lessons we can learn from the life of King David." Name four topics you would put in your talk. After each topic, name a story in David's life (and where it is found in the scriptures) that you would use to teach that topic.

---

1 Kings 3

What Shall I Give Thee?

If you could have anything you wanted from the Lord, what would you ask for? Why? Chapter 3 of 1 Kings records that Solomon had this opportunity. See how his desire compares to your own.

Understanding the Scriptures 🗝

1 Kings 3

Statutes (vv. 3, 14)—Laws

Thy servant (v. 7)—Me (referring to self)

Discern (vv. 9, 11)—Tell the difference

Delivered of a child (v. 17)—Gave birth

Thine handmaid (v. 20)—I (referring to self)

Give my child suck (v. 21)—Feed my child

Bowels yearned (v. 26)—Emotions were strong

Studying the Scriptures ✏

(A) Before, During, and After

In 1 Kings 3, Solomon had a special experience with the Lord in a dream. Answer the following questions about this experience:

Before. What had already happened to show Solomon how difficult it is to be king?

During. Why do you think Solomon asked for an understanding heart rather than anything else? What things did the Lord seem pleased that Solomon *did not* ask for?

After. How did Solomon demonstrate that he had received this spiritual gift at the beginning of his reign?

(B) How Do I Develop Wisdom?

Read the following scriptures and list what they say you can do to increase your wisdom and understanding: Alma 37:35–37; Doctrine and Covenants 89:18–21; 136:32–33.

1 Kings 4

Solomon Organizes the Kingdom

In 1 Kings 4 a brief description of how Solomon organized the government of his kingdom into twelve districts is given (see Bible map 8). Chapter 4 also gives some description of the wealth and prosperity of Solomon and Israel in those days. Solomon and Israel's wisdom and prosperity became so well-known that leaders of many other nations came seeking Solomon's wisdom and counsel.

1 Kings 5–7

Solomon Builds a Temple

Because he was a man of war, David was not permitted by the Lord to build a temple. The Lord promised David, however, that his son would reign in peace and build a temple (see 1 Chronicles 22:8–10). Chapters 5–7 of 1 Kings tell about the building of that temple, which has come to be known as Solomon's temple.

In 1 Kings 5 we are told about an agreement made between Solomon and Hiram, king of Tyre. Solomon got cedar wood from Lebanon (part of the land Hiram ruled) in exchange for wheat and oil from Israel. In addition, we read that Solomon put in effect a "labor tax" that required men in Israel to spend a certain amount of time in Lebanon preparing the cedar wood to be taken to Jerusalem for the temple.

In 1 Kings 6 is a description of some of the furnishings of the temple and the materials they were made of. The chapter also records the Lord's promise to Solomon that if the people would live the laws associated with the temple, the Lord would dwell among them in his house.

Chapter 7 in 1 Kings mentions that Solomon also built a house for himself that took thirteen years to complete, while the temple only took seven. Chapter 7 also reemphasizes the idea that the very finest workmanship was put into the temple. The same is true today. The way we build a house of God is a reflection of how we worship the Lord.

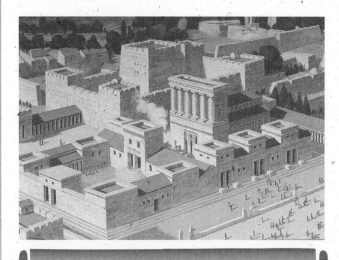

1 Kings 8

The Temple Is Dedicated

President Joseph Fielding Smith said, "When we dedicate a house to the Lord, what we really do is dedicate ourselves to the Lord's service, with a covenant that we shall use the house in the way He intends that it shall be used" ("Hyrum Smith Honored By Pres. Smith," Church News, 12 Feb. 1972, 4).

In our day, each temple built by the Church is dedicated by a prayer given by a member of the First Presidency. The Prophet Joseph Smith prepared by inspiration the first dedicatory prayer in our dispensation and read the prayer at the dedication of the

Kirtland Temple. The prayer is recorded in section 109 of the Doctrine and Covenants. Since that time, the Presidents of the Church have followed the pattern set by the Prophet Joseph.

The dedication of the temple built under Solomon's direction is found in 1 Kings 8. As you read, look for statements that teach us about the importance of temples.

Understanding the Scriptures 🔑

1 Kings 8

Oracle (vv. 6, 8)—Inner, most holy place of Solomon's temple

Staves (vv. 7–8)—Poles used to carry the ark (see illustration on p. 52)

Take heed (v. 25)—Are careful

Be verified (v. 26)—Come true

Supplication (vv. 28, 30, 33, 38, 45, 47, 49, 52, 59)—Humble prayer

Afflictest (v. 35)—Humbles

Maintain (vv. 45, 49, 59)—Help

Perversely (v. 47)—Wrongly

Incline (v. 58)—Turn, draw, entice

Hallow (v. 64)—Make sacred

1 Kings 8:12—"The Lord Said That He Would Dwell in the Thick Darkness"

The Hebrew words translated as "thick darkness" are words that represent the veiled glory of God (see R. Laird Harris, ed. *Theological Wordbook of the Old Testament*, 2 vols. [1980], 2:698 [1701b]). In other words, God promised that he would dwell quite close to his people but would be hidden from view.

1 Kings 8:22–54—The Blessings of the Temple

The prayer Solomon offered to dedicate the temple is found in 1 Kings 8:22–54. Solomon prayed that the temple would be a blessing to the people in some specific ways. Many of these ways still apply to our temples today. President Ezra Taft Benson said, "I promise you that, with increased attendance in the temples of our God, you shall receive increased personal revelation to bless your life as you bless those who have died" (in Conference Report, Apr. 1987, 108; or *Ensign*, May 1987, 85).

President Howard W. Hunter said, "I invite the Latter-day Saints to look to the temple of the Lord as the great symbol of your membership. . . .

"All of our efforts in proclaiming the gospel, perfecting the Saints, and redeeming the dead lead to the holy temple. This is because

the temple ordinances are absolutely crucial; we cannot return to God's presence without them" (in Conference Report, Oct. 1994, 8, 118; or *Ensign*, Nov. 1994, 8, 88).

Studying the Scriptures ✏️

Ⓐ Write an Eyewitness Account

Suppose you have been chosen to write an eyewitness account of the temple dedication for your local newspaper. Because of space limitations, your article must be fifty words or less. Write the article in your notebook.

Ⓑ Blessings of the Temple

List at least four blessings Solomon prayed would come to the people because of the temple (see 1 Kings 8:22–54).

Ⓒ Optional Activity—Temple Influence

Write about your best experience having to do with the temple. Consider getting a picture of a temple nearest you and hanging it where you can see the temple often.

---

1 Kings 9

The Lord Appears to Solomon

President Heber J. Grant said, "There is but one path of safety to the Latter-day Saints, and that is the path of duty. It is not testimony, it is not marvelous manifestations, it is not knowing that the Gospel of Jesus Christ is true, . . . that will save you and me, but it is the keeping of the commandments of God, the living the life of a Latter-day Saint" ("The President Speaks: Excerpts from the Utterances of Heber J. Grant," Improvement Era, *Nov. 1936, 659*).

Solomon and the Israelites had great spiritual experiences at the dedication of the temple, but spiritual experiences do not guarantee salvation (see D&C 3:4). Chapter 9 of 1 Kings records what the Lord told Solomon regarding what the Lord requires in order to be with his people. Look for these requirements as you read.

Understanding the Scriptures 🔑

1 Kings 9:1–9

Hallowed (vv. 3, 7)—Made sacred

Perpetually (v. 3)—Always

A proverb and a byword (v. 7) —Something people will talk about and make fun of

Hiss (v. 8)—Speak with disrespect or insult

Studying the Scriptures ▦▰✏

Ⓐ Identify Commandments and Consequences

If	Then

Make a chart like the one shown here and fill it in with what the Lord told Solomon in 1 Kings 9:1–9.

1 Kings 10

The Queen of Sheba Visits

If someone from a different country came to visit you and watched you in your daily activities, would they gain or lose interest in your God and religion? In 1 Kings 10 we learn about a special visitor (the queen of Sheba) who came to visit Solomon because she did not believe all the great things she heard about him. After visiting Solomon, Sheba was very impressed, especially with his wisdom and riches. The rest of chapter 10 describes things Sheba probably saw and noticed that made Solomon a very impressive king.

1 Kings 11

Solomon Turns from the Lord

If we could learn anything from the stories of Israel's first two kings, it would be this: no matter how good or favored you are in the beginning, you must endure to the end. This truth makes the story of Solomon all the more puzzling. Why didn't he endure faithfully to the end? As you read 1 Kings 11, notice what happened because of Solomon's unfaithfulness to the Lord.

Understanding the Scriptures 🔑

1 Kings 11

Strange (vv. 1, 8)—Foreign

Clave (v. 2)—Became close

Concubines (v. 3)—Women married to a particular man but with a lesser status than a "wife," usually performing servant-type duties in the household

Rend (vv. 11–13, 31)—Tear

Howbeit (vv. 13, 22, 34)—But

Adversary (vv. 14, 23, 25)—Enemy

Victuals (v. 18)—Food

Abhorred (v. 25)—Hated

Breaches (v. 27)—Gaps in the wall where it wasn't finished

Industrious (v. 28)—A good worker

Clad (v. 29)—Clothed

1 Kings 11:4—Was David's Heart Really "Perfect" with the Lord?

The Joseph Smith Translation changed 1 Kings 11:4 to say that Solomon's heart was not perfect with the Lord and he became like his father David.

Studying the Scriptures ▦▰✏

Ⓐ Marriage out of the Covenant

1. In 1 Kings 3:1 we read that Solomon married a non-Israelite wife. She was the daughter of the Egyptian pharaoh. Marrying Pharaoh's daughter seemed like a wise thing to do because a king would not usually attack another king who was married to his daughter. Marriage was a very common way of making treaties in those days. In Deuteronomy 7:1–4 the Lord gave counsel about marrying outside the covenant. How does the counsel in Deuteronomy apply to Solomon in 1 Kings 11:1–8?

2. Give an example of how this principle applies today in your age group.

Ⓑ What Are the Consequences?

Name at least two things that happened because Solomon's heart was turned from the Lord (see 1 Kings 11:11–40).

1 Kings 12

A Divided Kingdom

In 1 Kings 11 we read that the prophet Ahijah told a man named Jeroboam, of the tribe of Ephraim who worked closely with Solomon, that Jeroboam would be king over ten of the tribes of Israel. Solomon knew of Jeroboam's rebellion and sought to take his life, but Jeroboam fled.

When Solomon died, his son Rehoboam was made king. At the time Solomon died, many people in Israel were unhappy about the many taxes Solomon had put on them. They were waiting to support Rehoboam until he told them what he would do about the taxes. This is when the events in 1 Kings 12 took place.

In 1 Kings 12 Rehoboam sought advice from different groups of people concerning what he should do. Who are the different people in your life who give you guidance? Whose counsel do you listen to, and why? As you read, try to imagine you were in Rehoboam's place. Whose advice would you have chosen and why? Whom may we turn to for guidance and inspiration in our daily lives?

Understanding the Scriptures 🔑

1 Kings 12

Yoke (vv. 4, 9–11, 14)—Burden
Grievous (v. 4)—Difficult
Consulted (vv. 6, 9)—Asked advice
Forsook (v. 8)—Rejected
Loins (v. 10)—Waist

Chastised (vv. 11, 14)—Disciplined
Remnant (v. 23)—Others, the remaining part
Devised (v. 33)—Made up

Studying the Scriptures ✏️

A What Should He Do?

1. Make a chart like the one shown here and fill it in so that it tells the story found in 1 Kings 12:1–20.

The problem (see vv. 1–5)	
Advice from the "old men" (see vv. 6–7)	
Advice from the "young men" (see vv. 9–11)	
What Rehoboam did (see 1 Kings vv. 8, 12–15)	

2. Why do you think Rehoboam decided to take the young men's advice?

3. What groups of people try to influence your decisions? How do you choose which counsel to follow? Why is prayer essential in the decision-making process? (see D&C 30:1–2).

B What Would You Do?

1. In the story in 1 Kings 12:25–33, what was Jeroboam worried about?

2. If you were living in Israel at the time, what would be the right thing to do, and why?

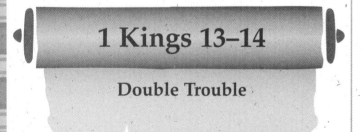

1 Kings 13–14

Double Trouble

In 1 Kings 13–14 we are told how both Jeroboam and Rehoboam led their people to sin. Interestingly, chapters 13–14 both contain accounts of experiences Jeroboam had that could have helped him recognize the power of God. Nevertheless, we read that Jeroboam "returned not from his evil way" (1 Kings 13:33).

Chapter 13 of 1 Kings also contains a story of a prophet that can help us understand the importance of obedience.

In 1 Kings 14 we learn that, like Jeroboam, Rehoboam also allowed idol worship in the land. Losing the protecting hand of the Lord because of his disobedience, Rehoboam was unable to

keep the king of Egypt from capturing and taking away treasures from the temple in Jerusalem.

1 Kings 15–16

New Kings, Old Problems

Chapters 15–16 of 1 Kings tell about the kings in Israel and Judah after Jeroboam and Rehoboam. Only one is mentioned as not being wicked—Asa, king of Judah. During his time, he destroyed idols in the land, including his own mother's idol. Even Asa, however, could not get rid of the "high places" (see Bible Dictionary, s.v. "high places").

In 1 Kings 15 we also read about the fulfillment of a prophecy concerning Jeroboam: all his descendants were destroyed and his family line ended.

At the end of 1 Kings 16 we are introduced to a king in Israel named Ahab. Ahab not only allowed idol worship, but he married a non-Israelite woman named Jezebel who was an idol worshiper. The king of Israel began worshiping Baal, one of the most abominable of all false gods in the sight of God.

1 Kings 17

Elijah the Prophet

When people will not listen to the message of the Lord's servants, the Lord will sometimes use something more dramatic to bring them to repentance. At the end of 1 Kings 16, we learned that Israel was becoming increasingly wicked, was led by a wicked king, and did not listen to the servants of God inviting them to repent. In 1 Kings 17 we learn about a prophet named Elijah who was sent by God with power to seal shut the heavens and cause a drought in Israel (to learn more about the prophet Elijah, see Bible Dictionary, s.v. "Elijah").

President Spencer W. Kimball wrote a book entitled Faith Precedes the Miracle (1972). 1 Kings 17 gives some great examples of that principle. Both Elijah and a widow exercised faith in some way before they later experienced a miracle. Look for the miracles as you read.

Understanding the Scriptures

1 Kings 17

But according to my word (v. 1)—Unless I say

Flesh (v. 6)—Meat

Sustain (v. 9)—Feed and house

Cruse (vv. 12, 14)—Jug

Waste (vv. 14, 16)—Be empty

Fail (vv. 14, 16)—Be empty

Studying the Scriptures

A Demonstrations of Faith

The miracle of raising a young man from the dead in 1 Kings 17:17–23 is one of the most rare and impressive miracles in the scriptures. Those types of events occur only when the faith of all involved is great and when the event is according to the Lord's will. We demonstrate our faith when we obey what the Lord and his servants tell us because we believe what they tell us— even though we may not fully see or understand why we should or how certain actions will turn to our good. This principle was best expressed by Nephi in 1 Nephi 3:7.

1. Write about ways Elijah showed faith in the Lord.

2. Write about ways the widow showed faith in the Lord.

3. List ways the Lord cared for or blessed Elijah and the ways he cared for or blessed the widow.

B Use the Principles

Consider the following modern situation: The Jones family were not members of the Church. They were very poor and often struggled to provide for their basic needs. When they were taught the gospel, they felt the Spirit and wanted to learn more and join the Church. Then the missionaries taught them about tithing, and they became discouraged because they felt they could not afford to pay it.

1. What gospel principles would you teach this family?

2. Think of a time you or someone you know had to rely on faith to obey a commandment, and write about it.

1 Kings 18

Elijah versus 450 Priests of Baal

Three years of drought did not seem to soften the hearts of King Ahab or the Israelites. In 1 Kings 18 we read about a dramatic event where the Lord, through Elijah, powerfully showed that he is a living God, as opposed to the powerless idol Baal that most of the people worshiped.

Of special importance in this story is the idea that Baal was supposed to be the god of fertility, meaning he was the god that made crops grow by giving rain, sun, good soil, and so on. Baal should have been able to send the people rain, but he couldn't

because he is a false god and has no power (see D&C 29:28–29). So there was no rain for three years—just as Elijah had said. The incident in this chapter when Elijah and the priests of Baal met on Mount Carmel is really a way to show that the Lord— not Baal—has power over the elements.

Understanding the Scriptures

1 Kings 18

Fountain (v. 5)—Springs of water that come out of the ground

Groves (v. 19)—Places where false gods are worshiped through immoral practices

Halt (v. 21)—Pass over

Bullock (vv. 23, 25–26)—Male cow or ox

Girded up his loins (v. 46)— Tucked his cloak in his belt so he could run faster

Studying the Scriptures

A What's Wrong with This Question?

1. What do we learn about Ahab from the question he asked Elijah in 1 Kings 18:17?

2. Give an example of how you think some people today have the attitude Ahab showed.

B "How Long Halt Ye between Two Opinions?"

1. What impresses you most in this story found in 1 Kings 18:19–46?

2. As Elijah did, modern prophets have asked us to choose between the Lord's ways and the ways of the world that have no power to save. Give three examples of issues where modern prophets have asked us to choose between ways of the world and the ways of the Lord.

The World's Way	"How long halt ye between two opinions?" (1 Kings 18:21).	The Lord's Way

C Convinced?

Notice the reaction of the people in 1 Kings 18:39. Write about what most convinces you that "The Lord, he is the God."

1 Kings 19

Elijah Learns More about the Holy Ghost

It would seem that the events recorded in 1 Kings 18 would convince anyone who witnessed or heard about them that Elijah's God is the true God. Not every one was convinced, however, because true conversion only occurs through the Holy Ghost—not through mighty miracles. The Spirit was likely present at the events in 1 Kings 18, but only those who were receptive to it had a change of heart. A change of heart does not occur because of fire out of heaven but rather because of quiet burning in the heart. Look for how the Lord reminded Elijah of this principle in 1 Kings 19.

As you read you may also want to consider how you feel when you've done the right thing but then suffer in some way for your decision. If you have ever felt as if you have suffered unjustly, you can especially relate to Elijah in 1 Kings 19. Notice in 1 Kings 19 what and how the Lord taught Elijah when he was discouraged. Perhaps knowing Elijah's story may help you at a time when you stand for the right but feel like you are standing alone.

Understanding the Scriptures 🔑

1 Kings 19

Withal (v. 1)—All about

Jealous (vv. 10, 14)—Provoked to anger

Mantle (vv. 13, 19)—Overcoat or cloak that also became a

symbol of his authority and power

Instruments (v. 21)—Plowing equipment

1 Kings 19:11–12—What Was the Most Powerful Manifestation of the Lord?

Elijah was discouraged that the miracles on Mount Carmel did not change the hearts of Jezebel and many others. The Lord then taught Elijah that spiritual heart-changing experiences are not in a "strong wind," or "earthquakes," or "fires," or other loud and physical things but in "the still small voice" (1 Kings 19:11–12).

Elder Boyd K. Packer taught, "The Spirit does not get our attention by shouting or shaking us with a heavy hand. Rather it whispers. It caresses so gently that if we are preoccupied we may not feel it at all" ("The Candle of the Lord," *Ensign*, Jan. 1983, 53).

Studying the Scriptures ✏️

Do two of the following activities (A–C) as you study 1 Kings 19.

A Discouragement

Look at 1 Kings 19:1–4, 9–10 and explain why Elijah was discouraged.

B Overcoming Discouragement

1. Write about at least three things the Lord did in 1 Kings 19 to help lift Elijah from his discouragement.

2. For each item you list, explain how you think it lifted Elijah in some way. In what ways does the Lord help us through our own discouragements and disappointments today?

C What Did He Learn?

How could Elijah's experience in 1 Kings 19 help him understand why things didn't turn out as he hoped after the events of chapter 18?

1 Kings 20–21

Ahab's Continued Disobedience

In 1 Kings 20 we read about battles Ahab and Israel had with Syria and their leader Ben-hadad. The Lord helped Ahab and Israel win the battles. After capturing Ben-hadad, however, Ahab made a treaty with Ben-hadad instead of killing him, as a prophet commanded him to do. As a result, Ahab was told he would be punished for his disobedience.

Another story of how wicked Ahab and Jezebel were is found in 1 Kings 21. Ahab wanted a piece of property owned by an Israelite who would not sell it to him. Jezebel decided to get the property for Ahab by paying false witnesses to testify against the property owner in court and have him sentenced to death. All this happened, and Ahab took possession of the property. Afterward he was met by Elijah who told him that he would meet the same kind of death as the man he had put to death.

1 Kings 22

The Prophet Micaiah

The story of Ahab's death is found in 1 Kings 22. Not surprisingly, Ahab's death occurred because he refused to follow the counsel of a true prophet, who told him not to go into battle. Instead, Ahab listened to four hundred false prophets who told Ahab whatever they thought he wanted to hear.

On this subject of following prophets, Elder Harold B. Lee said: "You may not like what comes from the authority of the Church. It may contradict your political views. It may contradict your social views. It may interfere with some of your social life. But if you listen to these things, as if from the mouth of the Lord himself, with patience and faith, the promise is that 'the gates of hell shall not prevail against you; yea, and the Lord

God will disperse the powers of darkness from before you, and cause the heavens to shake for your good, and his name's glory.' (D&C 21:6)" (in Conference Report, Oct. 1970, 152–53).

The Second Book of the Kings

The book of 2 Kings is the fourth and final book in the series of books that relates the history of the Israelites during the time they had kings. In 2 Kings we read of the fall and conquest of both Israel (Northern Kingdom) and Judah (Southern Kingdom).

Sad Endings

The Assyrians conquered the kingdom of Israel in approximately 725–20 B.C. and took most of the people north to Assyria. After this "scattering" of these ten tribes of Israel, we have no record of what happened to them except for a reference in the Book of Mormon that says the Savior visited some of them (see 3 Nephi 17:4). They are known as the lost ten tribes of Israel. Then 2 Kings ends with the account of the Babylonians conquering the kingdom of Judah and carrying the people away captive into Babylon. The Babylonian captivity occurred approximately between 605–587 B.C.

Getting Ready to Study 2 Kings

Because the book of 2 Kings tells about the fall, conquest, and captivity of the Lord's covenant people, we should pay special attention as we read to what led the Israelites to these troubles so we can avoid making those same mistakes. For example, what did their prophets teach them? Did they listen and obey? What do our prophets teach us today? If we don't listen and obey, will the same things happen to us as happened to the Israelites? These are important questions to consider as you read and study.

Outline of Major Events in 2 Kings	
Kingdom of Israel	**Kingdom of Judah**
Chapter 2—Elijah translated; miracles of Elisha	
Chapter 4—Elisha raised a child from the dead	
Chapter 5—Elisha healed a Syrian general	
Chapters 6–9—War with Syria; the Lord fought their battles and protected Elisha.	
	Chapter 12—The temple repaired
Chapter 13—Death of Elisha	
	Chapter 16—Judah made an alliance with Assyria
Chapter 17—Israel taken captive by Assyria	
	Chapters 18–20—Righteous reign of Hezekiah; Hezekiah sought counsel from the prophet Isaiah

	Chapter 21—Idolatry returned
	Chapters 22–23—Josiah reigned in righteousness; the scriptures found in the temple help the people repent
	Chapters 24–25—Judah taken captive by Babylonians

2 Kings 1

The King Seeks Help from Idols

The story of how Ahaziah, the son of Ahab, was injured and sought advice from an idol is found in 2 Kings 1. The Lord told Elijah what was happening. Elijah then met the king's servants, chastised them and King Ahaziah for not seeking counsel from the living God through the prophets, and prophesied that Ahaziah would die. Ahaziah heard of the prophesy and sent soldiers to get Elijah. A captain of fifty soldiers finally stopped trying to capture Elijah but not before one hundred soldiers were killed by the Lord as they tried to carry out Ahaziah's orders. As prophesied, Ahaziah never recovered from his injury, and he died.

2 Kings 2

Elijah Taken into Heaven

When we first met Elijah in 1 Kings 17, he already held the power and authority to seal shut the heavens, creating a drought in Israel. But unlike Isaiah, Jeremiah, or another of the well-known prophets, Elijah left no writings that we know of to tell us more about him. We do know that the prophet Malachi said Elijah would come before "the great and dreadful day of the Lord" (Malachi 4:5) to prepare people for the coming of the Messiah.

Because of Malachi's prophecy, people of some other faiths today still await his coming. The New Testament records, however, that Elijah as a translated being appeared on a mountaintop to Peter, James, and John, three of Jesus' Apostles (see Matthew 17:1–4). In addition, Elijah as a resurrected being appeared in our dispensation on 3 April 1836 in the Kirtland Temple shortly after it was dedicated. He said he came in fulfillment of Malachi's prophecy, and he restored the keys of the sealing power to the earth in preparation for the coming of the Lord (see D&C 110:13–16).

No one could be resurrected until Christ came forth from the tomb. So Elijah, in order to perform his special mission, needed to be translated. Translation means to be changed in a way that your body is no longer subject to sickness, death, or physical pain. Translation is not resurrection. This condition allows individuals to continue performing ministries that require a physical body, such as the laying on of hands for priesthood authority. Later, translated individuals will be "changed" again to be resurrected. In 3 Nephi 28:36–40 Mormon describes some Nephites who were translated. In 2 Kings 2 we read the story of Elijah's being translated.

Understanding the Scriptures

2 Kings 2

Hold ye your peace (vv. 3, 5)— Don't speak of it.
Mantle (vv. 8, 13)—Cloak or outer robe that signifies a prophet, or a prophet's authority

Parted them both asunder (v. 11)—Went between them
Naught (v. 19)—Bad
Barren (vv. 19, 21)—Unable to grow things
Cruse (v. 20)—Container

2 Kings 2:8–15—Elijah's Mantle Falls upon Elisha

Elijah's mantle symbolized his power and authority. This experience was necessary since Elijah was such a great prophet and the people needed some extra help understanding that Elisha would take his place. A similar situation happened in our dispensation. After the death of the Prophet Joseph Smith, there was some confusion about who should lead the Church. At a meeting in Nauvoo, Brigham Young told the Church that the keys of authority were with the twelve Apostles. As he spoke, many testified that the sound of his voice—and even his appearance—resembled the Prophet Joseph's. This experience was a special testimony to those present that the "mantle" had fallen on Brigham Young.

2 Kings 2:9—"Let a Double Portion of Thy Spirit Be upon Me"

When Elisha asked for a "double portion" of Elijah's spirit, he was asking to receive Elijah's same power and authority to act as a prophet to the people. The "double portion" statement refers to the idea that the birthright son received a double inheritance from his father for the purpose of taking care of the father's posterity.

2 Kings 2:23–24—"Go up, Thou Bald Head"

Having more details to the story in 2 Kings 2 would be very helpful. The "children" referred to were extremely disrespectful to the Lord's appointed servant, telling him in effect to leave. Notice that Elisha simply cursed them in the name of the Lord, which God's servants are authorized to do (see D&C 24:15–16), and then the Lord determined the punishment.

Studying the Scriptures

Do activity A or B as you study 2 Kings 2.

A "If Ye Have Desires"

1. Write about at least two things that show how much Elisha wanted to serve the Lord in the way Elijah did.

2. Identify qualities of leadership you see in the life of the Savior or the prophet and explain why these qualities are important.

B Respecting the Lord's Servants

1. What does the story in 2 Kings 2 teach us about the Lord and his servants?

2. Name at least three things you can do to show respect and reverence for the Lord's chosen servants.

2 Kings 3–4

Miracles

The scriptures testify that the Lord is a God of miracles (see Mormon 9:10–11, 15–20). Consequently, those who represent him may also perform miracles if they have faith and act according to the Lord's will. The prophet Elisha was one whose obedience and faith allowed him to participate in many miracles. You read about some of Elisha's miracles in 2 Kings 1, and you will read about several more in the chapters ahead.

As you read these chapters, notice the efforts Elisha made in exercising his faith and how the miracles were used to bless and teach the faithful to allow the Lord to assist them. Remember that miracles seldom convert but rather confirm the hope of those who believe and bless the faithful with special outpourings of grace from a loving God (see D&C 63:7–12).

The story of how Elisha performed a miracle to help give water to the combined armies of Israel, Judah, and Edom is told in 2 Kings 3. Chapter 4 of 2 Kings contains several miracles.

Understanding the Scriptures

2 Kings 4

Creditor (v. 1)—A person who loans money to others
Bondmen (v. 1)—To be a servant to another in order to pay them back for a debt

Vessels (vv. 3–6)—Containers

Of the rest (v. 7)—On what is left over

Constrained (v. 8)—Urged

Turn, turned in thither (vv. 8, 10)—Stopped here

Perceive (v. 9)—Know and feel

Chamber (vv. 10–11)—Room

Careful (v. 13)—Been nervous enough to make great effort

About this season, according to the time of life (v. 16)—About this time next year

Embrace (v. 16)—Hold (like a baby)

Fell (v. 18)—Happened

Reapers (v. 18)—People who harvest

Slack (v. 24)—Slow

Bid (v. 24)—Tell

Yonder (v. 25)—Over there

Vexed (v. 27)—Bitter

Gird up thy loins (v. 29)—Dress ready for travel

Salute (v. 29)—Greet

Twain (v. 33)—Both

Seethe pottage (v. 38)—Cook soup

Servitor (v. 43)—Servant

Understanding the Scriptures 🔑

2 Kings 5

Host (v. 1)—Army

Deliverance (v. 1)—Victory over enemies

Valour (v. 1)—Courage

Leper; Leprosy (vv. 1, 3, 6–7, 27)—Infectious, contagious disease (see Bible Dictionary, s.v. "leprosy")

Waited on (v. 2)—Was a servant to

Would God (v. 3)—I wish

Raiment (v. 5)—Clothing

Rent (vv. 7–8)—Tore (as a sign of being upset)

Wroth (v. 11)—Angry

Rage (v. 12)—Angry feeling

Bid (v. 13)—Command

Blessing (v. 15)—Some payment or present

Two mules' burden of earth (v. 17)—The amount of dirt that two mules can carry

Pardon (v. 18)—Forgive

Spared (v. 20)—Saved him the embarrassment for having his gift rejected

Bestowed them (v. 24)—Put them away

Studying the Scriptures ✏️

Ⓐ Elisha's Priesthood Blessings

1. Make a chart in your notebook like the one below. Read the following references from the life of Christ and tell how they are like something that happened in 2 Kings 4:

Things Jesus Did	Priesthood Blessings of Elisha in 2 Kings 4
Matthew 14:15–21	
Luke 7:11–16	
John 2:1–11 (see also JST)	

2. Considering the activity you just completed, how did Elisha leave a testimony for future Israelites that Jesus is their Messiah?

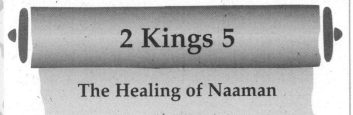

2 Kings 5

The Healing of Naaman

What one "small thing" that has the potential to greatly improve your life should you begin doing on a regular basis? Why haven't you started yet? Elder Rex D. Pinegar said, "The great work of the Lord is primarily accomplished through small, kind acts that exemplify the basic teachings of His gospel" (in Conference Report, Oct. 1994, 106; or Ensign, Nov. 1994, 80).

Sometimes the small commandments are the ones ignored or neglected in our lives, when actually they are the commandments that could make large differences in our lives. Chapter 5 of 2 Kings contains a story that illustrates this principle.

Studying the Scriptures ✏️

Ⓐ Little People, Large Faith

Sometimes we think that what we do and say doesn't really make a difference because we are not very important. There seem to be two such heroes in the story of Naaman. One is the little maid and the other is Naaman's servant. We do not know the names of either of these people, but their faith blessed Naaman's life.

1. Compare the faith of the little maid, who was in a foreign land, to the faith of the king of Israel.

2. Compare Naaman's reaction to Elisha with the counsel of his servant.

3. Write about a time when someone of little importance helped you in a big way, or explain how the story of Naaman is an example of the principle found in Alma 37:6–7, 46.

4. Name two things our modern prophets have asked us to do that could be considered little, and explain how they really can make a big difference.

2 Kings 6–7

Trust the Prophet

Sometimes trusting in the counsel of our prophets and being obedient to their teachings takes much faith. In 2 Kings 6–7 we are given examples of how the Lord gives power to his prophets and brings to pass the fulfillment of their words. As you read, notice what happens to those who believe in the prophets and compare with those who doubt the Lord's prophet.

Understanding the Scriptures 🔑

Thence (v. 2)—There

Beam (vv. 2, 5)—Wooden post or pole

Felling (v. 5)—Cutting down

Compassed (vv. 14–15)—Surrounded

Besieged (v. 24)—Surrounded and kept anything from going in or coming out

Cab (v. 25)—About one and a half liter

What aileth thee (v. 28)—What troubles you

Sackcloth (v. 30)—A rough cloth covering of goat's hair, dark in color, and worn by those in mourning

Ere (v. 32)—Before

2 Kings 6:16–17—"They That Be with Us"

In moments of difficulty we often overlook this truth that "they that be with us are more than they that be with them" (see also D&C 38:7; 84:88).

Studying the Scriptures ✏️➡️

A Use the Scriptures to Solve Problems

Consider the following situations and write about how something from 2 Kings 6 could help in each situation:

1. You are on a mission and there is much opposition to your work. Almost no members live in the area and it seems that nearly everyone you talk to is against the Church.

2. A person at your school or in your neighborhood doesn't like you and is often unkind to you. In a rare opportunity, you have the chance to get back at them.

3. You want to keep the standards of the Church but doing so is difficult because you are one of only a few Church members in your area.

2 Kings 8

Righteousness amid Great Wickedness

Elisha's continued kindnesses to the Shunammite woman whose son he raised from the dead is told in 2 Kings 8. Chapter 8 also contains some brief explanations of the changes in leadership in Syria, Israel, and Judah. The writer helps us realize that these countries were led by wicked men who led the people to greater wickedness.

2 Kings 9–10

Ahab's Descendants Destroyed

In 2 Kings 9–10 we read an account of prophecy again being fulfilled. This time the prophecy was the one Elijah gave concerning Ahab and Jezebel and their descendants. These sobering chapters testify to the awful end of those who fight against God. The prophecy's fulfillment didn't seem to have the desired effect on the people, however. King Jehu, the man who fulfilled the prophecy by killing Jezebel and Ahab's posterity, also killed the priests of Baal but would not give up the idols of Jeroboam, the first king of divided Israel. So Elijah's prophecies were fulfilled, but Israel continued in a form of idolatry although it was different than Baal worship.

2 Kings 11–14

More Wicked Kings, Part 1

The story of the kings in Israel and Judah continues in 2 Kings 11–14. The brief history of each king simply tells a short story or two that gives the reader an idea about what his kingdom was like. Note that the book of Kings never tells of a king in Israel that completely did away with idolatry. On the other hand, there are a few kings in Judah that are noted for their righteousness—but only briefly. For example, in 2 Kings 12 Jehoash is praised for his program to repair parts of the temple. We also read, however, that he took some of the most precious items from the temple made of gold and silver and gave them to the king of Syria as part of a treaty.

The prophet Elisha's death is described in 2 Kings 13.

WANTED
A righteous king for Israel or Judah.
Idol worshipers need not apply.

2 Kings 15–16

More Wicked Kings, Part 2

In 2 Kings 15–16 the account continues of the different kings in Israel and Judah over the years and is similar to the four previous chapters. Of special note in these two chapters is that the country of Assyria began to be a threat to the two kingdoms. The kings of Judah paid the Assyrians to not attack and destroy them (see 2 Kings 15:17–20; 16:5–9). King Ahaz (see 2 Kings 16) even took precious things from the temple and gave them to the king of Assyria as a payment for protection.

In the kingdom of Israel, Assyria attacked and carried away many people from the northern part of Israel as prisoners (see 2 Kings 15:27–29).

2 Kings 17

The Northern Kingdom (Ten Tribes) Taken Captive

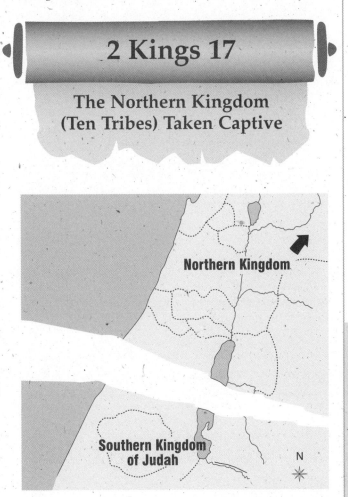

There is a story of two young men in a rowboat floating down a river. Although the river was calm where they floated, they were approaching an area where the water increased in speed and roughness as it headed toward a very steep, tall waterfall.

A man along the shore noticed the two men on the river and called out, "Hello! The rapids are in front of you and are followed by the waterfall!"

The young men heard the warning, but they felt fine about what they were doing and the boat was easily controlled. They continued laughing and joking, paying no attention to the man on the shore or the danger ahead.

The man on the shore shouted again with some urgency, "The rapids and falls will soon be upon you!"

The two men still did not seem to care. As the water began increasing in speed, however, the men became a little worried and tried to get the boat to shore. But it was too late. The current was too powerful, and over the falls they went to their death. Their fate could have been avoided had they listened to the warning voice (see David O. McKay, Gospel Ideals [1953], 912).

This imaginary story is much like the situation of the Israelites in 2 Kings 17, especially the position of the Northern Kingdom, where, as you have read in 1–2 Kings, virtually every king in some way promoted idolatry. From the time of the splitting of the two kingdoms after Solomon until the time of the events in 2 Kings 17 was about two hundred years. In other words, the Lord gave Israel two hundred years to change and put him and his laws above all other things, but they would not. Surely the Lord was merciful in allowing such a long time for the Israelites to repent. Chapter 17 of 2 Kings is also where we read how the Lord allowed the Assyrians to take the Israelites captive, removing them from their land of promise.

The Assyrians were one of the most brutal of all conquering kingdoms in history. They treated their captive prisoners in some of the most savage ways known to man. In addition, in order to extend their own kingdom and culture, they did everything they could to separate those whom they captured from their culture. Consequently, when the Assyrians captured thousands of Israelites from the Northern Kingdom, we never really find out what happened to them. Although some remained in the land and intermarried with their Assyrian captors, most became "lost" from our knowledge and are known as the "lost ten tribes of Israel."

As you read, look for reasons why the Israelites lost the Lord's protection and were taken captive by the Assyrians.

Understanding the Scriptures 🗝

2 Kings 17

Conspiracy (v. 4)—A plan to be a traitor

Besieged it (v. 5)—Surrounded it, preventing anything from going in or out

Statutes (vv. 8, 15, 34, 37)—Laws

Heathen (vv. 8, 11, 15)—Those who do not worship the true God

Vanity (v. 15)—Things that have no eternal value

Vain (v. 15)—Focused on self and things of the world rather than things of eternal value

Charged (vv. 15, 35)—Commanded

Molten images (v. 16)—Idols made by man

Divination (v. 17)—To get false revelation through communication with evil spirits

Enchantments (v. 17)—Supposed magic spells

Spoilers (v. 20)—Enemies who steal and ruin

2 Kings 18:5–18—Israel Attacked by the Assyrians and Removed

In the Church we speak of the "lost ten tribes" (see Articles of Faith 1:10). These lost tribes refer to the Northern Kingdom of Israel, which included the lands of inheritance of ten full tribes. In 2 Kings 18 we learn why and how many were carried away into Assyria and never heard of again as a people. The Lord is gathering the house of Israel in the latter days. To learn more about the ten tribes, look up scriptures found in the Topical Guide under the headings "Israel, gathering of"; "Israel, restoration of"; and "Israel, ten lost tribes of."

Studying the Scriptures

Do two of the following activities (A–C) as you study 2 Kings 17.

A A Warning Fulfilled

When the Lord first gave the Israelites their promised land, he gave them some warnings:

1. Summarize the prophecy the Lord gave Israel in Deuteronomy 4:24–28.

2. In what ways was that prophecy being fulfilled in 2 Kings 17? Be specific in your answer.

B Let Me Count the Ways

1. List the ways Israel sinned against the Lord (look in 2 Kings 17:7–23).

2. Read Doctrine and Covenants 1:14–16 and describe how people in our day could be considered guilty of the same sins as the children of Israel.

C Lost, but Not Forgotten

Read Deuteronomy 4:29–31, and summarize the promise the Lord made to the people and their descendants who were scattered.

2 Kings 18–19

Righteous King Hezekiah

At the time Assyria was conquering Israel, Hezekiah became king in Judah. He was able to lead the people toward increased righteousness, perhaps because they saw what was happening to Israel and feared the threat of the Assyrians to their own nation. As often happens to those who turn from sin to righteousness, however, Hezekiah and Israel had their commitment tested. For example, when a person who hasn't paid tithing begins paying it, there may come a month when it doesn't look like he or she can afford to pay a full tithe. The person may have to ask, "Can I trust the Lord enough to go ahead and pay my tithing and trust that he will bless me in whatever way I need?" Read Ether 12:6. Note the way the Lord has directed us to follow in such challenging times.

Hezekiah and his kingdom's trial of faith is told about in 2 Kings 18–19. As you read, consider how you would feel if you were in Hezekiah's situation, both during and after this trial of faith.

Understanding the Scriptures

2 Kings 18

Clave (v. 6)—Stayed very close
Return (v. 14)—Turn back
Appointed (v. 14)—Taxed
Conduit (v. 17)—Small channel that carries water

Vain words (v. 20)—Words that have no value and will not come to pass
Pledges (v. 23)—Money paid for protection
Cistern (v. 31)—Place for collecting water

2 Kings 18:26—Speak "in the Syrian Language"
The Assyrians were speaking in Hebrew outside the walls of Jerusalem so that all inside would understand their message. The Jewish men on the wall asked the Assyrians to speak in Syrian. They did not want many people to understand the frightening message of a group of very confident soldiers in what, at the time, was the most powerful army in the world.

2 Kings 19

Rent (v. 1)—Tore
Sackcloth (vv. 1–2)—Dark-colored clothing made from a goat hide and worn as a cloak in times of mourning
Rebuke (v. 3)—Punishment
Blasphemy, blasphemed (vv. 3, 22)—Express great disrespect for God
Reproach (vv. 4, 16, 22–23)—Ridicule, speak disrespectfully
Reprove (v. 4)—Correct
Remnant (vv. 4, 30–31)—Part left over, the remainder
Blast (v. 7)—Thought
Which dwellest between the cherubims (v. 15)—Reference to the ark of the covenant in

the Holy of Holies of the temple, symbolizing the place where God dwells
Despised (v. 21)—Disliked
Laughed thee to scorn (v. 21)—Mocks you
Lodgings of his borders (v. 23)—Furthest boundary
Dismayed (v. 26)—Fearful
Confounded (v. 26)—Put to shame
Blasted (v. 26)—Destroyed
Rage (vv. 27–28)—Anger
Tumult (v. 28)—Pride
Zeal (v. 31)—Strong feelings
Bank (v. 32)—Mound of dirt that allows an enemy to come over the wall

Studying the Scriptures

Do two of the following activities (A–C) as you study 2 Kings 18–19.

A A Formula for Success

How does 2 Kings 18:1–8 illustrate the truth of Proverbs 3:5–6?

B In Your Own Words

Summarize the story found in 2 Kings 18–19 by writing in your own words:

1. What Rab-shakeh said to Hezekiah's servants (see 2 Kings 18:19–35).

2. Hezekiah's reaction to the Rab-shakeh's words (see 2 Kings 19:1–5).

3. Isaiah's message to Hezekiah (see 2 Kings 19:6–7).

4. What Isaiah said to Hezekiah in response to Hezekiah's prayer (see 2 Kings 19:20–34).

5. What happened to the Assyrians (see 2 Kings 19:35–37).

C How Does It Happen Today?

What lesson could modern-day Israelites learn from the story in 2 Kings 18–19? As you write, consider the following questions: In what ways do you feel like you are in the position of Hezekiah and the people of Jerusalem? Does it take faith to believe that some of the things the prophets tell us will actually come to pass? How does the story of Hezekiah in these two chapters relate to Ether 12:6?

2 Kings 20

More about Hezekiah

In 1 Kings 20 we read about a time when Hezekiah was close to death. He prayed in faith that he might live a few more years, and the Lord gave him his desire. Chapter 20 also tells how Hezekiah showed the king of Babylon the treasures in the temple. Isaiah said this was a mistake because in future years the Babylonians would remember the great riches inside the temple, come to conquer Jerusalem, and take away those precious things.

2 Kings 21

Wicked King Manasseh

In 2 Kings 21 we read about Hezekiah's son Manasseh who, after the righteous reign of his father, reigned as one of the most wicked rulers in the history of Judah. The end of chapter 21 tells us that Manasseh's son Amon reigned only a short time before he was killed. The people found and slew the men who killed Amon and then put another king in power. This event suggests that if the people really wanted to, they could have overthrown wicked Manasseh and put a righteous king in his place. Manasseh's reign was so wicked because the people allowed his wickedness and were wicked themselves. A wicked man in power can do much harm. If the majority of the people are righteous, however, they can bring about much good, even in the midst of wickedness.

2 Kings 22–23

The Power of the Word

In the Book of Mormon, the Lord commanded Nephi to obtain the brass plates and to devote much of his life to writing the First Book of Nephi and the Second Book of Nephi. This illustrates how the Lord feels about the importance of scriptures.

How would your life be different if you had never read the scriptures or known of them? What difference are they making in your daily life now?

In 2 Kings 22 the scriptures are referred to as the "book of the law." As you read this chapter, consider what the writer was trying to teach us about the importance of the scriptures, and notice what effect the scriptures had on King Josiah and his people.

Understanding the Scriptures

2 Kings 22

Scribe (v. 3)—A clerk or secretary to the king, the high priest, or the city (at this time in history)

Sum (v. 4)—Gather all

Reckoning (v. 7)—Accounting for

Communed (v. 14)—Spoke

Quenched (v. 17)—Satisfied

2 Kings 23

Sepulchres (vv. 16, 30)—Tombs to place the bodies of the dead in

Tribute (v. 33)—Tax given to a ruler to keep him from attacking you

2 Kings 22:8—The Book of the Law Found in the Temple

There were no printing presses at the time of 2 Kings 22. Each copy of a book had to be written out by hand. Consequently, there were very few copies; finding the book of the law, or the scriptures, in the temple was a great discovery. In our day, obtaining a copy of the scriptures is much easier. Our challenge is not to find the scriptures, but to find out what they say. President Spencer W. Kimball taught about the story of the scriptures being found in the time of Josiah, and then said, "I am convinced that each of us, at some time in our lives, must discover the scriptures for ourselves—and not just discover them once, but rediscover them again and again". ("How Rare a Possession—the Scriptures!" *Ensign*, Sept. 1976, 4).

Studying the Scriptures

A The Power of the Word

Do three of the following four activities:

1. What was King Josiah's response when he heard the words of the book of the law? (see 2 Kings 22:11, 19; 23:4–14, 21, 24–25).

2. What was the people's response when King Josiah read these same words to them? (see 2 Kings 23:1–3).

3. Write about a time when the scriptures have had an important effect on your life.

4. Read 2 Timothy 3:15–17; 1 Nephi 15:23–24; 2 Nephi 32:3; Alma 31:5; Helaman 3:29–30, and make a list from these scriptures of the power the scriptures can have in our lives.

2 Kings 24–25

Judah Taken Captive by Babylon

In the last few verses of 2 Kings 23, we read that Josiah's son was a wicked king, leading the people back into wickedness. During that time, the Egyptians forced the kings of Judah to pay them money for protection. They had such influence that they put in a new king for Judah while the old one was still alive.

By the beginning of 2 Kings 24 Egypt's power had grown weaker than that of an emerging world power—Babylon. Led by King Nebuchadnezzar, the Babylonians attacked Jerusalem and took captive many rich, educated, and powerful families in Jerusalem. Chapter 24 in 2 Kings marks the "beginning of the end" for Judah.

During this time, the prophet Lehi warned the people about the total destruction of Jerusalem by Babylon. Knowing that Nebuchadnezzar had already successfully attacked Jerusalem prior to the beginning of 1 Nephi in the Book of Mormon makes the people's rejection of Lehi's warning seem even more amazing. The Book of Mormon begins in the "first year of the reign of Zedekiah" (1 Nephi 1:4), who is referred to in 2 Kings 24:17–20.

True to the prophecies of Lehi and others, Nebuchadnezzar returned to Jerusalem and completely "broke up" the city (see 2 Kings 25). Zedekiah's eyes were put out (blinded) after he was forced to witness the death of his sons. The Book of Mormon records that one of Zedekiah's sons named Mulek was saved and traveled with a group to the western continent. The Nephites later discovered the descendants of these "Mulekites" and called them the people of Zarahemla.

The account of the Babylonian captivity of the Lord's chosen people by the wicked is documented in 2 Kings 25. Israel's "golden" era began when Moses led them out of Egyptian bondage and made sacred covenants with the Lord. It concluded with the Assyrian capture and scattering of the Northern Kingdom, and with the Babylonian capture of the Southern Kingdom after the Israelites had become continually wicked. Thus we see that both the Northern and Southern Kingdoms of Israel and Judah were conquered as the Lord's prophets had foretold. For approximately six hundred years, Israel was essentially a free people, able to worship the God of their fathers Abraham, Isaac, and Jacob. But they forsook their God and were taken captive and scattered among those who did not worship the true and living God.

The First and Second Books of the Chronicles

In approximately 540–35 B.C., the Medes and Persians defeated Babylon and became the major power in the Middle East and Asia. Shortly after coming to power, Cyrus, king of Persia, invited the Jews to return to their homelands after over fifty years in Babylonian captivity. The books of 1–2 Chronicles were written sometime after the return of the Jews. Originally, 1–2 Chronicles were one book, but later translators separated them into two.

Getting Ready to Study 1–2 Chronicles

The writers of Chronicles sought to retell the history of the Jews during the time of the kings, so Chronicles covers the same time period as 1–2 Samuel and 1–2 Kings. In fact, some of Chronicles seems to simply quote from those books. Occasionally, however, Chronicles emphasizes different points. For example, Chronicles includes much more detail about temple articles and temple events since at the time Chronicles was written the Jews had a temple but no kings.

Because so much of Chronicles contains information you have already studied, this study guide does not discuss each chapter. You will only receive reading helps for 2 Chronicles 15; 20 since they contain stories not found in 1–2 Kings. For other selected parts of 1–2 Chronicles, you will only complete activities.

1 Chronicles 22:5–19

Preparing to Build the Temple

Studying the Scriptures

A) David and the Temple

1. List what 1 Chronicles 22:5–19 says David did to prepare for the building of the temple.

2. According to verses 5–19, why was David not allowed to build the temple?

1 Chronicles 29:29

"The Acts of David the King"

Studying the Scriptures

A How Can It Help?

How could 1 Chronicles 29:29 help you answer someone who criticizes the Book of Mormon by saying that all the writings of God's prophets are found in the Bible and there cannot be any other books of scripture?

2 Chronicles 3:1

Solomon Begins to Build the Temple

Studying the Scriptures

A What Is the Importance of This Place?

1. According to 2 Chronicles 3:1, where did Solomon have the temple built?

2. Read verse 1, footnote *b* and Genesis 22:2, and explain what other important event happened on Mount Moriah.

3. Why do you think this is a good place for a temple?

2 Chronicles 7:1–12

The Glory of the Lord

Studying the Scriptures

A Write an Eyewitness Account

Imagine you are a newspaper reporter. Using information from 2 Chronicles 7:1–12, write a front page story about what happened following the dedication of Solomon's temple as if you were there.

2 Chronicles 11:13–17

The Levites Return

Studying the Scriptures

A Tell Who Is Where and Why

When Israel split into two nations, we generally say that the tribes of Judah and Benjamin were in the Southern Kingdom, the other ten tribes were in the Northern Kingdom, and the Levites were spread throughout the tribes. But we know that Lehi in the Book of Mormon was not of the tribe of Judah or the tribe of Benjamin, yet he lived in Jerusalem. Read 2 Chronicles 11:13–17 and explain who moved to Jerusalem at the time the kingdoms split and why they moved there.

2 Chronicles 15

Asa Obeys a Prophet's Counsel

When the prophet gives counsel, how do you respond? What if his counsel requires you to do something unpopular? Chapter 15 of 2 Chronicles tells what Asa, king of Judah, did when he heard counsel from a prophet of God. As you read, consider what you could learn from Asa's response.

Understanding the Scriptures

2 Chronicles 15

Vexations, Vex (vv. 5–6)—Troubles, to trouble

Fell to him out of Israel in abundance (v. 9)—Placed themselves under his leadership

Spoil (v. 11)—Possessions they obtained through battle

Studying the Scriptures

A Problems and Solutions

Problems in Judah	What the People Should Do

Make a simple chart like the one shown that tells what the prophet Azariah said the people of Judah had done wrong and what they could do to correct the situation. You will find the information to fill in the chart in 2 Chronicles 15:1–7.

B It Takes ____ to Follow a Prophet

1. What word in 2 Chronicles 15:8 describes what is often required in order to follow a prophet's counsel?

2. What did Asa and the people do that showed how much they desired to obey the Lord?

3. Describe some specific ways that you could be more like Asa and his people. How could Church members generally be more like him?

2 Chronicles 20

Asa's Son Jehoshaphat

In 2 Chronicles 20 we find another example of the blessings of trusting in the Lord and his prophets. This time the story occurs during the reign of King Jehoshaphat of Judah. The complete story of Jehoshaphat in the scriptures is found in 2 Chronicles 17–20.

Understanding the Scriptures

2 Chronicles 20

Heathen (v. 6)—Those who do not worship the true God

Sanctuary (v. 8)—Temple

Dismayed (vv. 15, 17)—Afraid

Ambushments (v. 22)—Surprise attacks

Had made an end (v. 23)—Completely destroyed

2 Chronicles 20:7–9—The Promise of Praying in the Temple

Although we know that God will hear our prayers wherever we pray to him, in 2 Chronicles 20:7–9 Jehoshaphat asked for the fulfillment of the special promises found in the dedicatory prayer of Solomon's temple (see 1 Kings 8:37–40, 44–45).

Studying the Scriptures

A How to Receive the Lord's Help

Make a list of things Jehoshaphat and his people did to receive the Lord's help when faced with a great challenge.

B Give an Example

Write a modern example of how you or someone you have read about, perhaps in the scriptures, applied the counsel in 2 Chronicles 20:20 and learned of its truth.

2 Chronicles 26:14–21

Uzziah Becomes a Leper

Studying the Scriptures

A What Is the Problem?

1. Why did king Uzziah get leprosy?

2. What does the way the Lord punished Uzziah teach us about how the Lord feels about priesthood keys and authority?

2 Chronicles 29:1–11

"Be Not Now Negligent"

Studying the Scriptures

A Make a List

1. List what the Lord said to or about the following groups in 2 Chronicles 29:1–11: the Levites, "our fathers," and "my sons."

2. How might we apply Hezekiah's counsel in 2 Chronicles 29:9–11 so that we might prosper as a people before the Lord? (see also D&C 97:10–21).

2 Chronicles 36:11–16

Wickedness in Jerusalem

Studying the Scriptures

A Compare Two Different Books of Scripture

In 2 Chronicles 36:11–16 it tells about the time period when Lehi was in Jerusalem. How are verses 11–16 and 1 Nephi 1 similar?

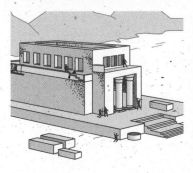

From approximately 605–586 B.C. the Babylonians conquered the Jewish nation and took the Jews captive into Babylon. During this captivity (see Psalm 137:1–4), they violated their covenants with God and appeared to have lost the blessings promised to them as part of the Abrahamic covenant.

New Hope

About fifty years after the Babylonian invasion, the Medes and the Persians united in defeating the Babylonians and created an empire in Asia and the Middle East. This Medo-Persian empire was led by a king named Cyrus who made policies that showed kindness to his subjects, including the Jews in Babylon. Shortly after conquering Babylon in 539 B.C., Cyrus announced that Jews in Babylon could return to Jerusalem and rebuild their temple (see 2 Chronicles 36:22–23; Ezra 1). This announcement brought great excitement to many Jews in captivity. As the Psalmist wrote, "If I forget thee, O Jerusalem, let my right hand forget her cunning" (Psalm 137:5; see also 137:6). New hope was born in the hearts of the Jews.

There were three major returns to Jerusalem: one approximately 538 B.C. under the direction of Zerubbabel, a second approximately 465–25 B.C. under the direction of Ezra, and a third 444 B.C. under the direction of Nehemiah.

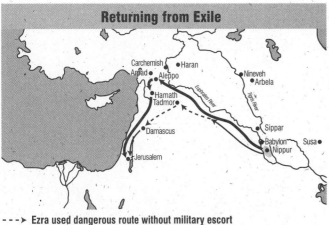

Returning from Exile

- - - ▶ **Ezra used dangerous route without military escort**
⟶ **Return under Ezra and Nehemiah (457–28 B.C.)**
⟹ **Return of exiles in days of Sheshbazzar and Zerubbabel (537–15 B.C.)**
▨ **Judean exiles concentrated in area around Nippur**

Getting Ready to Study Ezra

Ezra was a priest and a descendant of Aaron, the brother of Moses. He was also called a scribe, which was a person who studied, wrote, and taught the scriptures a great deal. Ezra led the second major group of Jews back to Jerusalem sometime around 465–25 B.C.

Some have called Ezra the "father" of modern Judaism because of his emphasis on studying the law (the scriptures). He led the Jews at a time when they began focusing more on becoming a church rather than a nation. Ezra apparently either wrote some of the book of Ezra or the original writer quoted directly from a record Ezra wrote because in the last four chapters, Ezra speaks in the first person ("I said," "I sent them," and so on).

After retelling the story of Cyrus allowing the Jews to return to Jerusalem (originally told in 2 Chronicles 36), Ezra tells the story of a group, led by Zerubbabel, who returned and sought to rebuild the temple and reestablish the Jewish way of life. This group became discouraged but were later encouraged to finish the temple by the prophets Haggai and Zechariah. The temple is one of two important themes emphasized in Ezra. The other idea is the importance of the law, or the sacred records we call the scriptures. Ezra tried to help the Jews become righteous from the inside out by teaching them the law. For more information on Ezra, see the Bible Dictionary, s.v. "Ezra."

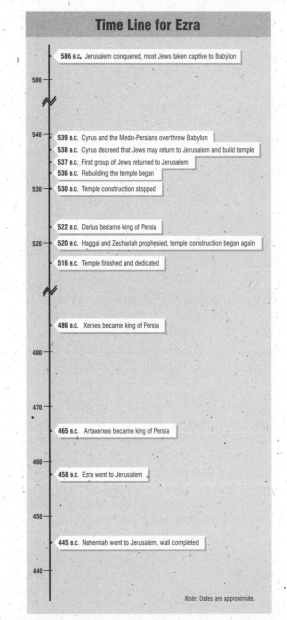

Time Line for Ezra

586 B.C. Jerusalem conquered, most Jews taken captive to Babylon

580

540 — **539 B.C.** Cyrus and the Medo-Persians overthrew Babylon
538 B.C. Cyrus decreed that Jews may return to Jerusalem and build temple
537 B.C. First group of Jews returned to Jerusalem
536 B.C. Rebuilding the temple began
530 — **530 B.C.** Temple construction stopped

522 B.C. Darius became king of Persia
520 — **520 B.C.** Haggai and Zechariah prophesied, temple construction began again
516 B.C. Temple finished and dedicated

486 B.C. Xerxes became king of Persia
480 —

470 —

465 B.C. Artaxerxes became king of Persia
460 —
458 B.C. Ezra went to Jerusalem

450 —

445 B.C. Nehemiah went to Jerusalem, wall completed
440 —

Note: Dates are approximate.

Ezra 1

Cyrus Fulfills Prophecy

Ezra 1 tells us that not only did Cyrus encourage the Jews to return to Jerusalem, but he also promised to return all the items Nebuchadnezzar took from the temple and placed in the temples of Babylon. Ezra encouraged others in his kingdom who had temple items to return them so the Jews could put them back in the rebuilt temple. Cyrus felt that God was inspiring him to make this decree. The decree of Cyrus fulfilled prophecies made by Isaiah and Jeremiah (see Isaiah 44:28—45:1).

Ezra 2

Who Returned?

Ezra 2 gives the number of people who returned to Jerusalem under the leadership of a man named Zerubbabel, who was a descendant of the kings of Judah and who became governor of the land when the Jews returned. The people listed in this chapter were grouped according to the city they were from in Israel and then according to family in that city. Ezra 2 also notes that the priests who returned were required to search their family history to prove they were Levites and could officiate in the priesthood.

Ezra 3–6

The Building of the Temple

In Ezra 3 we read how the returned Jews, under the direction of Zerubbabel and Jeshua (the leader of the priests), began rebuilding the temple. They began with the altar so they could perform the sacrifices commanded in the law of Moses. Then they began the foundation. When the foundation was complete they had a celebration. Those who could remember the temple of Solomon wept when they saw this temple because they knew it would not be nearly as beautiful as the one they remembered.

President Brigham Young said, "We completed a temple in Kirtland and in Nauvoo; and did not the bells of hell toll all the time we were building them? They did, every week and every day" (Journal of Discourses, 8:356). Ezra 4 shows the truth of

that statement. A group of people called Samaritans wanted to help the Jews rebuild the temple. The Jews would not allow their help, which angered the Samaritans. From that time the Samaritans tried everything they could to stop the building of the temple.

> A Samaritan was a descendant of Assyrian settlers and Israelites. The Jews considered Samaritans unclean because of intermarriage.

Ezra 5–6 tells the story of how the Jews regained permission to continue rebuilding the temple in Jerusalem after the Samaritans successfully stopped the building project. The prophets Haggai and Zechariah encouraged the people to keep building even though they had been asked to stop (see Ezra 5:1–2). Non-Jews in the land questioned whether the Jews had permission to build, and when the Jews quoted King Cyrus's decree as their permission for building, the non-Jews wrote to king Darius and asked him to see if the decree of Cyrus was true. Ezra 6 records that the decree was found and Darius permitted the building to continue.

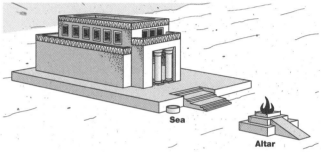

At the end of Ezra 6 we read that the temple was finished and dedicated. The temple dedication brought joy to the people because they were strengthened to continue the work of the house of God (see v. 2). Note that the happy events of these two chapters were the result of the people's willingness to obey the counsel of the prophets Haggai and Zechariah.

Ezra 7

Ezra—Teacher of the Law

Ezra 7 introduces Ezra the priest, who was also a scribe, or teacher. The list of names in the first five verses of chapter 7 tell us that Ezra was a direct descendant of Aaron, brother of Moses. We also learn from this chapter that Artaxerxes allowed Ezra to take a group of Jews from Babylon to Jerusalem. Furthermore, Artaxerxes provided money for the temple and had Ezra take treasures from the temple in Babylon and return them to the temple in Jerusalem. We also read that Ezra was given power to appoint judges among the people to serve in the Jews' local government.

Studying the Scriptures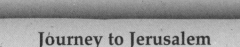

Ⓐ The Source of Ezra's Strength

1. According to Ezra 7:10, what three things did Ezra do? ("Law of the Lord" refers to the scriptures.)

2. Explain at least two benefits Ezra received because he did these things.

3. Give an example of how you can do each of these three things.

Ezra 8

Journey to Jerusalem

This first part of Ezra 8 contains a list of the groups of people who went with Ezra from Babylon to Jerusalem and the number of people in each group. Chapter 8 then tells the story of the Jews' journey to Jerusalem, including how they fasted and prayed for protection along the way and how the Lord heard and answered their prayers.

Ezra 9–10

Marriages to Non-Israelite Wives

Perhaps the biggest reason Israel and Judah were scattered and taken captive was that they worshiped idols. Ezra and other Jewish leaders tried to keep the people from making these same mistakes again as they returned to their promised land. But, as you will read in Ezra 9–10, many Jews had married outside of the covenant, increasing the temptation to worship the gods of their spouses. As you read these two chapters, consider how you might apply what these writings teach about marrying in the covenant.

Understanding the Scriptures

Ezra 9

Abominations (vv. 1, 11, 14)—Things that are wrong in the sight of God

Holy seed (v. 2)—Covenant people

Mingled (v. 2)—Intermarried

Chief in this trespass (v. 2)—Leaders in doing wrong

Astonied (vv. 3–4)—Surprised and saddened

Heaviness (v. 5)—Heavy burden

Blush (v. 6)—Humiliated

Iniquities (vv. 6–7, 13)—Sins

Space (v. 8)—Period of time

Reviving (vv. 8–9)—Hope

Affinity (v. 14)—Close relationship

Ezra 10

Swear (v. 5)—Promise

Substance should be forfeited (v. 8)—Property should no longer belong to that person.

Pleasure (v. 11)—Will

Ezra 10:9—"Trembling Because of This Matter, and for the Great Rain"

The incident described in Ezra 10:9 occurred during the coldest, rainiest time of the year. The people shivered because of the cold and also because they felt the Lord was upset with them because of their sins.

Studying the Scriptures

Ⓐ Interview Ezra

Imagine you are a newspaper reporter at the time of the events in Ezra 9. Choose three questions you would ask Ezra, and write how you think he would answer based on what you read in Ezra 9.

Ⓑ Identify Principles of Repentance

1. The people listened to Ezra and many tried to be more righteous. Write in your notebook and underline in your scriptures three principles of true repentance you find in Ezra 10.

2. Tell why each principle you found above is important to the repentance process.

The Book of Nehemiah

The book of Nehemiah continues the story that began in Ezra. In the earliest Jewish scriptures Ezra and Nehemiah were one book. For helpful information on Nehemiah and the book of Nehemiah, see the introduction to Ezra in this study guide and the Bible Dictionary, s.v. "Nehemiah."

Getting Ready to Study Nehemiah

As you read, consider the symbolism of the walls of Jerusalem that Nehemiah worked so hard to build. Why was it so important to build these walls? How were the walls like the Jews?

The Lord answered Nehemiah's prayer recorded in Nehemiah 1. Nehemiah 2 tells that Nehemiah had an opportunity to tell King Artaxerxes why he was sad and that the king's heart was softened toward him. The king then allowed Nehemiah to return to Jerusalem to help rebuild the walls of the city. Artaxerxes even provided financial support and gave Nehemiah letters to carry to governors of the provinces to show Nehemiah had the king's approval. With King Artaxerxes' permission, Nehemiah then traveled to Jerusalem, analyzed the situation, and realized more than ever that he must help build the walls of Jerusalem.

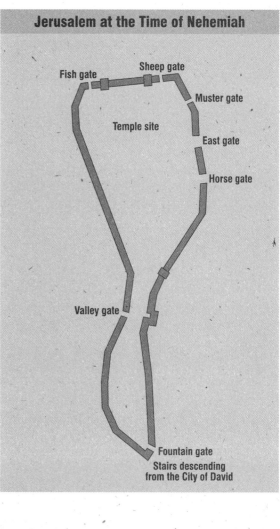

Nehemiah 1

Nehemiah's Prayer

How do you react when you hear about the problems people face in your area or in different parts of the world? Nehemiah 1 records what Nehemiah did when he heard about the suffering of others.

Understanding the Scriptures 🔑

Nehemiah 1

Were (are) left of (vv. 2–3)—Survived

Remnant (v. 3)—Survivors

Affliction (v. 3)—Trouble

Reproach (v. 3)—Disapproval

Be attentive (vv. 6, 11)—To listen with careful attention

Uttermost (v. 9)—Farthest

This man (v. 11)—The king

Studying the Scriptures ✏️

A **Look for Important Words**

Choose what you think are the four most important words in Nehemiah 1. Make sure you choose at least one word that describes Nehemiah's actions and one that is important to what he said. Explain why you chose each word.

Nehemiah 2

Nehemiah Goes to Jerusalem

(A) An Example of Faith

1. What did Nehemiah say to encourage the people?

2. How did the people respond?

3. How did Nehemiah respond to the "mockers"?

4. How could we apply what Nehemiah did when trying to accomplish something the Lord or his servants ask us to do?

Nehemiah 3–4

The Builders Face Opposition

Nehemiah 3 lists the names and groups of people who worked on rebuilding the walls of Jerusalem and tells what part of the wall they worked on.

Nehemiah 4 tells how Sanballat, governor of the Samaritans, continued to mock and oppose the rebuilding of Jerusalem's walls. When he discovered he could not stop the work by mocking the people, he attempted to physically attack the workers to stop them. But Nehemiah and the people prayed for the Lord's help and put half of the workers on "guard duty." The Lord protected them so they could continue their labors. These Jews had great faith in the Lord even in the midst of Satanlike mocking and opposition to their good works.

Nehemiah 5

Nehemiah: A Great Leader

Nehemiah 5 tells how Nehemiah, like King Benjamin in the Book of Mormon (see Mosiah 2), led his people without taxing them. He also made laws that prevented the Jews from charging unusually high or excessive interest to each other on loans (called "usury"), stopping the practice of Jews enslaving other Jews who were in debt to them.

Nehemiah 6

Nehemiah Finishes the Walls

Sometimes it can be hard to tell who really wants what is best for us. Men with evil intentions may try to trick us so they can personally gain from our misfortune. If we are obedient to God and trust the guidance of the Spirit, however, we may avoid deception. Nehemiah 6 tells us what Nehemiah did in a situation where others sought to harm him and disrupt his work.

Understanding the Scriptures ⚷

Nehemiah 6

Breach (v. 1)—Holes, gaps

Mischief (v. 2)—Harm

Feignest (v. 8)—Makes up, pretends

Perceived (vv. 12, 16)—Realized

Reproach (v. 13)—Speak evil of

Cast down in their own eyes (v. 16)—Discouraged

Was wrought of (v. 16)—Came from

Nehemiah 6:10–13—Why Would Nehemiah Not Go into the Temple?

Shemaiah was seemingly part of a plan to stop Nehemiah's efforts, and Shemaiah's being "shut up" in his house was part of the plan. Shemaiah made it sound like Nehemiah's life was in danger and told Nehemiah that he should go to the temple, grab the horns of the altar, and plead that his life be protected, which was an action spoken of in the law of Moses (see Exodus 21:14; 1 Kings 1:50–51; 2:28; 2 Kings 11:15). Nehemiah recognized the plot against him and chose to trust the Lord for protection. Another reason Nehemiah did not go into the temple was because he was not a priest. Shemaiah and others hoped to ruin Nehemiah's reputation with the people, but they failed.

Studying the Scriptures ▬▬▶

(A) Avoid Deception

1. Name the people in Nehemiah 6 who tried to do harm to Nehemiah, and explain how.

2. What things did Nehemiah do to avoid falling into their "traps"?

3. Write what the following scriptures say about what we can do to avoid being deceived: Helaman 3:29–30; Doctrine and Covenants 43:2–6; 46:7–8; Joseph Smith—Matthew 1:37.

Nehemiah 7

The Names of Those Who Returned

Nehemiah 7 is a record of the people who came to Jerusalem with Zerubbabel (see Ezra 2). Just as in Ezra, Nehemiah 7 notes that those who were not able to show by their genealogy that they were of the proper lineage were not permitted to have the priesthood.

Nehemiah 8

Ezra Reads the Scriptures to the People

How would your life be different if you could never hear, read, or even have a copy of the scriptures? In the days of Nehemiah, scriptures were hand-written onto scrolls, hence it would require great effort and sacrifice to obtain one. Anyone who had a complete copy was considered fortunate. The people of Nehemiah's day had not read or heard the scriptures for several years. As you read Nehemiah 8, compare what the people felt and did when they heard the scriptures with what you feel and do when you have an opportunity to read or hear the scriptures.

Understanding the Scriptures 🔑

Nehemiah 8

Were attentive (v. 3)—Listened carefully

Distinctly (v. 8)—Clearly

Sense (v. 8)—Meaning

Tirshatha (v. 9)—Governor

Portions (v. 10)—Some

Grieved (v. 11)—Pained

Nehemiah 8:13–18—They Read in the Scriptures That They Should Dwell in "Booths"

The Jews in Ezra's time discovered in the scriptures a commandment to "dwell in booths." The commandment refers to the Feast of the Tabernacles, which was a sacred celebration the Lord first gave to Moses and the children of Israel (see Leviticus 23:33–44; Bible Dictionary, s.v. "feasts").

Studying the Scriptures ✏️

Ⓐ Find Important Words

1. Read Nehemiah 8:2–12 and make a list of the words you think best describe how the people felt about hearing Ezra read and explain the scriptures to them. You may want to highlight these words in your scriptures.

2. Choose one of the words you wrote in your list and tell about a time when you felt the same way; or, choose one of the words in the list and tell why you think the people responded the way they did when Ezra taught the scriptures.

3. Which words in Nehemiah 8:2–12 do you think describe what Ezra did to help the people have a great experience with the scriptures?

Nehemiah 9–10

The Power of the Word

We read in the Book of Mormon that "the preaching of the word . . . had more powerful effect upon the minds of the people than the sword, or anything else" (Alma 31:5). Nehemiah 9–10 contains examples of this truth.

In Nehemiah 9 we read that because they heard the word of God (see Nehemiah 8), the people fasted, confessed their sins, and worshiped the Lord. The priests then gave the people an overview of their history from the time of Abraham, showing how merciful the Lord had been to them up to their day.

In Nehemiah 10 we read that the priests made covenants to fully keep the commandments. The rest of the people followed the example of their priests and also made this covenant. The events recorded in chapters 9–10 show some of the blessings of reading, studying, pondering, and applying the scriptures in our lives.

Nehemiah 11–12

The Dedication of the Wall

Nehemiah 11 gives the names of the leaders of the people in Israel and which of them were assigned to live in Jerusalem. Chapter 11 also mentions others who were assigned to live in other cities in the land.

The first section of Nehemiah 12 contains the names of the priests and Levites (priesthood holders) who returned to Jerusalem in Zerubbabel's group (vv. 1–9). The next section contains the names of the priests and Levites at the time of Nehemiah, who were descendants of the original group (vv. 10–26). The rest of the chapter tells about the dedication of the walls of Jerusalem (vv. 27–47).

Nehemiah 13

Nehemiah Continues to Preach Repentance

Some time after the dedication of the walls of Jerusalem, Nehemiah returned to be with King Artaxerxes in Babylon.

Nehemiah 13 tells the story of what he found when he came back to Jerusalem. Three things greatly disappointed him: (1) a foreigner, who did not believe in the God of Israel was allowed to dwell in the house of the Lord, (2) the people were not keeping the Sabbath day holy, and (3) the people—even the priests and Levites—were marrying out of the covenant. Nehemiah encouraged the people to be faithful to the Lord by keeping these commandments. We too show our faithfulness to God today by worthily attending the temple, keeping the Sabbath day holy, and marrying in the covenant.

The Book of Esther

The Story of a Jewish Heroine

Esther did not write the book of Esther, but her entire story is found in the book. The story took place during a time when many Jews were in Persia (approximately 460–30 B.C.) and tells how Esther's courageous actions saved her people from destruction. The Jewish people still celebrate this wonderful event with a happy holiday they call Purim. The Jews reread this story; some of the people clap and cheer for the heroes and curse the villains. Because the book of Esther is a story, the "Understanding the Scriptures" and "Studying the Scriptures" sections cover the entire book. For further information on the book of Esther, see the Bible Dictionary, s.v. "Esther, book of."

Getting Ready to Study Esther

Cyrus was the first king of the Persian Empire. He was succeeded by his son Cambyses, who ruled for a short time. After Cambyses' death, a man named Darius was king for many years. After Darius died, his son Xerxes ruled as the fourth king of the Persian Empire. Xerxes, which was his Greek name, is known in the book of Esther by his Persian name, Ahasuerus.

Although Esther comes after Nehemiah in your Bible, the events in Esther actually occurred about thirty years before the events in Nehemiah. Xerxes, or Ahasuerus, was the king in Nehemiah's time who seemed to be so friendly to Nehemiah and the Jews. Perhaps this is because of what happened in the book of Esther. If not for the events in Esther, there may not have been a book of Nehemiah!

Understanding the Scriptures

Esther 1

Expired (v. 5)—Finished

Diverse (v. 7)—Different

Abundance (v. 7)—Great amount

Compel (v. 8)—Force

Pleasure (v. 8)—Desire

Chamberlains (vv. 12, 15)—Governor over the king's interest

Wise men, which knew the times (v. 13)—Astrologers

Come abroad (v. 17)—Be known

Contempt (v. 18)—Disrespect

Wrath (v. 18)—Anger

Altered (v. 19)—Changed

Estate (v. 19)—Position and possessions

Esther 2

Wrath (v. 1)—Anger

Appeased (v. 1)—Calmed

Purification (vv. 3, 9, 12)—Treatments to make the women more beautiful

Preferred (v. 9)—Favored

Shewed her people, shewed her kindred (vv. 10, 20)—Told what group of people she belonged to

Charged (vv. 10, 20)—Commanded

Wroth (v. 21)—Angry

Lay hand (v. 21)—Kill

Certified (v. 22)—Told

Inquisition (v. 23)—Investigation

Esther 3

Thought scorn (v. 6)—Rejected the suggestion

Lot (v. 7)—Something that allows you to choose a number by chance, as with dice

Diverse (v. 8)—Different

Suffer (v. 8)—Allow, tolerate

Have the charge of the business (v. 9)—Who carry out the action

To take the spoil of them for a prey (v. 13)—To take their goods as a reward

Perplexed (v. 15)—Confused

Esther 4

Grieved (v. 4)—Very grieved or pained
Charge (v. 8)—Command
Make supplication (v. 8)—Humbly ask

Sceptre (v. 11)—A staff that is a symbol of authority
Altogether holdest thy peace (v. 14)—Do not say anything

Esther 5

Petition (vv. 6–8)—Desire
Indignation (v. 9)—Anger
Refrained (v. 10)—Controlled
Availeth me nothing (v. 13)—

Does me no good
Gallows (v. 14)—A place to kill someone by hanging

Esther 6

Apparel (vv. 8–11)—Clothing
Array (v. 9)—Clothe

Withal (v. 9)—Completely

Esther 7

Durst presume (v. 5)—Does think

Pacified (v. 10)—Calmed

Esther 8

Besought (v. 3)—To ask with great feeling
Mischief (v. 3)—Wicked plan
Device, devised (v. 3)—Plan, planned
Stand for their life (v. 11)—Defend themselves

Assault (v. 11)—Attack with intent to hurt
Spoil (v. 11)—Goods
Prey (v. 11)—Reward

Esther 9

Execution (v. 1)—Effect
Contrary (v. 1)—Opposite of the way it was

Ordained (v. 27)—Established
Confirm (vv. 31–32)—Establish
Enjoined (v. 31)—Ordered

Esther 10

Tribute (v. 1)—Tax

Studying the Scriptures

A Use Their Example

Write about what you think a person your age could learn from the examples of each of the following three people in the book of Esther: Queen Vashti, Mordecai, and Esther. For each individual, give specific examples and references from the scriptures as part of your explanation.

B An Important Verse to Remember

1. Read Esther 4:14 and then write it in your own words.

2. Mordecai's question to Esther in Esther 4:14 might well be asked of you today. President Ezra Taft Benson helped answer the question when he said, "For nearly six thousand years, God has held you in reserve to make your appearance in the final days before the second coming of the Lord. Some individuals will fall away; but the kingdom of God will remain intact to welcome the return of its head—even Jesus Christ. While our generation will be comparable in wickedness to the days of Noah, when the Lord cleansed the earth by flood, there is a major difference this time. It is that God has saved for the final inning some of His strongest children, who will help bear off the kingdom triumphantly. That is where you come in, for you are the generation that must be prepared to meet your God" (*The Teachings of Ezra Taft Benson* [1988], 104–5).

President Benson also said, "In all ages prophets have looked down through the corridors of time to our day. Billions of the deceased and those yet to be born have their eyes on us. Make no mistake about it—you are a marked generation. There has never been more expected of the faithful in such a short period of time than there is of us" (*Teachings of Ezra Taft Benson,* 105). Write a journal entry to your class telling why it is important for them to remember that they have come to the kingdom "for such a time as this."

The Book of Job

Why Do Bad Things Happen to Good People?

Each day, tragedy and suffering may come into people's lives. Loved ones die or are permanently harmed by disease, accident, or natural disaster. How could God allow these things to happen? How could they happen even to those who serve the Lord diligently? Does God cause all this suffering, sorrow, and death?

In addressing these kinds of questions, President Spencer W. Kimball said, "Answer if you can. I cannot, for though I know

God has a major role in our lives, I do not know how much he causes to happen and how much he merely permits. Whatever the answer to this question, there is another I feel sure about.

"Could the Lord have prevented these tragedies? The answer is, Yes. The Lord is omnipotent, with all power to control our lives, save us pain, prevent all accidents, drive all planes and cars, feed us, protect us, save us from labor, effort, sickness, even from death, if he will. But he will not" (*Faith Precedes the Miracle* [1972], 96). Why won't the Lord protect and save us from all of the adversities and opposition of life's experiences? (see Abraham 3:25). Would doing so strengthen or weaken us?

The book of Job deals with difficult questions. Job tells the story of a righteous man who suffers greatly. How he deals with his adversity and what he learns from his experiences can teach us important lessons about our suffering and the sorrows of those around us. The Lord used the story of Job to teach the Prophet Joseph Smith about tribulation at a time when the Prophet was in Liberty Jail and wondered why he was suffering (see D&C 121:1–33). As you read Job, consider what you learn about Heavenly Father's plan and what purpose suffering has in that plan.

Getting Ready to Study the Book of Job

Although we know very little about Job (pronounced Jōb), he probably lived in the time of the patriarchs (Abraham, Isaac, and Jacob). His book is placed in the "poetry" section of the Bible because the story is told in poetic form, which makes it perhaps one of the more difficult Old Testament books to read and understand. The poetry, however, helps the story come across with more feeling. Since poetry is meant to be read aloud, you may want to read aloud a few verses you like and see if doing so helps you understand the feeling and meaning of Job. For an overview of the book of Job, see the Bible Dictionary, s.v. "Job, book of."

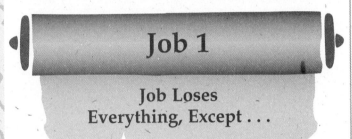

Job 1

Job Loses Everything, Except . . .

When something bad happens to you, how do you react? How do you feel toward God? Do you feel differently toward God or yourself if a bad thing happened to you and you "did nothing wrong"? Job 1 tells how Job reacted to what happened to him. Consider how you would react in the same situation.

Understanding the Scriptures 🗝

Job 1

Upright (vv. 1, 8)—Righteous
Eschewed, escheweth (vv. 1, 8)—Avoided, avoid
Sanctified (v. 5)—Made clean before God through ordinances
Nought (v. 9)—For nothing
Hedge (v. 10)—Like a fence built to protect

Made out three bands (v. 17)—Formed three groups
Rent his mantle (v. 20)—Tore his robe
Charged (v. 22)—Accused

Job 1:6–12—Do God and Satan Really Make Agreements?

Of course the Lord has power over Satan and has no need to "bargain" with him. In Job 1:6–12 we learn that the Lord was pleased with the way Job was living but that he still allowed Satan to tempt and cause trials for Job. Job 2 contains a similar situation. Notice that both times Job was tried, the Lord set the "rules" for what Satan could and couldn't do. We can feel confident knowing that as long as we are faithful to the Lord, he will never allow Satan to cause more trials for us than we are able to overcome (see 1 Corinthians 10:13).

Studying the Scriptures ✏️➡️

A Write a Recommendation for Job

If Job were applying for work and asked you to write a recommendation letter about the kind of person he was, what would you say about him based on what you read in Job 1?

B Same or Different?

Describe how Job responded to what happened to him and how his reaction compares to the way you think righteous people would have responded.

Job 2

More Trials for Job

Job passed the test he was given in Job 1, but the Lord allowed Satan to afflict Job even more. Job 2 will again show how Job responded to his trials.

Understanding the Scriptures 🗝

Job 2

Holdeth fast his integrity (v. 3)—Remained faithful
His crown (v. 7)—The top of his head
Potsherd (v. 8)—Piece of broken pottery
Withal (v. 8)—All over his body

Retain thine integrity (v. 9)—Stay faithful
Knew him not (v. 12)—Could not recognize him
Grief (v. 13)—Sadness and great sorrow

Studying the Scriptures ✏️➡️

A Give Your Opinion

Of everything that happened to Job in Job 1–2, write about the one thing that would be the hardest for you to experience, and explain why you think it would be so hard.

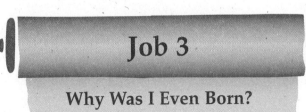

Job 3

Why Was I Even Born?

Although Job did not blame God for his troubles, Job 3 gives us an idea of how discouraged he was.

Understanding the Scriptures

Job 3

Seize (v. 6)—Take hold

Solitary (v. 7)—Alone

Raise up (v. 8)—Awaken

Studying the Scriptures

(A) Find Symbolic Words

Make a list of three words in Job 3 that you think describe how Job may have felt, and explain why you chose those words.

Job 4–31

Job's Friends Give Him Counsel

Job 4–31 contain conversations between Job and three friends who came to see him (see Job 2:11–13). Each friend, in his own way, told Job that God punishes sinners, so Job must have sinned. You know from what you learned in Job 1, however, that Job did not sin. When Job tried to defend himself and his righteousness, these "friends" accused him of boasting. Job explained that he knew of many wicked men who had not experienced the kind of punishment he received. The "friends" responded by encouraging him to repent so that God could remove his trials. But Job continued to argue that he was innocent of wrongdoing.

Studying the Scriptures

(A) Scripture Mastery—Job 19:25–26

1. Read Job 14:14, find a question Job asked, and write the question in your notebook. Then read Job 19:23–27 and summarize how Job later answered the question.

2. Why do you think Job's testimony in Job 19:25–26 was so important to him at the time he said it?

(B) Find Other Testimonies

Using your Topical Guide, find two other scriptures that answer Job's question in Job 14:11.

Job 32–37

A Fourth Friend

Job 32–37 contains the words of a man named Elihu. We are not sure when he joined the group, but apparently he listened to the conversation between Job and the other three men. He did not speak up because he was younger and had respect for his elders (see Job 32:4). When Elihu finally chose to speak, he criticized Job because Job claimed to be innocent. Elihu believed Job was suggesting that God was unjust or imperfect to allow him to suffer by saying he was innocent. Elihu also criticized Job's friends because they really didn't provide Job with an answer as to why he was suffering other than to condemn him as a sinner. Elihu offered a third point of view. He proclaimed the greatness of God and man's inability to understand the mind of God in a way that provides an explanation for everything that happens. He suggested that suffering is not always a punishment for sin, but since God does good things for his children, suffering could benefit a person in some way.

Job 38–39

The Lord Speaks

The Lord finally answered Job's prayers. He did not seem, however, to answer the questions Job and his friends raised, like: Why was Job suffering? Instead, the Lord gave answers in the form of more questions. The answers to the Lord's questions give us perspectives about God and life that are very important to people facing trials in their lives.

Speaking of life's challenges, Elder Richard G. Scott said, "When you face adversity, you can be led to ask many questions. Some serve a useful purpose; others do not. To ask, Why does this have to happen to me? Why do I have to suffer this now? What have I done to cause this? will lead you into blind alleys. It really does no good to ask questions that reflect opposition to the will of God. Rather ask, What am I to do? What am I to learn from this experience? What am I to change? Whom am I to help? How can I remember my many blessings in times of trial? . . .

"This life is an experience in profound trust—trust in Jesus Christ, trust in His teachings, trust in our capacity as led by the Holy Spirit to obey those teachings. . . . To trust means to obey willingly without knowing the end from the beginning (see Proverbs 3:5–7). To produce fruit, your trust in the Lord must be more powerful and enduring than your confidence in your own personal feelings and experience" (in Conference Report, Oct. 1995, 18–19; or Ensign, Nov. 1995, 17).

Job 38–39 gives us an idea of what would help Job have more confidence in the Lord so that he would more fully trust that whatever trials he experienced would be for his benefit.

Understanding the Scriptures 🔑

Job 38

Gird up now thy loins (v. 3)—Prepare yourself

Demand (v. 3)—Ask

Issued (v. 8)—Came

Garment thereof (v. 9)—Clothing (of the earth)

Swaddlingband (v. 9)—A covering wrapped around babies

Hitherto (v. 11)—Here

Stayed (v. 11)—Stopped

Dayspring (v. 12)—Sunrise

Perceived the breadth (v. 18)—Understood the size

Gendered (v. 29)—Gave birth to

Pleiades, Orion, Mazzaroth, Arcturus (vv. 31–32)—Constellations of stars

Dominion (v. 33)—Control

Studying the Scriptures ✏️

A Answer the Lord's Questions

1. How would you answer the questions the Lord asked Job?

2. Tell what you think Job should have learned as he answered the questions the Lord asked.

Job 40–42

Job Passes the Test

When you truly begin to understand the greatness of God, how do you feel?

Job 40 records Job's answers to the Lord's questions when he took an opportunity to briefly answer the Lord (see Job 38–39). Job simply declared his humility in response to what the Lord said to him. The Lord then continued to teach Job until the end of chapter 41. The Lord's message was much like the message of chapters 38–39, which was that the Lord is in control of all things and all things will be for our blessing and happiness as we are humble and obedient.

Job 42 records that Job spoke again and expressed what he learned from the Lord and how he felt about what he learned.

Then the Lord told Job's friends to repent. The last few verses tell what eventually happened to Job.

Understanding the Scriptures 🔑

Job 42

Withholden (v. 2)—Kept back

Uttered (v. 3)—Spoke

Abhor (v. 6)—Hate

My wrath is kindled (v. 7)—I am very angry

Folly (v. 8)—Foolish acts

Turned the captivity (v. 10)—Released from suffering

Bemoaned (v. 11)—Showed concern

Job 42:6—Is It Right to Hate Yourself?

When Job said he abhorred himself in Job 42:6, he was expressing in a poetic way that he was very sorry for past prideful actions. This remorse is an important part of repentance and growth to be more like God.

Studying the Scriptures ✏️

A Say It in Your Own Words

Write Job 42:5 in your own words, then write a paragraph that tells what you think Job may have meant when he said what he did.

B What Did He Learn?

What do you think Job came to understand through his experience? Before you answer, consider the following questions and statement:

- When did Job get relief from his trials? What changed first, things outside of Job or inside of him?

- How does what Job obtained later in his life (see Job 42:10–17) compare to what he had originally (see Job 1:2–3)? What might the increase symbolize?

- Elder Richard G. Scott said: "I testify that you have a Heavenly Father who loves you. I witness that the Savior gave His life for your happiness. I know Him. He understands your every need. I positively know that as you accept Their will without complaint, They will bless and sustain you" (in Conference Report, Oct. 1995, 21; or *Ensign*, Nov. 1995, 18).

The Book of Psalms

An Ancient Hymn Book

The book of Psalms is a collection of sacred poems that are praises and prayers to God. The title of this book in Hebrew, *Telhillim*, means "praises." The title of this book in Greek is *Psalms*, which means "songs." Most of the poems in this book were written as songs and were intended to be sung with a stringed-instrument accompaniment. Singing was a part of temple worship services and public events, such as funerals, marriages, and other celebrations.

As mentioned above, many psalms are written to simply praise the Lord. In addition, you will find psalms that are specifically about the law, the temple, nature, or historical events. Some of the most beautiful and important psalms teach about the Messiah, Jesus Christ. The book of Psalms is quoted in the New Testament more than any other Old Testament book. For a list of Old Testament scriptures quoted in the New Testament, see the Bible Dictionary, s.v. "quotations."

We do not know the author of all of the psalms, although many do note an author. King David is mentioned the most as a writer of various psalms. Others are also mentioned: Moses, Solomon, Asaph (David's musician), and Levite priests (the sons of Korah). Sometimes the author is anonymous.

Getting Ready to Study Psalms

Understanding a little about Hebrew poetry can help you better understand Psalms. Most poetry is written in the language of emotion. Poets do not try to "report" events as much as they express their feelings. To express themselves, they often use symbolic language and may exaggerate. In addition, they may also try to express their feelings or impress their audience by using some kind of pattern or rhythm.

Hebrew poetry creates a sense of rhythm by repeating ideas in a style called "parallelism." Sometimes the writer will say the same kind of thing in different ways, while at other times he will put two ideas in opposition to one another. Consider the following example from Psalm 1. This psalm is written below so that the repeated ideas are grouped together. Notice that sometimes the ideas are additional examples of the first idea, while other times later ideas are opposites of the first.

- Psalm 1:1–2 is an example of the opposite style of parallelism:

"Blessed is the man that walketh not in the counsel of the ungodly, nor standeth in the way of sinners, nor sitteth in the seat of the scornful."

"But his delight is in the law of the Lord; and in his law doth he meditate day and night."

- Psalm 1:3–4 shows symbolic language for both opposites:

Idea. "And he shall be like a tree planted by the rivers of water, that bringeth forth his fruit in his season; his leaf also shall not wither; and whatsoever he doeth shall prosper."

Opposite idea. "The ungodly are not so: but are like the chaff which the wind driveth away."

- Psalm 1:5 is an example of a repeated idea:

"Therefore the ungodly shall not stand in the judgment, nor sinners in the congregation of the righteous."

- Psalm 1:6 is another example of opposite parallelism:

"For the Lord knoweth the way of the righteous: but the way of the ungodly shall perish."

Notice in the example above that the writer used images that seem to paint pictures with words. This kind of writing gives greater power to the ideas. We might just say that the man who is godly and delights in God's laws will be blessed. But the psalmist instead gave the image of a tree, planted very close to a river, that receives constant nourishment and refreshment and continually grows and bears fruit. That image brings more power to the mind and heart of the reader or listener than just saying that the man is blessed.

If you read the book of Psalms keeping in mind these ideas about Hebrew poetry, you will find the psalms much more interesting and their teachings will come with greater power to your heart.

Because it is not possible to study the entire book of Psalms, this study guide will direct you to several of the important psalms quoted by New Testament writers, psalms that are about the Savior, or psalms that have a special insight on an important doctrine of the gospel. But you are welcome to read all of the psalms. Perhaps a psalm not mentioned in this study guide will become one of your favorites.

Psalm 22

A Psalm about Jesus Christ

Psalm 22 contains the words King David spoke or sang in response to what seemed like continual attacks from his enemies. Look for ways this psalm foretells what would happen to the Savior when he came in the flesh.

Understanding the Scriptures

Psalm 22

Forsaken me (v. 1)—Turned away from me and left me alone

Inhabitest (v. 3)—Lives with

Confounded (v. 5)—Challenged

Reproach of (v. 6)—Rejected

Despised (vv. 6, 24)—Hated

Laugh me to scorn (v. 7)—Mock me

Shoot out the lip (v. 7)—Insult

Compassed (vv. 12, 16)—Surrounded

Beset me round (v. 12)—Surrounded me

Gaped (v. 13)—To open the mouth wide

Ravening (v. 13)—Reckless or careless eating

Potsherd (v. 15)—Piece of broken pottery

Cleaveth (v. 15)—Sticks

Cast lots (v. 18)—Play a game of chance

Vesture (v. 18)—Clothing

Haste (v. 19)—Hurry

Abhorred (v. 24)—To completely dislike

Affliction, afflicted (v. 24)—Troubles, troubled

Pay my vows (v. 25)—Keep my promises

Studying the Scriptures ✏️➡️

Ⓐ Look for Things about the Savior

Verses in Psalm 22	What Happened	References in Matthew 27
1		
6–8		
16		
18		

1. In addition to Psalm 22, read Matthew 27:27–50. Make a chart in your notebook like the one shown here and record how verses from Psalm 22 were fulfilled in the life of Jesus as recorded in Matthew 27.

2. Beginning with verse 19 in Psalm 22, David expressed more hopeful feelings. Verses 19–31 are like a prayer, but they contain important truths. Choose something in verses 24–31 that explains why we would "declare" (v. 22), "praise" (vv. 22–23), "glorify" (v. 23), or "fear" (v. 23) the Savior for suffering in the way described in verses 1–18.

Psalm 23

"The Lord Is My Shepherd"

Psalm 23 is a famous psalm that is the source for the words of "The Lord Is My Shepherd," a hymn in the Latter-day Saint hymnbook (no. 108) that teaches us about the loving care of the Lord.

Understanding the Scriptures 🔑

Psalm 23

Want (v. 1)—Be in need of anything

Thy rod and thy staff (v. 4)—The straight and hooked-end stick used by shepherds.

Studying the Scriptures ✏️➡️

Ⓐ Explain the Images

You are one of the Lord's lambs in Psalm 23. Put in your own words what you think the following phrases mean in this psalm: "The Lord is my shepherd" (v. 1), "He maketh me to lie down in green pastures" (v. 2), "He restoreth my soul" (v. 3), "thy rod and thy staff they comfort me" (v. 4), and "my cup runneth over" (v. 5).

Ⓑ Choose Your Favorite Phrase

Choose a phrase from Psalm 23 that expresses how you feel about the Lord. Explain your choice.

Psalm 24

The Joy of the Lord's Coming

Psalm 24 is about being with the Lord when he comes.

Understanding the Scriptures 🔑

Psalm 24

Fulness thereof (v. 1)—Everything in it

Ascend (v. 3)—Go up

Vanity (v. 4)—Meaningless, temporary and not satisfying

Sworn deceitfully (v. 4)—Lied

Psalm 24:6, 10—What Is "Selah"?

The Hebrew word translated *selah* in the psalms comes from a root word that means "to lift up" (see Bible Dictionary, s.v. "selah").

Studying the Scriptures

A What Difference Does It Make?

Describe what difference you think it makes when a person really believes the truth expressed in Psalm 24:1.

B Scripture Mastery—Psalm 24:3–4

1. Make a list of what Psalm 24:4 says we must do to enter the Lord's house and his presence. Describe in your own words each word or phrase you listed.

2. Read Doctrine and Covenants 97:15–17 and tell what the verses say about how we can be in the presence of the Lord. You may want to write the reference in the margin of your scriptures next to Psalm 24:3–4.

C Help from the Joseph Smith Translation

What important insights does the Joseph Smith Translation add to Psalm 24:7–10?

Selected Verses from Psalms

The following study section will help you learn some specific, important verses from various psalms. You are not required to read each psalm, although you may wish to anyway.

Studying the Scriptures

Do at least four of the following activities (A–F) for Psalms.

A Compare the Ideas

1. Read Psalms 8:3–4; Moses 1:8–10. How was Moses' experience like that of the writer of Psalm 8?

2. Write about what helps you to realize the greatness of God and encourages you to be more humble.

3. Answer the question asked in Psalm 8:4.

B A Prophecy about Christ

Explain how the ideas and feelings in Psalm 41:9 were fulfilled in the life of Jesus (see Matthew 26:14–16; John 13:18–26).

C Explain the Meaning According to a Prophet

Read Psalm 118:22, then Acts 4:10–12. Write in your own words what Peter said Psalm 118:22 is about.

D The Power of the Word

1. List all the ways the writer of Psalm 119:97–105 said he benefitted because he had the word of the Lord and knew his teachings.

2. Tell about ways you think the word of the Lord is a "lamp" for your feet and a "light" to your path. Read 1 Nephi 17:13.

E Names and Descriptions of God

1. Make a list of at least five different names for God that you find in Psalms (there are at least twenty-seven).

2. Why do you think Psalms gives so many different names?

3. List at least five different phrases that describe God in Psalms (there are at least thirty-two).

4. Choose a phrase from the list you just made that best describes your feelings about the Lord.

F Find a Quote

Look through several psalms of your choice. Look for an idea you think would make a good poster saying. Write the phrase down and explain why you chose it.

The Proverbs

A proverb is a short saying that teaches proper and moral behavior. The book of Proverbs gives rather practical advice for living one's religion and behaving in a proper, moral way. We can all benefit from following the counsel given in this book.

Getting Ready to Study Proverbs

We read in 1 Kings 4:32 that Solomon spoke many proverbs; Proverbs 1:1 says Solomon is the author of the proverbs in this book, although other authors are also mentioned (for example, see Proverbs 30:1; 31:1).

Proverbs contains expressions on a wide variety of topics. One verse may not have anything to do with the verse (proverb) before or after it. Most of the proverbs are written in the Hebrew poetry style described in the introduction to the book of Psalms.

You will study the book of Proverbs like you did the book of Psalms. Rather than studying each chapter, you will study and consider some important verses.

Proverbs

An Overview

Studying the Scriptures ▰▰▰✏

Do six of the following twelve activities (A–L) as you study the book of Proverbs.

A Make up a Title

1. Some people feel that Proverbs 1:7; 9:10 are the theme of the book of Proverbs. Read these verses. Based on what you read, write a title for the book of Proverbs. (*Note:* The word *fear* as used in these verses means reverence or deep respect for God.)

2. From what you have experienced and learned, explain that what these two verses teach is true.

B Scripture Mastery—Proverbs 3:5–6

1. Draw something that represents the meaning of Proverbs 3:5–6. For example, you could draw a diagram or a picture with a short, catchy phrase. Show your drawing to your family and see if they understand the meaning, then read the scripture and explain the meaning to them.

2. Who have you read about in the Old Testament who was an example of Proverbs 3:5–6? Explain why.

C Give an Example

In Proverbs 3:11–12 the phrase "to chasten" is to punish for the purpose of correcting. Write a brief situation or story that shows the truth of this proverb.

D Make a Chart

Make a chart like the one below and fill it in with information from Proverbs 6:16–19 and from your own thoughts and experiences about what the Lord "hates" (there should be seven characteristics listed in Proverbs).

Characteristics the Lord Hates	Why You Think He Hates Them

E Give Advice to a Friend

Imagine you are helping someone who is struggling with why he or she should live the law of chastity. What verses in Proverbs 6:23–33 would you read to him or her? For each verse you choose, tell how you would explain what the verse teaches. For example, if you were to choose verse 32, you might ask "What understanding do you think a person who commits adultery lacks?"

F Try It Out

Try living the principles taught in Proverbs 15:1, 18; 16:32 for two or more days, and write in your notebook about your experience.

G Write It in Your Own Words

Write Proverbs 27:12 in your own words. How might verse 12 apply to the counsel we get from the prophets in the booklet *For the Strength of Youth* (34285)?

H Write the Opposite

Rewrite Proverbs 30:11–14 so that the verses express ideas opposite from the ones found in the scriptures. So, instead of the verses speaking of an unrighteous generation, they will tell about a righteous generation of Latter-day Saints. What could you do to help bring about this righteous generation?

I For Great Women

Proverbs 31:10–31 gives a description of a godly woman. List what you think are the five most important qualities mentioned, and explain why each one you chose is important.

J If You're So Wise . . .

Solomon is supposedly the author of most of the proverbs. Considering what you know about Solomon's life, find a proverb you think could have saved him from the problems he had later in his life.

K Proverbs about Riches

Read the following proverbs and summarize what they say about riches: 11:4, 28; 13:7–8; 15:16; 19:17; 21:6, 17; 22:1–2, 4, 7, 9, 16, 22–23; 28:6, 8, 11, 20, 22, 27; 30:7–9.

L Proverbs about Work

Read the following proverbs and summarize what they say about work: 6:6–11; 10:4, 26; 12:24, 27; 13:4; 14:23; 19:15; 20:4, 13; 21:25–26; 24:30–34; 26:13–16; 28:19.

Ecclesiastes or, the Preacher

Life without Knowledge of the Plan

How would your opinions and attitudes about life be different if you believed that this life was our only existence—that there is no accountability to our life after death?

The writer of Ecclesiastes wrote most of his book as if he believed that this life is all there is. By writing from that point of view, he showed how frustrating life can be without the gospel. In the last chapter the writer admitted that he really did believe that life continues after death and that because life goes on forever, life has no lasting meaning or happiness unless we serve God and prepare for the Judgment—where all that seemed like "vanity" (temporary and not satisfying) will be seen for what it really is.

For more information on Ecclesiastes, see the Bible Dictionary, s.v. "Ecclesiastes."

Ecclesiastes 1–2

"All Is Vanity"

Ecclesiastes 1–2 records what the "preacher" (as he calls himself) told about his search to find some lasting feeling of joy and happiness. As you read, think about how you feel about the things he saw and did and what he sought.

Understanding the Scriptures 🔑

Ecclesiastes 1

Vanity (vv. 2, 14)—Meaningless, temporary and not satisfying

Profit (v. 3)—Reward

Taketh (v. 3)—Does

Under the sun (vv. 3, 9)—On earth

Hasteth (v. 5)—Hurries

Circuits (v. 6)—Patterns

Whence (v. 7)—Where

Thither (v. 7)—There

Exercised therewith (v. 13)—Troubled with

Vexation (vv. 14, 17)—Troubling

Wanting (v. 15)—Lacking

Estate (v. 16)—Inheritance

Madness and folly (v. 17)—Foolishness

Ecclesiastes 2

Prove thee (v. 1)—Test the idea that there is nothing but vanity in the world

Mirth (vv. 1–2)—Fun, enjoyment that comes from lighthearted activities with others

What doeth it? (v. 2)—What good does it do?

Give myself unto wine (v. 3)—Experiment to see if wine added any quality and meaning to life

Yet acquainting mine heart with wisdom (v. 3)—Still trying to learn wisdom

Lay hold on folly (v. 3)—Do foolish things

Above (v. 7)—More than

Portion (vv. 10, 21)—Wage or payment

Wrought (vv. 11, 17)—Made

Folly (vv. 12–13)—Foolishness

Excelleth (v. 13)—Is greater than

Perceived (v. 14)—Realized

One event happeneth to them all (v. 14)—Some things happen to everyone, no matter how wise or foolish the person is.

Grievous (v. 17)—Bad

Travail (vv. 23, 26)—Work

Grief (v. 23)—Sadness

Heap up (v. 26)—Store

Studying the Scriptures ✏️

A Make a List

List at least five items from Ecclesiastes 1–2 that the writer said should have made him happy but did not. After each item on your list, write the reference of the verse where you found it. You may want to highlight in your scriptures the five things you chose to list.

B Do You Agree or Disagree?

Read Ecclesiastes 1:18. Write to the preacher and tell him why you agree or disagree with his statement there.

Ecclesiastes 3

Make the Best of Life While You Can

Ecclesiastes 3 tells how life has frustrations; the wicked and the righteous and the wise and the foolish all have good and bad happen to them. Chapter 3 concludes that even though good and bad times happen to all, a person is happier if he or she lives a good life and seeks joy—even if that joy does not last. In others words, if good and bad happen to all, we might as well enjoy the good while it lasts.

Ecclesiastes 3:1–8 are some of the most often quoted verses in Ecclesiastes. They can, however, be misunderstood. By saying that everything has a season, the preacher is simply saying that there are certain events that happen to all. He was not suggesting that all of us have a time to kill or a time to hate or do other negative things. There is never an appropriate time to disobey the commandments.

Ecclesiastes 4–5

What Makes You Happy?

Is there a way of life that makes people happy even when they do not believe or accept truths about God, his commandments, and eternal life? Even though the preacher saw so much "vanity" in the world, in Ecclesiastes 4–5 he admitted that there were still things worth doing that lead to greater happiness in a world that didn't make much sense to him otherwise (without an understanding of God's plan).

Understanding the Scriptures 🔑

Ecclesiastes 4

Oppressions (v. 1)—Bad things that happen to people

Travail (vv. 4, 6, 8)—Business, work

Envied of his neighbor (v. 4)—His neighbor is jealous of him

Prevail (v. 12)—Overpower

Admonished (v. 13)—Taught and corrected

Ecclesiastes 5

Be not rash with thy mouth (v. 2)—Do not speak harshly.

Hasty (v. 2)—Quick

Multitude of business (v. 3)—Jobs or tasks

Vow (vv. 4–5)—Promise

Divers (v. 7)—Many

Violent perverting (v. 8)—Terrible twisting or changing

Marvel not (v. 8)—Do not be surprised.

Regardeth (v. 8)—Sees it

Profit (v. 9)—Riches

Abundance (vv. 10, 12)—A great number

Saving (v. 11)—Except

Travail (v. 14)—Work

Comely (v. 18)—Right

Portion (vv. 18–19)—Reward or gain

Studying the Scriptures

A Find Some Good Advice

Ecclesiastes mentioned several deeds that still make sense to do even if "all is vanity." Write about two things you read about in Ecclesiastes 4–5 that would be good advice even to someone who does not believe in God. Explain the advice as if you were giving it to a person who does not believe in God.

Ecclesiastes 6

All Is Still Vanity

Ecclesiastes 6 contains more examples of how riches, honor, and children cannot completely bring happiness. The chapter concludes that if worldly wealth, praise, and posterity are all there is, then life is meaningless.

Ecclesiastes 7–11

Finding Some Contentment in Life

Having said that "all is vanity," or that nothing really brings a fulness of joy, the preacher used Ecclesiastes 7–11 to tell what he thought could bring a person some temporary happiness. Even though "all is vanity," he preached that there are still some ways of living that bring more happiness than others.

Studying the Scriptures

A Summarize the Teachings

Read the following verses from Ecclesiastes 7–11 and summarize what the preacher said a person should know or do to have some amount of happiness and contentment in life: 7:1, 11–12, 17–22; 8:12–13; 9:4–10; 10:8, 12–14; 11:1, 8–10.

Ecclesiastes 12

The Conclusion

If you knew you were going to die one week from today, what would you do in your last days?

Ecclesiastes 12 contains the preacher's concluding message. He reminded the young to live well while they are still able, for the day will come that they will die. The last two verses of Ecclesiastes 12 give us the first real idea that he believed in the eternal nature of life. These verses suggest that in the previous eleven and one-half chapters the preacher tried to prove that life without God has little meaning, but that living a good life still makes sense. Living a good life makes even more sense when we know that life is eternal and that we will someday stand before God and be judged. For this reason, the last two verses of Ecclesiastes 12 are the real message of the book.

Understanding the Scriptures

Ecclesiastes 12

Draw nigh (v. 1)—Come near

Keepers (v. 3)—Watchmen

Tremble (v. 3)—Become old

Flourish (v. 5)—Be rejected

Be a burden (v. 5)—Drag along

Long home (v. 5)—Death

Cistern (v. 6)—Well

Gave good heed (v. 9)—Paid attention

Set in order (v. 9)—Wrote

Goads (v. 11)—Sharp, pointed sticks

Admonished (v. 12)—Warned and taught

Is a weariness of the flesh (v. 12)—Makes you tired

Studying the Scriptures

A Make a Poster

1. Make a poster (at least the size of one page in your notebook) of what Ecclesiastes says is the whole duty of man.

2. According to Ecclesiastes 12:13–14, what reason is there for us knowing and doing this "whole duty"?

See the note for Song of Solomon 1:1 under footnote a in the LDS edition of the King James version of the Bible.

The Book of Isaiah

The book of Isaiah has received more attention and praise from other writers of scripture than any other book. Nephi used Isaiah's writings to "more fully persuade [his brethren] to believe in the Lord their Redeemer" (1 Nephi 19:23), and said "my soul delighteth in his words" (2 Nephi 11:2). Furthermore, Nephi said that the words of Isaiah would cause people to "lift up their hearts and rejoice for all men" (2 Nephi 11:8). Nephi's brother Jacob taught that those who are of the house of Israel should liken the words of Isaiah to themselves (see 2 Nephi 6:5; 11:8). The Savior himself offered the greatest praise of Isaiah's writings.

"Great Are the Words of Isaiah"

Isaiah is quoted more often in the New Testament than any other prophet. The writers of the Book of Mormon quoted or paraphrased 35 percent of the book of Isaiah. The Doctrine and Covenants makes approximately one hundred references to Isaiah by either quoting, paraphrasing, or interpreting its teachings. At the time Christ visited the Nephites after his Resurrection, Jesus told the people they should "search these things diligently; for great are the words of Isaiah" (3 Nephi 23:1).

Important Background to Isaiah

Isaiah lived and prophesied from approximately 740–700 B.C. During that time, the Assyrians conquered the Northern Kingdom of Israel. The Southern Kingdom of Judah, where Isaiah lived, was under tribute to Assyria and also faced destruction. They were spared, however, because Judah's King Hezekiah obeyed Isaiah's counsel. Isaiah warned Judah that they must continue to repent or they would also be destroyed—but by Babylon instead of Assyria.

Isaiah spoke about the first and second comings of Jesus Christ more than any other prophet in the Old Testament. He had a unique, inspired way of teaching; many of his prophecies apply not only to his time, but to the time of Jesus Christ, to our day, and to the future. Sometimes even the same verse or group of verses can apply to more than one time period.

How to Read Isaiah

Isaiah was a prophet of God, a gifted writer, and a poet to the tribes of Israel. For this reason, some of his writings can be difficult to understand when translated from Hebrew into other languages. Remember what you learned about Hebrew poetry in the introduction to Psalms (see pp. 131–32). The ideas noted there along with the Spirit of the Holy Ghost will help you understand the book of Isaiah. Through the use of images and symbols, Isaiah powerfully taught his message. You will read about the moon being ashamed, a land that is so joyful that the trees clap their hands, and a book that speaks from the dust. If you read beyond these and other images to understand the feelings and principles Isaiah wrote about, his words will take on much greater meaning. As you seek the help of the Holy Ghost, you will find that Isaiah will become one of the most inspiring and powerful books in all scripture.

For more information on the prophet Isaiah and his writings, see the Bible Dictionary, s.v. "Isaiah."

Overview of Isaiah							
General Themes	Judgments				Historical Portion	Promise of a Messiah		
Reference	1:1	13:1	24:1	28:1	36:1	40:1	49:1	58:1	66:24
Topics	Judah	The nations	Day of the Lord	Judgment and blessings	Jerusalem preserved from destruction; Hezekiah's life lengthened	Israel's deliverance	Israel's deliverer	Israel's glorious future

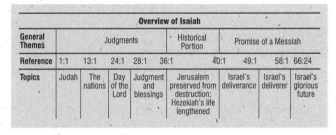

Isaiah 1

Isaiah Calls Israel to Repentance

We are not sure if Isaiah wrote the chapters in his book in the order they appear in the Bible. It seems, however, that the chapters were carefully ordered to best communicate Isaiah's full message. Isaiah 1 is like a preface to the book of Isaiah that previews and summarizes the entire book by telling: (1) what the people have done that is offensive to the Lord (vv. 1–9), (2) why they thought they did not need to repent (vv. 10–15), (3) what the Lord promised if they would repent (vv. 16–19, 25–27), and (4) what would happen if they did not repent (vv. 20–24, 28–31).

As you read, remember Nephi's and Jacob's counsel: Because we are of the house of Israel, we should liken these words to ourselves (see 1 Nephi 19:23; 2 Nephi 6:5). Many of Isaiah's teachings and prophecies apply to us as if he spoke them today.

Understanding the Scriptures

Isaiah 1

Nourished (v. 2)—Cared for, fed, clothed

Laden with iniquity (v. 4)—Carrying a heavy load of sin

Corrupters (v. 4)—Sinners

Provoked (v. 4)—Stirred up, offended

Soundness (v. 6)—Free from injury or disease

Putrifying (v. 6)—Open, fresh

Desolate (v. 7)—Destroyed

A cottage in a vineyard, a lodge in a garden of cucumbers (v. 8)—A temporary shelter

Besieged city (v. 8)—City under attack

Remnant (v. 9)—Remaining group of people

Who hath required this at your hand, to tread my courts? (v. 12)—Who invited you to be in my house?

Vain oblations (v. 13)—Meaningless offerings

Spread forth your hands (v. 15)—Pray

Relieve the oppressed (v. 17)—Give hope to those who are burdened, help lift their burdens

Dross (vv. 22, 25)—Impure matter in a metal

Purge (v. 25)—Refine

Quench (v. 31)—To put out a fire

Studying the Scriptures

A Israel Is Like a . . .

1. Read Isaiah 1:2–9, 21–22, 30–31 and list all the images, or symbols, Isaiah used to describe the people of Judah and their sins.

2. Which of the sins of Judah are sins of people today?

B Scripture Mastery—Isaiah 1:18

Although the Lord was stern and used strong language with the Israelites, we can sense his love in the way he invited them to repent. The Lord's solutions to our sins and problems may not always be quick or easy, but they will give us a lasting solution.

1. Summarize the Lord's solution for Judah's troubles (see Isaiah 1:16–19).

2. Read Doctrine and Covenants 58:42–43 and tell how the Lord made the same promise in these verses as he did in Isaiah 1:18 and what we must do to fulfill that promise.

Isaiah 2

Come to the Mountain of the Lord

The Second Coming of Jesus Christ will usher in a thousand-year period of peace on earth called the Millennium. The wicked will be destroyed at the time of the Savior's Coming, but those prepared to receive him will be spared and rejoice with him. What must we do to prepare? In a very well-known prophecy, Isaiah told ancient and modern Israel what they must do to prepare to meet the Lord and live in the Millennium. This prophecy is "dualistic," meaning that it can apply to more than one time and place. As such, the prophecy not only teaches general principles of what ancient Israel must do to establish his kingdom but also suggests a specific location of that kingdom in the last days prior to the Second Coming and Millennium.

In the Book of Mormon, Nephi quoted Isaiah chapters 2–14. Locating footnotes in your Bible as well as comparing these chapters to the ones in 2 Nephi may help you better understand what you read.

Understanding the Scriptures

Isaiah 2

Exalted (vv. 2, 11, 17)—Put above

Rebuke (v. 4)—Judge or correct them

Soothsayers (v. 6)—People who predict the future with signs and omens

Majesty (vv. 10, 19, 21)—Greatness and power

Lofty (vv. 11–12)—High, prideful

Haughtiness (vv. 11, 17)—Pride

Clefts (v. 21)—Holes

Isaiah 2:2–4—The Mountain of the Lord

The "mountain of the Lord" refers to the temple. In Isaiah 2:2–4, Isaiah reported a vision and made a prophecy that has been fulfilled in many ways. He said that when the time comes that the Lord's people put him and his house above all things, and when they actively seek counsel from him by going to his house, then Zion will be established among them and they will have peace and the promise of eternal life. Modern prophets have taught us the same doctrine. President Howard W. Hunter said, "Let us make the temple, with temple worship and temple covenants and temple marriage, our ultimate earthly goal and the supreme mortal experience" (in Conference Report, Oct. 1994, 118; or *Ensign*, Nov. 1994, 88).

Another fulfillment of this prophecy has to do with the Lord's house being established in the "top of the mountains" (Isaiah 2:2). Not only does the prophecy have symbolic reference to putting the temple in the highest place in our lives, but it also has a literal fulfillment in the location of the Church headquarters in the latter days. Regarding this prophecy of Isaiah, Elder Bruce R. McConkie said, "This has specific reference to the Salt Lake Temple and to the other temples built in the top of the Rocky Mountains, and it has a general reference to the temple yet to be built in the New Jerusalem in Jackson County, Missouri" (*A New Witness for the Articles of Faith* [1985], 539).

Elder B. H. Roberts taught the importance of the law going forth from Zion when he said, "To me that is, in part, the law of Zion—the basic principle of the civil law of the land—a principle of the law that is going forth from Zion—the civil law that is to be established and maintained upon this blessed land of liberty, and that, eventually, will directly or indirectly bless and make free every land in all the world" (in Conference Report, Apr. 1908, 108).

Studying the Scriptures

A Make a Drawing or Sketch

Draw a representation of the ideas found in Isaiah 2:2–3.

B Give a Modern Example

The basic message of Isaiah 2:2–4 is that Zion will be established when Israel places the temple and its ordinances and laws above everything else in their lives.

1. Read Isaiah 2:6–9 and list what the Lord said was preventing the people from receiving the blessings of the temple at that time. Give a modern example of each item listed. (Make sure you compare verse 9 to 2 Nephi 12:9.)

2. According to Isaiah 2:10–22 what will happen at the Second Coming of Jesus Christ, to all who will not accept him because of their pride?

Isaiah 3

Prophecies against the Proud

Isaiah 3 contains Isaiah's further description of Israel's and Judah's wicked condition in his day and what would happen because of their wickedness. Isaiah used one of his most descriptive images as he compared the house of Israel to prideful women completely decorated in the most fashionable styles of the day. These women, very concerned with appearing beautiful on the outside, had neglected true inner spirituality. We can liken these teachings to ourselves as a warning of what will happen to us if we are prideful and wicked.

Isaiah 4

Blessings for the Humble

Isaiah 4 acts as a contrast to chapter 3 by telling what happens when Israel turns to the Lord in humility.

Understanding the Scriptures

Isaiah 4

Reproach (v. 1)—Shame
Purged (v. 4)—Cleansed
Assemblies (v. 5)—People meeting together
Tabernacle (v. 6)—Shelter

Refuge (v. 6)—Place of peace and safety apart from a dangerous or undesirable situation
Covert (v. 6)—Place of shelter

Studying the Scriptures

A Interpret the Images

Pay careful attention to the images Isaiah created in this short chapter. Unlike the women at the end of Isaiah 3, the women described in Isaiah 4 are humble.

1. According to verses 2–6, what are the results of these women's humble actions?

2. What can we do to be like the women so that we can be relieved of our shame, be cleansed from filth, become a "beautiful and glorious" people, and be guided and protected by the Lord? (see vv. 5–6). You may want to look at the following scriptures before you answer: 2 Nephi 31:13, 17; 32:1–3; Alma 7:14–15; Moses 6:52, 57.

Isaiah 5

The Sins of Israel

Isaiah 5 contains Isaiah's continued description of Israel's sins and the consequences of those sins. As you read, consider how the people's sins in Isaiah's day are like people's sins in our day and what the Lord said will happen to those who refuse to repent.

Understanding the Scriptures

Isaiah 5

Betwixt (v. 3)—Between
Hedge (v. 5)—Fence, wall
Trodden down (v. 5)—Walked on
It shall not be pruned, nor digged (v. 6)—Taken care of
Briers (v. 6)—Thorns or thorn bushes
Judgment (v. 7)—Justice, fairness
Behold (v. 7)—Saw
Oppression (v. 7)—Bloodshed
Woe (vv. 8, 11, 18, 20–22)—Sadness, or calamity

Desolate (v. 9)—Empty
Inhabitant (v. 9)—Someone who lives in a certain place
Bath, ephah (v. 10)—Units of measurement (see Bible Dictionary, s.v. "weights and measures")
Exalted (v. 16)—Lifted up, set up high
Waste places of the fat ones (v. 17)—The lands used by animals for grazing will be destroyed.

Prudent (v. 21)—Careful and of good judgment

Despised (v. 24)—Turned away from, hated

Ensign (v. 26)—Flag or banner an army gathers under and marches behind

Studying the Scriptures

Do activity A or B as you study Isaiah 5.

A **Interpret the Parable for Today**

The parable in Isaiah 5:1–7 is about those who are given the gospel. What is the message of the parable for members in our day? You may want to consider Doctrine and Covenants 1:27; 82:3; 105:6 as you write your response.

B **Woe!**

List all the people who the Lord says will experience "woe" according to Isaiah 5:8–25, and describe each group of people in your own words.

Isaiah 6

Isaiah Sees the Lord

Isaiah 6 tells how Isaiah was called to be a prophet and what the Lord said about his prophetic mission. Verses 1 and 5 contain Isaiah's testimony that he saw the Lord.

Isaiah 7–8

Trust the Lord

Isaiah 7–8 tells about a specific historical event in the kingdom of Judah, but the prophecy not only applied then but also foretold the birth of Jesus Christ over seven hundred years later.

Isaiah 7 explains that the king of Israel (the Northern Kingdom, also called Ephraim) and the king of Syria had combined together for greater military strength. Together they hoped to conquer the kingdom of Judah (see vv. 1–2, 5–6). Their actions scared Ahaz, king of Judah (see v. 2). The Lord told Isaiah to tell Ahaz not to be frightened because the Assyrians would come from the north and conquer both Syria and Ephraim. Isaiah said that the fulfillment of this prophecy would be a testimony to Judah that the Lord would continue to preserve them as a people. Then Isaiah gave Ahaz a sign as a testimony that his words were true. He said that a virgin would conceive, have a son, and name him Immanuel, which means "God with us." The name Immanuel symbolized the fact that God would be

with his people Judah. Isaiah also prophesied that before the child would be old enough to know the difference between good and evil, the Assyrians would capture the kings of both Syria and Ephraim (see vv. 14–16).

This prophecy in Isaiah 7:10–16 has a much deeper meaning. One reason God would preserve Judah as a people was because he promised to send his Son to earth through the tribe of Judah and the posterity of King David. This Son of God would be an Immanuel. Isaiah was telling Ahaz that God would preserve Judah in their current challenge with Syria and Ephraim as well as for the many years leading up to the Messiah's birth.

Isaiah 8 continues the story begun in Isaiah 7. Isaiah told the people of Judah not to worry about Syria and the Northern Kingdom of Israel because Assyria would destroy them. The new worry, however, was that Assyria would attack Judah as well. The people of Judah considered joining with other nations in a "confederacy" to fight against Assyria (see vv. 9–10). Isaiah told the people that if they trusted the Lord, he would be their security, or "sanctuary" (vv. 13–14). He also warned them about listening to people who claim revelation but do not receive it from God (see vv. 19–22).

Studying the Scriptures

A **Prophecies about Jesus Christ**

1. Use the study helps in your scriptures and write where and how a New Testament writer used Isaiah 7:14.

2. Read Isaiah 8:13–14 and explain how Jesus is both the rock upon which we build a sure foundation (see Helaman 5:12) and a "stone of stumbling" and a "rock of offence" (v. 14).

Isaiah 9

A Prophecy about the Coming of the Messiah

Isaiah 9 contains another well-known prophecy about the coming of Jesus Christ. Verse 1 describes the northern part of the Northern Kingdom of Israel, which was the first area attacked when nations like Assyria came from the north. Isaiah prophesied that this area—known as "the Galilee"—would not always be so troubled. Isaiah promised that God would send them light and joy through the birth of a child who would break the "yoke of [their] burden" (Isaiah 9:4) and be called "Wonderful, Counsellor, The mighty God, The everlasting Father, The Prince of Peace" (v. 6). All of these names refer to the Messiah—the King of Kings—and this prophecy was most completely fulfilled when Jesus spent most of his mortal ministry in this Galilee area (see Matthew 4:12–16). The prophecy continues to be fulfilled as the government, or rule, of Jesus Christ continues to eternally expand when individuals accept him as their king and become eligible for the blessings of eternal life (see Isaiah 9:7).

Isaiah 10

The Destroyers Shall Be Destroyed

In Isaiah 9, the Lord made it clear that he would allow Assyria to conquer the children of Israel in the Northern Kingdom. Isaiah's prophecies also seemed to imply that Assyria would destroy some of the kingdom of Judah as well. Why would the Lord allow a nation of wicked unbelievers like Assyria to conquer his covenant people? In Isaiah 10 the Lord answered this question. He said that because Israel was so wicked and hypocritical, he would no longer protect them. Isaiah 10 clearly states, however, that the Assyrians would also be punished because of their wickedness. They would not be allowed to completely destroy Judah because God would yet fulfill his promise concerning the coming of his "anointed," or the Messiah (see Isaiah 10:27–34).

Isaiah 11

Events in the Future

One reason Isaiah is an important book for our day is that so much of what occurred in Isaiah's time occurs in our own. We also live in a wicked time, and the Lord has promised the wicked will experience the consequences of their actions—just as in the days of Isaiah. While our day and Isaiah's day differ in details, the principles are the same. The importance of Isaiah 11 was taught by the Prophet Joseph Smith when he said, "In addition to these, he [Moroni] quoted the eleventh chapter of Isaiah, saying that it was about to be fulfilled" (Joseph Smith—History 1:40).

Those who love the Lord and try to live righteously may get discouraged living among so much wickedness. At times of discouragement, it is important to look at the "bigger picture" of Heavenly Father's plan and realize that righteousness will eventually prevail and that he has provided a way to redeem all his willing children. Isaiah 11 is about that "bigger picture" and contains a message of hope concerning what the Lord will do for those who seek to know him and do his will.

Understanding the Scriptures 🗝

Isaiah 11

Rod (v. 1)—Branch or twig

Stem (v. 1)—Trunk

Reprove (vv. 3–4)—Gently correct someone

Equity (v. 4)—Justice

Meek (v. 4)—Lowly or humble

Rod (v. 4)—A staff a ruler holds to signify his power

Girdle of his loins, girdle of his reins (v. 5)—A belt

Sucking (v. 8)—Very young

Ensign (vv. 10, 12)—Flag or banner an army gathers under and marches behind

Dispersed (v. 12)—Scattered

Envy (v. 13)—Jealousy

Adversaries (v. 13)—Enemies

Vex (v. 13)—Trouble

Spoil (v. 14)—Destroy a place and take the riches found there

Dryshod (v. 15)—Without getting wet

Studying the Scriptures ✏

Do activity A or B as you study Isaiah 11.

A Interpret Isaiah with the Help of Other Scripture

1. According to Doctrine and Covenants 113:1–2, what is Isaiah 11:1–5 about?

2. According to Doctrine and Covenants 113:5–6, who is the "root of Jesse" in Isaiah 11:10?

3. According to Joseph Smith—History 1:40, when will the events in Isaiah 11 generally occur?

B The Last Days and the Millennium

Isaiah 11:1–9 speaks of events mostly in the future. Isaiah 11:10–16 tells about what the Lord will do to bring about the events spoken of in verses 1–9.

1. Which prophecies in Isaiah 11 have you seen that are already fulfilled or beginning to be fulfilled?

2. Write about a teaching in Isaiah 11 that encourages you to stay faithful to the Lord.

Isaiah 12

Praise the Lord

Isaiah 12 is a short poem to praise the Lord for what he does to save his people. Isaiah 12 seems to have come in response to the great truths spoken of in Isaiah 11 concerning the Messiah, the gathering of Israel in the last days, and the Millennium. The teachings in chapter 12 can also be applied to any individual who comes to know the Lord, gathers to the Lord's Church, and receives the peace that only Jesus Christ can give.

Studying the Scriptures ✏

A Names for Jesus Christ

Read the following verses from the first 12 chapters of Isaiah, and list all the different names Isaiah uses for Jesus Christ: Isaiah 1:24; 2:3; 3:1; 5:16; 5:24; 7:14; 8:14; 9:6; 11:1; 12:2. Tell what you think is significant about using the particular name in each verse. What does the name emphasize about the Lord's character or actions?

Isaiah 13–14

Babylon and Lucifer

Isaiah 13–14, like Isaiah 10, contains prophecies about the destruction of a country that conquered the Lord's covenant people. In Isaiah 10, the prophecy was about Assyria, the country that conquered the Northern Kingdom between approximately 725–21 B.C. Isaiah 13–14 tells about Babylon, the country that conquered Judah between approximately 600–588 B.C. Ancient Babylon was one of the wealthiest and most worldly empires in history. Consequently, the Lord used Babylon as a symbol of people who focus on the things of the world and as a contrasting image of Zion and heaven. The prophesied destruction of Babylon in Isaiah 13 symbolizes what will happen to those who fight against the people of God and those whose hearts are set upon the things of the world instead of the things of God.

Isaiah 14 is more especially about the king of Babylon, whom Isaiah compared to Lucifer, or Satan. Because of the writings in this chapter, we learn more about how Lucifer became Satan and also about what will yet happen to him and his followers.

Understanding the Scriptures

Isaiah 14

Cleave (v. 1)—Join together

Captives (v. 2)—Prisoners

Oppressors (vv. 2, 4)—Those who rule over and hurt others

Sceptre (v. 5)—Staff representing authority to rule

Hindereth (v. 6)—Stops

Pomp (v. 11)—Pride

Viols (v. 11)—Musical instruments

Renowned (v. 20)—Spoken of

Bittern (v. 23)—A porcupine (animal with sharp quills on its back)

Disannul (v. 27)—Stop

Rod (v. 29)—Weapon of war

Dissolved (v. 31)—Destroyed

Studying the Scriptures

A Why Would You Follow Him?

1. Isaiah 14:12–14 tells us about how Lucifer became Satan. What do you find most interesting about what Isaiah said?

2. Read Doctrine and Covenants 76:25–27; Moses 4:1–4 and write about additional concepts you learn about the fall of Lucifer.

3. According to Isaiah 14:4–11, 15–20, what will eventually happen to Lucifer?

4. What additional information do you learn from Doctrine and Covenants 76:30, 33, 36–38, 44–46?

5. One of the reasons we try to learn about Jesus Christ is so we can follow his example and be more like him. The scriptures briefly mention how Satan became the devil so we can identify what we must do to *avoid* following him. As you think about what you read in Isaiah 14 about Lucifer's fall, write about why what you learned makes you want to follow Jesus Christ's example more fully. Also write about how you will be better able to avoid Satan and his temptations because of what you learned.

Isaiah 15–23

Prophecies against Nations That Do Not Serve the Lord

Isaiah 15–23 contains several prophecies about the destruction of nations surrounding Israel. By revealing to Israel and Judah that all surrounding nations would be destroyed, the Lord gave them good reasons to trust him instead of trusting in any treaties or alliances with these neighboring countries.

Isaiah 15–16 contains prophecies about Moab (see map 9 in the Latter-day Saint edition of the King James Version of the Bible). The country is named after Moab, who was the son of Lot's eldest daughter (see Genesis 19:37) and who settled in that country with his family. The Moabites often battled with the Israelites, but at this time the Israelites might have considered an alliance with Moab helpful in overcoming their enemies.

Isaiah 17 gives a prophecy directed to Damascus (Syria) and Ephraim (the Northern Kingdom). Damascus and Ephraim joined together in an alliance to conquer Judah, but before they could attack, the Assyrians came from the north and destroyed the two would-be conquerors. Isaiah 17 records a prophecy of the destruction of these two nations and some of the destruction's effects upon the two nations.

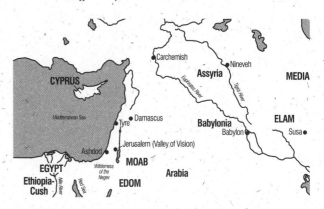

Isaiah 18 speaks to a land "beyond the rivers of Ethiopia" (v. 1). Most translators name this land Cush (see footnote 1c), which some think was a nation south of Egypt. Chapter 18 is more hopeful than many of the chapters in this section, and there is much disagreement about what chapter 18 refers to or means.

Isaiah 18 records Isaiah's prophecy that although the people of this nation would be "scattered and peeled" and "trodden under foot," they would be invited to gather to Mount Zion, where they will seemingly be well received. The last verse of the chapter may be of special interest because it speaks of giving the Lord a "present" of people who were "scattered." Gathering the people of the earth and preparing them to meet the Lord is one of the great purposes of the Church in the last days.

Isaiah 19–20 records prophecies about Egypt, which was one of the most powerful nations in the world in Isaiah's day. Isaiah prophesied of ways Egypt would be troubled and how the Egyptians would not be able to solve their troubles through their own abilities or false gods. Isaiah 19 also contains the remarkable prophecy that at some future time, Egypt and Israel will worship the same God and Egypt will be healed by the Lord. Even further, the prophecy suggests that Assyria will also be united with Israel and Egypt in worshiping God.

Isaiah 20 speaks specifically about the time when Assyria would take Egypt captive—again showing the people of Judah a reason why they should not join together with another country against Assyria.

Isaiah 21 speaks about the eventual destruction of three nations: Babylon (vv. 1–10), Edom (vv. 11–12), and Arabia (vv. 13–17).

In verse 10 the Lord seemed to specifically speak to members of the house of Israel who would be captives in Babylon nearly two hundred years after Isaiah's time and who would need the encouragement offered by this prophecy of Babylon's destruction.

Isaiah 22 refers to the fall of Jerusalem and speaks of a time when this "burden," or message of gloom, would be removed and Jerusalem would permanently be at peace. In this prophecy, Isaiah not only explained what would happen as a part of Jerusalem's destruction, but he also explained why Jerusalem would be destroyed. He noted that the people were very proud about tunnels and canals they built to solve their water problems but did not worship the Maker of the water nor recognize that all blessings come from him (see v. 11). He also criticized them for holding parties to celebrate messages that surrounding nations would be destroyed instead of reacting humbly and repenting (see vv. 12–14).

Isaiah 22 also contains a short historical story that has important symbolic significance. The story is about Shebna, the keeper of the treasury of Jerusalem, who is a symbol of the attitudes of the people of Jerusalem at the time. Isaiah accused Shebna of being prideful about Jerusalem's wealth. Then Isaiah said that not only would the Assyrians take many of Jerusalem's treasures but the nicest riches from Jerusalem would be the "cheapest" items in the house of the king of Assyria (see v. 18). Furthermore, Isaiah said that a man named Eliakim, which in Hebrew means "God shall cause thee to arise," would replace Shebna. There was important symbolism in the meaning of this name and story. Only by replacing love of treasures with love of God could Jerusalem be redeemed from destruction. And when Jerusalem turns to God, it will arise again as a holy city. The name Eliakim had even greater symbolic meaning because it pointed to the Atonement. Because of the Atonement of Jesus Christ, God will cause all men to arise and have the opportunity to overcome all the destruction, disappointments, and death of

this world. In the last verse of chapter 22, Isaiah testified of the great power of this redemption, comparing it to fastening a nail "in a sure place" so that it could not be moved. This image symbolized the permanent redemption Jesus Christ offered and the way he died and surely secured salvation for all mankind.

Isaiah 23, which contains a prophecy about Tyre, a city of Phoenicia, is the last of the chapters prophesying the overthrow of nations surrounding Israel and Judah. (See map 9 in your Bible to locate Tyre.) Tyre was a city focused on the buying and selling of the treasures of the world. The things of the world were always more important to the inhabitants of Tyre than anything, including God. Isaiah referred to Tyre as a harlot. This is because, in a sense, the people sold themselves and their sacred relationship with God for money—much in the same way a harlot sells her sacred virtue for money.

Isaiah 24

A Wicked World Destroyed

After several chapters that spoke of the destruction of different nations (see Isaiah 13–23), Isaiah 24 speaks of a more general destruction on all the earth. Isaiah 24 especially applies to the Israelites and what would happen to them because of their wickedness, but it also applies to the last days before the Second Coming.

Although Isaiah 24 seems very discouraging because it speaks so much about destruction, it also contains a small message of hope concerning the righteous who are spared. This hopeful message is even stronger in the next few chapters.

Understanding the Scriptures

Isaiah 24

Maketh it waste (v. 1)—Destroys

Abroad (v. 1)—Outside of one's country

As with (v. 2)—Whatever happens to

So with (v. 2)—Shall also happen to

Usury (v. 2)—Interest payments for loans

Utterly (vv. 3, 19)—Completely

Languisheth (vv. 4, 7)—Loses strength

Haughty (v. 4)—Proud

Defiled (v. 5)—Made filthy, polluted

Ordinance (v. 5)—Sacred ceremonies

Everlasting covenant (v. 5)—The laws and promises of the gospel

Devoured (v. 6)—Destroyed

Desolate (v. 6)—In a state of punishment

Mirth (vv. 8, 11)—Happiness

Majesty (v. 14)—Greatness

Uttermost (v. 16)—Farthest away

Treacherous (v. 16)—Deceitful

Snare (vv. 17–18)—Trap
Dissolved (v. 19)—Broken up
Reel to and fro (v. 20)—Move
back and forth

Removed (v. 20)—Moved
around as in shaking or
bending
Confounded (v. 23)—Ashamed

Studying the Scriptures

A Learn from Related Scriptures

1. Read Doctrine and Covenants 5:19; 84:96–98 and write about how and why the Lord will do what he said he would do in Isaiah 24:1.

2. Read Doctrine and Covenants 1:17, 35–36; 45:31–35; 97:22–28 and explain how a person can be saved in the midst of the destructions prophesied in Isaiah 24:1–12, 19–23.

3. List the ways the Lord said the people of the earth sinned in Isaiah 24:5. Compare what he said in Isaiah to what he said in Doctrine and Covenants 1:15–16, and tell what you think Isaiah 24:5 means.

B Part of the Plan of Salvation

1. According to Isaiah 24:21–22, what will happen to those destroyed at the time this chapter comes to pass?

2. According to Doctrine and Covenants 138:29–35, how will these people be "visited"?

Isaiah 25

Isaiah Praises the Lord

Isaiah 25 records Isaiah's gratitude for what the Lord has done and will do, including the eventual destruction of the proud and wicked and the rewarding of the humble, faithful, and obedient. He said that those who "wait" for the Lord in faithfulness (meaning that they remain faithful to the Lord while they wait for him to fulfill all his words—even when it may not seem that doing so is worth it at the time) will be rewarded in time, and their reward will be glorious.

Isaiah 26

Isaiah's Song of Praise

What song would you sing to express your gratitude to God? Isaiah 26 is a song of gratitude for what the Lord does for his

people. The resurrection of Jesus Christ mentioned in verse 19 would be a major reason for our gratitude.

Isaiah 27

The Lord and His Vineyard

Isaiah 27 records Isaiah's comparison of the way the Lord works with his people to the way one cares for a vineyard (see Isaiah 5:1–7; Jacob 5). In this comparison the Lord explained that the wicked are like dead branches that he will cut down and burn, while the righteous are like strong vines that take root even deeper, blossom, and "fill the face of the world with fruit" (Isaiah 27:6).

Isaiah 28

Counsel for a Prideful People

Isaiah 28 identifies pride as the major sin of the Israelites. Pride separated the people from the blessings the Lord wanted to give them. In verses 23–29, Isaiah compared a farmer's knowledge of how to plant and harvest crops to the Lord's even greater knowledge about how to properly work with his children.

Isaiah 29

A Marvelous Work and a Wonder

Sometimes people who are familiar with the Bible and are not members of the Church will ask us something like "If the Book of Mormon is such an important part of the work of God, why is it not mentioned in the Bible?" There are several answers to that question, and one of them is "It is!" Isaiah 29 is one place in the Bible where the Book of Mormon is referred to, even though it is not mentioned by name. As you read this chapter, look for prophecies of the coming forth of the Book of Mormon and the impact this book will have on the world.

Understanding the Scriptures 🔑

Isaiah 29

Ariel (vv. 1, 3, 7)—Jerusalem

Distress (vv. 2, 7)—Trouble

Heaviness (v. 2)—Sadness

Camp against thee (v. 3)—Set up an army against you

Lay siege against (v. 3)—Attack

One that hath a familiar spirit (v. 4)—Someone who invokes the dead to speak

Terrible (vv. 5, 20)—Those who are mighty, powerful, and wicked

Chaff (v. 5)—Light outer coating of a kernel of grain

Munition (v, 7)—Forts, strongholds

Appetite (v. 8)—Hunger

Stay (v. 9)—Wait or delay

Stagger (v. 9)—Stumble while you walk

Covered (v. 10)—Blocked the sight

Forasmuch as (v. 13)—Since

Precept (v. 13)—Rules

Perish (v. 14)—Be destroyed

Prudent (v. 14)—Wise and intelligent

Counsel (v. 15)—Plans, decisions

Esteemed (vv. 16–17)—Considered

Potter's (v. 16)—Belonging to a person who makes objects out of clay

Obscurity (v. 18)—Darkness

Meek (v. 19)—Humble and obedient

Brought to nought (v. 20)—Becomes nothing

Scorner (v. 20)—One who mocks

Consumed (v. 20)—Destroyed

Lay a snare (v. 21)—Set a trap

Reproveth (v. 21)—Corrects

Nought (v. 21)—Nothing

Wax pale (v. 22)—Lose its color

Erred (v. 24)—Made mistakes

Isaiah 29:11–12, 18–24—What Is "the Book" Referred to in This Chapter?

Those familiar with the restored gospel will probably see that these verses refer to the Book of Mormon and the role it plays in the Restoration of the gospel in the latter days. Elder Bruce R. McConkie said:

"Few men on earth, either in or out of the Church, have caught the vision of what the Book of Mormon is all about. Few are they among men who know the part it has played and will yet play in preparing the way for the coming of Him of whom it is a new witness. . . .

". . . The Book of Mormon shall so affect men that the whole earth and all its peoples will have been influenced and governed by it. . . .

". . . There is no greater issue ever to confront mankind in modern times than this: Is the Book of Mormon the mind and will and voice of God to all men?" (*The Millennial Messiah* [1982], 159, 170, 179).

Studying the Scriptures ✏️

Ⓐ Prophecy Fulfilled

1. Isaiah 29:1–6 tells about a group of people who "speak out of the ground" after the destruction of Jerusalem. Isaiah said they would be "visited . . . with earthquakes, and great noise, with storm, and tempest, and the flame of devouring fire" (Isaiah 29:6). Read 2 Nephi 26:15–17; 33:13; 3 Nephi 8:2–19; Mormon 8:23, 26, 34–35, and write about ways the Book of Mormon fulfills the prophecy in Isaiah 29:1–6.

2. Read Joseph Smith—History 1:61–65 and tell how the event recorded was a fulfillment of Isaiah 29:11–12. You may also want to read 2 Nephi 26:9–22 and see how these verses explain more about this prophecy.

Ⓑ Scripture Mastery—Isaiah 29:13–14

"Apostasy" means "a falling away," and we refer to "the Apostasy" as the time when the fulness of the gospel and the priesthood authority to administer the ordinances of the gospel was taken from among men on the earth. "The Restoration" refers to the fulness of the gospel and priesthood authority being brought back to the earth.

1. Read the following verses in Isaiah 29 and tell whether they are about the Apostasy or the Restoration, then explain what the verses teach about the Apostasy or the Restoration: vv. 9–10, 13–14, 15, 18–21, 24.

2. Compare Isaiah 29:13–14 to Joseph Smith—History 1:18–19. What do you think the "marvellous work and a wonder" is? (see also vv. 33–34).

3. Isaiah 29:11–12, 18–24 tell about a book that will play an important role in the "marvellous work and a wonder." List the truths those verses say this book will do, and then tell what book you think it refers to.

Isaiah 30–32

Trust in the Lord

Isaiah 30–32 was written when Assyria threatened to attack Israel after having conquered other neighboring countries. Fearful, many in Israel sought Egypt's help in defending themselves against the Assyrians. But the Lord helped the children of Israel escape wicked Egypt in the days of Moses; he fought their battles and helped them obtain their promised land. To join with Egypt in a treaty instead of relying upon the Lord who delivered them in the past showed how little faith the Israelites had in their God. Isaiah's counsel in chapters 30–32 was to trust the Lord, not Egypt, for deliverance. Isaiah also told the children of Israel of the blessings they would receive if they put their trust in the Lord and warned of the consequences of not trusting him.

How do you decide whether or not to trust someone? Have you ever trusted someone and had them take advantage of you? Whom should we trust? Do we fear what others can do more than we trust that the Lord will bless us for being faithful to him? Do we trust in our own power to solve problems instead of trying the Lord's way? These may seem like foolish questions, but because many people think the commandments are "too hard" or don't see the immediate rewards of keeping the commandments, they trust in their own power and judgment, or the power and judgment of others, and disregard the commandments.

Understanding the Scriptures 🔑

Isaiah 30:15–21

Pursue (v. 16)—Chase

Beacon, ensign (v. 17)—Signal

Adversity, affliction (v. 20)—
Trials and troubles

Studying the Scriptures ✏️

Ⓐ In Your Own Words

In Isaiah 30:15–21, the Lord explained to the Israelites why they should trust in him instead of in their own strength, the strength of others, or objects designed to help in battle. After you read these verses, respond to the following questions in your own words:

1. What did the Lord say would happen if the Israelites trusted in their own strength? (vv. 16–17).

2. What should the Israelites trust? (v. 15).

3. According to verses 18–21, what did the Lord ask of the people, and then what would the Lord do for them?

4. In what kind of situation do you think this counsel would be helpful today?

Isaiah 33–34

The Second Coming of Jesus Christ

When you think of the Second Coming of Jesus Christ, how do you feel? Do you look forward to it, or are you afraid? Isaiah 33 records Isaiah's words that some should fear the Second Coming because of their wickedness and because they are unprepared to be with the Lord. Isaiah also spoke of those who would dwell with the Lord and described what they would be like. Those who want to live with the Lord would do well to highlight these qualities and strive to develop them.

Up to this point, Isaiah 34 seems to be the harshest of all the chapters that speak of destruction. Chapter 34 describes the judgments upon the wicked that would surely take place, both in the time of Isaiah and just before the Second Coming. We should remember, however, that this awful judgment only comes upon those who have been warned and who have chosen to be wicked anyway. The Lord does not desire any of his children to experience these kinds of punishments (see 2 Nephi 26:23–28), but the consequences of a just law broken must be fulfilled (see D&C 63:33–34).

Studying the Scriptures ✏️

Ⓐ Make a List

1. Read Isaiah 33:14–17 and make a list of the kinds of people Isaiah said would survive the destruction at the time of the Second Coming of Christ.

2. Tell what each of the items on the list means.

3. According to verse 17, what else will happen to these people?

Isaiah 35

A Message of Hope

Some of the previous chapters have held gloomy messages of destruction. But Isaiah finished this section of his writings with a hopeful chapter concerning the blessings that come to people who are faithful to the Lord. When we consider the great blessings the Lord offers the righteous, we can gain the strength we need to walk the path of repentance and to overcome future temptations.

Isaiah 36–39

The Story of King Hezekiah

Much of Isaiah 36–39 is almost exactly like 2 Kings 18–20. The only significant difference is a "psalm" of Hezekiah recorded in Isaiah 38. If you want to review what happened in chapters 36–39, you could read the chapters in Isaiah and look at the help in this guide for 2 Kings 18–20 on pages 116–17.

Isaiah 40

The Lord's Power and Greatness

After recording historical events in chapters 36–39, Isaiah returned in chapter 40 to his prophetic and more poetic style of writing. Many of the verses in Isaiah 40 have become the words to wonderful musical works because this chapter richly describes the Lord's power and how he will redeem his people. After Isaiah and other prophets often prophesied of destruction, Isaiah 40 is a great, hopeful message to those who will trust the Lord. The prophecies of chapter 40 foretell both the first and second comings of the Messiah. If we "liken" the teachings in chapter 40 to ourselves, they can be a beautiful and powerful testimony of the Lord and his power in our personal lives.

Understanding the Scriptures

Isaiah 40

Make straight (v. 3)—Literally to make a level pathway; symbolically to prepare the way before. (This "straightening" was usually done to prepare a path for an important individual like a king.)

Withereth, fadeth (vv. 7–8)—Dies

Tidings (v. 9)—News

Meted out (v. 12)—Measured

Span (v. 12)—Width of his hand

Directed (v. 13)—Measured

Sufficient (v. 16)—Enough

Vanity (vv. 17, 23)—Worthless

Graven image (vv. 19–20)—Idol made with man's hands and tools

Impoverished (v. 20)—Poor

Oblation (v. 20)—Offering (In this verse the offering is to a false god.)

Cunning (v. 20)—Skillful

Foundations (v. 21)—Beginnings

Stock (v. 24)—Tree trunk

Stubble (v. 24)—Short pieces of a plant remaining after it has been cut down or burned

Fainteth not (v. 28)—Doesn't get weak

Faint (vv. 29–31)—Becoming physically weak, tired, or weary

Mount (v. 31)—Go up

Studying the Scriptures

Do two of the three following activities (A–C) as you study Isaiah 40.

A Help from the New Testament

Read JST, Luke 3:4–11 in the appendix of the LDS edition of the King James Bible.

1. Describe what Luke said Isaiah 40:3–5 applied to.

2. What additional information is found in the Joseph Smith Translation.

You may want to write this reference next to Isaiah 40:3–5.

B Apply It to Yourself and Others

1. In what ways could you personally apply the message in Isaiah 40:3?

2. Describe a way you think the Lord will literally fulfill Isaiah 40:4. You may want to read verse 5 and consider how all flesh can "see it together."

3. Describe a way you think verse 4 is or will be fulfilled in a spiritual and more personal way.

4. How could these verses apply to someone who is worried whether righteousness is worth the effort, if they personally can return to live with God, or what will happen in the future?

C Answer Scriptural Questions

Isaiah 40:12–31 contains many questions that neither the Lord nor Isaiah answered because the answers should be obvious. Read the following verses and answer the questions to yourself: 12, 13, 14, 18, 21, 25, 27, 28. Write about what you think Isaiah's message is in these verses.

Isaiah 41–47

Redeemer of Israel

Worshiping idols was perhaps the children of Israel's most offensive and obvious sin in Isaiah's day. Isaiah 41–47 tells how the Lord spoke to his people about why they should trust in and worship him instead of idols. He testified to them that, among many other important titles and names, he was their Redeemer (meaning someone who would redeem them from spiritual bondage with his atoning sacrifice; see Isaiah 41:14; 43:1, 14; 44:6, 24; 47:4), their Savior (see Isaiah 43:3, 11; 45:15, 21), and their Creator (see Isaiah 42:5; 43:1, 7, 15, 21; 44:24; 45:9, 11, 18). To the children of the covenant he emphasized: "I am the Lord thy God, . . . thy Saviour . . .

". . . Your redeemer . . .

". . . Your Holy One, . . . your King" (Isaiah 43:3, 14–15).

Although these chapters call the children of Israel to repent and return to the Lord, they are filled with hope in the promise that the Lord would receive them if they would choose to follow him and that he has power to save and redeem them from all their sins and afflictions.

Although the messages of these chapters can certainly be applied to our day, they had special meaning to the Jews who were captive in Babylon about 150 years after Isaiah's death. They had been taken captive because they, as a people, refused to repent of worshiping idols. They needed the saving and redeeming power the Lord offered, and they especially took courage in the promise of King Cyrus of Persia as their deliverer (see Isaiah 45) and in the prophesied destruction of Babylon (see Isaiah 47).

Understanding the Scriptures

Isaiah 42:1–7

Bring forth judgment (vv. 1, 3)—Make right any wrongs, bring about justice

Lift up (v. 2)—Shout

Have set judgment (v. 4)—Made right, see that justice is done

Isaiah 47:5–10

Daughter of the Chaldeans (v. 5)—People of Babylon

Lady of kingdoms (v. 5)—The greatest of kingdoms

Wroth (v. 6)—Angry

Ancient (v. 6)—Older people

Laid thy yoke (v. 6)—Put burdens

Lay these things to thy heart (v. 7)—Think about one's situation

Remember the latter end of it (v. 7)—Think about the future

Art given (v. 8)—Attracted to, enticed by

Sorceries, enchantments (vv. 9, 12)—Practices of magical arts, dealings with false spirits, and predictions based on signs, motions of stars, and so on

Isaiah 45:1—Who Was Cyrus?

As you read earlier in the Old Testament, the Babylonians conquered Judah between 600–586 B.C. In approximately 540 B.C., the Medo-Persian empire, under the direction of King Cyrus, conquered the Babylonians. Cyrus made a decree shortly thereafter that allowed the Jews to return to Jerusalem and rebuild their temple.

Studying the Scriptures

Do two of the following activities (A–D) as you study Isaiah 41–47.

A Who Is It?

1. Read Isaiah 42:1–7; Matthew 12:14–21 and tell who is the servant Isaiah wrote about.

2. List two concepts from Isaiah 42:1–7 that especially impress you as a description of this servant, and explain why they impress you.

B Help from the Joseph Smith Translation

1. Read the JST for Isaiah 42:19–23, especially verses 19–20, and write about what the Lord said he would do for people blind and deaf to spiritual matters.

2. Give an example of how this happens today.

C Write a Note to a Friend

Write a note using at least two truths contained in Isaiah 43:1–7 that might bring hope to someone who is discouraged.

D Find the Problem

Isaiah 47:5–10 compares Babylon to a queen who has lost her glory, and it explains why she fell.

1. List at least two phrases that describe why this "lady" fell. Tell in your own words what these phrases mean.

2. Write about a situation today in which someone could make the same mistakes as the "lady," and tell what you think the consequences would be.

Note: This chapter is the beginning of several chapters in a row quoted by the writers of the Book of Mormon. You may want to compare what is written in the Book of Mormon to what is written in Isaiah, making note of any changes and how those changes might add to the meaning. The Latter-day Saint edition of the Bible refers you to the Book of Mormon in the chapter summaries and in the footnotes.

Chapter in Isaiah	Where Quoted in the Book of Mormon
48	1 Nephi 20
49	1 Nephi 21
50	2 Nephi 7
51	2 Nephi 8
52:1–2	2 Nephi 8:24–25; see also 3 Nephi 20:36–38
52:7–10	Mosiah 15:18, 29–31; see also 3 Nephi 16:17–20; 20:40
52:11–15	3 Nephi 20:41–45
53	Mosiah 14
54	3 Nephi 22

Isaiah 48

An Invitation to Come Back

Isaiah 48 helps us understand how the Lord deals with those who have made covenants with him but treat those covenants and their Church membership lightly. As you read, consider what this chapter teaches us about the Lord's concern for those who stray from him. Think also of how you might use these teachings to keep yourself true to the faith and help others who struggle in their commitment to the Lord.

Understanding the Scriptures

Isaiah 48

Swear by (v. 1)—Promise in

Former things (v. 3)—What happened in the past

Sinew (v. 4)—Tendons that hold muscles and bones together and assist in their movements

Not from the beginning (v. 7)—Not long ago

Treacherously (v. 8)—Betraying or breaking promises, to deceive

Defer (v. 9)—Put off, delay

Refrain (v. 9)—Hold back

Refined (v. 10)—Removing an impure substance from metal by heating it to a very high temperature

Spanned (v. 13)—Measured with the hand (meaning he created it)

Them (v. 14)—Idols, false gods

Hearkened (v. 18)—Listened and obeyed

Utter (v. 20)—Speak

Clave (v. 21)—Split

Studying the Scriptures

Do two of the following activities (A–C) as you study Isaiah 48.

A Note the Changes

1. Compare Isaiah 48:1–2 with 1 Nephi 20:1–2. How are they different?

2. Having made the comparison, who do you think the Lord is speaking to in these verses?

B Choose a Word

In Isaiah 48 the Lord told the Israelites why he was upset with them. For each of the following verses, write one word you think best describes what the Lord said about the Israelites: 4, 6, 8. (The words do not have to be from the verses.)

C How Does the Lord Help His People?

1. Make a list from Isaiah 48:9–22 of promises the Lord made to the straying Israelites.

2. Give an example of how the Lord fulfills these promises for people today.

3. Write in your own words what the Lord said we must do in order to have peace and happiness (see Isaiah 48:16–22).

Isaiah 49

A Message to Scattered Israel

In 1 Nephi 19:23, Nephi said he read some of Isaiah's writings to his brothers to "more fully persuade them to believe in the Lord their Redeemer." Nephi followed this statement by recording Isaiah 48–49 from the brass plates to his "small plates" (see 1 Nephi 20–21). Nephi's explanation about what chapters 48–49 mean is found in 1 Nephi 22. If you read 1 Nephi 22 you will better understand the message of Isaiah 48–49.

Knowing that Nephi read these writings to more fully persuade his brothers to believe in Jesus Christ gives us clues as to what to look for when we read. As you read Isaiah 49 as well as chapters 50–53, look for teachings that strengthen your faith in the saving power of Jesus Christ.

Understanding the Scriptures

Isaiah 49

Shaft (v. 2)—Arrow

Quiver (v. 2)—Container for arrows carried on a person's belt or back

Nought (v. 4)—Nothing

In vain (v. 4)—For no good

Preserved (v. 6)—Saved alive

Gentiles (v. 6)—Those who are not members of the family of Israel

Despiseth (v. 7)—Looks down on, dislikes

Abhorreth (v. 7)—Hates

Desolate heritages, desolate places (vv. 8, 19)—Empty places

Way(s) (vv. 9, 11)—Roads

Afflicted (v. 13)—Troubled

Sucking child (v. 15)—Baby fed at a mother's breast

Graven (v. 16)—Engraved

Make haste (v. 17)—Hurry

Waste (vv. 17, 19)—Destroyed

Go forth of thee (v. 17)—Leave you

Ornament (v. 18)—Decoration

Narrow (v. 19)—Small

Swallowed thee up (v. 19)—Conquered you

To and fro (v. 21)—Here and there

Standard (v. 22)—Banner, flag, ensign

Prey (vv. 24–25)—Captured (Prey is commonly used to describe what an animal captures for food.)

Studying the Scriptures

Do two of the following activities (A–C) as you study Isaiah 49.

A Look for Items That Teach You about Jesus Christ

Choose verses in Isaiah 49 that you think sound like they describe Jesus Christ—his ministry, his power, or his love—and explain why you chose the verses you did.

B An Important Addition

1. There is a very important addition to Isaiah 49 in 1 Nephi 21:1. Read 1 Nephi 21:1 and write who the Lord was speaking to in this chapter.

2. In what ways do you think the description of these people could symbolize people in our day?

C Redeeming Israel

The basic theme of Isaiah 49 is the gathering, or the redemption, of Israel. Find a verse (or verses) that answers the following questions about the redemption of Israel: Who? How? Why? Write these questions in your notebook and write the verses that apply after each question. You may also want to underline these verses in your scriptures and write what question each verse answers in the margin next to the verse.

Remember that while we often speak of the Israelites gathering as a group, we should realize that the gathering occurs as each individual is personally gathered to the Lord and his Church. We can look at the gathering of Israel out from among their enemies in ancient times as similar to our own personal gathering to the Lord from the captivity of sin and unrighteousness.

Isaiah 50

Return to the Lord

Isaiah 50 continues with the same ideas begun in Isaiah 49.

Understanding the Scriptures

Isaiah 50

Bill (v. 1)—Legal document

Creditors (v. 1)—People you owe money to

Rebuke (v. 2)—Voice

Sackcloth (v. 3)—Black goatskin covering worn at a time of sadness

In season (v. 4)—At the right time

Smiters (v. 6)—People who beat other people

Confounded (v. 7)—Put to shame

Flint (v. 7)—A very hard stone that can spark when struck with steel

Justifieth me (v. 8)—Declares that I am right

Contend with me (v. 8)—Argue against me

Adversary (v. 8)—Enemy

Stay (v. 10)—Depend

Compass (v. 11)—Surround

Isaiah 50:6—"I Gave . . . My Cheeks to Them That Plucked off the Hair"

If a person wanted to humiliate another person, he could pull the hair out of someone's beard as a sign of disrespect.

Isaiah 50:10—Who Can Truly Follow the Lord and Not Be Blessed and Happier?

The invitation in Isaiah 50 to follow the Lord is similar to the one King Benjamin gave to his people in Mosiah 2:41.

Studying the Scriptures

Complete activity A or B as you study Isaiah 50.

A What Do You Learn about Jesus Christ?

Read Isaiah 50:5–7; 1 Nephi 19:9; Doctrine and Covenants 19:16–19 and write what these scripture passages teach you about:

1. What the Savior endured to accomplish the Atonement.

2. What motivated him to do such an incredibly difficult and painful thing.

B Give an Example

1. Describe the two kinds of people Isaiah spoke of in verses 10–11.

2. Think of a situation faced by people your age. Give an example of how each of the two kinds of people Isaiah described would act in that situation.

Isaiah 51–52

Awake! And Come unto Him

Following the same hopeful theme of the previous chapters, Isaiah 51–52 is filled with encouraging words for those who trust the Lord. In chapters 51–52 we read of the Lord's great power over all things—but especially over the enemies of Israel. Individuals in bondage to sin may liken these scriptures to themselves and receive this message: the Lord will give powerful help to his children who have strayed but who now put their trust in him and keep his commandments.

Isaiah 53

Jesus Christ's Suffering Foretold

Many people love and quote Isaiah 53 because of its moving testimony of the mission of Jesus Christ. This chapter contains Isaiah's prophecy of a Messiah who would save his people, not by the sword and war, but through humble suffering. Read Isaiah 53 carefully and be sensitive to what Isaiah was trying to help us feel and understand about the Messiah.

Understanding the Scriptures

Isaiah 53

Tender (v. 2)—Young

Form (v. 2)—Impressive appearance

Comeliness (v. 2)—Glory

Grief(s) (vv. 3–4, 10)—Sickness

Esteemed him not (v. 3)—Did not consider him important

Borne (v. 4)—Carry on the shoulders or back

Did esteem (v. 4)—Considered

Stricken (vv. 4, 8)—Punished

Chastisement (v. 5)—Punishment

Stripes (v. 5)—Wounds

Oppressed (v. 7)—Taken advantage of

Shearers (v. 7)—People who cut the wool off a sheep

Deceit (v. 9)—False speaking, dishonesty

Travail (v. 11)—Suffering

Justify (v. 11)—Make right

Bear (v. 11)—Carry

Spoil (v. 12)—Items or goods taken from others

Intercession (v. 12)—Acting in another's behalf

Studying the Scriptures

A Scripture Mastery—Isaiah 53:3–5

Make a chart in your notebook like the one below. After reading the verses referred to in the second column, find a verse in Isaiah 53 that seems to prophecy of the event you read about. In the third column, briefly explain why you chose the verse from Isaiah 53 and what it says about the Savior.

Verse in Isaiah 53	Fulfillment	Explanation
	Matthew 13:54–58	
	D&C 19:16	
	Luke 22:54–62	
	John 1:11	
	Matthew 26:36–46	
	Mosiah 3:7	
	2 Nephi 9:21	
	Alma 7:11–13	
	Mark 15:25–28	
	John 19:4–12	
	John 19:38–42	
	D&C 45:3–5	

B How Does It Make You Feel?

Having read all of the scriptures above and all of Isaiah 53, write a paragraph or two about what impressed you most in chapter 53 and how you feel about what the Savior has done for you and all mankind.

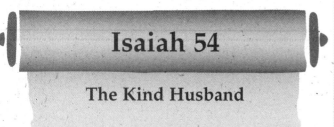

Isaiah 54

The Kind Husband

In speaking to the scattered and captive children of Israel in Isaiah 54, the Lord compared his relationship with them to a marriage relationship. Although they were separated for a time, he promised to receive them back with mercy and kindness and to be their "husband" forever (Isaiah 54:5). This promise can also be taken as a personal message of hope for individuals in sin who think that the Lord would never take them back even if they repented.

Isaiah 55

An Invitation from the Lord

Isaiah 55 is another call from the Lord to come to him. In chapter 55 he gives more reasons why scattered Israel and all of us would want to trust and follow him. The very first word, "ho," is a call for someone to pay attention and come. "Ho" would normally be combined with the waving of the hand in an invitation to come.

Understanding the Scriptures

Isaiah 55

Wherefore (v. 2)—Why

Incline your ear (v. 3)—Listen

Abundantly (v. 7)—Freely, in great number

Thither (v. 10)—Where it came from

Void (v. 11)—Empty, serving no purpose

Isaiah 55:3–4—Why Is He Talking about David?

The "David" here actually refers to Jesus Christ, who was a legal heir to the throne of David. Interestingly, the name *David* in Hebrew means "beloved." Usually when the later Old Testament prophets refer to David, they are talking about the throne of David and are speaking about the Messiah.

Studying the Scriptures

A In Your Own Words

1. Compare Isaiah 55:1–2 to 2 Nephi 9:50–51 where Jacob seemed to be using the words of Isaiah. In your own words, explain what these verses mean to you.

2. How do you think a person could "buy" and "eat" the food the Lord is offering in these verses? As you write your answer, read John 4:10–14 or John 6:29–35, 47–51 for help.

B Scripture Mastery—Isaiah 55:8–9

1. Draw a diagram that represents the message of these two verses.

2. How is the message of these verses one of comfort?

3. Read Jacob 4:8 and tell how we can come to understand God's thoughts and ways.

Isaiah 56

The Lord Saves All Nations

Isaiah 56 records that the Lord said he would save the children of Israel and would also offer the same blessings to anyone else who desired them. Notice the "sons of the stranger" in verse 6 and "others" in verse 8.

Isaiah 57

The Lord Has Power to Heal

In the last four verses of Isaiah 56, Isaiah began speaking directly to the people about their sins. His warnings continue through chapter 59. Isaiah 57 records the strong words he spoke against idol worshipers. He again used the symbol of marriage to represent the covenant relationship between Israel and the Lord. If those who made covenants with the Lord were symbolically married to him, then those Israelites who worshiped other gods were "adulterers." Isaiah spoke of what would happen to them because of their sins and showed that sometimes we are punished just as much by our sins as we are for them. Isaiah also spoke of what the Lord would do for those who stayed true. Staying true at that time was difficult because most of the people had forsaken the Lord, and the whole nation was feeling the effects. Consequently, the Lord used words like "revive" (v. 15), "heal" (vv. 18–19), and "comforts" (v. 18).

Isaiah 58

Fasting and the Sabbath

Before and as you read Isaiah 58, think about the following questions:

What is the purpose of fasting? What is the most meaningful fast you've ever had? Why? What is the purpose of keeping the Sabbath day holy? What blessings have you received from keeping the Sabbath day holy?

Understanding the Scriptures

Isaiah 58

Spare not (v. 1)—Do not hold back

Takest no knowledge (v. 3)—Do not notice

Bulrush (v. 5)—Tall grass, reed

Yoke (vv. 6, 9)—Wood or metal device fitted around the neck and shoulders of two animals that helps them combine their strength to pull a wagon or plow. "Yoke" in this verse symbolically represents burdens, such as poverty or sin.

Deal (v. 7)—Share

Flesh (v. 7)—Family

Vanity (v. 9)—Speaking ill of another

Draw out thy soul (v. 10)—Give

Satisfy (vv. 10–11)—Give relief to

Waste (v. 12)—Empty, destroyed

Breach (v. 12)—Broken

If thou turn away thy foot from (v. 13)—If you keep from trampling under your feet

Heritage (v. 14)—Blessings

Studying the Scriptures

A) Make a Chart

In your notebook, make a chart like the one below, and fill it in with what you find in Isaiah 58:3–12.

What We Should Do When We Fast	What We Should Avoid When We Fast	Blessings the Lord Promises for Fasting in the Way He Has Commanded

B) Give Examples

1. In Isaiah 58:13–14 the Lord gave us principles that help us know how to keep his Sabbath day holy. List these principles. Read Doctrine and Covenants 59:9–14 and add to your list principles of keeping the Sabbath day holy.

2. For each principle you listed, give an example of how someone could follow that principle on the Sabbath. Then give an example of how someone might violate that principle on the Sabbath.

3. List the Lord's promised blessings for keeping the Sabbath day holy according to Isaiah 58:13–14.

Isaiah 59

Sins and Consequences

We are often punished *by* our sins in addition to being punished *for* them because all sins have consequences. In Isaiah 59:1–15, the Lord told Israel their sins and explained that as long as they continued in sin he could not help them; they must continue to experience the consequences of those sins. On the other hand, in verses 16–21, the Lord spoke about the help he will give the righteous.

Isaiah 60

Let Your Light Shine

Elder Boyd K. Packer prophesied: "Across the world, those who now come by tens of thousands will inevitably come as a flood to where the family is safe. Here [in the Church] they will worship the Father in the name of Jesus Christ, by the gift of the Holy Ghost, and know that the gospel is the great plan of happiness, of redemption" (in Conference Report, Apr. 1994, 26–27; or Ensign, May 1994, 21).

Elder Packer's prophecy is much like the one in Isaiah 60. In chapter 60, Isaiah speaks of a day of darkness on the earth when Zion will be rebuilt, and stand out as a bright light, and have all nations of the earth honor her and look to her for leadership.

Isaiah 61

The Mission of the Lord and His Servants

Isaiah 61 is another chapter that speaks of the blessings that can come to God's people if they are faithful to him. In the first three verses, Isaiah spoke of his mission to lift and bless the house of Israel. However, the mission more fully applies to the Savior, and Isaiah simply represented him to the people. These verses can help describe the mission of all who are called to represent the Savior.

Understanding the Scriptures

Isaiah 61:1–3

Tidings (v. 1)—News

Meek (v. 1)—Humble

Bind up (v. 1)—Give healing to

Day of vengeance (v. 2)—Day when God punishes the wicked and rewards the righteous

Beauty for ashes (v. 3)—Refers to the custom of pouring ashes on one's head when deeply saddened. The Lord promised here a beautiful head covering, meaning the people will no longer mourn.

Studying the Scriptures

A. Explain the Fulfillment

1. Read Luke 4:16–21 and explain what Jesus said about Isaiah 61:1–3.

2. Write about ways you know the Savior fulfilled the prophecies in these verses or ways he continues to fulfill these prophecies.

Isaiah 62

The Redemption of the House of Israel

Isaiah 62 again describes the blessings that will come to the house of Israel in their day of redemption. These promises could also apply to individuals who have repented and gathered to Jesus Christ and the Church—the blessings are the same.

Isaiah 62 also teaches that Isaiah and other servants of the Lord will not stop preaching, laboring, and working in behalf of the Lord's people until all the blessings spoken of have come to pass (see vv. 1, 6–7, 10).

Isaiah 63

The Second Coming of Jesus Christ

Isaiah 63 tells about events that will occur at the time of the Second Coming of Jesus Christ.

Understanding the Scriptures

Isaiah 63:1–9

Apparel (vv. 1–2)—Clothing

Vengeance (v. 4)—Judgment

Fury (vv. 5–6)—Anger

Bestowed on (v. 7)—Blessed

Affliction (v. 9)—Troubles and pains

Redeemed (v. 9)—Paid a price to free someone from bondage

Studying the Scriptures

A. Find Information about the Second Coming

Read also Doctrine and Covenants 133:45–53 and find answers to the following questions about the Second Coming:

1. How will the Lord be dressed?

2. Why will he dress this way?

3. What will the Lord say?

4. What emotions will the Lord feel?

5. What will "the redeemed" say when he comes?

Isaiah 64

The Prayer of the Righteous

Isaiah 64 is written in the form of a prayer. The prayer expresses a desire for the Lord to come and destroy the wicked and reward the righteous. Doctrine and Covenants 133:38–45 helps us understand that the Lord's servants will offer this prayer in the last days.

Isaiah 65

The Millennium

One of the reasons Isaiah's writings are so great is that they explain so much of the great plan of God and the central role of Jesus Christ as our Savior in that plan. In Isaiah we read about events that occurred in the premortal life as well as those that will occur during the Millennium. Isaiah 65–66 speaks about the Millennium. In verses 1–16 of Isaiah 65, however, the Lord concluded his message to the Israelites of Isaiah's day. He told them he had always been available to help and redeem them (see vv. 1–2, 12), but they chose wickedness instead (see vv. 3–4, 11).

Because the Lord loved the Israelites, he promised to not completely destroy them (see vv. 8–10). He also promised he would try to give the same blessings they rejected to future generations of Israelites and to others as well (see vv. 13–15). Even in punishing Israel, we sense the great love that the Lord has for them and for all people.

Understanding the Scriptures

Isaiah 65:17–25

Thence (v. 20)—From then on

Inhabit (vv. 21–22)—Live in

Studying the Scriptures

A Learn about the Millennium

1. List what you learn from Isaiah 65:17–25 about the Millennium.

2. From what you wrote, what do you think you would most like to experience if you were to live during the Millennium? Why?

Isaiah 66

The Hope of Zion

Isaiah 66 summarizes the Lord's message through Isaiah: If you are faithful, the day will come that you will be rewarded, even though you suffer persecution and trials at this time. Wait upon the Lord and you and the whole world will know the day when everything is made right—the wicked punished and the righteous rewarded.

The Book of Jeremiah

Jeremiah's mission began approximately 626 B.C. He was one of several prophets whose ministry was during King Josiah's reign (see 2 Kings 22–23).

The Beginning and the End

During Jeremiah's ministry, the Babylonians conquered the Assyrians and became the great world power. The leaders and people of Judah worried that Babylon would also conquer their small nation, so for protection they attempted to form an alliance with Egypt. Jeremiah warned the nation to repent and seek deliverance from the Lord instead of from Egypt or any other country.

In a series of attacks over many years, the Babylonians carried away many Jews from their promised land into Babylon. The prophets Daniel and Ezekiel were among those carried away. Lehi and his family were warned by the Lord to flee Jerusalem to escape the destruction that soon happened at the hands of the Babylonian army. As a point of interest, the brass plates Lehi's family brought with them contained prophecies of the prophet Jeremiah (see 1 Nephi 5:13). Jeremiah continued to preach repentance, but his preaching had little effect on the people. The last king in Jerusalem, Zedekiah, disliked Jeremiah's messages and had him arrested and imprisoned. When the Babylonians came one last time and destroyed Jerusalem and took Zedekiah away captive, Jeremiah fled for his life and lived in Egypt.

Getting Ready to Study Jeremiah

Like Isaiah, Jeremiah was a very expressive writer, using much poetry and symbolism in his teachings. Like the prophet Mormon in the Book of Mormon, Jeremiah had the difficult mission of delivering messages of warning and promises of destruction to a people who simply would not repent and were about to be destroyed. Jeremiah was greatly persecuted because of his preaching.

Although Jeremiah's message seems gloomy much of the time, he also speaks of hope and of God's love for his covenant people. After the judgments that Jeremiah prophesied were fulfilled, the Lord promised he would again have mercy on the children of the covenant and gather them back to him, which is a pattern the Lord has followed to this day.

For more information on Jeremiah and the book of Jeremiah, see the Bible Dictionary, s.v. "Jeremiah."

Jeremiah 1

Jeremiah's Call

Some missions of the Church have had comparatively few convert baptisms in the past 150 years. How would you react if you were called to go on a mission to a place where very few people would listen to you and you would experience much persecution and many trials and have little hope for success? What could inspire you to fulfill this mission? Jeremiah 1 records what the Lord told Jeremiah about his mission. As you read, consider how you would feel if you were in Jeremiah's position. Take time to also think about what the Lord has called you to do and the preparation that you need to make in order to succeed.

Understanding the Scriptures

Jeremiah 1

Sanctified thee (v. 5)—Set you apart

Rod (v. 11)—Staff or stick

Hasten my word (v. 12)—Give a warning voice

Gird up thy loins (v. 17)—Get ready

Dismayed (v. 17)—Afraid

Lest (v. 17)—Or else

Confound (v. 17)—Confuse and make afraid

Defenced (v. 18)—Walled

Brasen (v. 18)—Bronze

Jeremiah 1:5—"Before Thou Camest Forth out of the Womb I Sanctified Thee"

The Prophet Joseph Smith taught, "Every man who has a calling to minister to the inhabitants of the world was ordained to that very purpose in the Grand Council of heaven before this world was" (*Teachings of the Prophet Joseph Smith*, sel. Joseph Fielding Smith [1976], 365).

Studying the Scriptures

A Scripture Mastery—Jeremiah 1:4–5

Jeremiah was foreordained to be a prophet. Foreordination is an important principle that helps us understand the premortal life and how it relates to this life. Read Jeremiah 1:4–5; Alma 13:3; Abraham 3:22–23 and write your understanding of foreordination.

B Before We Came to Earth

1. Jeremiah's calling was a difficult one, but what did he learn about his calling? (see Jeremiah 1:5).

2. What effect might it have had on Jeremiah to know he was chosen before he was born? In the margin of your scriptures you may want to write the statement of the Prophet Joseph Smith found in the "Understanding the Scriptures" section above.

3. How can a patriarchal blessing and the teachings of the prophets help you see what you were foreordained to do?

C Promises from the Lord

1. What was Jeremiah's response to his call from the Lord? (see Jeremiah 1:6).

2. Find and describe what the Lord said to Jeremiah in Jeremiah 1:7–11, 17–19 that you think helped him overcome his worries about preaching the gospel. How could this help a modern missionary with the same worry?

Jeremiah 2–3

Judah's Sins and Jeremiah's Message

Jeremiah 2–3 records what the Lord told Jeremiah to say to the people after he was called to preach to them. Much of what the Lord told Jeremiah to say deals with ways the children of Israel sinned before the Lord. Jeremiah 2:13 best describes their problems: they not only rejected the living waters (the living God), but their cisterns (water containers), symbolic of their spiritual lives, had holes in them and could hold no water. In other words, their lives were so full of sin that they could not receive the Lord's blessings.

Jeremiah 3 contains another example of the Lord using marriage as a symbol of his relationship with his covenant people. He said Israel and Judah were sisters who were both symbolically married to the Lord. Israel was unfaithful to her husband (the Lord), so he divorced (or rejected) her (see v. 8). The warning in Jeremiah 3 is to Israel's "sister" Judah, who did not seem to learn from Israel's mistakes.

Jeremiah 3 also contains promises that the Lord will take Israel and Judah back if they will repent and humble themselves before him. This return is what we call the gathering of Israel (see vv. 14–25). When Israel returns—if they will humble themselves and be true to their "marriage" covenants—the Lord promises to "heal" them.

Jeremiah 4–6

"We Have No Need to Repent"

One of the challenges Jeremiah faced in preaching to the people of Judah was that they thought they were already righteous and did not need to repent. They participated in different forms of idolatry, but they also offered sacrifices and practiced other "outward" parts of their true religion. Because they observed parts of their religion, they considered themselves righteous and claimed that the Lord would not allow anything to happen to a righteous people.

Through Jeremiah, the Lord told Judah that he was not pleased with them and proclaimed destruction upon them because of the way they pretended to be righteous. You will find examples of what Jeremiah said about the Jews' hypocritical religious practices at that time in Jeremiah 4:2, 14; 5:3, 12; 6:14–15, 20. Most of the rest of chapters 4–6 speak of God's judgments that will come upon Judah because of her sins.

Jeremiah 7

Jeremiah's Temple Sermon

If you want to be with your family eternally and enjoy eternal life, you must be married in the temple. Just being married in the temple, however, does not guarantee us a place in the celestial kingdom with Heavenly Father and our families. We must keep the commandments and covenants that are a vital part of that important ordinance, and we must endure faithfully to the end.

The Jews in Jeremiah's day believed that participating in temple ordinances and other religious ceremonies meant they were righteous, regardless of whatever else they did in their lives. As you read, look for what Jeremiah said defines true righteousness.

Understanding the Scriptures

Jeremiah 7

Amend (vv. 3, 5)—Change

Execute judgment (v. 5)—Deal fairly

Oppress not (v. 6)—Do not treat badly

Profit (v. 8)—Do good

Delivered (v. 10)—Safe, acceptable in the sight of God

Abominations (vv. 10, 30)—Actions or practices that disgust God

Intercession (v. 16)—Plea in another's behalf

Quenched (v. 20)—Put out

Inclined their ear (vv. 24, 26)—Paid close attention

Lamentation (v. 29)—Words of sorrow and remorse

Carcases (v. 33)—Dead bodies

Mirth (v. 34)—Happiness

Desolate (v. 34)—Empty

Jeremiah 7:3–4—"The Temple of the Lord"

Jeremiah did not tell the people that the temple was unimportant; the people felt that because they worshiped in the temple they were justified before God no matter what they did. Elder Bruce R. McConkie taught: "After we have been baptized, after we have been married in the temple, after we have taken all these covenants, we have to keep them. Every promise that we receive is conditioned upon our subsequent faithfulness" (in Conference Report, Oct. 1950, 16–17).

Jeremiah 7:12–14—Where Is Shiloh?

Shiloh was the site of the tabernacle and the ark of the covenant in the days of the judges. When the priests and the people became wicked in the days of Eli the priest, the Lord allowed the Philistines to destroy the tabernacle and capture the ark. Later, Israelites of the Northern Kingdom built at Shiloh a temple for idol worship that the Assyrians destroyed. Through the prophet Jeremiah the Lord said he would allow the temple in Jerusalem to be destroyed if the people did not repent. See the map section of your Bible to find Shiloh.

Studying the Scriptures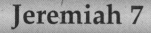

A Worthily Attending the Temple

1. List what Jeremiah said in Jeremiah 7:1–22 that the people had to do to worthily attend the temple.

2. What are the requirements to worthily enter the temple today? (Ask one of your leaders if you do not know.)

3. According to Jeremiah 7:8–15, what did the Lord say would happen if the people continued to attend the temple unworthily? Elder J. Ballard Washburn said: "We cannot go to [the Lord's] holy house unworthily without bringing upon ourselves the judgments of God. . . .

   ". . . If a man who is *dishonest* in his personal life, as it pertains to his wife and children or his business dealings, goes to the temple, he is heaping damnation upon his own soul and is in great need of repentance" (in Conference Report, Apr. 1995, 12–13; or *Ensign*, May 1995, 11–12).

B What the Lord Really Wants

1. The people of Judah offered sacrifices in the temple, but they did not obey the Lord in their daily lives. Elder J. Ballard Washburn reminded us that "we go to the temple to make covenants, but we go home to keep the covenants that we have made" (in Conference Report, Apr. 1995, 13; or *Ensign*, May 1995, 12). According to Jeremiah 7:21–28, what were the sins of Judah?

2. What did the Lord want the Jews to do in addition to worshiping in the temple?

3. Apply this principle to sacrament meeting. What do you think the Lord really wants from us *in addition to* our attendance at sacrament meeting? (see D&C 33:12–14).

Jeremiah 8

More Judgments against Judah

Jeremiah 8 speaks more of the judgments that would come upon the people of Judah, especially their wicked leaders. As in other chapters, chapter 8 teaches that one of the biggest problems among Judah and her leaders was that they believed they had no sin, and that they would be protected against their enemies.

Jeremiah 9–10

Jeremiah Weeps and Prays for Judah

Some have called Jeremiah the "weeping" prophet because of the sad message he delivered and because he saw his prophecies fulfilled concerning the destruction of the people of Judah. Like all men of God, Jeremiah loved the people and tried to prevent their destruction, but he could not avoid telling them the truth about what would happen if they did not repent. Jeremiah 9 is an example of Jeremiah's "weeping" over Judah's approaching destruction because they continued to worship and trust in idols. Jeremiah 10 ends with a prayer of sadness.

Studying the Scriptures

A What Pleases the Lord?

1. According to Jeremiah 9:23–24, what do many people "glory" in?
2. What did the Lord say he glories or delights in? How can we make this become *our* glory and delight?

Jeremiah 11–15

The Judgments of God

Although it may seem like Jeremiah repeated his message of God's judgment upon Judah, each chapter or sermon contains a slightly different view or teaching about these judgments.

Jeremiah 11 is about the importance of making covenants with the Lord. The Lord reminded the people of Judah that he made special covenants with them as a people from the time Moses led them out of Egypt. Because they continually broke those covenants, they would be punished. Jeremiah 11 ends with a reference to people in Jeremiah's hometown who wanted to kill him because of his message. The Lord said judgments would especially come upon those people.

Jeremiah 12 tells how the Lord explained to Jeremiah why the wicked sometimes seem to prosper. The Lord assured him that justice will eventually come upon the wicked. In addition, he said that the righteous are also eventually rewarded for their works.

The story of the Flood in the days of Noah can teach us that people can be so wicked that their sins "bind" them (2 Nephi 26:22), which can make them incapable of changing. The Lord

destroyed the people because of this inability to change. The Book of Mormon speaks of people who refused to repent until it was "everlastingly too late" (Helaman 13:38). Jeremiah 13 holds the basic message that because the people were so "accustomed to do evil" they could not change their wicked ways, just as a leopard could not change his spots (see Jeremiah 13:23).

Jeremiah 14 records Jeremiah's deep feelings for his people as he pleads with the Lord for them. Verses 1–6 tell what Jeremiah learned from the Lord about why they were having a "dearth" (famine) in the land. Verses 7–9 record Jeremiah's pleading with the Lord to turn away the famine, and verses 10–12 give the Lord's answer. Jeremiah speaks in verse 13, and the Lord again speaks in verses 14–18. The final four verses of chapter 14 record Jeremiah's words, which sound like a prayer.

Jeremiah 15:1–14 holds the Lord's proclamation of the destructions that would come upon Judah. Jeremiah worried that he was included in the judgments the Lord described. In verses 15–18, he told the Lord how faithful he had been. In verses 19–21 the Lord told Jeremiah that his life was accepted but that he should not try to defend his people.

Jeremiah 16

Hope in the Latter Days

For hundreds of years before Jeremiah's time, the Lord, through his prophets, pleaded with the children of Israel to trust and obey him, promising that he would bless them with peace and prosperity. They chose, however, the seemingly easier and more worldly ways of idol worship and other false religions. The Lord continued to give the Israelites evidence of his power, such as when Elijah met the priests of Baal on Mount Carmel (see 1 Kings 18). But the people still would not wholly follow the Lord; his ways seemed too difficult. What they did not realize was that his way is the only way of peace and salvation. Unfortunately, the time comes when the only way the Lord can show people that he is the only true and living, all-powerful God is to allow them to be cast out where they must trust in their false gods for deliverance, knowing the gods cannot save anyone because they have no life or power. The Lord promised to use this method in Jeremiah 16.

The message in Jeremiah 16 is not all negative, however. The Lord promised to receive Israel back again in the latter days and help them to know that he is their God. The gathering of Israel is something we can participate in today.

Understanding the Scriptures 🔑

Jeremiah 16

Grievous deaths (v. 4)—Deadly diseases

Cut themselves, nor make themselves bald (v. 6)—Ways people sometimes mourned the dead

Consolation (v. 7)—Comfort for someone who mourns

Recompense (v. 18)—Reward

Defiled (v. 18)—Polluted

Detestable (v. 18)—Disgusting

Refuge (v. 19)—Safe resting place

Studying the Scriptures ✏️➡️

A. What? and Why?

A stranger to Israel comes upon the land vacated by the Jews when they were taken into Babylon. When he asks you what happened and why, what would you tell him? Look in Jeremiah 16:10–13 for help.

B. Scripture Mastery—Jeremiah 16:16

1. Read Jeremiah 16:14–16 and tell what the Lord promised to do in the latter days for Israel.

2. According to these same verses, how impressive would the Lord's action be to them?

3. Who do you think the "fishers" and "hunters" are in verse 16?

4. Why do you think the Lord used the terms "fishers" and "hunters" to describe what he would do?

Jeremiah 17

The Sins of Judah

Jeremiah 17 records that the Lord and Jeremiah spoke about what removed Judah from favor in the sight of God. The people seemed to be permanently fixed on sin (see vv. 1–4), would not trust in the Lord (vv. 5–8), and did not keep the Sabbath day holy (vv. 19–27). Jeremiah prayed for the people (vv. 12–18).

Understanding the Scriptures 🔑

Jeremiah 17:5–8, 19–27

Maketh flesh his arm (v. 5)—Puts his trust in the strength of a mortal man

Parched (v. 6)—Very dry

Be careful (v. 8)—Watch out for, or be concerned

Hallow (vv. 22, 24, 27)—Make sacred

Studying the Scriptures ✏️➡️

A. Draw a Picture

Draw one or more pictures that represent what Jeremiah 17:5–8 says about those who trust in the Lord and those who don't.

B. Write a Sentence

Use the following words to write a sentence that summarizes what the Lord taught in Jeremiah 17:19–27 about keeping the Sabbath day holy: *burden, work, diligent, hallow.*

Jeremiah 18–19

Pottery and Judah

Jeremiah often used objects to teach his message. He used one in each of these two chapters. In chapter 18, Jeremiah was told to go to the potter's house. When a potter makes an object that doesn't look like he wants it to, he throws the clay back on the wheel in a lump and tries again. The Lord said that all people are like clay being worked by a potter and that he was reworking the people of Judah.

Jeremiah 19 tells about a finished piece of pottery. After Jeremiah explained the sins of Judah and what would happen because of those sins, he broke the piece of pottery. He taught the people that the Lord would "break" them and that just as it would be impossible to put broken pottery back together again and make the object look as it originally did, this particular generation of the people of Judah would not be restored as a people to their lands or to their relationship with the Lord.

Jeremiah 20

Jeremiah's Troubles

Most of the book of Jeremiah contains his prophecies. Jeremiah 20, however, tells us a little about his life. We learn that because of his prophecies, Jeremiah was put in stocks, a wooden frame with holes to lock in the head, arms, legs, and feet of someone accused or convicted of a crime.

Jeremiah prophesied against the man who put him in stocks, but he also said things that sounded like he was discouraged about his situation. He did what the Lord wanted him to do and said what the Lord wanted him to say, but he was suffering for his obedience. Sometimes those who follow the Lord with all their hearts

face this trial. We learn about the greatness of Jeremiah's character when we read that he did not quit preaching because he said the Lord's word was "a burning fire shut up in my bones" (Jeremiah 20:9). Jeremiah determined to continue to trust in the Lord and preach the word regardless of the consequences. His courage is a model for us all.

Studying the Scriptures

A What Would You Say?

Jeremiah felt bad because of his trials. He was suffering for doing what he knew was right. Write what you would say to him at this time to comfort and encourage him.

Jeremiah 21–22

Prophecies for Two Kings

Jeremiah 21–22 records prophecies Jeremiah made to kings of Judah; they are not written in historical order. Chapter 21 is for Zedekiah, the last king of Judah before Babylon destroyed Jerusalem and the temple and took the people captive. Chapter 22 is for Shallum and Jehoiakim, who were sons of King Josiah, the king at the time Jeremiah began his ministry. As far as we know, Shallum was never a king, but he could have been had the Babylonians not taken him captive.

The message to Zedekiah in chapter 21 was that destruction by Babylon was inevitable. There was no "if" involved in the prophecy. The only choice Jeremiah gave the Jews was to stay in Jerusalem and die at the hands of the Babylonians or to leave the city and be taken captive.

Jeremiah 22 was recorded some years earlier and contains the message that deliverance was still possible for some Jews if they would repent. Perhaps the order of the two chapters teaches us that the very stern punishments from the Lord came only after many years and many opportunities to repent. Earlier, the Lord extended the possibility for deliverance, but when the people refused to repent the judgments became certain.

Jeremiah 23

False Prophets

When we think of prophets, we usually think of the President of the Church or great men in the scriptures who taught the Lord's word. All prophets are teachers. There are also false prophets or teachers, however, who do not teach the truth. Jeremiah 23 tells

that the Lord spoke about false prophets among the people. He revealed their false teachings and spoke of how these false prophets led people to sin and to believe false ideas. We also learn from this chapter about some differences between true and false prophets.

President Ezra Taft Benson said, "The prophet tells us what we need to know, not always what we want to know" ("Fourteen Fundamentals in Following the Prophet," in Brigham Young University 1980–81 Devotional and Fireside Speeches [1981], 28). Look for how this statement might apply to Jeremiah's teachings in this chapter.

Jeremiah 22:5–8 is of great importance because Jeremiah prophesied about the Savior.

Understanding the Scriptures

Jeremiah 23

Pastors (vv. 1–2)—Literally "shepherds," but in this case "leaders"

Remnant (v. 3)—What is left when everything else is gone

Folds (v. 3)—Safe, fenced areas to keep sheep

Dismayed (v. 4)—Terrified

Execute, executed (vv. 5, 20)—Perform

Swearing (v. 10)—A curse

Folly (v. 13)—Foolish things

Return (vv. 14, 20)—Turn away

Wormwood (v. 15)—Bitterness

Gall (v. 15)—A bitter liquid, poison

Vain (v. 16)—To think you are better than you really are

Counsel (vv. 18, 22)—In Hebrew, "council"—a group gathered together to instruct or make decisions

Perceived (v. 18)—Seen

Marked (v. 18)—Listened to

At hand (v. 23)—Nearby

Deceit (v. 26)—Lies

Lightness (v. 32)—Acting without much thought, reckless

Burden (vv. 36, 38)—Message

Perverted (v. 36)—Changed, overturned

Reproach (v. 40)—Disgrace

Perpetual (v. 40)—Everlasting

Studying the Scriptures

A How Can You Tell a False Prophet?

1. Read Jeremiah 23:1–2, 9–11, 13–14, 16–27, 29–32 and list what the Lord said false prophets were saying and doing.

2. Choose one item you listed and explain why that action or teaching would make someone a false prophet.

3. Why do you think people follow false prophets?

4. Why is it vital to know and follow a true prophet? How can you discern a false prophet? (see Deuteronomy 18:20–22; D&C 42:11–12; 46:7).

B The Cure for False Prophets

What did the Lord say in Jeremiah 23:3–8 he would do for those who were led astray by their leaders in Judah? (Note that this prophecy will be fulfilled mostly in the latter days.)

Jeremiah 24

Good and Bad Fruit

Jeremiah 24 tells how the Lord, through Jeremiah, taught through the image of a basket of good figs and a basket of rotten figs that some Jews would be taken captive to Babylon for their good and then be able to return to their homeland at some future time. Others would be shamed and destroyed because of their wickedness.

Jeremiah 25–26

Rejecting Prophets Leads to Captivity

Jeremiah 25–26 is similar to the order and theme of Jeremiah 21–22. In chapter 25, Jeremiah prophesied with certainty that Babylon would conquer Judah because they rejected the words of Jeremiah and other prophets (such as Lehi). Furthermore, Jeremiah prophesied that Judah would serve Babylon for seventy years, at which time another kingdom would conquer Babylon. The rest of the chapter is about the destruction of other wicked nations. This chapter teaches that God punishes unrighteous people, regardless of what nation they are in or from.

Jeremiah 26 records events prior to and helps explain some history of chapter 25. Jeremiah 26 tells how Jeremiah prophesied that the people must repent or be taken captive. Because of his message, which still left some hope for deliverance through repentance, leaders in Judah wanted Jeremiah killed. We also read of a prophet named Urijah who was killed for delivering a similar prophecy. This fact helps explain why the judgment was so certain in chapter 25.

Jeremiah 27–28

The Yoke of Babylon

Jeremiah 27–28 is one story. As directed by the Lord, Jeremiah made a yoke and put it on his neck. A yoke is something put on the neck for the purpose of carrying burdens (see picture below). The yoke symbolized captivity or slavery. Jeremiah taught the people that Judah and her surrounding nations would be under the "yoke" of Babylon. He warned that false prophets might teach otherwise, but the captivity would certainly happen. Jeremiah told King Zedekiah that if he and the people would humbly submit to the "yoke" of Babylon, they would not be destroyed. As a sign that his words would be fulfilled, he prophesied that Nebuchadnezzar, king of Babylon, would carry away the rest of the treasures and holy articles from the temple. The prophecy was fulfilled.

Jeremiah 28 tells of another man, Hananiah, who also claimed to be a prophet. He prophesied that God would break the yoke of Babylon within two years. Jeremiah said that time would prove whether he was right or wrong. The Lord, however, inspired Jeremiah to tell Hananiah that his prophecies were not true and that he would shortly die. Hananiah died just as Jeremiah said.

Studying the Scriptures

A How Can You Tell?

Jeremiah 27–28 gives an example of a true prophet and a false one. Read Deuteronomy 18:20–22; Doctrine and Covenants 42:11–12; 46:7; Articles of Faith 1:5. Then tell how we can know whether a person is truly sent from God to preach.

Jeremiah 29

Jeremiah's Letter to the Captives

Jeremiah 29 contains a letter from Jeremiah to the people of Judah who were taken captive and lived in Babylon. He told them to build houses, plant gardens, and be prepared to live there and enjoy Babylon the best they could. He again said they would be there for seventy years. He promised them that if they sought the Lord with all their hearts (see v. 13; Deuteronomy 4:26–31), the Lord would bring them back to Jerusalem.

Jeremiah cursed those who were still in Jerusalem and trusted in the teachings of false prophets who promised immediate deliverance from the Babylonians. He also cursed a false prophet who was sending false messages to the Jews in Babylon.

Studying the Scriptures

(A) How Could It Help?

Read Jeremiah 29:11–14 and write about how this message to Jews captive in Babylon because of their unfaithfulness could be used as a message of hope to someone today who is in the captivity of sin.

Jeremiah 30

The Lord Promises Help

At the time the Babylonians conquered the kingdom of Judah and took them captive, the people of Judah wondered if God had forsaken them and the covenant he made with Abraham to give them the land of Canaan and to be a blessing to the rest of the world through the truths and blessings he gave them. They also questioned whether he had done away with the covenant he made to establish the descendants of David as kings in Israel (see 2 Samuel 7:13). Jeremiah 30–33 contains the Lord's assurance to the children of Israel who were scattered and in captivity that he had not forsaken them or his covenants.

Jeremiah was told to write rather than speak the prophecy in Jeremiah 30–33. Since Jeremiah was in jail at the time, the written word would still allow the words of a prophet to reach the people. Also, although the people did not listen to Jeremiah at the time this revelation was given, if it were written down the people who were in captivity might be more teachable and could read it at a later time. Also note that the prophesy is directed to both Judah and Israel. Israel was taken by the Assyrians over 120 years before the time the Lord gave Jeremiah the message in this chapter.

As you read Jeremiah 30, look for what the Lord said about Judah's captivity and what he would do for them if they would trust in him. This message could also apply to someone captive to sin who feels lost to God. Perhaps he might feel the Lord had also forsaken him. As you read, look also for a personal message someone could get from this chapter.

Understanding the Scriptures

Jeremiah 30

Bring again the captivity (vv. 3, 18)—Bring back from captivity

Doth travail (v. 6)—Be in labor

Dismayed (v. 10)—Worried, terrified

Measure (v. 11)—Justice

Chastisement (v. 14)—Correction

Devour, devoured (v. 16)—Conquered and destroyed

Spoil (v. 16)—Destroy

Heap (v. 18)—Ruins

Afortime (v. 20)—Before

Proceed (v. 21)—Come

Engaged (v. 21)—Pledged

Jeremiah 30:12–13—How Can the Lord Help Them If Their Wounds Are "Incurable"?

The Joseph Smith Translation of the Bible helps us understand that verse 12 should say the bruise is *not* incurable, although it is very bad. And in verse 13 of the Joseph Smith Translation, the Lord again indicated that Judah's wounds were *not* incurable, but the people thought they were.

Jeremiah 30:9—Which King David Would the People Serve?

This "David" refers to the Messiah and King whom God promised would be David's descendant. The promise was fulfilled at the coming of Jesus Christ and will be fulfilled again at the Second Coming.

Studying the Scriptures

(A) List the Consequences

1. Read Jeremiah 30:5–7, 12–15 (including the JST in the footnotes) and describe what happened to the Israelites because they forsook their God and worshiped idols.

2. How are the consequences of idol worship like the consequences of sin today?

(B) Make a Comparison

Read Jeremiah 30: 8–11, 16–17. How is what the Lord promised to do for Judah in captivity like what he could do to help someone captive to sin?

Jeremiah 31

The Gathering of Israel

Jeremiah 31 continues the message begun in chapter 30. Chapter 31 contains great promises concerning the gathering of Israel, both the gathering to Jerusalem from captivity in ancient times and the gathering to Jesus Christ and his Church in the latter days from all places in the world where Israel had been scattered.

Understanding the Scriptures

Jeremiah 31

Which were left of (v. 2)—Survivors

Drawn (v. 3)—Gathered

Adorned (v. 4)—Decorated

Tabrets (v. 4)—Musical instruments

Remnant of Israel (v. 7)—Israelites not destroyed, scattered, or in captivity

Supplications (v. 9)—Prayers of pleading

Redeemed, ransomed (v. 11)—Pay for someone's freedom from bondage

Satiate (vv. 14, 25)—Satisfy

Rahel (v. 15)—Rachel (wife of Jacob [Israel] and mother of Joseph and Benjamin)

Refrain (v. 16)—Stop

Unaccustomed (v. 18)—Not used to

Confounded (v. 19)—Ashamed

Bear the reproach (v. 19)—Carry the shame

Bowels (v. 20)—Feelings

Waymarks (v. 21)—Signs on the road

Compass (v. 22)—Surround

Habitation (v. 23)—House

Husbandman (v. 24)—Farmer

Replenished (v. 25)—Filled up

Sow (v. 27)—Plant

Plucked up (vv. 28, 40)—Pull up, uproot

Teeth are set on edge, teeth shall be set on edge (vv. 29–30)—Pucker

Ordinances (vv. 35–36)—Regular motions

Depart from before me (v. 36)—Removed

Jeremiah 31—The Gathering of Israel

The entire chapter of Jeremiah 31 is about the gathering of the house of Israel. Israel is gathered in two ways: physically and spiritually. For individual members of the house of Israel the two gatherings may occur at the same time, or they may occur separately. Because these two gatherings have occurred at different times throughout history and will yet occur in the future, scriptures about the gathering of the house of Israel can be confusing. Jeremiah 31:1–30 certainly applies to the physical gathering of the family of Israel from the lands in which they were scattered and captive to their promised lands. But these verses may also apply to those who are spiritually gathered to the Lord and his Church. Jeremiah 31:31–34 seems to have special application to the spiritual gathering (see D&C 45:56).

Jeremiah 31:9—"Ephraim Is My Firstborn"

Ephraim was not literally the firstborn of Israel since he was Jacob's grandson, the son of Joseph who received the birthright from Jacob, or Israel (see Genesis 48–49). The reference in Jeremiah 31:9 to Ephraim being the firstborn refers to this position of heir to the birthright.

Jeremiah 31:31–34—The "New Covenant"

Elder Dallin H. Oaks explained the following about the "new covenant": "The 'new covenant,' . . . was the covenant contained in the Book of Mormon and in the 'former commandments' [see D&C 84:57]. . . . These former commandments must have been the Lord's prior revelations, as contained in the Bible (the Old and New Testaments) and in those modern revelations already given to the Saints. . . .

"The covenant described in [the] scriptures, made new by its renewal and confirmation in these latter days, refers to our covenant relationship with Jesus Christ. It incorporates the fullness of the gospel. . . .

". . . The 'new covenant' contained in the Book of Mormon and the former commandments is that central promise of the gospel, rooted in the atonement and resurrection of Jesus Christ, which gives us the assurance of immortality and the opportunity for eternal life if we will repent of our sins and make and keep the gospel covenant with our Savior. By this means, and through his grace, we can realize the great promise 'that through the Atonement of Christ, all mankind may be saved, by obedience to the laws and ordinances of the Gospel' (Articles of Faith 1:3)" (Dallin H. Oaks, "Another Testament of Jesus Christ" [CES fireside address, 6 June 1993], 4–5).

Studying the Scriptures

A Illustrate an Idea

Draw a picture or make a diagram of some kind that represents an idea you read about in Jeremiah 31:1–30. Write a brief explanation for your picture or diagram.

B Describe the Difference

1. According to Jeremiah 31:31–34, when did the Lord make the old covenant with the house of Israel?

2. Describe how and why the new covenant is different than the old covenant.

Jeremiah 32

Jeremiah Buys Land

Jeremiah 32 records that in order to impressively teach that the children of Israel would be gathered back to their promised lands, even after the Babylonian destruction, the Lord commanded the imprisoned Jeremiah to buy land. He then told Jeremiah to keep the title in a safe place as evidence of this prophecy. The power of the Babylonians made this seem impossible, but with God nothing is impossible (see v. 27). It is important to remember that with mortals many things seem impossible, but to an all-powerful God the words "Is there any thing too hard for me?" apply (Jeremiah 32:27).

Jeremiah 33

Peace in Jerusalem

Jeremiah 33 contains some special promises concerning Jerusalem that have not yet been completely fulfilled. Chapter 33 speaks of a great day of peace in Jerusalem when all the people who live there will worship the Lord. This prophecy has not been fulfilled, but Jeremiah said it would be in the days when "the Branch" (Jesus Christ) reigns as King on David's throne (see vv. 15–16). In other words, Jerusalem will never know complete peace and safety until all her inhabitants accept Jesus Christ as their King.

Studying the Scriptures

A What Do You Learn about Jesus Christ?

Read Jeremiah 33:15–18. These verses say that in some future time Israel will not "want" (lack or need) a man to sit and rule on David's throne, nor will they "want" men to perform sacrifices. In what ways does Jesus Christ eternally fulfill the roles of king, priest, and sacrifice for his people? (see Luke 1:32–33; John 18:36–37; Hebrews 2:17; 7:11, 22–27; 8:1–6; 9:11–15; 10:10–17; 3 Nephi 9:19–20).

Jeremiah 34

Condemnation of Zedekiah and the Jews

Jeremiah 34 contains prophecies Jeremiah made about what would happen to King Zedekiah and also about what would happen to the people of Judah. In Jeremiah 34 the Lord specifically condemned the people of Judah for having slaves and servants who were Jews and for breaking the commandment given in the law of Moses to set all servants and slaves free every seventh year.

Jeremiah 35

The Rechabites

Jeremiah 35 records events that actually occurred several years before those in previous chapters. We know this because Jehoiakim (mentioned in v. 1) was king before Zedekiah (mentioned in chapters 33–34). This kind of "flashback" occurs several times in the book of Jeremiah.

Jeremiah 35 speaks of a group of people called Rechabites. They lived outside of the cities in tents and never settled in one place. The Rechabites followed certain traditions given by the leader of their group. These traditions were not part of their religion, but they followed the rules and traditions very faithfully. The Lord used these people as an object lesson. The lesson was this: the Rechabites faithfully keep human traditions, but the people of Judah cannot keep the commandments of a living God—commandments that have real and eternal blessings attached to them. The Lord promised to bless the Rechabites for their sincerity and faithfulness.

Jeremiah 36

Baruch the Scribe

Jeremiah 36 records that the Lord told Jeremiah to write all the prophecies he made against Israel, Judah, and other nations. Because Jeremiah was under arrest, a scribe named Baruch wrote all of Jeremiah's prophecies and then read them on the steps of the temple. Some of the king's men heard the prophecies, got the writings, and read them to the king. The king commanded that the writings be burned and he sought to have Jeremiah and Baruch killed, but the Lord hid them. Jeremiah made one more prophecy and sent it to the king. The prophecy was that no descendant of Jehoiakim would be king—a prophecy which came to pass.

Jeremiah 37–44

Babylon Conquers Judah

Jeremiah 37–44 is mostly historical. This section briefly tells the story of Jeremiah during the time Judah was destroyed by Babylon and many people were taken captive.

Jeremiah 37 tells that the Egyptian army marched to Judah at the time the Babylonians (sometimes called Chaldeans in these chapters) were conquering the land of Judah. When the Babylonians heard Egypt was coming, they left for a while. This withdrawal gave Judah the false hope that Egypt would save them. Jeremiah told Zedekiah this would not happen. Because of this prophecy, Jeremiah was put in a dungeon. Later, Zedekiah allowed him to be released, but he still remained under arrest.

Jeremiah 38 records that the leaders in Jerusalem thought they could withstand the Babylonians. They did not like Jeremiah's continual message that they should allow themselves to be taken into Babylon and all would be well. They thought the message was especially bad for the morale of the fighting men, so they had Jeremiah thrown into a dungeon that was worse than the first one. An Ethiopian eunuch named Ebed-melech had Jeremiah removed from the dungeon, and Jeremiah once again appeared before Zedekiah. He reminded the king that if he were obedient, all would be well. But the king did not heed the counsel.

Jeremiah 39 tells about the destruction of Jerusalem, the capture of King Zedekiah, the slaying of his sons as Zedekiah looked on, and the torture Zedekiah experienced when the Babylonian invaders put his eyes out. From the Book of Mormon we learn that one of Zedekiah's sons was saved. The group who saved him traveled to the Western Hemisphere and are commonly known as the people of Zarahemla in the Book of Mormon (see Omni 1:14–19; Helaman 8:21). The Babylonians treated Jeremiah well. At the end of chapter 39, the Lord promised to bless Ebed-melech for his kindness to Jeremiah.

Jeremiah 40 records that the Babylonians completely freed Jeremiah. They suggested that he go live with Gedaliah, whom they assigned to govern the land, and Jeremiah did. Jews from surrounding lands began to gather to Mizpah, where Gedaliah dwelt. A man named Johanan found out that some Jews planned to kill Gedaliah, but Gedaliah would not let Johanan do anything to thwart the plan.

Jeremiah 41 tells how a man named Ishmael killed Gedaliah. Ishmael and his men also killed all who were living with Gedaliah, whether they were Jews or Babylonians. Johanan organized an army and attacked Ishmael's men, killing many, taking others as prisoners, and freeing prisoners taken in the attack on Gedaliah. Worried about the Babylonians' reaction to the Jews because of what happened, all the Jews moved from Mizpah to an area close to Bethlehem called Chimham. From there they intended to go to Egypt for safety.

Jeremiah 42 names Jeremiah among the group that moved to Chimham. Johanan went to Jeremiah and asked if he would inquire of the Lord concerning their plans to go to Egypt. They promised that whatever the Lord said, they would do. Jeremiah said they should not go to Egypt. He said if they stayed in the land of Judah, the Lord would protect them, but if they went to Egypt, they would die by the sword, by famine, or by some other disaster.

Jeremiah 43 tells that Johanan and the other proud leaders of this group of Jews did not believe Jeremiah's counsel. They went to Egypt anyway, and they took Jeremiah with them as a prisoner. When they got there, Jeremiah prophesied that Nebuchadnezzar, the Babylonian king, would conquer Egypt as well.

Jeremiah 44 records that Jeremiah told the Jews that they would be destroyed in Egypt because they continued to practice forms of idol worship and because they would not obey the Lord; only a few would survive and return to Judah as a witness that the Lord's word was fulfilled. This prophecy was fulfilled among yet another group of Jews who could have received blessings at the Lord's hand if they would have obeyed his prophet. But instead they trusted in their own judgment.

Jeremiah 45

The Righteous Also Have Trials

Jeremiah 45 is a revelation to Baruch, the scribe who wrote Jeremiah's revelations and read them on the steps of the temple in the days of King Jehoiakim. Apparently, Baruch had hoped the Lord would take away his trials and troubles because he did the Lord's work. The Lord, however, promised him no deliverance from trials, only that he would not die in the near future.

We too should remember that we cannot expect that just because we are living right the Lord will take away trials, persecution, and other difficult experiences. Like those who have been true and faithful to the Lord since the beginning of time, we must be faithful in good times and in bad.

Jeremiah 46–51

Destruction of Nations

Jeremiah 46–51 records prophecies about the destruction of several nations surrounding Israel and why each would be destroyed. Jeremiah prophesied that Egypt (see Jeremiah 46), Philistia (see Jeremiah 47) Moab (see Jeremiah 48), Ammon (see Jeremiah 49:1–6), Edom (see Jeremiah 49:7–22), Damascus (see Jeremiah 49:23–27), Kedar (see Jeremiah 49:28–29), Hazor (see Jeremiah 49:30–37), Elam (see Jeremiah 49:34–39), and Babylon (see Jeremiah 50–51) would all be destroyed.

Perhaps the purpose for all these messages of destruction is to teach, especially to the house of Israel, that not only will the Lord punish the wickedness of his people, he will also punish the wickedness of all people, regardless of their nation. The good news for Israel is that although the Lord will destroy all these other nations, he promised to preserve his people and not completely destroy them (see Jeremiah 46:27–28). The messages of destruction are also symbolic of the destruction of the wicked in the last days.

Jeremiah 52

Jeremiah's Last Writings

Jeremiah 52 is a fitting end to the book of Jeremiah. Chapter 52 gives an account of when Babylon conquered Jerusalem, the capital of Judah, and either killed or took captive a large number of the people of Judah.

Understanding the Scriptures 🔑

Jeremiah 52

Pitched against it (v. 4)—Camped around in preparation for war

Besieged (v. 5)—Surrounded and cut off from anything and anyone going out or coming in

Residue (v. 15)—Rest

Vinedressers (v. 16)—People who take care of vineyards

Husbandmen (v. 16)—People who work in and take care of fields of crops

Pillars of brass, bases, brasen sea, caldrons, snuffers, basons, firepans, chapiter of brass (vv. 17–22)—Precious items from the temple

Eunuch (v. 25)—Officer (see Bible Dictionary, s.v. "eunuch")

Principal (v. 25)—Main, chief

Mustered (v. 25)—Enlisted people in the army

A) List the Events in Order

Jeremiah 52 tells about events in the fall of Jerusalem. Consider the following events and use what you read in the chapter to list them in order: King Zedekiah's eyes put out; Nebuchadnezzar puts the city under siege; thousands of Jews taken captive; temple destroyed; walls of Jerusalem destroyed. After each event, give the verse that describes the event.

B) Write an Explanation

Write a letter to the people of Judah who were captive in Babylon. Explain why their city was destroyed and why they were in captivity. Give at least two good reasons each for the Jews' destruction and captivity, and give a scripture reference for each answer.

The Lamentations of Jeremiah

The word *lamentation* means weeping or crying with great sorrow. Traditionally, Jews wrote and sang lamentations for close relatives and friends who died. This small book contains Jeremiah's lamentations, written in poetic form, for Jerusalem, the temple, and the people of Judah. As you read, you might look for the following points:

- We cannot sin without consequences.
- Heeding false prophets is often easier than heeding true ones.
- Thinking the powers of the world can help you escape God's punishment is foolish.
- Sinners who are punished often think God is unfair.
- True remorse usually comes only after some amount of suffering.
- Hope comes from acknowledging our sins.
- Because of God's love and mercy, there is a time of forgiveness and renewal for all who repent.

For more information, see the Bible Dictionary, s.v. "Lamentations, book of."

Lamentations 1

The Consequences of Sin

Elder Theodore M. Burton said, "The scriptures and instructions from our spiritual leaders teach us how to avoid the heartache which always results from sin" (in Conference Report, Oct. 1985, 81; or Ensign, Nov. 1985, 64).

Lamentations 1, as well as all of the chapters in Lamentations, give examples of the heartache Elder Burton spoke of. Heartfelt sorrow and remorse are the parts of sinning we don't often see or think about when we are tempted to do wrong.

As you read, think about how the words in chapter 1 might be like the words of those who wasted their days on earth and are now in the spirit world facing the eternal consequences of the poor choices they made on earth.

Understanding the Scriptures 🔑

Lamentations 1

Solitary (v. 1)—Alone

Provinces (v. 1)—Areas like states or counties

Tributary (v. 1)—Slave, subject to others

Treacherously (v. 2)—Offensively

Servitude (v. 3)—Slavery

Heathen (vv. 3, 10)—Those who don't know or worship the true God

Between the straits (v. 3)—While in distress

Desolate (vv. 4, 13, 16)—Alone, without strength

Adversaries (vv. 5, 7, 17)—Enemies

Harts (v. 6)—Deer

Last end (v. 9)—Future

Sanctuary (v. 10)—Temple

Vile (v. 11)—Worthless

Prevaileth, prevailed (vv. 13, 16)—Succeeds

Wreathed (v. 14)—Woven together

Trodden (v. 15)—Walked on

Bereaveth (v. 20)—Take away loved ones

Studying the Scriptures ✏️

A) Why?

In Lamentations 1:1–11 Jeremiah spoke as himself. In verses 12–22 he spoke as if he were the whole country of Judah.

Choose four phrases from Jeremiah's words (vv. 1–11) that you think explain why he "lamented."

Lamentations 2–4

Why Judah Was Punished

Lamentations 2–4 are expressions of sadness over what happened to the people of Judah. Lamentations 2 clearly states that the Lord punished his people because of their sins and for their good. Lamentations 3 contains the expressions of a people that feel forsaken by the Lord but still trust and find hope in the thought that he has not forsaken them forever. Lamentations 4 records Jeremiah's sorrow as he compares the way Israel lived as a righteous people with what they had become after the Babylonian conquest.

Lamentations 5

Jeremiah's Plea

When you sin, lose the companionship of the Holy Ghost, and feel the despair that comes from the consequences of sin and separation from the Lord, you really only have two choices. One choice is to cover your sins. We usually cover our sins by blaming others, excusing ourselves from responsibility, or by being dishonest and denying we did anything wrong. The other choice is to humble ourselves, repent, and begin to be reconciled to the Lord.

Lamentations 5 contains a lamentation of humility. In this prayer-like lamentation, Jeremiah speaks for the people who realized their sins and desired forgiveness.

Understanding the Scriptures

Lamentations 5

Reproach (v. 1)—Shame

Inheritance (v. 2)—Land, houses, and clothing

Aliens (v. 2)—Foreigners

Borne their iniquities (v. 7)—Suffered for their sins

Peril (v. 9)—Danger

Ravished (v. 11)—Abused

Grind (v. 13)—Millstones that crush grain

Studying the Scriptures

A How Can You Tell?

List words and phrases from Jeremiah 5 that indicate the people were truly repentant. Explain why you chose each word or phrase.

B What Can You Do?

Read and reflect on the second Article of Faith. There is, however, a difference between being punished for our sins and suffering as a result of other people's sins. What can you do if you find yourself in the circumstance described in verse 7, and how can the doctrine explained in the second Article of Faith help you?

The Book of Ezekiel

A Prophet in Captivity

The Babylonians attacked Judah on three major occasions. The second was approximately 597 B.C. Ezekiel was among the group taken captive to Babylon. About five years later he was called to be a prophet to the Jews in captivity. He tried to help the people learn from their mistakes.

Watchman on the Tower

While Jeremiah cried repentance in Jerusalem, Ezekiel worked with the people in Babylonian captivity. Jeremiah tried to save the people from destruction and Ezekiel tried to help his people understand that their captivity resulted from their wickedness. Both prophets taught that there was cause for hope in the future as the people returned to the Lord. Ezekiel was to be a watchman on the tower, a calling which will be discussed in chapter 33.

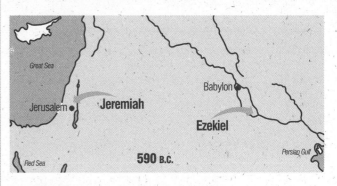

Getting Ready to Study Ezekiel

If we were to choose a main theme of the book of Ezekiel, it might be that eventually all people shall know that the Lord is God. This principle, indicated by phrases such as "then will they know that I am the Lord," appears over sixty-five times in Ezekiel.

The following outline shows six major topics in the book of Ezekiel:

1. Ezekiel's call to be a prophet (see Ezekiel 1–3)

2. Prophecies condemning the sins of the people in the land of Israel, especially in Jerusalem (see Ezekiel 4–11, 20–24)

3. Prophecies calling the Jews in Babylon to repentance (see Ezekiel 12–19)

4. Prophecies concerning the destruction of the countries surrounding Israel who were their enemies (see Ezekiel 25–32)

5. Prophecies about the gathering of Israel and other events in preparation for the Second Coming (see Ezekiel 33–39)

6. A description of Ezekiel's vision of a temple being built in Jerusalem at some future time (see Ezekiel 40–48)

For more information about the book of Ezekiel, see the Bible Dictionary, s.v. "Ezekiel."

Ezekiel 1

Ezekiel's Vision of God's Glory

Ezekiel 1, after a brief introduction, describes Ezekiel's vision of God and his glory. Because the glory of God and heaven are very hard to describe in the language of mortals, prophets often use symbolic terms and images to describe what they saw. Some people have tried to explain what the symbols represent, but the Prophet Joseph Smith said, "Whenever God gives a vision of an image, or beast, or figure of any kind, He always holds Himself responsible to give a revelation or interpretation of the meaning thereof, otherwise we are not responsible or accountable for our belief in it. Don't be afraid of being damned for not knowing the meaning of a vision or figure, if God has not given a revelation or interpretation of the subject" (Teachings of the Prophet Joseph Smith, 291).

Even if we do not fully understand the meaning of what Ezekiel saw, his dramatic description can still give us a feeling for how incredible the vision was and how great God's glory truly is.

Ezekiel 2–3

Ezekiel's Call to Serve

Ezekiel 2–3 begins to record what God said to Ezekiel as part of his vision of God's glory (see Ezekiel 1). In a way, these chapters contain his "mission call." As you read the way the Lord describes Ezekiel's mission and the people he is called to teach, consider how the prophet of God calls a missionary today.

Understanding the Scriptures

Ezekiel 2

Impudent (v. 4)—Proud

Forbear (vv. 5, 7)—Refuse to listen and obey

Briers and thorns (v. 6)—Prickly weeds (a symbol for the trouble people might give Ezekiel when he delivers his messages)

Scorpions (v. 6)—Poisonous creature (a symbol of wicked people that Ezekiel will preach to)

Dismayed (v. 6)—Afraid

Lamentations, mourning, woe (v. 10)—Sadness

Ezekiel 2:9–10; 3:1–3—The Lord Asked Ezekiel to Eat a Scroll

The description of Ezekiel eating a scroll is a symbolic one representing his calling to teach the Lord's word by literally making the word of God part of his being. The book of Revelation records a time when the Apostle John had a similar experience (see Revelation 10).

Ezekiel 3

Hearkened, hearken (vv. 6–7)—Listened and obeyed

Heat (v. 14)—Anger

Watchman (v. 17)—A man standing on the wall of a city watching for enemies and warning the people in the city

But his blood will I require at thine hand (vv. 18, 20)—You will be held responsible for his sins

Delivered (vv. 19, 21)—Saved

I lay a stumblingblock before him (v. 20)—I cause him to fall

Cleave (v. 26)—Stick

Dumb (v. 26)—Unable to speak

Reprover (v. 26)—One who corrects another

Studying the Scriptures

Do two of the following three activities (A–C) as you study Ezekiel 2–3.

A Summarize Ezekiel's Mission

To summarize Ezekiel's mission, explain the significance of the following words and phrases: "impudent children" (Ezekiel 2:4; see also 3:7); briers, thorns, and scorpions (2:6); the roll of a book (2:9–10; 3:1–3); a diamond (3:9); watchman (3:17–21); a reprover (3:26).

or

Draw at least four pictures in your notebook that represent the ideas listed above.

B A Difficult Mission

1. Search Ezekiel 2–3 and list reasons you think Ezekiel would have had a difficult mission. For each reason, list a verse to support your idea.

2. List what the Lord said Ezekiel's mission would be in Ezekiel 2–3 and what encouraged Ezekiel to fulfill his mission.

C The Watchman

1. Read Ezekiel 3:17–21 and describe the calling of a watchman.

2. Name a "watchman" in the Church today and explain why you chose who you did.

3. What does Ezekiel 3:17–21 teach us about the importance of fulfilling our callings? You may want to cross-reference these verses to Jacob 1:19.

Ezekiel 4–5

Prophecies of Jerusalem's Destruction

As with Jeremiah, the Lord had Ezekiel use objects and physical symbols to teach the people in ways they were more likely to notice and remember. Ezekiel 4–5 records symbols the Lord told Ezekiel to use to represent the wickedness of the Israelites or the destruction of Jerusalem.

Ezekiel 6–7

Sin and Destruction

Ezekiel 6–7 contains the Lord's forceful message about what would occur in the land of Israel when conquered by Babylon. Ezekiel was taken into Babylon before the complete fall and destruction of Jerusalem, so he speaks of this event as being in the future. In the prophecies in chapters 6–7, the Lord especially condemned Israel's idolatry and said Jerusalem would be destroyed so the Jews would "know that I am the Lord" (6:14). The survivors would be able to bear testimony that God truly is the living God and that his words were fulfilled.

Ezekiel 8–11

Why Jerusalem Was Conquered

Ezekiel 8–11 contains an account of a vision the Lord gave Ezekiel. Ezekiel was one of many Jews taken captive in the Babylonians' earlier attacks on Judah. This vision helped the exiles (people who were in captivity in Babylon) know what happened to Jerusalem and why it happened.

Ezekiel 8 tells about the wickedness of the people of Jerusalem, including their religious leaders. Ezekiel 9 records that the Lord had an angelic messenger "mark" the righteous to protect them from destruction (like Passover in Egypt). Ezekiel 10 makes it clear that the Lord permitted Jerusalem's destruction. Ezekiel 11 provides some hope for future generations by prophesying that the Lord would gather his people back to their promised lands and renew their covenant relationship.

Studying the Scriptures

A The Gathering

1. Find the words "will I" and "I will" in Ezekiel 11:16–20 to help you make a list of what the Lord said he would do for his covenant people.

2. How are you a part of what is spoken of in these verses, or how is the Lord fulfilling these promises today?

B Explain the Phrases

Read Ezekiel 11:19 and describe what you think the difference is between a person with a "stony heart" and a person with a "new spirit" and a "heart of flesh."

Ezekiel 12–17

Why Captivity?

Ezekiel 12–17 contains the Lord's revelations to Ezekiel that there would be more Babylonian attacks on Jerusalem and more Jews taken captive. The Lord also revealed why these events would happen and told Ezekiel to preach repentance to those in captivity.

Ezekiel 12 assures the Jews that more would be taken captive.

Ezekiel 13 tells that the Lord condemned false prophets who pretended to speak in his name and others who led people away from him in various ways.

Ezekiel 14 records that Jewish leaders came to Ezekiel seeking counsel. The Lord told them he would not counsel them until they stopped seeking answers from idols as well. He emphasized that each individual must be righteous in order to endure the coming judgments and that they could not rely on their leaders' righteousness.

Ezekiel 15 holds a comparison between the children of Israel and a burned vine, which is good for nothing. Many other times in the scriptures, the Lord compared the children of Israel to a vine or a vineyard (see Isaiah 5; Jacob 5).

Ezekiel 16, like other places in the Old Testament, contains a comparison between the Lord's relationship with Israel and the covenant of marriage. Chapter 16 goes into great detail to show how Israel (Jerusalem) was unfaithful to her "husband" and why she deserved her punishment.

Ezekiel 17 includes a parable the Lord revealed to Ezekiel that taught the people they should not seek deliverance from Egypt while in bondage but rather to submit to the Babylonians and the Lord would eventually redeem them.

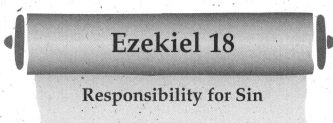

Ezekiel 18

Responsibility for Sin

In what ways are you like or unlike your parents? Why?

It is true that sometimes the "innocent are compelled to suffer for the iniquities of the guilty" (Teachings of the Prophet Joseph Smith, 34). Some people, however, continue to blame their parents or others for things they have power to change. The children of Israel felt their punishments resulted from their fathers' sins. They even had a common saying about suffering for their parents' sins which is found in Ezekiel 18:2. Their proverb (saying) was partially true. The fathers had not properly taught the children in the ways of the Lord nor had they created an environment where their children would be more likely to grow up faithful to the laws of God.

In every generation, however, the Lord sends prophets to teach the truth and teach people ways they must repent. Each generation has the opportunity to choose whether to listen and obey the words of the prophets or to follow the tradition of their parents. The Lord clearly taught this element of the principle of agency in this chapter.

Understanding the Scriptures

Ezekiel 18

Teeth are set on edge (v. 2)—Pucker

Eaten upon the mountains (vv. 6, 11, 15)—Participated in idol worship

Defiled (vv. 6, 11, 15)—Been immoral with

Come near to (v. 6)—Have sexual relations with

Oppressed (vv. 7, 12, 16, 18)—Been unfair to, placed burdens upon

Pledge (vv. 7, 12, 16)—Money someone owes

Given forth upon usury (vv. 8, 13)—Charged interest when giving loans

Increase (v. 8)—An unfair amount of money to charge

Executed (vv. 8, 17)—Performed

Bear (vv. 19–20)—Carry, be accountable for

Equal (vv. 25, 29)—Fair, just

Studying the Scriptures

(A) Apply the Scriptures

How could you use Ezekiel 18:1–18 to help someone who lives in a home where he or she is not encouraged in righteous activities? You may want to cross-reference these verses to the second Article of Faith.

(B) Identify Important Principles

Read Ezekiel 18:19–32 and find what the Lord taught about sin, repentance, enduring to the end, and how he feels about those in sin. Write at least four one-sentence statements that summarize the principles taught in these verses.

Ezekiel 19–20

Leaders Who Won't Listen

Ezekiel 19–20 is especially to and about the leaders of the Jews. In chapter 19, the Lord used two parables to teach that leaders with great potential lost blessings because of their foolishness. Chapter 20 tells how some leaders of the Jews in Babylon (where Ezekiel lived in captivity) wanted to receive instruction from the Lord through Ezekiel. The Lord called them to repentance for seeking the Lord while also seeking revelation from others gods. In Ezekiel 20:33–44 the Lord promised he would give a future generation of Israelites another opportunity to be led from bondage and know that he is their Lord and God, just like he did when he originally led the children of Israel out of Egypt. This time, however, he promised he would gather Israel from all nations where they were scattered.

The remarkable events mentioned as part of the gathering in these verses were only partially fulfilled in ancient days. Their complete fulfillment is happening in the last day as the children of Israel gather to the true Church, are cleansed from sin, and serve the Lord in his "holy mountain" (the temple). Then they truly come to know who they are and who their Lord and God is (see vv. 42, 44).

Understanding the Scriptures 🔑

Ezekiel 20:33–44

Mighty hand, stretched out arm (vv. 33–34)—Symbols of power

Purge (v. 38)—Clean

Sojourn (v. 38)—Live somewhere that is not your real home

Oblations (v. 40)—Sacrifices

Lothe (v. 43)—Hate

Ezekiel 20:37—"I Will Cause You to Pass under the Rod"

The rod in Ezekiel 20:37 is the shepherd's staff. To "pass under the rod" refers to coming under the care of the Shepherd, or as it says in Ezekiel, "into the bond of the covenant." Some have suggested that passing under the rod might also have reference to the way shepherds tithed their sheep, marking each tenth one with a rod and dedicating it to the Lord.

Studying the Scriptures ✏️

A Summarize Using Key Ideas

Ezekiel 20:33–44 tells that the Lord will gather Israel and that they will turn their hearts to him. Explain the message of these verses by describing the following key ideas in your own words: mighty hand (v. 33); gather (v. 34); face to face (v. 35); pollute (v. 39); mine holy mountain (v. 40); sanctified (v. 41); remember (v. 43); know (vv. 38, 42, 44).

Ezekiel 21–24

Wickedness Leads to Destruction

In Ezekiel 21–23 the Lord continued to explain why Jerusalem would be destroyed. Ezekiel 21 explains that some of the righteous will suffer in this destruction as well. This suffering, which some people may think unfair, happens because the Lord honors the agency of his children. The righteous may also suffer in some of the judgments of the last days, but the Lord has promised a great eternal reward for those who do (see D&C 58:2).

Another interesting prophecy in chapter 21 is found in verses 25–27 where Ezekiel prophesied of the overthrow of Judah's king, saying there would not be another until he "whose right it is," meaning Jesus Christ, reigns (v. 27). Since the time the Jews were captive in Babylon they have not reestablished their kingdom. Jesus Christ will be the only king in their future.

Ezekiel 22 discusses the many sins for which Jerusalem was destroyed. Looking at which sins caused the Lord to allow them to be destroyed helps us understand what is offensive in his sight.

Ezekiel 23 is another chapter where the Lord referred to the countries of Israel (Samaria) and Judah (Jerusalem) as women who chose to be harlots. The comparison shows us how strongly the Lord feels about his covenant people worshiping other gods.

Ezekiel 24 records that the Lord used the image of a boiling pot of meat to describe the Jews being "boiled" by the Babylonians. Chapter 24 also tells about the death of Ezekiel's wife. The Lord told Ezekiel not to mourn for her as a sign to the Jews that they should not mourn the destruction of Jerusalem and the kingdom of Judah because the great wickedness of Judah made her punishments deserved and fair.

Ezekiel 25–32

The Punishment of Other Nations

Like the prophets Isaiah and Jeremiah, Ezekiel spoke against the Israelites first and then spoke against the wickedness of the surrounding nations and prophesied of their destruction. Ezekiel 25–32 contains prophecies concerning these nations: the Ammonites, Moabites, Edomites, and Philistines (see Ezekiel 25); Tyrus and Zidon (Ezekiel 26–28); and Egypt (Ezekiel 29–32).

Prophesied Destruction of Lands

Map labels: Zidon, Tyrus, Canaan, Ammon, Philistia, Moab, Edom, Egypt

Ezekiel 33

Watchmen on the Tower

Why are parents and leaders at every level of Church government so concerned about teaching people and encouraging them to repent?

Throughout history people have had to guard against attack from neighboring tribes or nations. As part of their plan for protection they built towers on the walls of their cities and placed watchmen in the towers to watch for approaching enemies. If the people ignored the watchmen, they placed themselves at great risk. At the same time, if watchmen did not do their duty, an entire city could be destroyed. Ezekiel 33 records the comparison of leaders in Israel to watchmen.

Understanding the Scriptures 🔑

Ezekiel 33

Coasts (v. 2)—Borders

His blood (vv. 4–6, 8)—The responsibility

Pine away (v. 10)—Wasting away

Restore the pledge (v. 15)—Pay his debts

Statutes (v. 15)—Laws

Equal (vv. 17, 20)—Fair

Afore (v. 22)—Before

Wastes (vv. 24, 27)—Destroyed area

Ye eat with the blood (v. 25)—Refers to breaking the law, which said to not eat the blood of meats

Defile (v. 26)—Are immoral with

Desolate (vv. 28–29)—Empty

Pomp (v. 28)—Pride

Covetousness (v. 31)—Behavior caused by greed

Ezekiel 33:30–32—The Way the Jews Treated Their Prophets

Having a prophet is a great blessing—but only if we obey his counsel. In these last verses of Ezekiel 33, the Lord told Ezekiel that the people talked as if they loved the prophet and were anxious to listen to him speak, but then they did not obey what the prophet taught them. The end of verse 31 sounds much like the description the Lord gave to the Prophet Joseph Smith of people in apostasy (see JS—H 1:19).

Studying the Scriptures ✏️

Ⓐ Solve Problems Using the Scriptures

Ezekiel 33:1–9 explains the role and importance of a watchman. The Lord calls upon prophets, other priesthood and Church leaders, and parents to be watchmen for his people. Consider the following situations and answer the questions at the end of each according to the principles taught in Ezekiel 33:1–9:

1. One of the favorite activities of the youth is to watch movies on video. These videos are often below the standards of the Church. What should the parents do? The bishop? The Young Men and the Young Women presidents? The youth? Yourself?

2. In addition to other practice times, the soccer coach scheduled team practice every Sunday morning. He expects every player to participate. What should parents do? The bishop? The youth on the team?

Ezekiel 34

The Shepherds of Israel

Ezekiel 34 records additional responsibilities of Church leaders. The Lord this time compared leaders to shepherds over his sheep (people). During his earthly ministry, the Lord called himself the "good shepherd" (John 10:14). As you read Ezekiel 34, look for what the Lord said he does that makes him a good shepherd and for what he said the leaders of the people had done that made them bad shepherds. Look also for what he said about the sheep.

Understanding the Scriptures 🔑

Ezekiel 34

Prey (vv. 8, 22, 28)—Something hunted for food

Require my flock at their hand (v. 10)—Hold them responsible for the flock

Fold (v. 14)—Fenced area for keeping flocks

Residue (v. 18)—Other, what remains

Foul, fouled (vv. 18–19)—Make unclean

Shower (v. 26)—Rain

Broken the bands of their yoke (v. 27)—Taken away their slavery, captivity, and burdens

Plant of renown (v. 29)—Productive or prosperous

Ezekiel 34:23–24—"My Servant David"

"David" in these verses refers to the Messiah. The name *David* in Hebrew means "beloved." The wonderful conditions these verses describe will come about when the Jews accept God's beloved Son as their Messiah. See also Isaiah 9:6–7; Revelation 22:16.

Studying the Scriptures ✏️

Ⓐ What Makes a Good Leader?

1. According to Ezekiel 34:1–10, 18–19, why were Israel's leaders bad "shepherds" of the Lord's people?

2. List the qualities of a good shepherd found in Ezekiel 34:11–16, and explain how someone serving in the presidency of an Aaronic Priesthood quorum or Young Women class could apply each quality to his or her calling.

Ezekiel 35

Destruction of Edom

Ezekiel 35 is another chapter of judgment upon Edom, also called Mount Seir and Idumea, a nation surrounding Israel.

Ezekiel 36

A Message of Hope

Although the Israelites were put to shame in the eyes of all the surrounding nations, the Lord said in Ezekiel 36 that he allowed them to be shamed as a testimony that he will not allow his people to mock him and the covenants they made with him. Ezekiel 36 contains a promise that—as a testimony to the world that he is the only true and living God—the Lord would gather a future generation of Israelites back to their land and to their covenant relationship with him. He promised that he would wash them clean from their iniquities and give them a "new heart" and a "new spirit" (see v. 26), and that, unlike the many years before Ezekiel's time, they would keep the Lord's commandments.

Ezekiel 37

Two Visions of Restoration

One of the beautiful things about inspired symbolic teaching is that it can have more than one meaning and apply to more than one time or situation. Ezekiel 37 is a particularly good example of multiple meaning. The Lord gave Ezekiel two "object lessons" about the gathering of Israel in chapter 37. These object lessons also teach and testify of other great truths relating to God's plan and his kingdom in the last days.

Understanding the Scriptures

Ezekiel 37

Sinews (v. 6)—Tendons that hold muscles and bones together and assist in their movements

Heathen (v. 21)—Those who do not believe in God

Defile (v. 23)—Make unclean

Detestable (v. 23)—Disgusting

Sanctuary (vv. 26, 28)—Temple

Tabernacle (v. 27)—Place where God dwells

Ezekiel 37:15–20—The Stick of Judah and the Stick of Ephraim

Elder Boyd K. Packer said, "In ancient Israel records were written upon tablets of wood or scrolls rolled upon sticks. . . . The stick or record of Judah—the Old Testament and the New Testament—and the stick or record of Ephraim—the Book of Mormon, which is another testament of Jesus Christ—are . . . indeed one in our hands. Ezekiel's prophecy now stands fulfilled" (in Conference Report, Oct. 1982, 73; or *Ensign*, Nov. 1982, 51, 53).

Studying the Scriptures

A Find the Symbol

1. Ezekiel's vision recorded in Ezekiel 37:1–14 dramatically symbolized the Lord's promise to gather the children of Israel. Choose a word or phrase that you think represents the following people or conditions: the children of Israel, the spiritually lost condition of the children of Israel, the influence of the Holy Ghost upon the children of Israel, the gradual gathering of the children of Israel.

2. How does Ezekiel 37:1–14 testify of another, even greater "restoration" of the children of Israel? (see also Alma 11:42–45; D&C 138:16–17).

B Scripture Mastery—Ezekiel 37:15–17

1. Draw a picture or diagram of the objects in these scripture mastery verses.

2. The same two sticks, or records, that Ezekiel spoke of are mentioned in 2 Nephi 3:11–12. List what the Book of Mormon says will happen because of the "joining" of these two sticks.

3. As you read on in Ezekiel 37 to verse 22 you realize that these two "sticks" are important in the gathering of Israel. Explain how you think the linking of the Bible and the Book of Mormon help gather the house of Israel. In your answer consider the message of the Book of Mormon's subtitle: Another Testament of Jesus Christ.

Ezekiel 38–39

The Battle of Gog and Magog

Ezekiel 38–39 speaks of a great battle that will occur in Israel in the "latter days" and that will involve a people from "Magog" led by a king named Gog. Ezekiel described this war as being waged in the "mountains of Israel" against the children of Israel gathered to these lands. The Lord also told Ezekiel he would miraculously save his people from the armies of Magog so that all nations may "know that I am the Lord" (Ezekiel 38:23). Because of these descriptions, Ezekiel seems to be describing the great battle before the Second Coming commonly known as "Armageddon."

What can be confusing is that John the Revelator described a battle between good and evil at the end of the Millennium as the battle of Gog and Magog (see Revelation 20:7–9). So there are two battles referred to as Gog and Magog, the first right before the Second Coming and the other at the end of the Millennium. They are similar in that they will be massive battles involving great destruction that completely destroys the enemies of God and makes significant changes in the earth.

Ezekiel 40–42

Ezekiel's Vision of a Temple

Ezekiel 40–42 contains Ezekiel's detailed description of a tour he took through a temple in "the land of Israel" (40:2). His guide, a heavenly messenger, measured every part of the temple, so Ezekiel's description includes the size of the rooms, the walls, the doors, and so on. The temple he described was much like the temple of Solomon. We do not know when or if the temple he saw will be built.

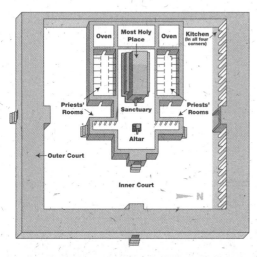

Ezekiel 43–44

The Glory of God Fills the Temple

How do you feel when you look at pictures of a temple or when you visit one and walk around it or go inside?

Ezekiel 43 records that Ezekiel saw the glory of the Lord enter the temple and make it holy and sacred. Ezekiel was told that the Lord would dwell in the midst of his people in the temple. He was also told to tell the people what he saw to make them ashamed of their iniquities (see v. 11) and help create a desire in them to return to the Lord and worthily enjoy the blessings of the temple, a privilege they lost because of their unrepented sins.

Ezekiel 44 sets forth the Lord's clear charge that no unclean thing enter and worship in the temple Ezekiel saw. The Lord has set the same standard for those who enter temples in our day (see D&C 97:15–17).

Ezekiel 45–46

More about the Temple

Ezekiel 45–46 contains the Lord's further description of rites associated with the temple, such as some of the ordinances the Jews performed in their temples which they had not properly performed at the time they were taken captive into Babylon.

Ezekiel 47

The Healing Waters of the Temple

Ezekiel 47 gives Ezekiel's vision of how water will yet flow from underneath the temple in Jerusalem and flow to the east, becoming larger and larger until it becomes a river of water. The river will flow into the Dead Sea and made it "alive" again with fish and vegetation. The Prophet Joseph Smith said, "Judah must return, Jerusalem must be rebuilt, and the temple, and water come out from under the temple, and the waters of the Dead Sea be healed. It will take some time to rebuild the walls of the city and the temple, . . . and all this must be done before the Son of Man will make His appearance" (Teachings of the Prophet Joseph Smith, 286).

This event is also symbolic of the spiritual renewal and rebirth that comes to individuals and families as they participate in the sacred, uplifting, and empowering ordinances of the temple that come from the source of "living waters," even Jesus Christ.

Ezekiel 48

Israel Gathers and the Lord Is with Them

At the end of Ezekiel 47, Ezekiel described the gathering of Israel to her homelands. Ezekiel 48 records that the Lord spoke of each tribe receiving a specific area as their inheritance and the Lord living in their midst.

The Book of Daniel

If you were in a foreign country where your religion was not practiced, how easy would it be to be true to your religion? What if practicing your religion required you to do things that were unpopular or even against the law of that land?

A Courageous Young Man

Daniel faced these situations. Daniel was a teenage boy who, along with other Jews, was taken captive in the first Babylonian conquest of Judah (approximately 605 B.C.). Because Daniel was courageous and true to his faith, the Lord blessed him with the gift of prophecy and with influence among leaders in a foreign land. His example is an inspiration and example to us in a day when we feel pressures like he felt and when we desire to have the positive influence he had.

Getting Ready to Study Daniel

Key People in the Book of Daniel

Daniel—Authored the book. He was a young man when the book began and in his eighties by the end of the book.

Shadrach, Meshach, Abed-nego—Three of Daniel's fellow Jews who were faithful to their religion.

Nebuchadnezzar—King of the Babylonian Empire from approximately 604 B.C. until his death in approximately 561 B.C. He was the king who conquered Judah and carried away many Jews into Babylonian captivity. For more information, see the Bible Dictionary, s.v. "Nebuchadnezzar."

Belshazzar—Nebuchadnezzar's son who ruled after his father and before the Persians conquered Babylon. For more information, see the Bible Dictionary, s.v. "Belshazzar."

Cyrus and Darius—Rulers of the Medo-Persian Empire that conquered Babylon in approximately 539 B.C. Cyrus ruled first. He was the king who decreed that the Jews could return to their homeland and rebuild their temple.

Key Events in the Book of Daniel

- Daniel and other Jews refuse to eat food that would cause them to break the law of Moses (see Daniel 1).
- Daniel interprets the dreams and the signs given to kings (see Daniel 2; 4–5).
- Three valiant men are put in a fiery furnace (see Daniel 3).

- Daniel is thrown in the lions' den (see Daniel 6).
- Daniel prophesies future events from his time until the end of the world (see Daniel 7–12).

Daniel 1

Faithful Young Israelites

The Babylonians believed that magicians and fortune-tellers had the power to know the future. Nebuchadnezzar, the king of Babylon, decided to see if he could train young captive Israelites to see the future. As you read, look for how the faithfulness of some of these young men brought the blessings of the Lord and amazed the king.

Understanding the Scriptures 🔑

Daniel 1

Besieged (v. 1)—Attacked

Eunuchs (vv. 3, 9–11)—Trusted household servants

Defile himself (v. 8)—Eat or drink what God had forbidden

Endanger my head (v. 10)—Risk my life

Prove thy servants, I beseech thee (v. 12)—Please test us

Countenances (v. 13)—Appearances, the way they looked

Consented to (v. 14)—Agreed with

Communed (v. 19)—Talked

Stood before the king (v. 19)—Became servants to the king

Astrologers (v. 20)—People who pretend to predict the future by watching the stars

Studying the Scriptures

A **Apply Their Example**

Daniel and the other young men provide a great example of being true to the faith and of how the Lord blesses those who are faithful to him. Consider the following situations and suggest a solution based on what you read in Daniel 1:

1. You and your classmates have important exams coming up. Some of them take pills to keep awake so they can study longer. They offer you some. What do you do or say?

2. You just got your first job. You want to make a good impression. At an important office party everyone is expected to toast the boss with an alcoholic drink. What do you do?

B **Physical and Spiritual Blessings**

Ways Daniel and His Friends Were Blessed

1. List the ways Daniel and his friends were blessed because of their faithfulness to the Lord.

2. How are the blessings these young men received like the blessings promised to those who obey the Word of Wisdom in our day? (see D&C 89:18–21).

Daniel 2

Nebuchadnezzar's Dream

Many people in the world are eager to give us advice. Daniel 2 teaches that King Nebuchadnezzar asked his magicians and astrologers for advice, but there was only one who could tell him the truth. Notice how this story is similar to what happened to Joseph in Egypt in Genesis 41:14–43.

Nebuchadnezzar's dream has special importance to us because it prophesies of the establishment of the kingdom of God in the latter days.

Understanding the Scriptures

Daniel 2

His sleep brake from him (v. 1)—He could not sleep

Magicians, astrologers, sorcerers, Chaldeans (v. 2)—People who pretend to do magic and know the future and the meaning of dreams

Gain the time (v. 8)—Stall for time

Chaff (v. 35)—The outer shell of a kernel of grain (such as wheat or barley)

Inferior (v. 39)—Not as great

Cleave one to another (v. 43)—Stick together

Consume (v. 44)—Take the place of

Offer an oblation and sweet odours (v. 46)—Offered a sacrifice to God and burned incense

Sat at the gate of the king (v. 49)—Stayed with the king as an advisor

Daniel 2:45—"The Stone Was Cut out of the Mountain without Hands"

Daniel explained that unlike all other kingdoms, the kingdom of God represented by the stone would be set up by God. "Without hands" means without *man's* hands.

Nebuchadnezzar's Dream

KINGDOMS REPRESENTED

Head of fine gold
Babylonian Empire

Breast and arms of silver
Medes' and Persians' Empire

Belly and thighs of brass
Macedonian Empire

Legs of iron
Roman Empire

Feet and toes of clay
Kingdoms that arose after the fall of the Roman Empire

Studying the Scriptures

A Finish These Sentences

1. Before the astrologers and magicians could interpret Nebuchadnezzar's dream, he said they first had to . . .

2. Daniel found out the meaning of the king's dream . . .

3. Daniel told the king he got the interpretation . . .

4. After Daniel told the king the interpretation . . .

B Scripture Mastery—Daniel 2:44–45

1. Daniel 2:44–45 symbolizes the Church in the latter days, which is the kingdom of God on earth. Draw a design for a poster that represents the ideas in these two verses. Write an explanation of your drawing on the back of the poster.

2. Read Doctrine and Covenants 65:1–2, 5–6 and write about how the Church is like the stone Daniel saw and about what has happened to the Church since it began with six members in 1830.

3. Using the diagram in the "Understanding the Scriptures" section above, you may want to mark the meanings of the symbols in your scriptures.

Daniel 3

Three Valiant Young Men

Have you ever gotten close enough to a fire that you were uncomfortable? Or have you ever been burned? If so, you can understand how frightening being thrown into a fire would be. Imagine, then, the kind of faith you would have to have to willingly walk into a furnace of fire rather than go against what God has taught you. Shadrach, Meshach, and Abed-nego had this great faith.

Understanding the Scriptures

Daniel 3

Threescore (v. 1)—Sixty (A "score" is twenty.)

Cubits (v. 1)—A distance (see Bible Dictionary, s.v. "weights and measures")

Cornet, flute, harp, sackbut, psaltery, dulcimer (vv. 5, 7, 10, 15)—Various musical instruments

Regarded (v. 12)—Obeyed

We are not careful (v. 16)—We are not worried

If it be so (v. 17)—If we are thrown into the furnace

Hosen (v. 21)—Coat, garment, or tunic

Urgent (v. 22)—Had to be done immediately

Astonied (v. 24)—Startled

Singed (v. 27)—Scorched

Yielded their bodies (v. 28)—Risked their lives

After this sort (v. 29)—In this way

Studying the Scriptures

A Explain the Problem

1. What did Nebuchadnezzar order everyone to do, and why was it wrong? (see Exodus 20:1–6).

2. What do you imagine less faithful Jews might have said to Shadrach, Meshach, and Abed-nego at the beginning of the story before they were thrown into the fiery furnace? What do you think the three would say in response?

B Give a Modern Example

Showing My Faith

At school

In community

With friends

Sometimes modern Church members are expected to bow down to the things of the world, or in other words, lower their standards to be acceptable in the eyes of the world. Give one example in each of the following settings where you think members of the Church today might show the faith of Shadrach, Meshach, and Abed-nego: (1) at school, (2) in the community, and (3) with friends.

C In Your Own Words

1. Write in your own words what the three young men said in Daniel 3:17–18.

2. What were the young men unsure about, and what were they sure about?

3. Based on what Shadrach, Meshach, and Abed-nego said and did, what would you say were the most important and powerful elements of their testimonies?

4. If you could talk with Shadrach, Meshach, and Abed-nego, what questions would you ask them, and why?

Daniel 4–5

Two Prideful Kings

Daniel 4 records that because Nebuchadnezzar again became prideful, God gave him another dream. Again, Daniel interpreted the dream. The Lord taught Nebuchadnezzar that he was king over a great empire only because the King of Heaven allowed him to be.

Between Daniel 4–5, over twenty years passed, and there was a new king in Babylon named Belshazzar. He was very proud also and mocked the God of Israel during a great feast in his palace. A hand appeared and wrote upon the wall. Daniel interpreted the writing, which said Babylon would fall. That night the Medes and Persians conquered Babylon.

Daniel 6

Daniel in the Lions' Den

Daniel 6 was written when Daniel was approximately eighty years old. Even though Daniel had been a counselor to the kings of Babylon, he also became a counselor to the kings of the Medo-Persian Empire who conquered Babylon. Look for how Daniel's enemies tried to destroy him and how the Lord continued to bless him because of his faithfulness.

Understanding the Scriptures

Daniel 6

Give accounts (v. 2)—Report

Sought to find occasion against Daniel (v. 4)—Tried to catch him doing something wrong

To establish a royal statute, and to make a firm decree (v. 7)—Get the king to make a law

Ask a petition (vv. 7, 12)—Ask for help

Aforetime (v. 10)—Before

Making supplication (v. 11)—Asking for help

Signet (v. 17)—Ring with an emblem of authority engraven on it

Lamentable (v. 20)—Voice of a person who is pained or grieving

Innocency (v. 22)—No wrongdoing

Dominion (v. 26)—King's empire

Stedfast (v. 26)—Dependable

Studying the Scriptures

A **Retell the Story**

Write the story of Daniel 6 so a young child could understand it.

B **And Thus We See**

Decisions in Daniel 6

○ What the king did

○ What other presidents and princes did

○ What Daniel did

1. Review all of Daniel 6 and look for what the king did, what the other presidents and princes did, and what Daniel did. Write about what happened to each of them because of their decisions.

2. Read 1 Nephi 1:20; Alma 30:60. To whom and how would the principles in these scriptures apply to the story in Daniel 6?

Daniel 7–12

Daniel's Prophetic Dreams and Visions

Daniel 7–12 contains the record of several of Daniel's visions about what was going to happen to his people, the house of Israel, and to the world. As the table below shows, some of Daniel's visions had the same meaning as Nebuchadnezzar's dream in Daniel 2. The Lord has not revealed to us the meaning of all that Daniel saw.

The Kingdoms in Daniel's Visions				
	Daniel 2	**Daniel 7**	**Daniel 8**	**Daniel 11–12**
Babylon	Head of gold See vv. 32, 37–38.	Lion See v. 4.		
Medo-Persia	Breast and arms of silver See vv. 32, 39.	Bear See v. 5.	Ram See vv. 3–4, 20.	See 11:1–2.
Greek-Macedon	Belly and thighs of brass See vv. 32, 39.	Leopard See vv. 6–7.	Goat See vv. 5–8, 21–22.	See 11:3–20.
Rome	Legs of iron See vv. 33, 40.	Terrible beast See vv. 7, 19.		
Many Kingdoms	Feet and toes of iron or clay See vv. 33, 41–43.	Ten horns See vv. 7–8, 20.		
Kingdom of God in the Latter Days	Stone See vv. 34–35, 44–45.	Adam and Jesus Christ See vv. 9–14, 22–28.		See 12:1–3.
The Power of Anti-Christ		Little horn from among the ten horns See vv. 8, 20–22.	Little horn from the four heads See vv. 9–12.	See 11:21–45.

The Book of Hosea

Historical Background

Although we do not know exactly when Hosea lived and preached, his writings suggest he lived between approximately 760–20 B.C. This would mean he lived at the same time as Isaiah, Micah, and possibly Amos. His message is generally directed to the Northern Kingdom, which was conquered and carried away by the Assyrians in 722 B.C. The people of the Northern Kingdom had grown increasingly wicked—especially in their worship of the idol Baal. This idolatrous religion was so wicked it even involved immoral acts as one part of "sacred" ceremonies. These practices were very offensive to God, and Hosea probably used such powerful and dramatic symbols and teaching as a result of these practices.

A Love Story

The book of Hosea begins with a marriage. Although the marriage is not one we all hope for, the story is told in such a way that we see love displayed in a truly remarkable manner. The story says Hosea is the husband, but the "real" husband is the Lord, and the wife is the children of Israel. The marriage represents the Lord's covenant with his people. The story is perhaps the most dramatic explanation in all scripture of the Lord's love for his children and his commitment to the covenants he makes with them. It also illustrates the responsibility of the children of Israel to keep their covenants with God and avoid all kinds of idolatry, anciently and today.

Teaching with Symbols

Hosea used many images and symbols to teach his message. For example, he used a husband, a father, a lion, a leopard, a she-bear, dew, and rain as symbols of the Lord. And he used a wife, a sick person, a grapevine, grapes, olive trees, a woman in childbirth, morning mist, and other symbols to represent Israel. Even the name *Hosea* is symbolic. It comes from the same Hebrew root as *Joshua*, which is the Hebrew name for *Jesus*. Hosea's name is appropriate because his message can help us learn about and feel more deeply the power of the Atonement of Jesus Christ. Other names in the book, such as the names of Hosea's children, also have symbolic meaning.

Hosea 1–3

A Marriage Covenant

As he did with the lives of Jeremiah and Ezekiel, the Lord used the life of the prophet Hosea to symbolically teach a powerful lesson. Hosea 1–3 contains a story whose meaning you will better understand if you remember that the Lord compared his covenant relationship with Israel to a marriage relationship. The comparison made in the book of Hosea is especially appropriate because the idolatry the Israelites practiced also involved committing immoral acts with harlots. Looking in the footnotes for the meanings of some of the names and other words and phrases in this story will also help you understand the Lord's message through Hosea.

As you read, put yourself in Hosea's place and imagine what it would take to do what he did. You may also want to imagine what you would be thinking if you were Gomer. Remember that Hosea represents the Lord, and Gomer represents Israel.

Understanding the Scriptures 🗝

Hosea 1

Conceived (vv. 3, 6, 8)—Became pregnant

Avenge (v. 4)—Give just punishment for something (in this case for Jehu's killing in Jezreel)

Hosea 1:2–3—Did the Lord Really Tell Hosea to Marry a Harlot?

"Whether the writer's interpretation of Hosea's marriages or some other be accepted, the religious significance of chapters 1–3 is quite clear. Hosea's wives represent Israel, the disloyal and harlotrous consort of Jehovah, who stipulates that unless Israel puts aside her harlotries and reforms she will meet with stern action. For her gross sins she will be checked and punished and thus learn in the crucible of bitter experience that her husband means more to her than she at first supposed" (Sidney B. Sperry, *The Voice of Israel's Prophets* [1952], 282).

To truly understand the message of the book of Hosea, we must consider what kind of strength Hosea had to have to actually do what is described in the story.

Hosea 2

Hedge up (v. 6)—Block
Overtake (v. 7)—Catch
Lewdness (v. 10)—Immoral behavior
Mirth (v. 11)—Fun, happiness, laughter

Allure (v. 14)—Invite by offering something good
Betroth (vv. 19–20)—The covenant one entered into when becoming engaged to be married

Hosea 3

Homer (v. 2)—A unit of measurement (see Bible Dictionary, s.v. "weights and measures")

Ephod, teraphim (v. 4)—In this case, objects associated with idol worship

Studying the Scriptures ▶

A Interpret the Symbolism

1. If Hosea represents the Lord, and Gomer represents Israel, what is the message of Hosea 1?

2. Hosea 2:5 explains why Gomer went after her idols. How are these reasons like the ones people give for breaking their covenants today?

3. Explain why you think what Gomer said in Hosea 2:7 is important, especially as it relates to someone who is in sin today (see Alma 30:60; 41:10).

4. Hosea 2:1–13 tells what the Lord would do to or for Israel (Gomer) because of what she did. List those promises and explain how they are an expression of his love for her (see D&C 95:1).

B "Come unto Me"

1. Elder Spencer W. Kimball said, "The image of a loving, forgiving God comes through clearly to those who read and understand the scriptures. Since he is our Father, he naturally desires to raise us up, not to push us down, to help us live, not to bring about our spiritual death" (*The Miracle of Forgiveness* [1969], 344). Choose two specific instances from Hosea 2:14–23 that illustrate the truth of what Elder Kimball said, explaining what impressed you about the verses you chose.

2. From Hosea 2:14 list some specific ways you know the Lord persuades us to come unto him.

3. In the story of Gomer, it seems that the mistakes she made somehow put her in bondage or slavery. So, even if Gomer (Israel) wanted to return to Hosea (the Lord), she was unable. The same is true for those in sin. On their own, they are unable to release themselves from the bondage of sin. According to Hosea 3:25, what did Hosea do for Gomer that symbolizes what the Lord does for his people?

4. Read also 1 Corinthians 6:19–20; 1 Peter 1:18–20 and tell how the verses relate to what Hosea did for Gomer.

5. According to Hosea 3:3–5, what was Gomer supposed to do to accept what Hosea did for her?

6. According to Luke 10:25–27 and Mosiah 2:21–24, what are we to do to accept what the Lord has done for us? (see D&C 59:8).

Hosea 4–5

The Sins of Israel and Judah

Hosea 4–5 marks where the Lord identified the sins of the children of Israel. He called the Northern Kingdom "Ephraim" after the tribe that led them, and he called the Southern Kingdom "Judah" after the tribe of their king.

Hosea 6

God Desires Sincere Repentance

Sometimes people think that they can sin and then do a few outward things, such as offer apologies, say a few prayers, pay their tithing, and attend all their Church meetings, to make up for their sins. While these are certainly important, repentance is a much deeper process. Repentance is a broken heart and a contrite spirit that brings a deep sorrow for our sins (see 3 Nephi 9:20). If we sincerely repent in this manner and renew our covenants with the Lord, the Spirit will cleanse us, bring us peace of conscience, help us lose the desire for sin, teach us how we can continue to draw near to the Lord, and give us strength to keep the covenants we have made.

Hosea 6:1–3 seems to be the children of Israel's expression about how quickly they hope to repent. The rest of this short chapter gives the Lord's response of disappointment in their attitude. Verse 6 expresses the Lord's desire for inward righteousness as well as outward displays of religion.

Hosea 7–10

Israel Reaps What She Planted

Hosea 7–10 records that the Lord spoke to Ephraim (the Northern Kingdom of Israel) about their sins. He used many objects as comparisons for their condition, such as "a cake not turned" (7:8), "a silly dove" (7:11), "a wild ass alone by himself" (8:9), "grapes in the wilderness" (desert; 9:10), and "an empty vine" (10:1).

The Lord's main message was that the people of Ephraim (Northern Kingdom of Israel) made gods and worshiped them, even though they could not save them. Realizing the gods' powerlessness, Ephraim turned to the true God and expected him to save them, and when he was slow to help, they said he was not a powerful God, even though they brought sorrow and destruction upon themselves by forsaking him. See Hosea 10:13 for a good summary of the Lord's message.

Hosea 11

Evidence of God's Love

Hosea 11 contains the Lord's reminder to Ephraim (the Northern Kingdom) of how he mercifully redeemed them from Egypt in the days of Moses. They had not fully followed him, however, and now some wanted to return to Egypt for protection from Assyria instead of trusting the Lord who led them out of Egypt to protect them. Even with this betrayal, the Lord said he would continue to offer mercy to them. He said he would allow Assyria to take Ephraim captive but not completely destroy them.

Hosea 12–14

A Call to Return to the Lord

Hosea 12–14 are the final chapters of Hosea's writings. In chapters 12–14 the Lord continued to speak of Ephraim's sins and their painful consequences. The Lord's final message, however, is one of hope and love for his children in sin (see Hosea 13:9–14; 14).

Understanding the Scriptures

Hosea 13:9–14

Travailing woman (v. 13)—
A woman in labor

Hosea 14

Render the calves of our lips (v. 2)—Give our words, or praise, as a sacrifice

Revive (v. 7)—Grow with life

Studying the Scriptures

A What Is Most Impressive to You?

Write about the phrases, verses, or ideas that most impress you in Hosea 13:9–14; 14 about how to repent and what the Lord will do if we repent.

The Book of Joel

Joel was a prophet of Judah. The book of Joel is a prophecy assuring the people that with repentance they will again receive the blessings of God. We know very little about the prophet Joel. Joel 1:1 tells us the name of his father, but no other information is given about his personal life. It is not likely that the Joel who wrote this book is the same Joel mentioned elsewhere in the Bible. Because Joel did not mention the nations of Assyria or Babylon, it is hard to tell when he lived and wrote. He seemed to be familiar with the country of Judah, however, so we assume he preached there.

"The Day of the Lord"

Joel's message centers around what he calls the "day of the Lord" (Joel 1:15; 2:1; 2:11; 2:31; 3:14). The "day of the Lord" refers to a day or time of judgment when the Lord delivers rewards and punishments. While we often refer to the Second Coming as the day of the Lord, there are other days of the Lord. For example, when Israel was conquered by the Assyrians, that was the day of the Lord's judgment on Israel. On an individual level, the day of the Lord may be the day a person dies.

Latter-day Application

Although Joel's prophecies must have had application to the people of his day and time, Moroni told Joseph Smith that a passage in Joel 2:28–32 would "soon" be fulfilled (see JS—H 1:41). Consequently, we should consider how Joel's prophecies apply to our day, especially regarding the "day of the Lord" we most often call the Second Coming of Jesus Christ.

Joel 1

Learn from a Locust Invasion

Natural disasters often make us feel weak and helpless in the face of their awesome, uncontrollable power. Joel 1 contains a graphic lesson Joel taught by using a natural disaster—a plague of locusts—to teach the people about how helpless they will feel if they do not repent before the "day of the Lord" comes and the wicked are judged. He specifically compared the locust invasion to the invasion of an army that would come into the land and destroy a people that would not repent as part of God's judgments. These kinds of judgments are also prophesied for the last days (see D&C 5:19; 45:31; 87). Joel suggested that the people gather to the house of the Lord in fasting and prayer for deliverance in their difficult time just as the Lord commanded the Saints in the last days to "stand in holy places" (D&C 45:32).

Joel 2

Who Can Survive the Day?

People often think about the Second Coming of the Savior with fear. But the Lord has said that "the righteous need not fear" (1 Nephi 22:17). Joseph Fielding Smith further added, "It will not be a day of dread and fear to the righteous" (Doctrines of Salvation, comp. Bruce R. McConkie, 3 vols. [1954–56], 1:173). Joel 2 records some dark prophecies that make some people fearful. As you read, also look for what the Lord will do in the last days and at the time of his Second Coming that can encourage you and give you hope.

Understanding the Scriptures 🗝

Joel 2

Nigh at hand (v. 1)—Coming soon

Devoureth (vv. 3, 5)—Completely destroys

Stubble (v. 5)—The small, short stalks left over after harvesting the grain

Battle array (v. 5)—Prepared and set up for battle

Ranks (v. 7)—Lines of marching soldiers

Thrust (v. 8)—Bump, run into

Executeth (v. 11)—Performs, will see that something happens

Rend (v. 13)—Tear, break

Heritage (v. 17)—Children

Reproach (vv. 17, 19)—Shame

Hinder (v. 20)—Back

Savour (v. 20)—Smell

Spring (v. 22)—Grow

Former rain, latter rain (v. 23)—Two rainy seasons of the year in the land of Israel

Studying the Scriptures ✏

A Answer Joel's Question

Who can abide the Lord's day?

The first ten verses of Joel 2 describe awful destructions that occur at the "day of the Lord." Verse 11 asks a question we might wonder about after reading such gloomy and terrible prophecies. After reading Joel 2:12–20; Doctrine and Covenants 45:57, write an answer to the question at the end of Joel 2:11.

B A Latter-day Prophecy

Read Joel 2:28–32; Joseph Smith—History 1:41. In what ways have you seen this prophecy fulfilled?

Joel 3

A Great Battle

Joel 3 greatly applies to the last days. In fact, it seems to describe a battle often referred to in the scriptures as Armageddon, which will occur just before the Second Coming of the Savior. Armageddon is a battle where all nations will fight against the Lord's people and where the Lord will fight for his people to help them win the victory. The battle is part of the judgment and destruction of the wicked before the Millennium.

Studying the Scriptures ✏

A Winning the War

We must not forget that the battle of Armageddon is certainly not the only time the Lord's people will be or have been engaged in a war. In fact, our war with Satan began in the premortal life (see Revelation 12:7–11). Satan was cast out at that time, but he still "maketh war with the saints of God" (D&C 76:29). This war is one of eternal consequence, and we must be aware that as the time of the Second Coming draws near, Satan will not only stir up men to physical warfare, but he will continue his battle to spiritually destroy Heavenly Father's children. So while we watch for Armageddon as one of the signs of the coming of the Savior, we must not forget that we are already involved in a great battle against the forces of evil, and we must be valiant in this effort. Read Joel 3:16–21; 1 Nephi 14:11–14; 22:16–17 and explain how the Lord has promised to help his people in the physical and spiritual wars of the last days.

The Book of Amos

A Prophet of Peace and Prosperity

Amos prophesied in the Northern Kingdom about 760–50 B.C., near the same time as the prophet Hosea. At the time, the Northern Kingdom of Israel experienced peace and prosperity. All did not share the prosperity, however, since some became very rich through a disregard of the laws of the Lord while others became poorer. In addition, most of the nation, including the kings, participated in idol worship, and very few were keeping the commandments. The Lord sent Amos to command the people to repent of these sins.

Background

Amos was a simple shepherd from a small town, but he had a powerful and important message about applying gospel principles in our lives, and about the judgments of God upon the proud. For more information on Amos, see the Bible Dictionary, s.v. "Amos."

Amos 1–2

Condemnation of Israel and Surrounding Nations

Amos began his prophecies with messages of the Lord's condemnation to several nations that surrounded Israel: Syria (identified by its capital, Damascus; see Amos 1:3–5), Philistia (identified by the major cities Gaza, Ashdod, Ashkelon, and Ekron; see Amos 1:6–8), Phoenicia (and its major city, Tyrus or Tyre; see Amos 1:9–10), Edom (see Amos 1:11–12), Ammon (see Amos 1:13–15), and Moab (see Amos 2:1–3). Each was condemned for its sins and for attacking Israel.

These condemnations must have gotten the children of Israel's attention, and they would have likely agreed with Amos's decrees, but he also condemned Judah (see Joel 2:4–5) and Israel (see Joel 2:6–16). Amos let the Israelites know that God's justice is the same for all who sin against him—they will all eventually be punished. The rest of the book of Amos is mostly a message to Israel warning them to repent.

Amos 3

The Role of Prophets

Many people in the world today believe that Heavenly Father no longer speaks to his children through prophets. Amos 3 records what Amos said about the Lord and prophets. Look for his teachings about prophets as well as what the Lord said would happen to Israel if they did not listen to their prophets.

Understanding the Scriptures

Amos 3

Hath no prey (v. 4)—Has not killed anything to eat

Snare (v. 5)—Trap

Tumults (v. 9)—Noise and confusion

Adversary (v. 11)—Enemy

Horns of the altar shall be cut off (v. 14)—Their worship of God had become a powerless and empty form. (Horns were a symbol of power.)

Winter house, summer house (v. 15)—Homes of the wealthy who had ignored God and his prophets

Amos 3:7—The Lord Always Calls Prophets to Deliver His Word

Amos 3:7 contains a truth that is very important to the message of the Restoration: God always works through prophets to establish his word and his works among men. After quoting Amos 3:7, Elder LeGrand Richards said: "Now if we understand that, no one can

Studying the Scriptures

A. Scripture Mastery—Amos 3:7

1. In Amos 3:3–6, Amos asked seven questions, the answers to which were obviously "no." He asked those questions to make a point in verse 7 that he felt was just as sure. What did Amos say would "surely" happen? (see also 1 Nephi 22:2).

2. Give an example of a "secret" the Lord has revealed in our day and how it has blessed the lives of those who listen and obey.

B. What Are the Consequences?

Read Amos 3:11–15; Doctrine and Covenants 1:11–16 and write what the Lord said would happen to those who refuse to listen and obey the prophets?

Amos 4

"I Tried to Help You"

Have you ever gone out of your way to do something nice for someone only to have him reject you and what you offered? Israel rejected the God who freed them from Egyptian bondage and gave them the land of promise (see Amos 2:9–10). Amos 4 tells what the Lord said he would do to get Israel to "return" to him. Look for what he said as you read.

Understanding the Scriptures

Amos 4

Kine of Bashan (v. 1)—Literally, cows of an area very rich in vegetation; symbolically, wealthy women who care only for themselves

Beth-el, Gilgal (v. 4)—Places of worship that had become corrupted

Leaven (v. 5)—Yeast (Offering leavened bread with burnt offerings was forbidden.)

Proclaim and publish the free offerings (v. 5)—A comment about Israel's righteousness since they liked the outward show of religion but did not want to be obedient to God's commandments

For this liketh you (v. 5)—You like to do this

Cleanness of teeth, want of bread (v. 6)—Famine

Blasting and mildew (v. 9)—Diseases that destroy crops

Pestilence (v. 10)—A terrible disease

Firebrand (v. 11)—Burning stick

Amos 4:2—How Would the Lord Take Away His People with "Hooks" and "Fishhooks"?

The Assyrians were known for putting hooks through the lips, noses, or cheeks of their enemies and linking them to one another with a chain. Linking captives made them easy to guard and "herd" away to captivity.

Studying the Scriptures

A How Would This Work?

1. In Amos 4:6–11 the Lord explained what he had done to persuade Israel to return to him. Make a list of what he said.

2. How do you think the Lord's judgments could influence Israel to return to him? (see Alma 32:13; Helaman 12:2–6).

3. Read Doctrine and Covenants 122:7–8 and think of some difficult times you have experienced. How can a trial become a blessing?

Amos 5

Seek the Lord and Live

Amos 5 tells how Israelites were again encouraged to seek the Lord and repent of their evil ways. In particular, the Lord condemned their greed and their idolatry. He said if they would "seek the Lord," they would "live" (see vv. 3–6, 14–15), but if they did not, they would be carried away into captivity.

Studying the Scriptures

A What Do You Think?

Read Amos 5:4–6, 14–15. Since we must all experience death sometime or in some way, explain the ways you think those who seek the Lord will "live."

Amos 6

Woe to Those at Ease

Are there people in the Church today who seem to think they will be saved just because they are members of the Church even if they do not really love and serve the Lord? The Israelites often made the mistake of thinking that the Lord would never let them be destroyed—even if they were not righteous—because they were God's chosen people (see Deuteronomy 7:6).

In Amos 6 the Lord condemned them because they thought more of their wealth and comforts than they did of justice, mercy, or their God (see also 2 Nephi 28:21–24). Because of these attitudes, the Lord said Israel would be carried away captive by their enemies.

Amos 7–9

Five Visions of Amos

Amos 7–9 deals with five visions Amos received from the Lord. Each vision showed that the Lord intended to completely destroy the kingdom of Israel if the people did not repent. The first two visions were of destructions that were avoided because Israel repented (see Amos 7:1–6). The next three visions revealed ways Israel had not repented (see Amos 7:7–9; 8:1–3; 9:1–4). The result of these sins would be that the Northern Kingdom of Israel would be conquered and taken captive. God, however, would not allow Israel to be utterly destroyed. In chapter 9, the Lord promised them that although they would be scattered among all nations, in the last days they would be gathered again to their lands of promise.

Studying the Scriptures

A Optional Activity—What Does It Mean?

1. Amos 8:11–12 describes an apostasy. Find out the meaning of the word *apostasy* and tell why these verses in Amos are a good description of a general apostasy on the earth.

2. Using the same symbols for the gospel that Amos used in Amos 8:11–12, make an advertisement to invite people to investigate the truth. You can simply write what the advertisement would say or draw what you might put on a poster.

A Message of Justice

Has someone ever taken advantage of you when you were in a difficult situation? Obadiah condemned the nation of Edom for taking advantage of Jerusalem. When a foreign power attacked Jerusalem, the Edomites helped defeat the Jews and steal their property. Obadiah prophesied of Edom's destruction because of their cruelty toward Judah and of Israel's eventual salvation upon Mount Zion.

Short Background to a Short Book

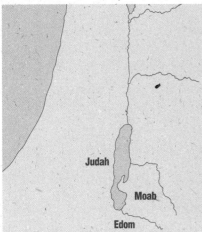

The name *Obadiah* means "servant (or worshiper) of Jehovah." His book was probably written about 586 B.C., shortly after the destruction of Jerusalem, and is the shortest of all the books of the Old Testament. For more background information see the Bible Dictionary, s.v. "Obadiah."

Obadiah

Redeeming the Dead

Understanding the Scriptures

Obadiah 1:21—"Saviours . . . on Mount Zion"

Modern prophets have pointed to Obadiah 1:21 as a prophecy of the latter-day temple work performed for those who died without hearing the gospel and receiving its ordinances. The Prophet Joseph Smith said: "But how are they to become saviors on Mount Zion? By building their temples, erecting their baptismal fonts, and going forth and receiving all the ordinances, baptisms, confirmations, washings, anointings, ordinations and sealing powers upon their heads, in behalf of all their progenitors who are dead, and redeem them that they may come forth in the first resurrection and be exalted to thrones of glory with them; and herein is the chain that binds the hearts of the fathers to the children, and the children to the fathers, which fulfills the mission of Elijah" (*Teachings of the Prophet Joseph Smith*, 330).

The Book of Jonah

An Unusual Prophet and Book

The book of Jonah is the only book in the Prophets section of the Old Testament that primarily records what happens to the prophet instead of recording his revelations and prophecies. Jonah most likely lived during the time Jeroboam II was king of Israel (about 793–53 B.C.). As you read the book of Jonah, consider what it teaches you about God's love. Also note that although the book is short, Jesus referred to two different parts of it during his mortal ministry (see Matthew 12:39–41; Luke 11:29–32). For more information on the book of Jonah, see the Bible Dictionary, s.v. "Jonah."

Jonah 1–2

Can You Run from the Lord?

What would you say or how would you feel if your leaders assigned you (alone) to share the gospel with the most wicked and cruel person you know? Jonah 1–2 tells how Jonah was called to go to Nineveh, the capital of Assyria, and warn the Assyrians to repent. The Assyrians were known for their great wickedness and cruelty and had already conquered Syria (see map 10 in your Bible) and threatened to conquer Israel.

Understanding the Scriptures

Jonah 1

Cry against it (v. 2)—Warn the people to repent

Tempest (vv. 4, 12)—Storm

Mariners (v. 5)—Sailors

Cast forth the wares (v. 5)—Threw out the ship's cargo

Perish (vv. 6, 14)—Die

Cast lots (v. 7)—A way people believed they could determine God's will (similar to drawing straws or flipping a coin)

Occupation (v. 8)—Job, mission

Wrought, and was tempestuous (vv. 11, 13)—Became more rough

Beseech (v. 14)—Ask with great feeling, plead

Ceased from her raging (v. 15)—Calmed down

Vows (v. 16)—Promises

Jonah 2

Affliction (v. 2)—Troubles

Floods compassed me (v. 3)—Water was all around me

Corruption (v. 6)—Death

They that observe lying vanities forsake their own mercy (v. 8)—Those who trust in idols lose the Lord's help

Jonah 1:2–3—Nineveh and Tarshish

Nineveh and Tarshish represent the two opposite ends of the Middle Eastern and Mediterranean world. When Jonah started for Tarshish, he was apparently trying to get as far away from Nineveh as possible.

Intended Voyage to Tarshish

Studying the Scriptures

A Look for Details

1. Why did the sailors wake Jonah up?

2. Whose idea was it that Jonah be thrown into the sea?

3. What did the Lord prepare to swallow up Jonah?

B What Do You Think?

Write about why a person might feel like running away from what God wanted him to do or decline callings in the Church. What can we learn from Jonah's experience in Jonah 1 about trying to run from the Lord? (see Moses 4:12–16).

C A Type of the Savior

How long was Jonah in the belly of the fish? Read also Matthew 12:38–41 and write how Jonah's experience is like what happened to the Savior.

Jonah 3–4

Jonah at Nineveh

Nineveh, the capital of Assyria, was a very large city for that day. It was about 96 kilometers (60 miles) around and had a population of about 120,000 (see Jonah 4:11). Nineveh was known to be a very wicked city. Jonah 3–4 records what the people do when Jonah tells them they will be destroyed because of their wickedness, and how Jonah reacts to their response. Notice what they do and what Jonah learns from his mission as well.

Understanding the Scriptures

Jonah 3

The preaching that I bid thee (v. 2)—The message I sent you to give

Three days' journey (v. 3)—Taking three days to walk across

Sackcloth (vv. 5, 6, 8)—Rough clothing worn to show humility or sadness

Sat in ashes (v. 6)—A sign of humility or sadness

Jonah 4

Was this not my saying (v. 2)—Didn't I say you would do this

Gracious, merciful (v. 2)—Forgiving through the power of the Atonement

Deliver him from his grief (v. 6)—Make him feel better

Withered (v. 7)—Died

Vehement (v. 8)—Very hot

Pity (v. 10)—Felt sorry for

Sixscore thousand (v. 11)—120,000

Cannot discern between their right hand and their left hand (v. 11)—Do not know right from wrong

Jonah 3:9–10—Does God Need to Repent?
Notice the Joseph Smith Translation for Jonah 3:9–10.

Studying the Scriptures

A Write a Proclamation

A Proclamation to the People of Nineveh

Jonah 3:5–8 says that when the king heard Jonah's message he made a proclamation to the people. Based on what you read in Jonah 3, write what you think the proclamation might have said and what you know about the people of Nineveh.

B What Was He Thinking?

Describe how Jonah may have felt about what God did in Jonah 3:10 and why you think he may have felt that way.

C What's the Point?

Tell what you think the message of the book of Jonah is (you can choose more than one).

The Book of Micah

A Messianic Prophecy

The name *Micah* means "who is like unto Jehovah." Micah came from a small town in southern Judah (see Micah 1:1) and prophesied between approximately 740–697 B.C. during the reigns of Jotham, Ahaz, and Hezekiah, kings of Judah; Micah prophesied at about the same time as Isaiah. Micah's message was to both Israel and Judah and contains words of doom and judgment as well as hope and a promise of a later, merciful restoration of the Lord's people. Micah is most famous for his remarkable prophesy of the birth of the Messiah (see Micah 5:2).

Micah 1–2

Both Israel and Judah to Fall

Micah 1–2 holds Micah's prophecies that the Lord would come in judgment upon both Israel and Judah because of their sins. He specifically mentioned the sins of idol worship and desiring riches and then obtaining those riches through violence and dishonesty. Micah did not leave Israel and Judah entirely hopeless, however. He prophesied that after the judgments, Israel would be gathered again.

Micah 3

Wicked Leaders Rebuked

What kind of people does God choose to be his servants? Micah 3 tells what Micah said was wrong with those who were supposed to be the leaders of Israel and the servants of God. Look for what he said as you read.

Understanding the Scriptures 🔑

Micah 3

Know judgment (v. 1)—Be able to judge fairly

Pluck off their skin, eat the flesh of my people, flay their skin, break their bones, chop them in pieces (vv. 2–3)—Phrases used to describe the cruelty of the leaders of Israel and Judah. The leaders did not really *eat* the people. They used their authority to make themselves rich by taking the people's food, clothing, and property.

Ill (v. 4)—Wickedly

Err (v. 5)—Sin

That bite with their teeth, . . . prepare war against him (v. 5)—False prophets will say "peace" to those who feed them but will fight against those who will not.

Divine (vv. 6, 11)—Foretell the future using means not ordained of God

Sun shall go down over the prophets, seers be ashamed, diviners confounded (vv. 6–7)—Phrases that mean that the false prophets will be silenced

Abhor judgment, and pervert all equity (v. 9)—Hate fairness and twist what is right

With blood, with iniquity (v. 10)—By murder and wickedness

Heads (v. 11)—Leaders

Become heaps (v. 12)—Be turned into a pile of stones

The mountain of the house as the high places of the forest (v. 12)—The temple will become as a hill overgrown with trees and bushes.

Studying the Scriptures ✏️

Ⓐ Turn It Around

1. List what Micah 3 says the leaders of the people were doing wrong.

2. Write about a Church leader you know or use a scripture example and describe his or her qualities in following the Lord and leading others.

Micah 4

The Lord Will Reign in Zion

Using the pattern of Micah's prophecies, Micah 4 follows the "bad news" in Micah 3 with some "good news." The first three verses are much like Isaiah's prophecy concerning the mountain of the Lord in the tops of the mountains (see Isaiah 2:1–4). Most of the rest of chapter 4 is about what Zion can become when we seek the Lord and his Zion.

Micah 5

The Coming of the Messiah

Micah 5 records that Micah foretold the first coming of the Savior and that in the last days the children of Israel would be delivered from their enemies and become righteous.

Studying the Scriptures ✏️

Ⓐ How Was It Fulfilled?

The prophecy in Micah 5:2 was given about 700 B.C. Read Matthew 2:1–6; Luke 2:1–7. Who fulfilled Micah's prophesy? The additional name *Ephratah* in Micah 5:2 was probably used to indicate the Bethlehem in Judea as opposed to the Bethlehem in Zebulun.

Micah 6–7

Israel's Sins and the Lord's Mercy

Micah 6 records that the Lord condemned Israel for their dishonesty and greed, their violence, and their idolatry. Micah 7 sets forth the Lord's promise that in the last days, when Israel repents and returns to the Lord, he will have mercy upon them.

A What Is Required?

1. According to Micah 6:7–8, what is required to be "good" in the Lord's sight?

2. Micah 6:7–8 is written for people many years ago. Rewrite verse 7 using examples of what people might give today that are not "good" unless accompanied by the Christlike qualities listed in verse 8.

The Book of Nahum

A Message of Comfort

Nahum means "comfort" in Hebrew. Since Nahum's short book is a prophecy of God's judgments upon Nineveh, the capital of Assyria, his message must have comforted the Israelites who suffered at the hands of the Assyrians.

Background

As with some of the prophets in the Old Testament, we know little about Nahum. The content of his book leads us to believe he wrote his prophecies sometime between 663–12 B.C., which was during the time when Assyria was the most powerful nation in the Middle Eastern world.

Nahum's prophecies about the destruction of Assyria also apply to the world just before and at the time of the Second Coming.

The Book of Habakkuk

A Prophet's Questions and God's Answers

Habakkuk apparently lived at a time when Judah grew increasingly wicked in spite of prophets' efforts to change the spiritual state of the nation. Habakkuk's short book contains two questions he asked the Lord, the Lord's answers, and a prayer he offered to acknowledge the Lord's perfect wisdom in the way he deals with his children. For more information about the prophet Habakkuk and his writings in the Old Testament, see the Bible Dictionary, s.v. "Habakkuk."

"How long shall I cry, and thou wilt not hear?"

more wicked than the Jews—to destroy his covenant people who had become wicked. In Habakkuk 2:2–20 the Lord answers by saying that the Babylonians would also be destroyed for their wickedness—even though they would seem to prosper for a time.

Habakkuk 3

Habakkuk's Prayer

Habakkuk 3 contains a prayer, written in Hebrew poetry, in which Habakkuk bore testimony of the power and goodness of God and his own personal commitment to follow the Lord even in his people's difficult times.

Habakkuk 1–2

Questions and Answers

Habakkuk 1:2–4 records that Habakkuk asked the Lord about the Jews' wickedness and why he allowed such wickedness among his people. The Lord answered him in Habakkuk 1:5–11, explaining that because of the Jews' wickedness, the Babylonians would soon conquer them. In Habakkuk 1:12–17, Habakkuk asked the Lord why he would use the Babylonians—a people

Studying the Scriptures

A In Your Own Words

My Commitment to
Follow the Lord
_____

Read Habakkuk 3:17–18 where Habakkuk expressed a commitment to follow the Lord even in difficult times. Write your own brief statement that expresses your commitment to follow the Lord.

The Book of Zephaniah

Zephaniah prophesied that the day of the Lord would come with great power upon the wicked but would provide a hopeful and wonderful future for those who seek the Lord and live righteously.

A Royal Prophet

The first verse of Zephaniah identifies him as a descendent of King Hezekiah, a righteous king of Judah who lived approximately one hundred years before this book was written. Zephaniah prophesied in the days of King Josiah, another righteous king in Judah, which means he lived about the same time as Habakkuk, Micah, and the young Jeremiah.

Getting Ready to Study Zephaniah

The book of Zephaniah contains two major ideas:

1. *The day of the Lord.* The Lord will come in judgment upon people involved in sin and hypocrisy. This truth applies to the nation of Judah in Zephaniah's time as well as to the wicked in all ages, especially those living at the time of the Second Coming.

2. *Restoration and purification.* God will draw to himself and purify people who humble themselves in the midst of his judgments.

Zephaniah 1–2

Judgment Day

Zephaniah 1 records Zephaniah's prophecy about what would happen to the people of Judah because of their sins, which included worshiping idols, doing evil to each other, and thinking they were righteous while they acted wickedly.

Zephaniah 2 tells that Zephaniah prophesied that not only would the Babylonians destroy the Jews but also all the wicked surrounding Judah, including the Philistines (see vv. 4–7), the Moabites and the Ammonites (see vv. 8–11), the Ethiopians (see v. 12), and the Assyrians (see vv. 13–15).

Zephaniah 3

Words of Encouragement

A person who has sinned may be tempted to give up on himself and think there is no way he can ever "come back." Because of these feelings of discouragement, it is important not only to speak clearly about what the sinner did wrong but also to speak words of hope that the sinner may be encouraged to repent and look to a better future. Zephaniah 3 holds the Lord's words of encouragement for the people of Judah.

Understanding the Scriptures

Zephaniah 3

Oppressing (v. 1)—Taking unfair advantage of or causing someone distress

Light (v. 4)—Not serious in thinking about or performing duties

Treacherous (v. 4)—Turning against promises made to others

Polluted the sanctuary (v. 4)—Made the temple unclean

Done violence (v. 4)—Go against

Corrupted all their doings (v. 7)—Sinned in all they did

Rise up to the prey (v. 8)—Punish or destroy enemies

With one consent (v. 9)—In unity

Suppliants (v. 10)—Worshipers

Dispersed (v. 10)—Scattered

Haughty (v. 11)—Prideful

Remnant (v. 13)—Those remaining

Judgments (v. 15)—Punishments

Slack (v. 16)—Limp with discouragement

Reproach (v. 18)—Shame

Turn back (v. 20)—Release

Studying the Scriptures

A Tell What Impresses You

Zephaniah 3:8–20 describes the latter days and the wonderful way the Lord will bring his covenant people back to him after their being scattered and taken captive because of their sins. As you read these verses, think about how they might apply to people today who need to come back to the Lord or who are worried and fearful about the last days. Write at least two truths the Lord said in this chapter that impress you the most, and explain why.

The Book of Haggai

Encouragement to Build the Temple

In 538 B.C. King Cyrus of Persia (also mentioned in the book of Ezra) decreed that the Jews could return to Jerusalem and rebuild their temple which the Babylonians destroyed. At first the Jews were very excited about this opportunity, but the difficulty and expense of the task, the opposition of their enemies, and the lack of support from the kings that followed Cyrus made the Jews feel discouraged. For sixteen years almost no work was done on the temple. Haggai prophesied in 520 B.C., teaching the people to make the temple a priority and encouraging them to continue rebuilding the temple in spite of these challenges.

Getting Ready to Study Haggai

Haggai gave a specific date for each part of his short book. The months were called by different names in the Old Testament but have been changed to current names to aid our understanding.

Haggai 1:1–15   29 August 520 B.C.

Haggai 2:1–9   17 October 520 B.C.

Haggai 2:20–23 18 December 520 B.C.

The story of the Jews' return to Jerusalem and the building of the temple is found in the books of Ezra and Nehemiah. For more information on Haggai, see the Bible Dictionary, s.v. "Haggai."

Haggai 1

Finish the Temple

Elder Claudio R. M. Costa told the following story about a man he knew of in Brazil:

"After being baptized with his family, he could hardly wait to complete a year's membership in the Church so he could take his wife and children to the temple. The São Paulo Brazil Temple is very far from the Amazon. It usually takes four days by boat and four days by bus to get to the temple—about a week's travel. This man was a cabinetmaker. How could he save enough money to pay for himself, his wife, and his children? Although he worked hard for many months, he made very little money.

"When the time came to go to the temple, he sold all his furniture and appliances, even his electric saw and his only means of transportation, a motorcycle—everything he had—and went to the temple with his wife and children. It required eight days of travel to reach São Paulo. After spending four glorious days in the temple doing the work of the Lord, this family then had to travel seven more days to return to their home. But they went back home happy, feeling that their difficulties and struggles were nothing compared to the great happiness and blessings they had experienced in the house of the Lord" (in Conference Report, Oct. 1994, 34; or Ensign, Nov. 1994, 27).

The story of this Brazilian family represents the spirit of Haggai's message in chapter 1. As you read, look for what Haggai says about the importance of the temple and what the people are doing to show they do not value the temple as they should.

Understanding the Scriptures

Haggai 1

Waste (vv. 4, 9)—Not built, still destroyed

Sown (v. 6)—Planted

Stayed from dew (v. 10)—Does not produce dew (the moisture on the ground in the morning)

Remnant (v. 14)—A small number remaining from a larger group

Studying the Scriptures

A The Importance of the Temple

1. What did Haggai say were the consequences of delaying building the temple? (see Haggai 1:6, 9–11). Consider the effect of the temple covenants, ordinances, and blessings on every part of our lives. What do you think it means to put your wages "into a bag with holes"?

2. What does Haggai 1:4–6 tell about the priority of the temple in the lives of the people?

B The People's Response

1. What did the people do because of Haggai's message? (see Haggai 1:12–15).

2. Like Haggai, President Howard W. Hunter told Church members "to look to the temple of the Lord as the great symbol of your membership" (in Conference Report, Oct. 1994, 8; or Ensign, Nov. 1994, 8). Explain how you are making the temple the symbol of your membership and how the temple affects the way you live today.

Haggai 2

Keep Building!

Haggai 2 was written when the people had already begun rebuilding the temple. Among those rebuilding the temple were Jews who had seen the previous temple and knew how beautiful and glorious it was. The temple they were rebuilding was not nearly as big or beautiful as the destroyed one. This fact discouraged many Jews. Haggai encouraged them with two main ideas. First, he told them to continue building and promised them that in the last days, the Lord would make a temple greater and more glorious than the one Solomon built, which was the one they remembered. Second, Haggai reminded the people that from the moment they began rebuilding the temple, they began to prosper. So, even though the temple was not as glorious as Solomon's temple, it still brought the same blessings from the Lord.

He Saw beyond His Day

Zechariah was from a priestly family in the tribe of Levi. He was born in Babylon and returned to Jerusalem about 538 B.C. with the Jews who were allowed to return from Babylonian captivity. He was called to be a prophet about 520 B.C. (see Zechariah 1:1), which means he lived about the same time as Haggai, the prophet, and Ezra, the priest. Like Haggai, Zechariah encouraged the people to continue rebuilding the temple. But he also challenged the people to rebuild their personal spiritual lives. Zechariah was also quite visionary. His visions are both Messianic (tell about the Savior's Second Coming) and apocalyptic (tell about the last days). Zechariah's prophecies about Jesus Christ in chapters 9–14 are quoted more in the four Gospels of the New Testament than those of any other Old Testament prophet.

Zechariah 1–6

Eight Visions of Zechariah

Zechariah 1–6 records eight visions the Lord gave Zechariah about the house of Israel:

- A vision of horses (see Zechariah 1:7–17), which teaches about the merciful way the Lord will deal with Jerusalem

- A vision of four horns and four carpenters (see Zechariah 1:18–21), which is about the powers (horns) that scattered Judah and what will happen to these powers

- A vision of the man with a measuring line (a surveyor; see Zechariah 2), which testifies of the Lord's protective power over his people

- A vision of the high priest (see Zechariah 3), which symbolizes how Judah can overcome Satan and be cleansed through the power of Jesus Christ ("the Branch" in v. 8)

- A vision of a lampstand and olive trees (see Zechariah 4), which symbolizes how the Lord would give power to his people by his Holy Spirit

- A vision of a flying scroll (see Zechariah 5:1–4), which taught that those who were dishonest in the land were condemned

- A vision of a woman in a basket (see Zechariah 5:5–11), which testifies that wickedness would be removed from the people

- A vision of four chariots (see Zechariah 6:1–8), which symbolizes spreading the Lord's power over the whole earth

Zechariah 6 concludes with the ordination of a man named Joshua to be the high priest as a symbol of the Savior who ministers for his people.

Zechariah 7–8

Present and Future Jerusalem

Zechariah 7 records that the Lord condemned the people of Jerusalem in Zechariah's day for pretending to be righteous by fasting and doing other outward ordinances without being kind, fair, or charitable to others. Zechariah 8 contains Zechariah's prophecy concerning the future of Jerusalem. He said that when the people repent and are gathered in righteousness to this holy city, the Lord would be with them and bless them beyond the ways he had in the past.

Zechariah 9

The Coming King

The prophet Jacob in the Book of Mormon said that all the ancient prophets testified of Jesus Christ (see Jacob 7:11). Some of these prophecies may be missing from the Bible (see 1 Nephi 13:24–28), but here in Zechariah we find some that have been preserved for us.

Studying the Scriptures

(A) A Prophecy Fulfilled

Compare Zechariah 9:9 with Matthew 21:1–11 and write about how the prophecy in Zechariah was fulfilled.

Zechariah 10

Latter-Day Promises

The people of Israel and Judah were scattered because of their disobedience to the Lord's commandments. Zechariah 10 tells us what the Lord promised to do for them in the last days. Look for these as you read.

Understanding the Scriptures 🗝️

Zechariah 10

Latter rain (v. 1)—Spring rains that were needed to ripen the wheat crop

Idols, diviners, they comfort in vain (v. 2)—False gods and false prophets cannot bless people or make them happy

Made them as his goodly horse in the battle (v. 3)—Made them as the horse ridden by the leader (usually the best horse)

The corner, the nail, the battle bow (v. 4)—References to the Savior. This prophecy indicates that the most important one in Israel will come out of the tribe of Judah. (You may want to write "Jesus Christ will come from the tribe of Judah" in the margin of your scriptures next to this verse.)

Mire (v. 5)—Mud

Confounded (v. 5)—Defeated

Hiss for them (v. 8)—Call for them

Redeemed (v. 8)—Saved, bought from captivity or slavery

Sow (v. 9)—Scatter

Place shall not be found (v. 10)—There will not be enough room.

He shall pass through the sea with affliction (v. 11)—Ephraim will return through much trouble.

Smite the waves in the sea, deeps of the river shall dry up (v. 11)—Phrases indicating that God will make it easier for his people to gather

Walk up and down in his name (v. 12)—Obey God's commandments in all they do

Studying the Scriptures ✏️

A) The Gathering of Israel

The gathering of Israel is both spiritual and physical. People are gathered first spiritually when they are converted to the gospel and leave worldliness behind. The Saints will also be gathered physically to their lands of promise when the prophets tell them to do so (see Alma 5:57; D&C 133:12–15). Read Zechariah 10:6–12; D&C 29:7–11; 101:63–68; 115:5–6 and write what you learn about the gathering of Israel and why it is so important.

Zechariah 11–13

The Jews and Their Savior

Zechariah 11–13 records prophecies of the future of the Jews. In chapter 11, Zechariah foretold what would happen to the Jews because of their wickedness at the time of Jesus Christ. Zechariah 12–13 contains prophecies about the Second Coming of Jesus Christ and what he will do for the Jews in the last days.

Studying the Scriptures ✏️

A) How Are They Fulfilled?

1. Read Zechariah 11:12–13; Matthew 26:14–16; 27:1–10 and tell how Zechariah's prophecy was fulfilled.

2. Read Zechariah 12:10; 13:6; Doctrine and Covenants 45:47–53. When and how will Zechariah's prophecy be fulfilled?

Zechariah 14

The Second Coming of Jesus Christ

When you think about the Second Coming of the Savior, are you thrilled, frightened, or a little of both? Zechariah 14 describes some of the events that will happen at the time of the Second Coming. As you read, look for verses that could help a person be less worried about the Second Coming of Jesus Christ, remembering that "if ye are prepared ye shall not fear" (D&C 38:30).

Understanding the Scriptures 🗝️

Zechariah 14

Spoil (v. 1)—Wealth

Rifled (v. 2)—Robbed

Ravished (v. 2)—Raped

The residue of the people (v. 2)—The rest of the people

Living waters (v. 8)—May literally mean fresh water, may symbolically mean knowledge from heaven

Former sea, hinder sea (v. 8)—the Dead Sea and the Mediterranean Sea

Turned as a plain (v. 10)—Made like a level valley

It shall be lifted up, and inhabited in her place (v. 10)—Jerusalem will be raised up but not moved out of her place.

Consume away (v. 12)—Rot

Tumult (v. 13)—Confusion or panic

Feast of tabernacles (vv. 16, 18–19)—A holiday to remember how the Lord prospered the children of Israel in the land of Canaan after he led them there

Zechariah 14:6–7—It Will Be Light at Evening Time
Compare Zechariah 14:6–7 to 3 Nephi 1:8, 15–17.

Studying the Scriptures ✏️

A) Events before the Second Coming

1. According to Zechariah 14:1–7, what great miracle will the Lord perform for the Jews at the Second Coming? (see also D&C 45:47–53).

2. According to Zechariah 14:20–21, how will the situation on earth be different when the Lord comes?

3. What events related to Zechariah's prophecy of the Second Coming help you anticipate when the Savior comes again? Read also Isaiah 11:4–9; Doctrine and Covenants 29:7–13; 133:17–35 for additional details on events prophesied in Zechariah.

4. Read Doctrine and Covenants 106:4–5 and identify what you can do to be prepared for the Second Coming if it comes in your day so that it will be a glorious day for you rather than a dreadful one.

The book of Malachi is the Old Testament book that was written last historically. Malachi (whose name in Hebrew means "my messenger") probably wrote these prophecies about 430 B.C., nearly one hundred years after Jews began returning from Babylon to the land of Israel. The Jews of the Old Testament had no prophets after Malachi that we know of, but the descendants of Father Lehi in the Western Hemisphere (Nephites) had numerous prophets right up to the birth of Jesus Christ, as recorded in the Book of Mormon.

The Last Known Old Testament Prophet's Message

By the time Malachi prophesied, many Jews hoped that God would more dramatically display his power by freeing them from Persian rule and allowing them to regain a kingdom. After one hundred years from the time they returned to their homelands, the Jews were still under Persian control. Many Jews became discouraged and did not work as hard to live a religious life, believing that God had forgotten or forsaken them so being righteous didn't really matter. Malachi's message addressed these circumstances. The principles Malachi taught, however, can apply to nearly any time in history, since people in all ages are tempted to be "lukewarm" in their religion.

Malachi's Message

Malachi spoke for the Lord in answering questions the people asked in his day. The following problems, sins, and challenges are ones he identified:

- How did the people despise and pollute the name of God? (see Malachi 1:6).
- Why didn't the Lord accept the people's offerings and prayers? (see Malachi 2:13–14).
- How did the people weary the Lord? (see Malachi 2:17).
- How should the people return to the Lord? (see Malachi 3:7).
- How does man rob God? (see Malachi 3:8).
- How had the people spoken against the Lord? (see Malachi 3:14–15).

Malachi is one of the most frequently quoted Old Testament prophets. New Testament writers quoted Malachi's writings, the resurrected Savior quoted some of Malachi's teachings to the Nephites so they would have them in their records, and the angel Moroni quoted some of Malachi to the young Prophet Joseph Smith, telling him that Malachi's prophecies would be fulfilled in the latter days.

For more information on Malachi, see the Bible Dictionary, s.v. "Malachi."

Malachi 1

Insincere Worship

During his mortal ministry, Jesus condemned Jewish leaders because they tried to appear extremely righteous when in truth they lived unrighteously. The book of Malachi helps us understand that this problem existed for at least four hundred years. Malachi 1 records that Jewish leaders were obedient to the Lord's commandment to sacrifice, but that instead of sacrificing the best of their flocks, they offered their injured or diseased animals (see Malachi 1:7–8, 12–14). This hypocrisy demonstrated their lack of respect for the Lord and the low priority religion held in their lives.

Malachi 2

The Priests Called to Repentance

Malachi 2 describes the Lord's direction to the descendants of Aaron, who were priests for the people in the temple. The Lord said they did not set a righteous example for the people nor did they help them walk in righteous paths. Instead, the priests broke the covenants of the priesthood, which the Lord compared to the covenants between husband and wife. The Lord said they would be punished for their disobedience.

Malachi 3–4

The Lord's Coming

When Moroni visited Joseph Smith on the evening of 21 September 1823 and told him about the Book of Mormon, he also quoted several scriptures to him, including "part of the third chapter of Malachi; and . . . the fourth or last chapter of the same prophecy" (JS—H 1:36). Malachi 3–4 are of great importance in the latter days.

Malachi 3–4 focuses on "the great and dreadful day of the Lord" (Malachi 4:5), or the Second Coming. Malachi testified to the people of his day and ours that the day of the Lord will come. Furthermore, although the wicked may seem to prosper, the day of the Lord will be a day of judgment wherein the righteous will be rewarded and the wicked will be burned.

As you read these two chapters, look for what we must do to prepare for the Second Coming, what can help us faithfully endure until that great day, and what can encourage us to have faith that the Second Coming will come.

Understanding the Scriptures 🔑

Malachi 3

Abide (v. 2)—Survive

Refiner's (v. 2)—Someone who separates pure metal from all other substances

Fullers' (v. 2)—Belonging to people who wash clothes as part of the process of making them

Purge (v. 3)—Cleanse

Sorcerers (v. 5)—People who seek to use magic and evil spirits to influence others

Oppress (v. 5)—Treat unfairly

Hireling (v. 5)—Worker, a person who is hired

Wherein (vv. 7–8)—In what ways

Prove (v. 10)—Test, try

Rebuke (v. 11)—Prevent, turn back

Devourer (v. 11)—Things that destroy

Vain (v. 14)—No benefit

Set up (v. 15)—Prosperous

Tempt God (v. 15)—Challenge God's commandments by not living them and seeing if there really is a punishment

Delivered (v. 15)—Saved from punishment

Spare (v. 17)—Have compassion on

Discern (v. 18)—Come to know or recognize

Malachi 4

Stubble (v. 1)—Short stalks left after a field is harvested. They are then burned.

Stall (v. 2)—Place where animals are fenced in

Tread down (v. 3)—Walk on

Horeb (v. 4)—Mount Sinai

Statutes (v. 4)—Laws

Studying the Scriptures ✏️

Complete three of the following five activities (A–E) as you study Malachi 3–4.

A) More Than One Fulfillment

Read Matthew 11:7–11; Doctrine and Covenants 45:9 and tell who or what the messenger is speaking of in Malachi 3:1. We would also be correct in saying that the Prophet Joseph Smith is a messenger to prepare the way of the Lord by restoring the Church of Jesus Christ in these latter days (see JST, Matthew 17:10–14; 2 Nephi 3).

B) One Fulfillment

Notice that in Malachi 3:1 we read about "my messenger" and "the messenger of the covenant." You identified "my messenger" in activity A above. Who do you think "the messenger of the covenant" is? Why?

C) Scripture Mastery—Malachi 3:8–10

1. List the blessings contained in Malachi 3:8–10 for those who live the law of tithing. Read verses 11–12 and add other blessings to your list.

2. How could not paying our tithes and offerings be considered "robbing God"?

3. Read what the Lord said about tithing in Doctrine and Covenants 64:23. How does what the Lord said compare to Malachi's message if you read on to Malachi 4:1?

D) In Your Own Words

1. In your own words, write the people's complaint found in Malachi 3:14–15.

2. What promises did the Lord give in Malachi 3:16–18 that answered the complaint and can help you in times when you don't seem to be blessed for your righteousness while those who do not keep the commandments seem to be doing just fine?

E) Scripture Mastery—Malachi 4:5–6

1. You may be interested to know that Malachi 4:5–6 contains the only verses quoted (although not word for word) in all four of the standard works of the Church (see 3 Nephi 25:5–6; D&C 2; 128:17; JS—H 1:36–39). From the many scriptures quoted by Moroni to the boy prophet in 1823, this prophecy about Elijah to return before the Savior's Second Coming is the only portion put into the Doctrine and Covenants. Elijah's return to restore sacred keys is most important. Read Doctrine and Covenants 110:13–16 and explain when and how this prophecy was fulfilled.

2. President Joseph Fielding Smith said, "Through the power of this priesthood which Elijah bestowed, husband and wife may be sealed, or married for eternity; children may be sealed to their parents for eternity; thus the family is made eternal, and death does not separate the members. This is the great principle that will save the world from utter destruction" (*Doctrines of Salvation*, comp. Bruce R. McConkie, 3 vols. [1954–56], 2:118). Knowing this truth, explain what "curses" you think come upon the earth and upon individuals and families who know about these teachings but do not live according to the blessings and covenants Elijah restored. In other words, how do the keys of the priesthood Elijah restored keep the earth from "cursings"? Why is it so important for us to share the wonderful news about these things? The following quotation from a proclamation by the First Presidency and Quorum of the Twelve Apostles may help you answer:

"We warn that individuals who violate covenants of chastity, who abuse spouse or offspring, or who fail to fulfill family responsibilities will one day stand accountable before God. Further, we warn that the disintegration of the family will bring upon individuals, communities, and nations the calamities foretold by ancient and modern prophets" ("The Family: A Proclamation to the World," *Ensign*, Nov. 1995, 102).

3. Explain what you think you could do to turn your heart to "the fathers" (your ancestors) or to your children in ways that would bless their lives forever.